# HARVARD ECONOMIC STUDIES

1. The English Patents of Monopoly. By W. H. Price.
2. The Lodging House Problem in Boston. By Albert B. Wolfe.
3. The Stannaries: A Study of the English Tin Miner. By George R. Lewis.
4. Railroad Reorganization. By S. Daggett.
5. Wool-Growing and the Tariff. By C. W. Wright.
6. Public Ownership of Telephones on the Continent of Europe. By A. N. Holcombe.
7. The History of the British Post Office. By J. C. Hemmeon.
8. The Cotton Manufacturing Industry of the United States. By M. T. Copeland.
9. The History of the Grain Trade in France. By Abbott Payson Usher.
10. Corporate Promotions and Reorganizations. By A. S. Dewing.
11. The Anthracite Coal Combination in the United States. By Eliot Jones.
12. Some Aspects of the Tariff Question. By F. W. Taussig.
13. The Evolution of the English Corn Market from the Twelfth to the Eighteenth Century. By N. S. B. Gras.
14. Social Adaptation. By L. M. Bristol.
15. The Financial History of Boston, from May 1, 1822, to January 31, 1909. By C. P. Huse.
16. Essays in the Earlier History of American Corporations. By J. S. Davis. 2 vols.
17. The State Tax Commission. By H. L. Lutz.
18. The Early English Customs System. By N. S. B. Gras.
19. Trade and Navigation between Spain and the Indies in the Time of the Hapsburgs. By C. H. Haring.
20. The Italian Emigration of Our Times. By R. F. Foerster.
21. The Mesta. By Julius Klein.
22. Argentine International Trade under Inconvertible Paper Money: 1880–1900. By J. H. Williams.
23. The Organization of the Boot and Shoe Industry in Massachusetts before 1875. By Blanche E. Hazard.
24. Economic Motives. By Z. C. Dickinson.
25. Monetary Theory before Adam Smith. By Arthur E. Monroe.
26. Canada's Balance of International Indebtedness, 1900–1913. By Jacob Viner.
27. The History of the United States Post Office to the Year 1829. By W. E. Rich.
28. The Theory of International Prices. By James W. Angell.
29. Forests and Sea Power. By R. G. Albion.
30. Banking Theories in the United States before 1860. By Harry E. Miller.
31. Karl Marx's Interpretation of History. By Mandell Morton Bober.
32. Grain Growers' Coöperation in Western Canada. By Harald S. Patton.
33. The Assignats. By S. E. Harris.
34. Economic and Social History of an English Village. By N. S. B. Gras and E. C. Gras.
35. Direct Taxation in Austria. By John V. Van Sickle.
36. The Greenbacks and Resumption of Specie Payments, 1862–1879. By D. C. Barrett.
37. The Street Railway in Massachusetts. By Edward S. Mason.
38. The Theory of Monopolistic Competition. By Edward Chamberlin.
39. Interregional and International Trade. By Bertil Ohlin.
40. The French International Accounts, 1880–1913. By Harry D. White.
41. Twenty Years of Federal Reserve Policy. By S. E. Harris. 2 vols.
42. The Illinois Central Railroad and Its Colonization Work. By Paul W. Gates.
43. American Treasure and the Price Revolution in Spain, 1501–1650. By Earl J. Hamilton.
44. German Monetary Theory, 1905–1933. By Howard S. Ellis.
45. Wages in Eighteenth Century England. By Elizabeth W. Gilboy.
46. The Theory of Economic Development. By J. A. Schumpeter.
47. The Supply and Control of Money in the United States. By L. Currie.
48. British International Gold Movements and Banking Policy, 1881–1913. By W. E. Beach.
49. State Control of Local Finance in Massachusetts. By Royal S. Van de Woestyne.
50. Fluctuations in American Business, 1790–1860. By Walter B. Smith and Arthur H. Cole.
51. Money, Prices, and Wages in Valencia, Aragon, and Navarre, 1351–1500. By Earl J. Hamilton.
52. The Development of the Business Corporation in England, 1800–1867. By B. C. Hunt.
53. Exchange Depreciation. By S. E. Harris.
54. A Study of Fluid Milk Prices. By J. M. Cassels.
55. Location Theory and the Shoe and Leather Industries. By Edgar M. Hoover, Jr.
56. Federal Subsidies to the Provincial Governments in Canada. By J. A. Maxwell.
57. Studies in Massachusetts Town Finance. By Eugene E. Oakes.
58. Market Control in the Aluminum Industry. By Donald H. Wallace.
59. The New York Bond Market, 1920–1930. By Charles Cortez Abbott.
60. The Commercial Paper House in the United States. By Albert O. Greef.
61. The Middlesex Canal, 1793–1860. By Christopher Roberts.
62. Fascist Economic Policy. By W. G. Welk.
63. Monopoly and Competition in the English Coal Trade, 1550–1850. By Paul M. Sweezy.
64. English Theories of Central Banking Control, 1819–1858. By Elmer Wood.
65. Politics, Finance, and Consequences. By Charles Jesse Bullock.
66. German Financial Policies, 1932–1939. By Kenyon E. Poole.
67. Monopolistic Competition and General Equilibrium Theory. By Robert Triffin.
68. The Newsprint Paper Industry, An Economic Analysis. By John A. Guthrie.
69. Exchange Control in Central Europe. By Howard S. Ellis.
70. The American Carpet Manufacture. By A. H. Cole and H. F. Williamson.
71. The American Maritime Industries and Public Policy, 1789–1914. By John G. B. Hutchins.
72. The Creation of Purchasing Power. By David McCord Wright.

# HARVARD ECONOMIC STUDIES

## VOLUME LXXIII

**LONDON : HUMPHREY MILFORD**
OXFORD UNIVERSITY PRESS

# Economic Fluctuations in the United States

A Systematic Analysis of Long-Run Trends
and Business Cycles, 1866–1914

BY

## EDWIN FRICKEY

ASSOCIATE PROFESSOR OF ECONOMICS, HARVARD UNIVERSITY

CAMBRIDGE · MASSACHUSETTS
HARVARD UNIVERSITY PRESS
1942

PRINTED AT THE HARVARD UNIVERSITY PRINTING OFFICE
CAMBRIDGE, MASSACHUSETTS, U. S. A.

To V. G.

# PREFACE

THE AUTHOR is indebted to the Harvard University Committee on Research in the Social Sciences for a grant of funds which made possible the research incorporated in this book, and for assistance in publication. Particular portions of the research were aided also by a grant from the Committee on Research in the Trade Cycle of the Economics Department of Harvard University.

A great variety of material from published sources has been used in the preparation of this volume. Individual acknowledgments are later made at appropriate points in the text. This opportunity is taken to express appreciation for the kindness of the various organizations, publications, and writers concerned.

Also acknowledged is the courtesy of the editors of the Review of Economic Statistics in permitting the inclusion of the substance of two articles which originally appeared in that publication.

The author desires to express his sincere gratitude to all those who had a part in the tedious task of carrying out the prolonged analytical work involved in this study. In particular, thanks are given to Dr. M. J. Fields, Mr. Edgar Eaton, Mr. Louis Weiner, and Mr. F. H. Sanderson, who at successive stages of the program exercised general supervision over the computing staff and performed essential research; to Miss Ruth Crandall, for indispensable aid in connection with the index of transportation and communication; to Mrs. Esther Morton and Mr. Frank L. Hall, for the construction of the published charts; to Mr. Edgar Eaton and Mr. F. H. Sanderson, for the verification, intercomparison, and audit of these charts; to Mrs. Anna H. Thorpe and Miss Lillian Buller, for the typing of the manuscript; to Mr. F. H. Sanderson, for aid in verification of the manuscript and the proof sheets, and for preparation of the index. Also gratefully acknowledged is the constant and helpful coöperation of Dr. Elizabeth W. Gilboy and Miss Althea MacDonald of the Harvard University Committee on Research in the Social Sciences, and Miss Dorothy Wescott of the Review of Economic Statistics.

The author is particularly indebted to his colleague, Professor

W. L. Crum, for a reading of the manuscript, and the making of many helpful suggestions.

One matter of terminology must be mentioned. This study pertains to the period 1866–1914; consequently the expressions "pre-war" and "post-war" are used with reference to the World War of 1914–18.

In the Introduction the purposes of the investigations described in this volume — together with a statement of the point of view, basic principles, and program of attack which it takes as point of departure — are set forth in the opening section dealing with the Nature of the Problem; following this, a Summary of the Findings is presented for the benefit of those who may wish to see the analytical scheme in broad outline before undertaking examination of the details.

EDWIN FRICKEY

Cambridge, Massachusetts
October 30, 1942

# CONTENTS

# TABLES

# CHARTS

## SKETCHES

# INTRODUCTION

# INTRODUCTION

## THE NATURE OF THE PROBLEM

THIS VOLUME deals with that branch of the general subject of *time-series analysis* which is called *time-series decomposition*. In time-series decomposition we are concerned with the development of procedures for separating the fluctuations of time series into component parts, and thus identifying and measuring different types of movements.

We shall, tentatively and as a point of departure, accept the conventional system for the classification of time-series fluctuations — i.e., into secular, cyclical, seasonal, and irregular movements. The following quotation, taken from Professor Warren M. Persons' fundamental monograph upon time-series decomposition,[1] will very well serve to indicate the generally accepted viewpoint.

"That several kinds of fluctuations appear in any time series is obvious. For example, we expect pig-iron production to be vastly greater in 1910 than in 1890, because of the growth of the industry in the interval. On the other hand, we know from experience that there are periods of prosperity and depression, and are not surprised, notwithstanding the large increase *for the whole period*, to find considerable ups and downs in the production of pig iron *during the period*. Irregular or accidental occurrences, likewise, cause fluctuations — a strike, a court decision, the outbreak of war. Within any given year, also, there are fluctuations. The round of the seasons is known to produce changes in the volume of production or of sales, as well as other related changes."

---

[1] This memoir — which presents the results of some of Professor Persons' most notable work in a field where he accomplished so much — was published in the *Review of Economic Statistics*, 1 (January and April 1919). The quotation is from p. 8 of the January issue.

As Professor Wesley C. Mitchell has pointed out,[2] we are prone to think of time-series analysis in general, and especially the methodological developments connected with the conventional classification of time-series fluctuations, as a twentieth-century phenomenon. "But," as Professor Mitchell adds, "the current classification of economic changes runs back at least to the times of classical economists, when 'commercial cycles' were recognized, when Ricardo speculated about the long-time trends of wages, rents and profits, when writers upon finance began discussing seasonal variations and when every economist abstracted from 'disturbing circumstances' for the same reason that analytic statisticians now seek to eliminate random perturbations."

## IMPORTANCE OF THE SUBJECT OF TIME-SERIES DECOMPOSITION

The subject of time-series decomposition is clearly of the greatest importance for economic analysis and reasoning. Professor Joseph A. Schumpeter, in his review of Professor Mitchell's 1927 *Business Cycles*, asserts that "there would be little overstatement in saying that trend-analysis will be the central problem of our science in the immediate future and the center of our difficulties as well." [3] Professor W. L. Crum, in a penetrating article upon "Statistical Normals and Economic Planning," [4] suggests that "one of the central quantitative problems, which we hope may be answered by statistics, has to do with the appraisal of economic normals," and further urges that this is true with respect to both "normal tendencies" and "normal relationships."

After setting forth his classification of time-series fluctuations (quoted above), Professor Persons continues by saying that all of the forces involved in the various types of movements — secular, cyclical, seasonal, and irregular — "may be at work simultaneously: and all of them play a part in determining the fluctuations which occur in a statistical series. Those fluctuations are thus a

---

[2] The great contributions of Professor Mitchell to the subject of time-series analysis — beginning with the 1913 *Business Cycles* landmark, and continuing to the present time — are well known to all students in this field. The quotation here presented is from his foreword to Professor Arthur F. Burns' *Production Trends in the United States since 1870* (New York: National Bureau of Economic Research, Inc., 1934), pp. xi–xii.

[3] *Quarterly Journal of Economics*, XLV (November 1930), p. 166.

[4] *Harvard Business Review*, XII (January 1934), pp. 176–185. The quotation is from p. 177.

confused conglomerate growing out of numerous causes which overlie and obscure one another. In view of this complexity the simple comparison of items within time series, in what may be termed their crude state, is of but little significance. How ascertain from such a conglomerate the particular meaning of any given change in the figures? How divide the given change into its constituent parts? In other words, how isolate and measure the influence of different sets of causes or forces? These are the difficult problems which render necessary the development of an adequate method for analysis and comparison of business conditions." [5]

Speaking somewhat more broadly, and considering the application to economic theory generally of statistical methods involving the use of time series, it is manifest that we must have a definitive solution to the problem of the statistical decomposition of time series before we are equipped to set up empirical tests or applications of theoretical schemata, employing time-series variations as a basis. To give a trite example, it is one of the stock criticisms in the field of statistical demand curves — both of the statistical work involved in any given piece of analysis, and of the explicit or implicit theoretical foundations thereof — that the analyst has failed to take proper account of the distinction between long-run and short-run tendencies. And if, adopting a more sophisticated theoretical starting point and setting more ambitious goals, we try to develop a system of equations (employing as basis the items of appropriate time series) which shall, through their solutions, indicate quantitatively the nature of relationships inherent in the economic system, we need all the more to be clear regarding the statistical decomposition of time series. Quite possibly, for example, the system of equations inherent in long-time secular relationships may be altogether different from the system inherent in short-time cyclical relationships, and by mixing the two types of variation (i.e., by using non-analyzed or improperly analyzed data) we may get in our results not truth, but confusion.

Even when one thinks in terms of partially or wholly managed economies, the topic of time-series decomposition still has indisputable importance. Even if, looking forward over a generation or more,[6] one anticipates the wide extension of economic planning

---

[5] Persons, *loc. cit.*

[6] Fixing attention, that is to say, not so much upon the years immediately ahead

in the world at large and in the United States in particular, this by no means spells lack of interest in the problems of time-series analysis. We can be certain that the development of a very extensive body of statistical materials and analyses would be required as a necessary guide to action in any sound and effective attempt at control. Only by painstaking and thoroughgoing investigation into the records of the past could a solid foundation be laid for exercise of such control.[7]

In particular, the important problem of statistical normals (and their relation to economic normals) would demand special attention — and this is true, to employ Professor Crum's terminology,[8] with regard to both normal tendencies over time and normal relationships at a given time. As Professor Crum suggests, the broad objectives of many of the prominent schemes for economic planning can be classified under two heads: stabilizing plans and reconstruction plans. "Some plans aim at keeping the economic system close to normal — they are stabilizing plans. Others aim to force changes in the normals — they are reconstruction plans."

With respect to the *stabilizing plans*, statistical normals (and their relation to economic normals) patently would be of the utmost concern: indeed, the whole object would be to maintain normal tendencies and normal relationships as nearly as might be possible. And for the *reconstruction plans*, a knowledge of statistical and economic normals would be a vital feature. As Professor Crum points out, the statistician may quite properly contend that "reconstruction plans which involve an excessively rapid modification of existing normals, or modifications in certain normals inconsistent with modifications in others, may produce maladjustments in the economic structure and perhaps lead to disastrous panics.

---

(which unfortunately promise to be characterized by great uncertainty and disturbance in economic affairs, and by violent and non-conventional fluctuation in economic time series) as upon the period to follow.

[7] Cf. Henry L. Moore, in his *Synthetic Economics* (New York: The Macmillan Co., 1929) : referring to his synthetic method — which, as he indicates (p. 4), aims "to give, by means of recent statistical methods, a concrete, practical form to the theoretical ideas of moving equilibria, oscillations, and secular change" — he says (p. 8) "by far the chief, advantage . . . is that it gives ground for the hope of introducing into economic life rational forecasting and enlightened control."

[8] Cf. Crum, *op. cit.*, p. 177. The quotations just below are from pp. 183, 184. The whole article is worthy of most careful reading in connection with the topic here touched upon.

He may even contend that forced modifications in normals will have normal consequences, unless the application of the same or different forces is continued. He will at least make out a good case for the decisive importance of a thorough knowledge of statistical normals as a foundation for plans aiming at the uprooting of those normals."

## SEASONAL AND IRREGULAR FLUCTUATIONS

In this volume we shall concentrate attention upon the study of secular and cyclical movements, in the conviction that just here we encounter the fundamental logical issue involved in time-series decomposition. Accordingly, we shall make no attempt to deal systematically or comprehensively with seasonal and irregular fluctuations.

Whenever in the present investigation we encounter the problem of seasonal variation, we shall proceed on the assumption that there are available a sufficient body of knowledge concerning the causes producing seasonal movements and a sufficiently developed statistical technique to make possible seasonal adjustments adequate for our ends. There is no intention, however, of taking a cavalier attitude toward the topic of seasonal variation. We agree that further perspicacious investigation in the field of seasonal variation constitutes a task worthy of able statistical analysts. But we are here preoccupied with a problem which is decidedly more difficult and which has implications believed to be more profound. Our contribution in this book to the subject of seasonal variation will consist mainly in expanding the body of statistical experience relating to seasonal movements in fundamental economic series extending over long time periods. In the statistical work of Chapter III, we employ methods of seasonal correction which are adequate for the purpose at hand and for most other practical uses as well. It would not, in these earlier stages of our study, be appropriate to develop more highly elaborate treatment of seasonal variation — such as, for example, that involved in setting up seasonal indexes variable with respect to the phase of the business cycle — for in so doing we should inevitably be obliged to beg certain questions which are fundamental to our main line of analysis, e.g., the question whether there *is* any unambiguous basis for marking off cyclical phases. With the completed findings of this volume in hand to furnish guidance, it will be possible to go back and undertake the refinement of the seasonal measurements here worked out.

We shall in the present book make no attempt at investigation of irregular variations. Preoccupied with a logical issue — the significance of secular and cyclical movements — which is believed to be of paramount importance, we shall merely accept the obvious fact that irregular variations do occur, even though the exact lines of demarcation from secular, cyclical, and seasonal movements, respectively, may by no means be clear, either as a matter of logical definition or of statistical isolation.

### The Problem of Secular Trend

We turn at once, then, to the fundamental *logical* problem of time-series decomposition — the nature of secular trend, and its relation to cyclical variations. In Part One of this volume we consider the problem broadly and give attention to certain questions of general methodological approach. In Chapter I, five viewpoints as to the nature of the problem of secular trend (representing successively more and more sophisticated concepts of the entity) are presented and discussed. The notion of secular trend as *a problem in mathematical curve fitting* is rejected as missing the essential point — the representation of the secular trend of the series, as opposed to the reproduction of the series itself, or at least its main fluctuations. The concept of secular trend as *a problem in statistical description* is also held to be inadequate, but it is suggested that until such time as our knowledge regarding economic causation shall be greatly increased, this concept can play a useful rôle in our analyses. Accordingly, some attention is devoted in Chapter I to the methodological question as to the best technique for the fitting of secular-trend representations. It is argued that for periods of moderate length (ten, fifteen, even twenty years) the conventional least-squares method is often untrustworthy, even judged by the narrow requirement of giving a "good fit" in the quasi-mechanical sense. A new technique — involving the use of the criterion "absolute sum of the deviations a minimum" — is suggested.

Going on to other viewpoints, it is urged that the idea of secular trend as *a problem in historical description* has at least the virtue of bringing us face to face with the issue, "What part of the fluctuation of the series is secular, and what part is cyclical?" The appearance of the final curve of "cyclical variations" palpably depends upon the previous decision as to how the secular trend is to be represented. Discretionary judgment inevitably enters. But upon what basis should this discretionary judgment be made? It is indicated that while the concept of secular trend as *a problem in the analysis of causation* gives us the clue to the answer, we should associate the idea of time-series decomposition not with the separation of causal influences into distinct sets or groups (for the forces which produce the cycles, let us say, may also be instrumental with respect to the trends), but rather with the delineation of paths of causal influence. Finally, the stand is taken that the problem of secular trend is essentially and fundamentally *a problem in economic theory*, and that our aim and endeavor should be to bring our statistical analyses into conformity with this conception as speedily as may be possible.

## THE LIMITATIONS OF CONVENTIONAL METHODOLOGY

If this volume indeed has distinctive features, it is certain that such features have their origin in the attitude taken with regard to certain general methodological questions, as set forth in the earlier part of Chapter II. In planning our statistical investigation, we should proceed by the *genetic* method — *ab initio* — setting aside all preconceptions. Our aim should be so to perform the analysis as to lead to complete conviction in the end that the results portray only relationships inherent in the original figures; ground must not be left for the suspicion that these results even *might have been* in whole or in part created by some process of adjustment or manipulation. We must, therefore, deny ourselves the use of moving averages and other smoothing devices which have in the past played a considerable part in time-series decomposition work. Further, and here we depart from most previous analysis in this field, *we expressly reject the notion of commencing the investigation by application of the conventional procedure for trend-cycle separation — fitting secular trends and computing cyclical deviations therefrom* — for in a study which undertakes to proceed by the genetic method, as ours does, employment of such procedure at the outset would mean begging the very question at issue, namely: "How *should* the statistical decomposition be performed?"

This last point is given emphasis in Chapter II by the presentation of "the pig-iron-production case." Twenty-nine different secular trends for the series pig-iron production are assembled — twenty-three trends mathematically fitted by various other investigators and six moving-average trends computed by the present writer. For each of these twenty-nine trends, the average length of "cycle" about the trend line is calculated; the average length of "cycle" thus secured varies, by more or less regular gradations, from 45–40 years to 3.2 years (cf. Tables 1 and 2). It is clear that the discovery, about a particular trend-representation for a given series, of oscillations which may conform more or less closely to a certain average length cannot in itself be taken as establishing the statistical or economic validity of such movements as cycles.

But we go still further. In the course of the investigations described in Part Two of this volume, we shall deny ourselves *even the concepts* "secular trend" and "cyclical variations." We shall refuse to admit these expressions to our working vocabulary until such time as we may have developed *analytically* cogent evidence that such variations are inherent in the material and that the terms are appropriate for their description.

## PRINCIPLES AND PROGRAM

### BASIC PRINCIPLES

We thus have rejected the customary and conventional modes of approach to the problem of time-series decomposition. What basic principles, then, should guide us in a new, genetic attack? In Chapter II it is urged: (1) that we shall have the best chance of success if we attack the problem as a unified whole — look at the whole picture at once (in so far as the evidence is available, and within practical limitations of time and expense) — rather than at fragmentary parts of it; (2) that we should be on the lookout for, and be guided by, consistencies and uniformities of behavior among our series; and (3) that we should bring to bear on the problem all of our theoretical equipment and all of our historical knowledge.

### A BROAD GENERAL PROGRAM OF ATTACK

It is next suggested that a broad general program of attack upon the problem of time-series decomposition (having as foundation the basic principles just set forth) would include: (1) as an initial step, the carrying out of a number of extensive statistical analyses, collectively covering as much of the available pertinent statistical material as is practically possible, involving a search for the "consistencies and uniformities of behavior" just mentioned, and presumably eventuating in some form of time-series decomposition (not necessarily along conventional lines) for the constituent series; (2) next, the interpretation of the results thus obtained, considered as a whole and in conjunction with other appropriate statistical evidence, in the light of economic theory and economic history; (3) last of all — after a synthesis of the elements provided by the preceding statistical, theoretical, and historical investigations — reconsideration and unification of the work earlier done, in the statistical analyses mentioned under "(1)" above, upon the statistical decomposition of the several time series, with a view to obtaining finally a systematic and connected composite array of statistical results, accompanied, correspondingly, by a systematic and connected theoretical and historical interpretation.

### INDISPENSABILITY OF THE EARLY, COMPREHENSIVE STATISTICAL ANALYSES

Toward the end of Chapter II, emphasis is laid upon the vital necessity for the first of the three steps just listed — i.e., the carrying out of early, comprehensive statistical analyses for the basic data — and it is urged that this step constitutes an indispensable prerequisite for the later synthesis of theoretical, historical, and statistical elements. Such extensive preliminary statistical studies are clearly necessary in order to derive from the confusing and bewildering mass of available statistical data a picture of the general tendencies inherent therein. The raw facts need classification, condensation, interpretation. The statistical series must be examined with respect to various criteria of homogeneity: technical excellence of construction, perfection of measurement of the phenomena which the several series purport to represent, reliability of sampling, comparability over time. The data thus require criticism, and often they in addition require revision. Further, these preliminary analyses are all the more urgent because we find in existing studies certain statistical summarizations which at least *appear to be* contradictory — cf. the question as to the existence, nature, and average length of "intermediate cycles," or "secondary trends." Still further, before we enter upon an attempt to develop a theoretical explanation for the flow of economic events, we need to know *what it is that we are trying to explain*. It makes a great deal of difference with respect to our theoretical explanation, for example, whether the expressions "secular trend" and "cyclical variations" are essentially arbitrary in their application — representing little more than a *façon de parler* — or correspond to lines of causal influence which really are inherent in the course of economic change, and which can be rather definitely distinguished and delineated. And it makes a great deal of difference with respect to the diagnosis, prognosis, and prescription in a given economic situation whether economic life is marked by a single wave-like form of fluctuation, or by two or more such movements each (though doubtless related to the other or others) having its own individuality and possessing its own peculiar theoretical counterpart.

### THE PRESENT VOLUME

The present volume is intended as a contribution toward the fulfillment of the broad general program of attack upon the problem of time-series decomposition outlined on preceding pages. This book is mainly devoted to an elaborate analysis of an extensive and significant body of data. Our basic material consists of significant economic series pertaining to the United States; our interval of study, the period from the close of the Civil War to the outbreak of the World War in 1914. In Part Two of this volume, we make a thoroughgoing search for "consistencies and uniformities of behavior" — look for patterns of fluctuation in time series. Guided by the results of our pattern analyses, we turn in Part Three to the task of effecting the explicit statistical decomposition of a group of leading time series. The investigations which form the principal subject matter of this book are described at length in Parts Two and Three, and are sketched briefly in the Summary of the Findings, to which we now turn our attention.

## SUMMARY OF THE FINDINGS

### The Standard-Pattern Investigation for the Thirteen Important Economic Series

We begin the pattern investigation of Part Two by choosing — on the basis of fundamental importance, continuity, and homogeneity — a group of thirteen series for intensive study (cf. Chart 1).[9] Believing, as has been set forth in this Introduction, that we have sufficient knowledge of the causes producing seasonal movements, and a sufficiently developed statistical technique, to make possible seasonal measurements satisfactory for our purposes, we apply seasonal adjustments to the various series where needed (for the seasonal indexes, see Table 3). The task is tedious, and necessitates careful study; for every series requiring adjustment, we find progressive or other changing seasonal tendencies. It is believed that significant contribution is here made to the historical information regarding the form of seasonal fluctuations over this long period, and also to the body of experience with the technical problems of seasonal-variation measurement for long series.

The group of series, freed of seasonal fluctuations, is ready for analysis. What type of procedure shall we adopt? Having in mind the danger of creating the appearance of relationship where none really exists, through the application of complex methodology, we resolve to begin the analysis by a search for relationships of the simplest sort: specifically, to give first consideration to simple period-to-period changes. Next, we make an extended analytical investigation of a question which up to this time has not received the attention it deserves: "Do the short-run fluctuations of time series, compared one with another, show greater constancy of dispersion ratio upon an *absolute* or upon a *relative* basis?" Our extended graphic studies (cf. Chart 2) and our analytical tests indicate the definite superiority of the relative basis. Accordingly, we decide to work with measures of period-to-period relative variation — link relatives. And, finally, we plan to examine link relatives of several periods — commencing with quarterly data, thence proceeding to annual, and so on.

[9] In examining this Summary of the Findings, the reader will find it convenient to refer to the list of charts, presented at the beginning of this volume, which gives page references.

We develop a general method of attack, capable of wide application in time-series analysis. This procedure is designed to discover and to represent such common patterns of movement as may be inherent in the data. Applying this procedure first to the quarterly link relatives, we discover a general pattern of short-run fluctuation unmistakably tracing itself through our array of series, and we derive a *standard pattern* representing this basic movement (cf. Charts 1, 3, and 4, Chapter III). The derivation of this pattern is of very great significance, for the reason that it affords *analytical* demonstration of the presence in the data of a smooth, wave-like fluctuation of particular form. This standard pattern could not possibly have been created by the methodology, for we have employed a simple procedure, and have avoided question-begging assumptions; the movements pictured have been shown, altogether cogently, to be inherent in the original material.

We next apply this same procedure to link relatives pertaining to successively longer time periods — annual, two-year, three-year, six-year, nine-year (cf. Charts 5, 7, 8, 9, and 10, in Chapters IV and V) — but we discover no new pattern; the basic pattern first developed maintains itself (cf. Chart 6). *We find analytical evidence of the presence of one, and only one, definite pattern of fluctuation.*[10] The work leading to this conclusion is of decided importance, for clearly the question whether there is more than one pattern of fluctuation inherent in our material must be settled analytically before it is permissible for us to proceed to the building of more complex methodological machinery for time-series decomposition.

Still another finding of this pattern investigation — one possessing the highest significance — must be recorded. We discover in our displays of link-relative curves unmistakable evidence establishing *analytically* — and once more without the employment of any preliminary question-begging assumptions — *the presence of some force, or complex of forces, of a long-run sort, which is operating upon our array of series, gradually destroying their cohesiveness and driving them away from one another.* The investigation of this disjoining force is clearly a task calling for attention as soon as we can turn to it.

We may, however, pause to suggest that, although the analysis

---

[10] It is, of course, quite conceivable that our standard pattern is a *composite*, reflecting the effect of two or more sets of causal influences.

as so far developed has of course not accomplished the statistical decomposition of the various time series under examination, the results nevertheless — even supposing the statistical analysis to be carried no further — should be of material value. The original series and patterns presented in Chart 1 and various other charts of Part Two, together with the generalizations which may be derived therefrom, make it possible to set up a method of attack the results of which shall at least have the merit of representing a unified and consistent theoretical interpretation of the general picture shown by this assemblage of curves — a procedure far superior to that of studying the series one at a time. Further, the standard pattern furnishes a background against which to compare segments of statistical data, otherwise perhaps awkward to handle, and thus to judge their proper places in the general scheme.

## THE PATTERN OF PRODUCTION, LINK-RELATIVE APPROACH

We turn now to the examination of various bodies of supplementary data, beginning with those for the field of production. In investigating the pattern of production, we give first attention to the *link-relative approach*, reserving the *fixed-base approach* for later consideration.

### THE PATTERN STUDY

In the link-relative approach, we begin the analysis by studying the structure of production, basing such study upon some one hundred annual series for individual industries. We apply to these series the general form of analysis previously carried out for the group of thirteen important economic series, but with such modifications in detail as seem appropriate for the data at hand.

We classify the production series by economic groups, and find that (setting aside agriculture, where the behavior is palpably individualistic) the several groups have definite, and similar, patterns of short-run movement (cf. Chart 12). Clearly, over our period of analysis *a well-defined pattern of short-time fluctuation is generally pervasive throughout the structure of the nation's industrial and commercial life.* This pervasiveness is brought out in most striking fashion by the lines upon Chart 13, especially the last nine curves. Each of these curves pertains to a particular sector of the array of production series, arranged in order of amplitude of short-run fluctuation.

We develop a composite curve to portray the general pattern in the structure of industrial and commercial production. The correspondence between this new pattern and that previously set up for the thirteen series (cf. the first two sections of Chart 12) is truly remarkable. It is all the more noteworthy when one considers that: (1) it appears in spite of numerous defects of the basic constituent series for each pattern; (2) the two patterns are derived from wholly distinct lists of series; and (3) even the *lists* were set up by independent investigators, each in entire ignorance of the other's work.

## THE AVOIDANCE OF "METHODOLOGY BIAS"

Two significant developments incidental to this study of the structure of production may now be mentioned. The first has perhaps some claim to novelty in statistical research. It relates to the emphasis laid upon "methodology bias." All statistical analysis requires, at one stage or another, some exercise of discretionary judgment; and even with the very best of intentions the investigator may, in the course of making these judgments, altogether unconsciously impress into the somewhat plastic mass of materials confronting him certain preconceptions as to what the results *ought* to show. We are, therefore, under obligation continually to exercise every effort to avoid such "methodology bias." In the case at hand, for example — the study of the pattern in the structure of industrial and commercial production — we employ a list of series independently developed by another investigator. Furthermore, we take pains to confirm our final results in various ways: by trying out a different system for economic grouping of the constituents; by reworking the pattern analysis, applying it to all non-agricultural series combined, without separating them into economic groups; by dividing the series into groups according to amplitude of short-run fluctuation.

## THE LONG-RUN TENDENCIES OF INDIVIDUAL PRODUCTION SERIES NOT CAPABLE OF ADEQUATE REPRESENTATION BY THE LOGARITHMIC PARABOLA

The second of the two significant developments to which reference is made just above has to do with the attention given to the problem of representing long-run tendencies in individual production series. *We find that such long-run tendencies are much*

*less simple than has sometimes been supposed. Our study of indi-
vidual production series leads unmistakably to the conclusion that
for very few individual production series indeed can it fairly be
said that there is indication of even rough approximation to a
constant rate of retardation in growth over the pre-war era.* The
logarithmic parabola is almost always a poor fit.[11] This is demonstrated not only by graphic survey of the original-item charts,
but also by the application of a new methodological technique,
involving the study of first and second logarithmic differences and
the utilization of the relation between the sine curve and its first
derivative (cf. Chart 11; note, in particular, how the "band"
between the curves of first and second differences for each of the
three series of Chart 11, Part B, systematically changes over
time — first steadily widening and then gradually narrowing).

Further evidence is found by comparing our rates of retardation in growth (for 1866–1914) with those of Professor Arthur
F. Burns (for 1870–1929).[12] Our retardation rates consistently
are appreciably lower. This discrepancy is significant, as it suggests that the general tendency for individual industries *is not
simply for the pre-war (1866–1914) retardation rate to continue
into the post-war years 1915–29, but rather is for the retardation
to become more severe in these later years.*

### New Production Indexes; the Pattern of Production, Fixed-Base Approach

We turn next to the *fixed-base approach.* We first give some
attention to the theoretical and practical difficulties connected
with the construction of production indexes. We then examine
critically existing long-range production indexes extending over
our pre-war period, notably (1) the Day-Persons index for manufacture, and (2) the Snyder deflated-clearings index of trade.
Finally, we construct entirely new production indexes for manufacture and for transportation and communication. (See the
graphic presentation of the various indexes in Chart 14.)

---

[11] The logarithmic parabola (log $y = a + bt + ct^2$) is a curve exhibiting constancy in rate of acceleration, or of retardation, as the case may be. However, the
case of retardation in growth is of principal interest in the study of long-time
movements for individual production series. For a numerical example of the logarithmic parabola and retardation in growth, see Table 4 in Chapter VII.

[12] Cf. his *Production Trends in the United States since 1870* (New York: National
Bureau of Economic Research, Inc., 1934), chapter IV.

### THE NEW INDEX FOR MANUFACTURE

A new annual index of manufacturing production, 1860–1914, is presented. The construction of this index involves an elaborate and extended analysis, including intensive examination (and, so far as feasible, improvement) of basic data, careful consideration of a variety of methodological issues, and a long-extended series of laborious computations. The new annual index is presented in Chart 14. While there is, of course, no thought of suggesting that all theoretical and practical difficulties have been overcome, or that we have here arrived at statistical measurements which are from all points of view unimpeachable, it would nevertheless appear that we may properly claim for our new index of manufacture some degree of merit, relative to that which lies within the realm of practically achievable possibility — especially as regards the qualities of continuity and comparability over time which are crucial with reference to the purposes of the present pattern investigation.

### THE NEW INDEX FOR TRANSPORTATION AND COMMUNICATION

So far as is known to the present writer, no production index for the field of transportation and communication has ever previously been worked out covering the pre-war interval 1860–1914. In developing our new index number, we naturally give first, and major, attention to railroad transportation. Many serious difficulties and many perplexing problems present themselves here. The available aggregate series — for tonnage, ton-miles, passengers, and passenger-miles — over the years prior to 1890 are found to pertain to constantly changing groups of roads. The only solution is to construct entirely new aggregates. This involves: (1) setting up a suitable "sample" list of railroad systems, with proper proportionate representation of geographical and economic groups; (2) tediously searching out the data for individual railroads in various manuals and reports; (3) studying the history of the several systems and making adjustments, to secure real, as opposed to apparent, homogeneity; (4) employing comprehensive "cross-section" aggregates at selected dates, as a safeguard against gradual drifts away from the truth in the relative movements of the sample totals. In addition to the work upon steam railroads, numerous problems have to be met in connection with other series — e.g., those pertaining to street-railroad traffic, postal traffic, and so on. Through these extended and elaborate studies, we obtain and present a new annual index for transportation and communication, 1860–1914 (Chart 14).

THE NEW INDEX OF INDUSTRIAL AND COMMERCIAL PRODUCTION

Finally, we develop a new index of the volume of industrial and commercial production (which we shall frequently indicate simply by the designation "production index"); this is an average of the two new indexes — for manufacture, and for transportation and communication — just described. And — once more with a view to avoiding "methodology bias" — we set up a "check production index," inferior technically to our own, but having the virtue of being based upon production indicators developed independently by *other analysts*. This "check production index" is employed throughout the remainder of our investigation as a "control" upon the various conclusions reached through the use of our own new production index.

### THE PATTERN OF PRODUCTION INDEXES

The production index — as well as its two components, and the "check production index," and indexes of mining and trade — shows close conformity of short-run fluctuation to the standard pattern for the thirteen important economic series, earlier derived, thus affording still further confirmation of this pattern (cf. Chart 16). So far as the *long-run* tendencies of the production index are concerned, our study indicates that these largely exhaust themselves in rather rapid growth, accompanied by very slight retardation in rate of growth (cf. Chart 17, showing the indexes with average rate of growth and average rate of retardation eliminated).

### OTHER PATTERNS

NEW EMPLOYMENT INDEXES; THE PATTERN OF EMPLOYMENT

We next give attention to pre-war employment data. The available indexes for Massachusetts, New Jersey, and New York are examined; and entirely new indexes are developed for Ohio and Pennsylvania, after going back to the original records and subjecting these records to careful study. In so far as the present writer is aware, no extended analysis has ever been made of the statistical data on employment prior to 1914 for these last two states. The basis for drawing conclusions regarding pre-war movements in the volume of employment has thus been appreciably broadened. In addition, a new general index number is constructed, 1889–1914, both annually (Chart 19) and quarterly (Chart 20). In the derivation of this new index, attempt is made to obtain continuity and comparability over time; the extension of the index back to 1889 is not accomplished by simple "splicing," but rather by a procedure which takes into account differences among the constituents with respect to average rate of growth, average rate of retardation, and average amplitude of short-run fluctuation. The short-time movements of the new general index — as well as those of its components (cf. Chart 21) — are found to conform closely to those of the production index and of the standard pattern for thirteen series (cf. Chart 22).

## COMMODITY PRICES; MISCELLANEOUS SERIES

Turning now to the field of commodity prices, we find that for commodity-price *index numbers* there is conformity in short-run fluctuation to the standard pattern (Chart 22). So far as the *structure* of commodity prices is concerned, limitations of time and expense make it necessary for us to confine ourselves to graphic examination of price series. This examination suggests that, while the situation with respect to the general nature of the pattern in the structure of commodity prices is roughly similar to that for production, we should probably expect to find more elements of diversity, of heterogeneity, in the price structure.

Finally, examination of a group of miscellaneous economic series not falling within any of the preceding rubrics of classification indicates that the general short-run tendencies among these series are clearly in conformity with those of the standard pattern for the thirteen series and the other patterns which we have found to be so closely correlated with it.

Of the findings of Part Two of this volume, there are three which possess fundamental importance — constitute "foundation stones," in fact — with reference to the work of Part Three. (1) We have established that for the United States over the pre-war interval 1866–1914 there is a clearly-defined pattern of short-run fluctuation (cf. Chart 22) permeating the whole structure of the nation's industrial and commercial life. (2) We have been able to find analytical evidence of the presence of one, and only one, such pattern. (3) We have, however, discovered clear indication of the existence of long-run disjoining tendencies in our array of economic series, gradually over the course of time overcoming their cohesiveness and driving them away from one another.

## The Fundamental Proposition Regarding the Nature of Secular and Cyclical Movements and Their Relation

When we turn to Part Three of this volume — which aims at the explicit statistical decomposition of certain leading time series — the methodological apparatus becomes so technical that detailed advance summarization is highly difficult. We can only outline very briefly. In Chapter XII we develop and demonstrate, through appropriate analytical treatment, a Fundamental Proposition: *For a group of leading economic series (exhibited upon Chart 23) and over our pre-war period, it is a good first approximation to the truth to say that the time-series variations (setting aside seasonal and irregular fluctuations) are resolvable into smooth, continuous, gradually-changing long-time movements which may appropriately be designated "secular trends," and wave-like short-time oscillations which may appropriately be designated "cyclical variations"; and it is further a good first approximation to assert that the relationship between these two types of variations is that of being logarithmically additive.*

There is, of course, nothing essentially new about the proposition itself — the claim of novelty rests not upon the *statement* of the proposition, but upon *demonstration* of it for an important range of data.

We are at last free to use the concepts "secular trend" and "cyclical variations," and to admit the terms to our working vocabulary. And now we push forward to still more ambitious goals. We endeavor to arrive at a good first approximation to the statistical decomposition of this group of leading economic series (see again Chart 23) — to accomplish, that is, the separation of the secular and cyclical movements. We attack the problem by two independent methods.

### The Separation of Secular and Cyclical Movements for Leading Time Series

#### THE FIRST METHOD: USE OF A PARTICULAR SERIES TO PRECIPITATE THE TREND-INDICATIONS

In the first method (Chapter XIII), we use a particular series to *precipitate* indications of secular tendency for the other series. More specifically, we determine that the production index is that series of the group under treatment for which the relationship between secular and cyclical variations is likely to be simplest. We find that the production index is essentially different from typical individual production series, as regards secular constancy of the retardation rate (see Chart 24; also compare Chart 25 with Chart 11). Then, employing the new technique (referred to above) involving the study of first and second logarithmic differences and the utilization of the relation between the sine curve and its first derivative (cf. Chart 25), we conclude that the prewar secular trend of the production index can be represented with reasonably close approach to precision by a logarithmic parabola of such form as to indicate rather rapid secular growth, accompanied by a very slight retardation in rate of growth. Through elimination of this secular trend from the original items, we obtain the curve of cyclical variation.[13] Taking this curve of cyclical variation for the production index as basis, we precipitate the *trend-indications* for the other series (cf. Chart 26 and Chart 27).

#### THE SECOND METHOD: GRADUAL ATTENUATION OF THE NON-CYCLICAL ELEMENTS IN THE STANDARD PATTERN

In the second of the two independent methods for effecting the statistical decomposition of the group of leading economic series, the procedure (Chapter XIV) involves the gradual attenuation of the non-cyclical elements in the standard pattern, developed in the earlier stages of this investigation (Chapters III and IV). More specifically, we begin by arguing — on the basis of the showing of the "chart of ranks" (Chart 28), and other evidence — that in the original calculation of the standard pattern the

---

[13] The "check production index" is used here (as throughout) to afford a "control" — as a guard against "methodology bias."

secular influences of the individual series must have been so weakened, so attenuated, that their rôle in this pattern is comparatively minor. We then proceed to the precipitation of *tentative trend-indications* for the several individual series (cf. Charts 29, 30, and 31, in Chapter XIV), by means of which we are able still further to reduce the influence of the secular element in the standard pattern. We continue this line of attack until the process of gradual attenuation of the secular elements in the standard pattern has eventuated in virtually complete elimination, so that we may regard the revised standard pattern finally obtained (third and fifth lines on Chart 32) as a faithful picture of the cyclical element in isolation. Using this new cyclical pattern as basis, we precipitate still further improved trend-indications for our array of leading economic series (Chart 31, Part D). These trend-indications, derived by this independent method, agree closely with those obtained by the first method (compare Charts 27 and 31).

Incidentally, through the use of this second, independent method we obtain complete confirmation (cf. Charts 29 and 30) of the conclusion — earlier reached by a different analytical process — that the secular trend of the production index may be suitably represented by a logarithmic parabola; indeed, the significant constants for the mathematical equation are almost identical in the two cases.[14] Further, there is a very close resemblance between the form of cyclical variation displayed by the newly improved standard pattern and the production index, respectively (cf. Chart 34). This resemblance is all the more striking in view of the fact that these two cyclical curves are based upon entirely distinct sets of statistical series and have been developed independently of each other.

Finally, we apply to the several leading economic series the procedure developed in Chapter XIII, but substituting the cyclical variations of the revised standard pattern in place of those of the production index. The resulting trend-indications are almost precisely identical with those obtained in the preceding chapter (cf. Chart 33).

[14] Here again we use the "check production index" as a guard against "methodology bias" (cf. Chart 30).

THE ARRAY OF SECULAR TRENDS AND CYCLICAL VARIATIONS
FOR LEADING ECONOMIC SERIES

We now turn to the task of developing lines of *trend-repre-sentation* for our array of leading economic series, 1866–1914. We accomplish this by transliterating the readings of the trend-indication lines of Chart 27 (virtually identical results might have been secured by using instead those of Chart 33). The equations of the lines of secular trend thus obtained are presented in Table 15, and the secular trends and cycles are graphically exhibited on Chart 34. In Chart 36 we replot the trend-indications, this time drawing the curves with *arithmetic* (as opposed to logarithmic) vertical scales. This chart is of some interest in relation to the Kondratieff "long-wave" hypothesis.

We are now at last in position to state a conclusion as to the true place of mathematical curve fitting in secular-trend deriva-tion for economic time series. Its rôle is minor. Far from being the principal element of the methodology (we can surely no longer speak of the secular trend as being *"determined* [e.g.] by the method of least squares"), its part is altogether subordinate and incidental. It enters not as the first step, but as the last in a long analytical process. It has its modest function, but is in no way fundamental.

The contrast between our new methodology and the conven-tional procedure is decided. Our results here rest primarily not upon discretionary judgment, but upon an extended, connected chain of analytical reasoning, involving the search for patterns (Part Two), the investigation into the fundamental nature of time-series variations (Chapter XII), and the precipitation of the trend-indications by two independent methods (Chapters XIII and XIV). Our point may be emphasized by inviting a contrast. Consider "the pig-iron production case" of Chapter II. Imagine the twenty-nine different trends which have been fitted to this series to be superimposed, in a single graph, upon the chart of original items, yielding a confused network of lines. Then in contrast set Chart 35, which shows the application of the present methodology to pig-iron production. The need for discretionary judgment in the selection of trend-representation has been reduced until it becomes almost a negligible factor. And, although for the array of leading economic series of Charts 27 and 34 the transliteration from trend-indications to trend-representations is not always so simple nor so clear-cut as it is for pig-iron production, nevertheless even for that array the difference in degree, as to dependence upon discretionary judgment, between the conventional procedure and our present methodology, is unquestionably still great enough to constitute a difference in kind.

# PART ONE

## THE NATURE OF THE PROBLEM, AND QUESTIONS OF GENERAL METHODOLOGY

# CHAPTER I

## THE PROBLEM OF SECULAR TREND

THIS CHAPTER treats the logical problem of the significance of trend-cycle separation in the analysis of economic time series.[1] We begin with a discussion of various points of view as to the meaning of secular trend.[2]

### A PROBLEM IN MATHEMATICAL CURVE FITTING

It might be urged that in establishing a representation for secular trend, closeness of fit of the curve to the data should be the criterion, and mathematical measures of "goodness of fit" might be set up, analogous to those employed for frequency series. A fundamental difficulty, however, immediately appears. In applying this principle to secular trends, we must "choose a curve which reproduces the underlying movement of the data without bending or twisting itself so as to conform to the extreme sinuosities, and which at the same time gives a good 'fit' as judged by some arbitrary criterion — say, the mean square error." [3] These two requirements, however, are mutually contradictory,[4] and evidently exercise of arbitrary judgment is required in effecting a compro-

---

[1] This chapter reproduces (with certain additions) the substance of the first part of an article by the present writer, published under the title "The Problem of Secular Trend," in the *Review of Economic Statistics*, XVI (October 15, 1934), pp. 199–206.

The reader may find it of interest to compare the present classification of secular-trend concepts with that of Professor Joseph A. Schumpeter, in his recent *Business Cycles* (New York and London: McGraw-Hill Book Co., Inc., 1939), pp. 200–212.

[2] In this connection, see the preliminary discussions of the Introduction. It is not maintained that the five concepts here set forth represent entirely independent categories; on the contrary, they merge into one another successively, and the transition point in each case is by no means definite.

[3] Henry Schultz, *Statistical Laws of Demand and Supply* (Chicago: University of Chicago Press, 1928), p. 47.

[4] "On the one hand we can obtain the curve which actually goes through the points — here the sum of the squares of the errors is zero, but the curve is composed of perturbations or sinuosities. On the other hand we can obtain a perfectly smooth curve . . . and we obtain a large mean square error." — E. C. Rhodes, "Smoothing," *Tracts for Computers*, No. VI (London: Cambridge University Press, 1921), pp. 43–44.

mise between them. In a word, our difficulty arises from the fact that we wish to represent the *secular trend* of the series, as opposed to reproducing the *series itself* (or at least its main fluctuations), and we are consequently unable to place sole reliance on mathematical tests. Additional criteria are required.

## A Problem in Statistical Description

The problem of secular trend might be thought of as a problem in statistical description. Just as we describe the essential characteristics of frequency series by the citation of, e.g., averages, standard deviations, and measures of skewness, so we might describe the general tendencies shown by time series through the computation of lines of secular trend. The secular trend has in fact often been defined in some such language as the following: the gradual and persistent movement of the series over a period of time which, contrasted with the cyclical fluctuations of the series, is long.

In fitting the trend line which is designed to furnish a statistical description of the fundamental movements of a particular time series, the decisions as to type of curve and trend interval are by no means matters of indifference. In particular, with reference to the trend interval it is patently inappropriate to combine segments from time periods which are clearly non-homogeneous — as would be the case, for example, if the years 1910–22 were selected for a commodity-price series. Furthermore, if intervals for trend fitting are chosen indiscriminately, the calculated line is likely to be distorted by the influence of the cyclical movements at the beginning and end of the computation period.[5] It is certain, then, that even if we accept the view that the problem of secular trend is one of statistical description, we have by no means reduced the problem to a mechanical basis, nor have we done away with the necessity for careful examination of the characteristics, and in particular the economic characteristics, of the original data.

With respect to the usefulness and validity of the concept of secular trend as a statistical description, there is possibility for contrary opinions. On the one hand, it may be maintained that such a statistical description can have little or no value unless the calculations are preceded by an extensive causal analysis of the

---

[5] In this connection, see fn. 11 in this chapter.

forces behind the movements of the series — such analysis to be obtained through a theoretical examination of the causal forces in question, or through historical investigation, or both; and still further, that in the absence of an exhaustive analysis of this sort, the determination and representation of secular movements should not be undertaken. The opposing opinion is that until such time as our knowledge regarding economic causation shall be greatly increased, there will still be room for a procedure which starts with the statistical summarization and perhaps works back from that summarization.[6]

Still further in defense of the concept of secular trend as a statistical description, it may be suggested that even though we do not present in advance a complete theoretical and historical causal explanation of the movements in an economic series, there is nevertheless justification for the employment of a procedure which will yield the answer to some significant question. By way of example, we may quote from Professor Frederick C. Mills' statement regarding the measurements of secular trend in his *Economic Tendencies*, and from Professor Arthur F. Burns' discussion of production trends in his book upon that subject.

Professor Mills says: "A detailed inspection of the series used indicates that, during the periods here studied, economic series have tended to increase (or decrease) by fairly constant percentage increments (or decrements), year by year. During an era marked by no sudden breaks in the general economic development of a country, sharp interruptions in the rates of change of individual series are the exception, not the rule. . . . There is a final justification for the employment of the procedure here described. This method yields, for each series, a single measurement which summarizes the direction and degree of change of that series during a stated period and which is directly comparable with similar measures derived from other series." [7]

Professor Burns says: "The nature of the problem leading to the measurement will then determine whatever definiteness and significance the primary [8] trend will have . . . if there is some

[6] In this connection, see the concluding sentences of Professor Warren M. Persons' *Forecasting Business Cycles* (New York: John Wiley & Sons, Inc., 1931), p. 284.

[7] Frederick C. Mills, *Economic Tendencies in the United States* (a publication of the National Bureau of Economic Research, Inc., in cooperation with the Committee on Recent Economic Changes, New York, 1932), p. 48.

[8] In the paragraph from which this quotation is taken, Professor Burns speaks

point in inquiring about the average annual rate of increase of wheat production in the United States since 1870, a primary trend embodying an answer to this question will also have some significance. . . . Suppose that growth at a declining percentage rate is considered as the outstanding characteristic of the history of pig-iron production in the United States, and that it is desired to give mathematical expression to this characteristic. In this case, the choice of a mathematical curve to represent the primary trend is limited to functions — such as the simple logistic, the Gompertz equation, or the 'logarithmic' parabola — which possess the characteristic of advance at a declining percentage rate. Suppose, now, that the aim is not only to indicate the presence of decline in the percentage rate of growth of pig-iron production, but also to measure the average rate of retardation per time unit over the period covered. In this case, a parabola fitted to the logarithms of the production data is the proper mathematical curve to represent the primary trend; for only this function can answer directly the question which has been asked." [9]

Admittedly, the concept of secular trend as a problem in statistical description is inadequate, but nevertheless until such time as our knowledge (and particularly our quantitative knowledge) regarding the operation of economic causation shall be greatly increased, this concept has a useful rôle to play. Accordingly, some attention may properly be devoted to the question of quasi-mechanical trend fitting (i.e., assuming that one has already, on the basis of some broad general analysis, decided upon the type of curve and the approximate time period of the fit). In the fitting of mathematical curves to represent secular trends, especially for short periods — say ten, fifteen, even twenty years — the method of least squares is not always trustworthy, even judged within the limits of the narrow requirement of giving a "good fit" in the quasi-mechanical sense. In many instances the criterion "absolute sum of the deviations a minimum" is superior.[10]

---

of that portion of the secular movement which he designates as the "primary trend." The argument, however, is quite applicable to the general problem now under consideration.

[9] Arthur F. Burns, *Production Trends in the United States since 1870* (New York: National Bureau of Economic Research, Inc., 1934), pp. 45–46.

[10] By "absolute sum" is meant, of course, the total of the values without regard to plus and minus signs. The fitting of a trend line by the criterion "absolute sum

Indeed, the method of least squares was developed with reference to quite a different problem from that which confronts us in the fitting of secular trends to time series, and the squaring process implied in the method powerfully accentuates the "pull" of even moderately large variations from the general tendency. The essential point may be brought out by a simple diagram, such as that of Sketch A. The upper part of the sketch, captioned "absolute-sum criterion," shows a straight line and deviations therefrom of actual items, indicated by vertical bars; in the lower part of the sketch, captioned "least-squares criterion," the lengths of the vertical bars are proportional to the *squares* of the deviations in the upper part.

In the particular case presented by Sketch A, the principal "pull" comes on the two central items, and the distorting influences approximately offset each other. But a new illustration could readily be set up in which these two extreme items are transferred to the boundaries of the time interval in such way as to distort a fitted least-squares line decidedly more than a line fitted by the "minimum-absolute-sum" criterion. The methodological point which this simple example brings to attention clearly has very wide applicability.[11]

---

of the deviations a minimum" is unfortunately a somewhat tedious operation, inasmuch as a direct analytical solution is apparently impossible, and resort must be had to the method of trial and error. However, the burden of the work can be materially lightened by employing the least-squares results as a first approximation, and then proceeding systematically, making intelligent use of interpolation as a guide to the approximate location of the minimum point. In fact, for many of the cases arising in actual practice it is sufficient to make a few tests by the "minimum-absolute-sum" criterion, merely to confirm that the least-squares results are at least reliable within reasonable "limits of tolerance" — i.e., to establish that the distortions produced by the squaring process in the least-squares approach are not serious enough to affect any substantive conclusions one might draw from the results of the fitting process.

[11] Whenever in the present volume mathematical curve fitting is necessary, the principles implicit in the discussion above will be followed.

Another methodological point which has some importance in connection with the question of quasi-mechanical trend fitting relates to the selection of the *precise* beginning and ending dates of the trend interval, supposing the approximate limits already to have been determined on the basis of some broad general analysis.

With reference to the determination of the level and slope of a straight-line trend (as indicated by the constants $a$ and $b$ in the equation $y = a + bt$), we quote from W. L. Crum, A. C. Patton, and A. R. Tebbutt, *Introduction to Economic Statistics* (New York and London: McGraw-Hill Book Co., Inc., 1938), p. 304. "The choice of beginning and terminal years in the interval generally is on the following principle. The cyclical movements at the beginning and at the end of the

## SKETCH A

### ABSOLUTE-SUM VERSUS LEAST-SQUARES CRITERION

Absolute-sum criterion

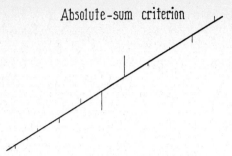

Least-squares criterion

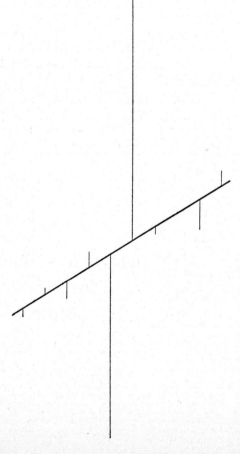

## A Problem in Historical Description

Another view is that we should regard the problem of secular trend as one of *historical* description. According to this view, the specific problem of secular trend is not different in essence from the general problem of historical description. The historian endeavors to develop, from his mass of material, a descriptive summary which will bring out clearly the nature of the fundamental factors which have been at work. Thus, Professor Arthur M. Schlesinger in the preface to the first edition of his *Political and Social History of the United States* says that in the writing of this volume "constant stress has been placed on the great dynamic currents which have shaped the nation's life. In the author's judgment, these were, and still are, (1) the growth of nationality; (2) the struggle for greater democracy; (3) changes in the methods of production and distribution (as evidenced, for instance, by the introduction of machinery and the social adjustments necessitated thereby); (4) the constant striving for social amelioration, including the contest for free public schools, improvement in the lot of women and children, and the successive movements for humanitarian reform; and (5) the expansion of the national boundaries. All these are envisaged as continuous and continuing processes." [12]

---

interval should be in symmetrical phases: if there is a rise at the beginning, there should be a decline at the end . . . ; if there is a peak at the beginning, there should be a peak at the end. . . . Moreover, if possible, the first and last years should be chosen so that the cyclical movement is in an intermediate phase rather than at the peak or trough. . . . If the terminals are thus in intermediate phases, however, the *level* of the line — but not its direction — may be somewhat in error in cases in which the interval is short."

With reference to the determination of the curvature of a parabolic trend (as indicated by the constant $c$ in the equation $y = a + bt + ct^2$), it would seem best to make (wherever possible) *two* computations — the first pertaining to a trend interval beginning at an intermediate phase of the cyclical movement going up and ending at an intermediate phase going down; the second pertaining to a trend interval beginning at an intermediate phase of the cyclical movement going down and ending at an intermediate phase going up — and then *compromise* between the two results (for the constant $c$) by averaging. Preferably, also, the series should be approximately in an intermediate phase at the center of the time interval, in each case.

The careful selection of precise terminal dates for the trend interval is a matter of vital concern when the time period covered is short — say, ten, fifteen, twenty years — but is less important if the period is comparatively long — say, thirty, forty, fifty years.

[12] Arthur M. Schlesinger, *Political and Social History of the United States, 1829–1925* (New York: The Macmillan Co., 1926), p. viii.

The problem of secular trend represents, it might be suggested, merely a special case of historical description. The historical materials consist of a considerable number of statistical series, supplemented by certain non-statistical information. The problem here, as in the general case, is to write the best *description* possible of the fundamental tendencies which these facts reveal. The statistician writes this description, not in words, but in lines or curves upon a chart.[13] Specifically, he writes it in terms of secular trends and cyclical fluctuations about these trends.[14]

The foregoing view brings us to the issue which (granted that the customary classification of time-series variations is acceptable) may be stated thus: "What part of the fluctuation of the series is secular, and what part is cyclical?" This question cannot be evaded, for our computed representations of secular and cyclical movements are palpably interdependent. The appearance of the curve which we finally set forth to represent "cyclical fluctuations" depends upon the previous decision as to how the secular movement is to be represented. We cannot dismiss the *logical* issue merely by saying that the cyclical fluctuations "are obtained by eliminating the secular trend," or that the secular trend "consists of the non-cyclical elements of the series." It is a necessary corollary of this view that every set of lines and curves labeled "secular trend" and "cyclical fluctuations" represents the use of someone's discretionary judgment. This raises the question, "Upon what basis should this discretionary judgment be made?"

[13] In the present chapter, attention will be directed to the basic problem of separating secular and cyclical movements; the problem of seasonal variation — which in general is not of the same order of difficulty — will be neglected.

[14] Cf. the review of Professor J. H. Clapham's *An Economic History of Modern Britain: the Early Railway Age, 1820–50*, by Professor Abbott Payson Usher, in the *Journal of Political Economy*, XL (April 1932), pp. 186–209, especially pp. 195–197, from which the following sentences are quoted.

"The secular trend supplies the realist with the focus of attention essential to any vigorous portrayal of the movement of economic phenomena. It imparts to a historical narrative the requisite unity without resort to any artificial device. . . . The primary task of the general economic historian is to establish the general characteristics of these basic secular trends and to furnish as substantial a commentary as is possible with the materials available. . . . The commentary upon the secular trend must needs include discussion of all the qualitative changes both in technology and in institutions, as well as the quantitative significance of changes in the utilization of natural resources. The scale of treatment of any period thus turns largely upon the elaboration of the commentary."

## A PROBLEM IN THE ANALYSIS OF CAUSATION

One view is that we can best give rationality to the statistical process of separating the various elements in a time series — referred to as the statistical decomposition of the series — by thinking of this process as one of analyzing the effects of particular groups of causes. This general conception would, of course, lead to different schemes for time-series decomposition according to the beliefs held as to the nature of the causal influences.

If the conventional classification of time-series fluctuations is accepted, the statement may be made more specific by saying that in computing lines of secular trend and curves of cyclical variation we are trying to separate, by statistical devices, the effects of two sets of causal influences — one set operating in general gradually and over comparatively long periods of time; the other set operating in a more oscillatory manner and producing fluctuations of shorter length. This point of view may be illustrated by a quotation from an article by Professor Allyn A. Young. This article deals with stabilization of the price level, but the statement is easily capable of a broader application to the problem of secular trend in general.

"Stability, furthermore, may imply primarily the elimination or the lessening of those wave-like general oscillations of prices which economists have come to call 'cyclical.' Or it may imply the absence of those long, slow movements upward or downward which economists have come to call 'trends.' The distinction between these two meanings of stability is not merely academic. It is not made merely to serve the convenience of statisticians and other analysts. It rests upon real differences in the nature of the various forces which make for instability, and upon corresponding difference in the character of the measures which have to be taken if a larger degree of stability is to be secured." [15]

The concept of trend-and-cycle analysis just set forth and illustrated — namely, that the purpose is to separate statistically the effects of two sets of causal influences — may very well meet with objection on the ground that the rate of change exhibited by the secular trend is in part a *result* of the presence of cyclical varia-

[15] Allyn A. Young, "Downward Price Trend Probable, Due to Hoarding of Gold by Central Banks," *Annalist*, XXXIII (January 18, 1929), p. 96.

tions.[16] With reference to industrial growth, for example, it may on the one hand be argued that cyclical fluctuations reduce the rate of growth, and on the other that it is the cyclical movements which generate the secular trend.[17]

Objections of this sort might be met by altering the wording of the statement to read, "In the statistical separation of trends and cycles the purpose is to analyze the fluctuations of time series with respect to various *paths* of causal influence"; and by saying, in the particular case at hand, that whatever influence of any permanence the cycle may have is to be assimilated by the secular trend and become a property of it.[18] By no means all of the critics of the point of view under consideration would, however, be satisfied by this answer. One group would argue that something much more fundamental is involved than a mere verbal difficulty. They would maintain that the attempted separation of causal influences into two types — long-run and short-run — very much oversimplifies a problem which is in fact highly complex; that quite formidable logical difficulties are bound to appear when an effort is made to apply this concept in a concrete case.

Still other critics would regard the proposed plan of analysis as not merely inadequate, but as positively wrong, in that it implies an incorrect view as to the nature of the basic causal forces which produce the fluctuations appearing in economic series; more specifically, they would object on the ground that the proposed plan combines, under the heading "long-run influences," causal impulses which are altogether different in character and in effect.

It may be that we shall be obliged to refine or revise our causal analyses, and to shape our definitions and distinctions with much more precision than in the past. It may be that we shall have to give up the attractively simple notion that the problem of trend-cycle separation is merely one of distinguishing short-run and

[16] A similar objection might be made to the often-quoted statement to the effect that "the secular trend represents the values which the given series *would have* attained if non-secular influences (notably, cyclical influences) had been eliminated."

[17] Compare the section on "The Business Cycle as a Source of Waste" in Professor Sumner H. Slichter's *Modern Economic Society* (New York: Henry Holt and Co., 1931), pp. 450–454, with the writings of Professor Schumpeter, referred to below; see also L. K. Frank, "Long Term Price Trends," *Journal of the American Statistical Association*, XVIII (September 1923), pp. 904–908.

[18] See O. Gressens, "The Quantitative Determination of Fundamental Changes in Economic Data," *Journal of the American Statistical Association*, XX (December 1925), p. 554.

long-run effects of causal influences, and that we shall have to make the statistical decomposition of time series correspondingly more complex. But, of course, it does not follow that we should discard this general point of view — that the problem of secular trend is one in the analysis of causation — which holds out such promise of assistance in rationalizing a process otherwise quite empirical.[19]

## A Problem in Economic Theory

Many would see no reason for distinguishing the view that secular trend is a problem in the analysis of causation from the view that it is a problem in economic theory. They would regard the application of economic theory as the process by which the causal analysis referred to in the preceding section should be carried out. But, since there is clearly lack of unanimous agreement among economists upon this point, it has seemed best to divide the discussion.

The argument for regarding the problem of secular trend as a problem in economic theory has been put most cogently by Professor Joseph A. Schumpeter. "If trend-analysis is to have any meaning, it can derive it only from previous theoretical considerations, which must not only guide us in interpreting results, but also in choosing the method. Failing this, a trend is no more than a descriptive device summing up past history with which nothing can be done. It lacks economic connotation. It is, in fact, merely formal. We can apply the familiar methods just as well to e.g. a few successive years of a prosperity-phase, as to the whole of the material we may happen to have (as, again, to a period of political commotion). The result has the same claim in every case to be called a trend in the statistical sense, and may in each case be decomposed into component elements in an indefinite number of

---

[19] Before bringing the discussion to a close, a special variation of this point of view may be mentioned: we may regard lines of secular trend as the embodiments of particular causal hypotheses which we desire to test, and we may use these fitted lines as an *aid* in the verification of the hypotheses (the mere fact that a curve fits the data well cannot, of course, in itself constitute such a verification). Thus Dr. Simon S. Kuznets, in his *Secular Movements in Production and Prices* (Boston and New York: Houghton Mifflin Co., 1930), first develops the hypothesis of retardation in industrial growth, and then fits to his production series curves — the logistic and Gompertz — embodying this hypothesis. See, in this connection, the discussion by Professor Wesley C. Mitchell in his *Business Cycles: The Problem and Its Setting* (New York: National Bureau of Economic Research, Inc., 1927), pp. 221–226.

ways which have no rational connection to each other — unless it be supplied by the theory of the subject under research." [20]

As to the precise nature of the theoretical analysis which is to accompany the statistical decomposition of time series, there are numerous and diverse opinions. Professor Warren M. Persons, in his *Forecasting Business Cycles*,[21] says: "These actual cycles are the composite results of two sets of forces. The first set of forces is economic in origin and is created by the unbalanced character, or 'disequilibrium,' of production, trade, wages, consumption, interest rates, security issues, and prices of commodities and securities. I shall call these forces 'internal' to the economic system. The second set of forces impinging upon production, trade, consumption and prices of all kinds is 'external' in origin. The forces are of various degrees of potency and may operate either to throw our economic system more out of balance or to restore equilibrium." [22]

In contrast with the preceding may be set the following quotation from Professor Wesley C. Mitchell: "Nor can the idea presented in many theories that business cycles represent an alternate rupture and restoration of economic equilibrium be included in our working conception. Men who take as their point of departure the theorem that economic forces tend to establish a stable equilibrium may conceive the main problem to be, how this fundamental tendency is overcome at times and how it presently reasserts itself. I have not chosen that point of departure. Hence it is no part of my task to determine how the fact of cyclical oscillations in economic activity can be reconciled with the general theory of equilibrium, or how that theory can be reconciled with facts." [23]

Professor Schumpeter suggests: "Yet it should not be difficult to show that keeping distinct such things as (a) *that element of growth, which is capable of being decomposed into infinitesimal steps* — such as increase in population or savings; (b) the effect

[20] Joseph A. Schumpeter, "Mitchell's Business Cycles," *Quarterly Journal of Economics*, XLV (November 1930), pp. 166–167.

[21] See, in Professor Persons' book, p. 79. Cf. also his pp. 80–82 and 283–284.

[22] The reader will find it of interest to compare the foregoing with the statement regarding "Growth and the Normal Level" and related topics in Professor Elmer C. Bratt's *Business Cycles and Forecasting* (Chicago: Business Publications, Inc., 1940); cf. especially his chapters III and IV.

[23] Mitchell, *Business Cycles*, p. 462.

of industrial and commercial innovation; (c) influences from outside the economic system — such as harvests, gold discoveries, wars, changes in social organizations or in the attitude of men towards business success — and the working out of theoretical schemata for every one of them, might go a long way towards answering many of the questions alluded to, and give additional definiteness both to the aims and results of 'realistic study.' " [24]

There are, of course, many other opinions as to the proper theoretical basis for the statistical analysis of time series which might, if space permitted, be cited at length and illustrated, for example, by such diverse views as the following: the belief that secular trends are mainly to be accounted for by changes in the quantity of money (particularly, the stock of gold), as well as, of course, the gradual growth of population and industry; the notion that cycles (and perhaps secular trends also) may represent merely the cumulative effect of random causes; the suggestion that business cycles are fundamentally the result of forces outside the economic system, operating in a periodic manner.

The stand taken by the present writer is that the problem of secular trend is essentially and fundamentally one of economic theory. Questions of mathematical technique in curve fitting are not to be neglected, but their place is decidedly a subordinate one. The notion of secular trend as a problem of statistical description is inadequate. The aim of those engaged in the analysis of economic time series should be to effect as rapidly as may be possible the replacement of this notion by the concept of secular trend as a problem in economic theory. In the meantime the various concepts discussed in this chapter — except perhaps the first — have a valuable and useful part to play in economic discussions.

---

[24] Schumpeter, *op. cit.*, p. 168. See, in addition, Professor Schumpeter's articles, "The Explanation of the Business Cycle," *Economica*, VII (December 1927), pp. 286–311, and "The Instability of Capitalism," *Economic Journal*, XXXVIII (September 1928), pp. 361–386, especially pp. 372–375 and 381–382 of the latter article; also see his recent *Business Cycles*.

## CHAPTER II

### FUNDAMENTAL METHODOLOGICAL QUESTIONS; GENERAL PRINCIPLES AND PROGRAM OF ATTACK

THE BASIC logical difficulty connected with the separation of secular and cyclical variations, discussed at length in the preceding chapter, finds its counterpart when the actual process of secular-trend representation is undertaken for a particular economic series. To illustrate the fundamental difficulty which arises in connection with such secular-trend representations, certain test computations are shown below, based upon the data for pig-iron production in the United States — a series selected because of the great frequency with which it has been subjected to statistical analysis.[1]

### THE PIG-IRON PRODUCTION CASE

Table 1 presents a list of the various mathematically-fitted secular trends which have at one time or another been calculated for this series. These trends have not been computed by the present writer, but are assembled from various published studies. Column 1 shows for each entry the type of curve fitted and the trend interval.

In each case, a count is made of the number of "cycles." This count is carried out in a quasi-mechanical manner, by merely observing the number of complete swings about the trend line exhibited by the actual figures — simply accepting, in other words, the definition that the term "cycle" denotes "a recurrence of different phases of plus and minus departures." In the pages which immediately follow, the expression has been placed within quotation marks to indicate that it is used in this special and quasi-mechanical sense, without any implication whatever as to the

---

[1] This chapter constitutes an expansion of the latter part of an article by the present writer, published under the title "The Problem of Secular Trend," in the *Review of Economic Statistics*, XVI (October 15, 1934), pp. 199–206. Since the statistical investigations of "the pig-iron production case" are intended only to illustrate a principle, it has not seemed worth while to go to the expense of formally bringing them up to date.

possession or non-possession of statistical or economic significance by the measurements secured.[2]

In the selection of the terminal dates shown in Column 2, the trend interval — that is, the entire period of time included in the calculation of the trend representation — is in each instance employed as a basic period, but the count of "cycles" is made for the interval extending from the first to the last "trough." [3] Whenever it is feasible to include in the count a "cycle" which stands unfinished at the beginning or end of the trend interval, the trend is extrapolated sufficiently to permit such inclusion. It thus happens that the terminal dates in Column 2 in general indicate periods not precisely coextensive with the trend interval, being sometimes longer and sometimes shorter. These variations are obviously called for by the nature of the test computations.

In carrying out the count of "cycles," reference is made to a chart showing the annual data for pig-iron production, 1854–1933. Since annual figures invariably conceal much significant detail in the movement of a series, it is desirable wherever possible to supplement them by items pertaining to shorter intervals. Accordingly, in the present case the available quarterly and monthly figures (1877–1933), corrected for seasonal variation, are plotted on the chart, superimposed upon the annual data.[4]

In the count of "cycles" difficulties arise, as indeed might easily be foreseen, owing to the fact that exercise of discretionary judgment is required in deciding whether a particular "thrust" of the actual figures above or below the trend line is to be included in the count, or is to be rejected as a comparatively minor and temporary fluctuation. These difficulties illustrate, of course, one of the uncertainties connected with attempts to measure the average length of "cycle" for a particular economic series. In the problem at hand we are interested, not in the absolute accuracy of the individual measurements, but rather in their intercomparison.

---

[2] The use of this convenient device for denoting the concept under examination does not, of course, imply acceptance of the definition cited as suitable for statistical or economic analysis.

[3] Except in the case of the first four entries, where it is necessary to measure from peak to peak, in order to obtain one complete "cycle." Were this alternative procedure employed throughout the whole of the table, the conclusions would not be altered in any significant manner.

[4] In interpreting this chart, allowance is made for the fact that prior to October 1901 the quarterly and monthly figures, being estimates, are not precisely consistent with the annual data, which represent actual production.

## TABLE 1

### MEASUREMENTS OF AVERAGE LENGTH OF "CYCLE" FOR PIG-IRON PRODUCTION, WITH REFERENCE TO MATHEMATICALLY-FITTED TRENDS

| Type of curve, and trend interval | Computations employing trend interval as basic period | | Computations employing 1877–1914 as basic period | |
| --- | --- | --- | --- | --- |
| | Interval from first to last "trough" * | Average length of "cycle" (years) | Interval from first to last "trough" * | Average length of "cycle" (years) |
| (1) | (2) | (3) | (4) | (5) |
| (1) Straight line, 1875–1920 (apparent length of "cycle" read from unsmoothed data) | 1875–80 to 1920 | 45–40 | 1875–80 to 1920 | 45–40 |
| (2) Straight line, 1871–1910 | 1872–1913 | 41 | 1872–1913 | 41 |
| (3) Straight line, 1860–1915† | 1872–1907§ | 35 | 1872–1907§ | 35 |
| (4) Straight line, 1879–1913 | 1880–1913 | 33 | 1880–1913 | 33 |
| (5) Logistic curve, 1854–1924 (actual items smoothed before making count of "cycles") | 1863–1932‡ | 23 | 1877–1933‡ | 27.5 |
| (6) Logistic curve, 1854–1924 (count of "cycles" made from actual figures) | 1861–1921 | 15.0 or 12.0 | 1876–1921 | 15.0 or 11.2 |
| (7) Straight line fitted to logarithms, 1854–1926 | 1861–1921 | 12.0 or 10.0 | 1876–1914 | 12.7 or 9.5 |
| (8) Parabola, 1860–1915† | 1865–1908 | 10.8 | 1876–1908 | 10.7 |
| (9) Compound-interest curve, 1879–1913 | 1876–1908 | 10.7 or 8.0 | 1876–1908 | 10.7 or 8.0 |
| (10) Modified Gompertz curve fitted to logarithms, 1854–1926 | 1861–1921 | 10.0 | 1876–1914 | 9.5 |
| (11) Third-degree parabola fitted to logarithms, 1854–1926 | 1861–1921 | 10.0 | 1876–1914 | 9.5 |
| (12) Compound-interest curve, 1860–1915† | 1865–1914 | 9.8 | 1878–1914 | 9.0 |
| (13) Logistic curve, 1884–1926 (actual items smoothed before making count of "cycles") | 1885–1921 | 9.0 | 1876–1914 | 9.5 |
| (14) Parabola fitted to logarithms, 1870–1922 | 1876–1921 | 9.0 or 7.5 | 1876–1914 | 9.5 or 7.6 |
| (15) Two straight lines fitted to logarithms, 1879–95 and 1902–15 | 1876–94 and 1904–14 | 7.0 or 5.6 | ........ | ........ |
| (16) Fourth-degree parabola, 1881–1913 | 1876–1914 | 6.3 or 5.4 | 1876–1914 | 6.3 or 5.4 |

| | Col1 | Col2 | Col3 | Col4 |
|---|---|---|---|---|
| (17) Two straight lines, 1879–96 and 1897–1913 ......... | 1879–1914 | 5.8 or 5.0 | 1879–1914 | 5.8 or 5.0 |
| (18) Four straight lines, 1877–84, 1885–97, 1898–1902, and 1903–16 .. | 1878–1914 | 4.5 or 3.6 | 1878–1914 | 4.5 or 3.6 |
| (19) Straight line, 1903–16 ......... | 1904–19 | 3.8 | ........ | ........ |
| (20) Straight line, 1899–1913‖ ......... | 1900–14 | 3.5 | ........ | ........ |
| (21) Compound-interest curve, 1901–13 ......... | 1904–14 | 3.3 | ........ | ........ |
| (22) Straight line, 1902–23 ......... | 1904–24 | 3.3 | ........ | ........ |
| (23) Straight line, 1904–14 ......... | 1904–14 | 3.3 | ........ | ........ |

* For the first four entries, interval extends from first to last *peak*.
† Fitted to per-capita data.
‡ Precise location of terminal date for smoothed series is uncertain.
§ 1872 selected as high point, since fit of line prior to 1870 is very poor.
‖ Fitted to pig-iron consumption.

Because of the emphasis later to be placed on this intercomparison, every effort is made to follow a uniform procedure throughout with reference to doubtful cases. Wherever two readings seem equally reasonable, both are included in the calculations leading to the results presented in Column 3.[5]

The computed average lengths of "cycle" shown in Column 3 have been arranged in order of magnitude. It will be seen that the results obtained exhibit great diversity; the averages range by more or less regular gradations from 45–40 years for the first entry to 3.3 years for the last. It may be objected at once, of course, that the measurements in Column 3 are not properly comparable, since they are based upon non-uniform time intervals. This objection calls attention to another uncertainty connected with attempts to state the average length of "cycle" for a particular series: the results obtained will vary, depending upon the time period employed in making the calculation.

In order to meet the objection just stated, a second set of computations is carried out (Columns 4 and 5). These computations are, so far as the nature of the procedure will permit, made with reference to a uniform time period. That is to say, a standard time interval (1877–1914) is chosen,[6] and this constant period is used as the basis in selecting terminal dates (Column 4) for the "cycle" count, in place of the variable trend intervals previously employed in selecting these dates (cf. Column 2). As before, the count of "cycles" is made from the first to the last "trough"[7] and short extrapolation of the trend is resorted to in certain cases as required.

The alteration of procedure does not produce any marked change in the general nature of the results. The average length of "cycle" — now computed with reference to a uniform standard time interval — again exhibits wide diversity; the averages range from 45–40 years for the first entry to 4.5 or 3.6 years for the last.

[5] The counts of "cycles," and the measurements of average length of "cycle" presented in Table 1 have been made by the present author, and there is, of course, no implication that the various investigators who originally fitted the trends would accept these measurements, or indeed that they would so much as give approval to the general process employed in Table 1.

[6] This interval, comprising all of the pre-war years for which monthly or quarterly data are avaliable for the series, is chosen as the standard because it is substantially the longest which could be applied to all of the trend representations listed in Column 1 (disregarding, of course, those which extend over only a comparatively short period, such as 1903–16), without extensive and doubtful extrapolations.

[7] With, as before, the exception of the first four entries.

Having completed the calculations pertaining to the mathematically-fitted secular trends for pig-iron production, we may now direct our attention to moving-average trends. It is not possible to assemble from published studies a sufficient number of such trends to permit a comprehensive comparison, and consequently Table 2, unlike Table 1, is based upon calculations made specifically for the purpose of this study.

The various moving averages of Table 2, following customary procedure, are in all cases centered, and at the extremities of the time interval resort is had to free-hand extension. The necessity for such extension, involving as its does arbitrary decisions on the part of the investigator, is one of the well-known difficulties connected with the use of moving averages for secular-trend representation.[8]

Two sets of calculations are shown in Table 2 — the first (Columns 2 and 3) based on the entire period 1854–1933, and the second (Columns 4 and 5) upon the pre-war years 1877–1914. It will be seen that, whether the results be examined for the longer or the shorter interval, the conclusion indicated is the same. Here, as in Table 1, great diversity is displayed by the average length of "cycle." The average length of "cycle" increases more or less regularly as the period of the moving averages is progressively lengthened from three years to twenty years.

The results shown in Tables 1 and 2 should not, of course, be interpreted as indicating that all the various trend-representations listed in these tables are lacking in statistical or economic significance. But the results here presented do point to certain unmistakable conclusions: first, that the average length of "cycle" for a series — and for that matter, the whole form of the supposed cyclical picture — may exhibit great variation depending upon the kind of secular trend which has previously been fitted; second, that the discovery, about a particular trend-representation which has been set up for a given economic series, of oscillations which may conform more or less closely to a certain average length

---

[8] With respect to the difficulties relating to bringing moving-average trends up to date, see Warren M. Persons, "Indices of Business Conditions," *Review of Economic Statistics*, 1 (January 1919), pp. 10–13. For a discussion of the technical difficulties with moving averages as trends, see Wesley C. Mitchell, *Business Cycles: The Problem and Its Setting* (New York: National Bureau of Economic Research, Inc., 1927), pp. 215–216, and Frederick C. Mills, *Statistical Methods Applied to Economics and Business* (New York: Henry Holt and Co., 1938), pp. 235–241.

## TABLE 2

### MEASUREMENTS OF AVERAGE LENGTH OF "CYCLE" FOR PIG-IRON PRODUCTION, WITH REFERENCE TO MOVING-AVERAGE TRENDS

| Type of curve | Computations employing 1854–1933 as basic period | | Computations employing 1877–1914 as basic period | |
|---|---|---|---|---|
| | Interval from first to last "trough" | Average length of "cycle" (*years*) | Interval from first to last "trough" | Average length of "cycle" (*years*) |
| (1) | (2) | (3) | (4) | (5) |
| 20-year moving average ................ | 1861–1932 | 10.1 or 8.9 | 1876–1914 | 9.5 or 7.6 |
| 15-year moving average ................ | 1861–1932 | 7.9 or 6.5 | 1876–1914 | 6.3 or 5.4 |
| 11-year moving average ................ | 1858–1932 | 5.7 or 4.9 | 1876–1914 | 5.4 or 4.2 |
| 7-year moving average ................ | 1858–1932 | 4.6 or 4.1 | 1876–1914 | 4.2 or 3.8 |
| 5-year moving average ................ | 1854–1932 | 3.9 or 3.7 | 1876–1914 | 3.8 or 3.5 |
| 3-year moving average ................ | 1854–1932 | 3.5 or 3.4 | 1876–1914 | 3.5 or 3.2 |

cannot in itself be taken as establishing the statistical or economic validity of such movements as cycles.

We now, in bringing to a close Part One of this volume, set forth a statement of certain conclusions with respect to fundamental methodology, basic principles, and program for attack upon the problem of time-series decomposition.

### Fundamental Methodological Decisions

Clearly, in conducting an investigation of this problem we should proceed by the *genetic method*. It is desirable to indicate the force of this expression in the present connection. We begin by referring to *Webster's* definition — genetic, "pertaining to, concerned with, or determined by, the genesis of anything, or its mode of production or development." [9] Paraphrasing the language of this definition, we may say that the earlier steps of our study *pertain to* the *genesis*, the intrinsic origin, of such expressions as "time-series decomposition," "secular trend," "cyclical fluctuation" (to avoid misunderstanding, it must be set forth at once that the earlier stages of our investigation have to do not with the outward appearance of things, but with inward realities; and we give our principal attention, not to recording what various writers may have said — or omitted to say — about the genesis of our problem, but rather to examining certain basic essentials, of which they may have been intuitively conscious, but which they in general did not treat explicitly). Further paraphrasing the definition, we indicate that we are *concerned with* the *mode of development* of the topic time-series decomposition — with the establishment, advancing analytically by orderly, systematic steps, of a set of fundamental principles for procedure. Paraphrasing still further, we predict that the form of our ultimate results will be *determined by* a *mode of production* — a technique — founded upon these same fundamental principles.

Alternatively, we may take as our point of departure the Funk and Wagnalls definition — genetic method, "a method of investigation, either in science, history, or philosophy, which endeavors to throw light upon the nature and laws of any kind of being by

---

[9] Quoted by permission from *Webster's New International Dictionary, Second Edition* (Springfield, Mass.: G. and C. Merriam Co., 1934 and 1939), p. 1045.

tracing its origin and early stages of growth." [10] Here again, it must be stressed that we do not apply the definition superficially in terms of a mere review of literature. We rather apply it with reference to tracing the rightful *intellectual* origin and the stage-by-stage development of the concept time-series decomposition — in a word, to *supplying* a statement of that which deeply underlies the surface. We build from the bottom, we proceed *ab initio*.

If then we are to proceed by the genetic method, *ab initio*, we must set aside all prejudices, all preconceptions. Our goal must be so to perform the analysis that in the end the results shall portray only relationships inherent in the original data. But even more than this is required: we must aim at producing complete conviction that the relationships *are* thus inherent. We must, so to speak, not only go along with the translators of the Revised Version and abstain from every form of evil, but also follow the injunction of the Authorized Version to abstain from all appearance of evil. Ground must not be left for the suspicion that our results even *might have been* in whole or in part created by some twist or turn of the methodology, by some adjustment or manipulation involved in the procedure.

This decision means that we must deny ourselves the use of moving averages and other smoothing devices which have in the past played a considerable part in time-series decomposition work. Moving averages can change the indication as to form of short-run movement in various unwarranted ways: they can, for example, transform sharp peaks into rounded curves, they can alter essentially the form and timing of movement. The material for an excellent case study upon these potentialities is afforded by certain charts in Professor Persons' fundamental memoir (*Review of Economic Statistics* for January 1919), previously cited. The possibilities for alteration of the form of movement and the timing can be abundantly illustrated by comparing the chart of twelve-month moving averages, on pages 34–35 of Professor Persons' article, with the charts portraying adjusted items derived in conventional fashion, on pages 104–107. The study of this case from the Persons memoir is extremely illuminating, but it does not tell the whole story. Moving averages may do more than to distort the delineation of short-run movement. They may — in the series

---

[10] Quoted by permission from the *New Standard Dictionary of the English Language* (New York and London: Funk and Wagnalls Co., 1935), vol. I, p. 1019.

we encounter in actual economic analysis, which characteristically behave capriciously as regards amplitude, contour, and timing of fluctuation — create *fictitious* "cycles" which have no discernible rational relation to the wave-like fluctuations exhibited by the series itself, and no ascertainable logical connection with the economic forces operating upon the series.

Time series can, of course, be smoothed by other methods than use of moving averages. Regarding time-series smoothing in general, we may perhaps accept Dr. Frederick R. Macaulay's dictum [11] that "the fitting of a mathematical curve to physical observations may be a rational operation; the 'smoothing' of economic time series is almost inevitably purely empirical." Dr. Macaulay adds that "in spite of the absence of any even hypothetically rational law, smoothing or 'graduation' seems useful for many purposes and therefore quite legitimate." Be this as it may, we have to say at once that — in view of our great anxiety to avoid any suspicion of question-begging — our study, at least, is most definitely one in which preliminary smoothing is *not* legitimate.

We have thus resolved to eschew the use of moving averages and other devices for preliminary smoothing of the data. And, when we come to consider the main line of procedure, we must at once depart from most previous analysis in this field. That is, *we expressly reject the notion of commencing the investigation by application of the conventional methods of trend-cycle separation.* In these conventional methods, at the very beginning some general form of curve (e.g., straight line, parabola, exponential) is selected to represent the secular trend; next this curve is fitted to the data (usually by mathematical methods), and the successive annual or monthly ordinates are obtained; last of all (the items meanwhile having been adjusted for seasonal variation, if deemed necessary), the percentage deviations of the items from the corresponding ordinates of trend are computed and are designated as "cyclical variations." Now, there is no thought here of condemning the use which has been made of these methods for attacking isolated problems involving time-series analysis. The methods in fact have been of great value in economic research, and important results have been secured by their aid. But in a study which undertakes

[11] In his monograph, *The Smoothing of Time Series* (New York: National Bureau of Economic Research, Inc., 1931). The quotations are from p. 20.

to proceed by the genetic method, as ours does, employment of the conventional procedure at the outset would mean begging the very question at issue, namely: "How *should* the statistical decomposition of time series be performed?"

As was indicated earlier in this chapter — in connection with "the pig-iron production case" — it is clear that the discovery, about a particular trend-representation for a given series, of oscillations which may conform more or less closely to a certain average length cannot be taken as establishing the statistical or economic validity of such movements as cycles. But we go still further. In the course of the investigations to be described in the chapters immediately following, we shall deny ourselves *even the concepts* "secular trend" and "cyclical variations." We shall refuse to admit these expressions to our working vocabulary until such time as we may have developed *analytically* cogent evidence that such variations are inherent in the material and that the terms are appropriate for their description.

## Basic Principles

We thus have rejected the customary and conventional modes of approach to time-series decomposition. What basic principles, then, should guide us in a new, genetic attack? What principles, that is, hold out the greatest promise of leading to helpful results in connection with the logical problem of the significance of trend-cycle separation, and the related practical problem of selecting, from a host of plausible possibilities, the most suitable trend-representation for a particular series? The following are set forth as fundamental.

(1) In the first place, we shall have the best chance of success if we attack the problem as a *unified whole* — look at the whole picture at once (in so far as the evidence is available, and within practical limitations of time and expense) — rather than at fragmentary parts of it. We should consider the complete array of economic series *simultaneously*, as opposed to particular series individually. The "one-thing-at-a-time" method (here, as in value theory) is not capable of furnishing conclusions logically satisfying. When we attack time series singly, we are, as has already been suggested, confronted with an embarrassment of riches: a host of possibilities appears. Further, in time-series decomposition we should look forward to obtaining a unified and consistent

interpretation of our array of analyzed series; such unity we can hardly hope to attain by dealing with the series one at a time. And, still further, we can easily foresee that the procedure of attacking series individually would lay us open to the criticism that our method is question-begging.

(2) Secondly, we should be on the lookout for consistencies and uniformities of behavior among our series [12] (and, needless to add, for divergencies and contrasts as well). This is not to be taken to imply that we should confine ourselves to a search for simple surface correlations; indeed, as the later stages of the study are reached, relationships of a highly complex sort may quite possibly be discovered. We argue here merely that early investigation of consistencies and uniformities should furnish valuable guides as to procedure in these later stages; furthermore, it is precisely in the course of the investigation of inconsistencies and departures from uniformity that we may hope to find those clues which, traced back, will enable us to surprise basic economic forces in the course of their operation.

(3) Finally, before we are entitled to consider our investigation in any broad sense complete we shall be obliged to bring to bear upon the problem all of our theoretical equipment and all of our historical knowledge. The problem can never be solved by statistical analysis alone — however ingenious or extensive. To illustrate by reference to a specific theoretical-historical issue, we shall need to consider the relation of statistical normals to the normals of economic theory. Shall we accept the view that there is a simple and direct correspondence between the two kinds of normals — as is implied in the following quotation from one of Professor Warren M. Persons' pioneer articles on time series analysis? "My concept of normal growth," Professor Persons says, ". . . is that of an element which can be represented by a smooth line or curve. . . . The normal line, of course, should 'fit' the original data and be determined by them. Marshall says that 'when "normal" prices are contrasted with temporary or market prices, the term refers to the dominance in the long run of certain tendencies under given conditions,' and that 'there are very gradual or *Secular* movements

---

[12] For an example of a highly effective application of this principle, see the work on cycles in the growth of industries, in Professor Arthur F. Burns' *Production Trends in the United States since 1870* (New York: National Bureau of Economic Research, Inc., 1934), pp. 179 ff.

of normal prices, caused by the gradual growth of knowledge, of population and of capital, and the changing conditions of demand and supply from one generation to another.' " [13]   The present writer predicts that in the last event the two kinds of normals — those of statistics, and those of economic theory — will be found to have not a simple and direct correspondence, but rather a highly involved and complex relationship — a relationship which will have to be worked out precisely, and with the very greatest care.

## A Broad General Program of Attack

A broad general program, based upon the fundamental principles just set forth, for attack upon the problem of time-series decomposition may be outlined as follows.

(1) The first step is the carrying out of a number of extensive statistical analyses. Ideally, these analyses should collectively accomplish the gathering of all pertinent statistical evidence, followed by simultaneous statistical treatment of the various bodies of data thus secured. Practically, we are confronted by limitations of time and expense. The most that we can expect is to secure a group of analyses for the most important parts of the available pertinent statistical material, developed from points of view which have some approach to unity and carried out by procedure essentially consistent. The analyses will, of course, involve in the first place the assembling of great masses of raw data, and the development of new indexes of various sorts. Further, the constituent material will need to be treated with a view to discovering the "consistencies and uniformities of behavior" referred to above (as well as divergencies and contrasts): inquiry must be made into forms and sequences of fluctuation, relative amplitudes, the presence or absence of common patterns of movement, the degree of conformity or incongruity — as well as many other matters involving more complex relationships. The analyses may quite possibly result in the emergence for the constituent series of trend-cycle separations of the conventional sort — i.e., the establishment of curves to represent secular trends, and the calculation of cyclical deviations therefrom — or, on the other hand, they quite conceivably may eventuate in the rejection of the notions now generally

[13] Warren M. Persons, "Construction of a Business Barometer Based upon Annual Data," *American Economic Review*, vi (December 1916), p. 744. See also Henry L. Moore's *Synthetic Economics* (New York: The Macmillan Co., 1929), pp. 22–23.

accepted regarding the fundamental nature of time-series fluctuations, and the development of a new and altogether different point of view as to the handling of the problem.

(2) Next in the broad general program of attack comes the interpretation of the results obtained in these preliminary statistical surveys — considered as a whole and in connection with other appropriate statistical evidence — in the light of economic theory and economic history. Most certainly, the attempt to supply such interpretation will involve the careful examination of a great range of problems. It is not possible, within the limits of the present volume, to undertake extended consideration of these problems, or even to outline them. The nature of the issues involved, and something of their scope, may perhaps be indicated by referring to such discussions as the following, which are arranged in order of original publication (the list is, of course, intended to be suggestive rather than exhaustive): Alfred Marshall on equilibrium of demand and supply, with reference to long and short periods; J. N. Keynes on the scope and method of political economy; Gustav Cassel on the steadily progressive economy; Wesley C. Mitchell on causal theory and analytic description, history and theory, and the concept of equilibrium; Henry L. Moore on economic equilibrium; Warren M. Persons on the relation of statistics and economic theory, and the connection between economic and non-economic forces and equilibrium; Abbott Payson Usher on the application of the quantitative method to economic history; Arthur F. Burns on the differences in the rates of development of individual industries in a progressive economy; J. M. Keynes on underemployment equilibrium; Erik Lundberg on the theory of economic expansion; Joseph A. Schumpeter on equilibrium and the theoretical norm of economic quantities, and the historical approach to the problem of economic evolution; J. R. Hicks on general equilibrium and dynamic economics.[14]

[14] See Alfred Marshall, *Principles of Economics* (eighth edition, London: Macmillan and Co., Ltd., 1922 [first edition is dated 1890]), pp. 363–380; J. N. Keynes, *The Scope and Method of Political Economy* (fourth edition, London: Macmillan and Co., Ltd., 1917 [first edition is dated 1890]), especially pp. 268–296 and 328–350; Gustav Cassel, *The Theory of Social Economy* (London: T. Fisher Unwin, Ltd., 1923), vol. I, pp. 34–42; Mitchell, *Business Cycles*, especially pp. 54–60, 186–188; Moore, *Synthetic Economics*, especially pp. 19–23; Warren M. Persons, "Statistics and Economic Theory," *Review of Economic Statistics*, VII (July 1925), pp. 179–197, and also *Forecasting Business Cycles* (New York: John Wiley & Sons, Inc., 1931), pp. 79–81, 283–284; Abbott Payson Usher, "The Application of the

Throughout these (and other) discussions pertinent to the general problem of the interpretation of time-series decomposition in the light of economic theory and economic history, there runs quite clearly and unmistakably one broad general theme: the concept of economic equilibrium and the problem of unifying its statistical, theoretical, and historical connotations. We shall, in the last event, be forced to make a choice among such points of view as are indicated by the following (or, alternatively, to substitute still some other mode of approach): Professor Henry L. Moore's principle that "the final equilibria become shifting ideal goals whose lines of motion trace out the *trends* of the system of economic quantities";[15] Professor Warren M. Persons' belief that "the irregular ebb and flow of trade, depicted by our actual records, is the composite result of (1) internal economic forces which are rarely in equilibrium and which, in action, produce oscillations above or below a datum line, or 'normal,' (2) momentous events and developments, such as war, currency instability, or natural catastrophes which may, at times, dominate the internal cyclical forces and actually mould the course of business over a span of years, and (3) lesser, but still important, events and developments, such as crop situations, which may interrupt, retard, or stimulate the current cyclical trend of production and trade";[16] Professor Wesley C. Mitchell's stand, "nor can the idea presented in many theories that business cycles represent an alternate rupture and restoration of economic equilibrium be included in our working conception";[17] Professor Joseph A. Schumpeter's decision that "we will, for our purpose, recognize existence of equilibria *only at those discrete points on the time scale at which the system approaches a state which would, if reached, fulfill equilibrium conditions.*" [18]

(3) The last step in the broad general program of attack — to

---

Quantitative Method to Economic History," *Journal of Political Economy*, XL (April 1932), pp. 186–209; Burns, *Production Trends*, chapter III; J. M. Keynes, *The General Theory of Employment, Interest and Money* (New York: Harcourt, Brace and Co., 1936); Erik Lundberg, *Studies in the Theory of Economic Expansion* (London: P. S. King & Son, Ltd., 1937); Joseph A. Schumpeter, *Business Cycles* (New York and London: McGraw-Hill Book Co., 1939), volume I, especially pp. 30–71 and 220–231; J. R. Hicks, *Value and Capital* (Oxford: Clarendon Press, 1939).

[15] Moore, *Synthetic Economics*, p. 23.
[16] Persons, *Forecasting Business Cycles*, p. 283.
[17] Mitchell, *Business Cycles*, p. 462.
[18] Schumpeter, *Business Cycles*, pp. 70–71.

be taken only after a synthesis of the elements provided by the preceding statistical, theoretical, and historical investigations — is the reconsideration and unification of the work earlier done, in the statistical analyses referred to under "(1)" above, upon the statistical decomposition of the several time series, with a view to obtaining finally a systematic and connected composite array of statistical results, accompanied, correspondingly, by a systematic and connected theoretical and historical interpretation.

Though the word "synthesis" is here used in referring to one important phase of our program, this program is nevertheless not to be identified with that of Professor Henry L. Moore in his *Synthetic Economics*,[19] which may be epitomized by the following quotations from that volume. "The title of this essay, *Synthetic Economics*, is intended to indicate a concrete, positive description of moving equilibria, oscillations, and secular change, by a method which presents all of the interrelated economic quantities in a synthesis of simultaneous, real equations." "There are three special characteristics which I should like the name *Synthetic Economics* to imply: (1) the use of simultaneous equations to express the *consensus* of exchange, production, capitalization, and distribution; (2) the extension of the use of this mathematical synthesis into economic dynamics where all of the variables in the constituent problems are treated as functions of time; and (3) the still further extension of the synthesis to the point of giving the equations concrete, statistical forms." [20]

The two approaches are, of course, by no means totally unrelated — both eventually involve careful consideration of the theo-

---

[19] The present writer wishes to record his deep and sincere admiration of the life and achievements of Henry L. Moore. To Professor Moore must be given a large share of the credit for the introduction of statistical methods into economic analysis, and for the increasing bond between theory and concrete fact. The list of scholars who, directly or indirectly, have been inspired along various lines of economic inquiry by Moore's original pioneer works is indeed extended and distinguished.

[20] Moore, *Synthetic Economics*, pp. 5, 6. In immediately following passages he says: "A first advantage of this method of treating as an ensemble the totality of prices and their determinants is the elimination of many controversies in economics as to the causes of phenomena." "A second advantage of the synthetic method is that it enables one to know when an economic problem has reached a solution." "A third, and by far the chief, advantage of the synthetic method is that it gives ground for the hope of introducing into economic life rational forecasting and enlightened control." It is interesting to compare this last sentence with the discussions of Professor W. L. Crum on "Statistical Normals and Economic Planning," in the *Harvard Business Review*, XII (January 1934), pp. 176–185.

retical ideas of "moving equilibria, oscillations, and secular change" — but, as the attentive reader will immediately recognize, the goals in the two cases are somewhat different, and correspondingly there are variations with respect to preliminary hypotheses, emphasis, and proposed procedure. In particular, the program of attack here presented does not start from the hypothesis that lines of secular trend fitted to economic series trace out the equilibria of economic theory, and it does not involve any commitment that the final results necessarily will be expressible in terms of formal mathematical equations.

### INDISPENSABILITY OF THE EARLY, COMPREHENSIVE STATISTICAL ANALYSES

A word may now be said as to the vital necessity for the first of the three steps mentioned in the outline of method of attack, as set down just preceding — that is, the carrying out of early, comprehensive statistical analyses for the basic data. The importance of this step can hardly be overemphasized. It constitutes an indispensable prerequisite for the later synthesis of theoretical, historical, and statistical elements.

(1) To begin with, such statistical studies are clearly necessary in order to derive from the confusing and bewildering mass of available statistical data a picture of the general tendencies inherent therein. We find ourselves confronted with a great body of numerical factual material. This body of material is lacking in order, is inchoate; we must classify and arrange it. In addition, the very bulk of the material is an obstacle to our progress; we must find means of condensation — perhaps through mere simple groupings, perhaps through more sophisticated treatment, say the calculation of group averages or index numbers (yet here we must, reversing the maxim, be very careful in contemplation of the forest not to lose sight of the trees; we must not content ourselves with the calculation of averages and index numbers, we must not forget also to look into the *structure* of each grouped array of series). And, obviously, the raw statistical facts require interpretation; we must searchingly inspect their origins — study thoroughly the source and nature of the data.

Further, we must concern ourselves with the homogeneity of our several series. For the time series with which economic analysts have to deal, this matter of homogeneity has many

aspects. The series need to be examined with respect to the technical excellence of their construction; thus, in scrutinizing an index
number, we may well ask whether the formula, weighting system,
and base period have been selected with a view to avoiding type
bias and weight bias. We need to consider in each case how nearly
the series approaches perfection of measurement of the phenomenon which it purports (or is generally taken) to represent; thus,
with reference to the common practice of using pig-iron production
as denotative of the growth of the iron and steel industry in the
United States, we must keep in mind the change over time in the
importance of steel scrap, and also the progressive increase in
degree of fabrication of iron and steel products. For many series,
the sampling process explicitly or implicitly involved requires
careful investigation; thus, in a series showing total building permits for a selected group of cities we must try to judge the representativeness for the country as a whole. And, more generally, for
almost all economic time series the question presents itself as to
the comparability of the successive items; thus, in interpreting
data on railroad freight-car or passenger-car output, we must keep
in mind the gradual shift in the relative importance of wooden
and metal cars. For many reasons, then, our constituent series
require careful examination and thoroughgoing criticism. And,
even more than this, they may require *revision*. Such revision may
take the form of mere detailed improvement of the existing
series, or it may involve complete reconstruction of a series which
is deficient in some essential respect.

(2) Again, the early, comprehensive statistical analyses are all
the more urgent in view of the fact that in existing studies we find
certain statistical summarizations which at least *appear to be* contradictory. As an example, we may take the question of "intermediate cycles" (alternatively referred to as "secondary trends").
Survey of the pertinent literature reveals significant divergence
of opinion as to the nature and average length of such movements,
and indeed their very existence as independent entities is in
dispute.

With respect to the average length of these "intermediate
cycles," wide differences appear. Clément Juglar described wave-
like movements in economic and social data for France, England,
and the United States, varying in duration, but averaging nine or
ten years. Joseph Kitchin suggested that the movements of eco-

nomic factors, whether made up of price or volume, are mainly composed of major cycles, which are aggregates usually of two, and less seldom of three, minor cycles (such minor cycles averaging $3\frac{1}{3}$ years). Charles A. R. Wardwell, after working with a group of diversified economic series for the United States, England, and Germany, concluded that there were cycles averaging about fifteen years in length for the United States, and somewhat less for England and Germany. Simon S. Kuznets, on the basis of a study of the movements in price and production series in the United States, Great Britain, Belgium, Germany, and France, for a large number of individual commodities, reported the discovery of secondary secular-trend oscillations having an average length of twenty-two or twenty-three years.[21]

There is thus decided divergence regarding the average duration of these "intermediate cycles," or "secondary trends";[22] but even more fundamentally, there is lack of accord as the very *existence* of such movements. Thus, Professor Persons throughout all of his extensive work on time series by implication denies their validity, and Professor Mitchell, in stating the conclusions of his statistical studies upon the duration of cycles, says (in his 1927 *Business Cycles*, page 417), "nor can I confirm the ingenious suggestion made by Professor H. S. Jevons and Mr. Joseph Kitchin, that long cycles are multiples of two or three short ones"; Professor Schumpeter, on the other hand, says (in his *Business Cycles*, pages 172 and 173–174), "we go on to postulate that . . . each Juglar [should contain] an integral number of Kitchins," and, "barring very few cases in which difficulties arise, it is possible to count off, historically as well as statistically, . . . three Kitchins to a Juglar — not as an average, but in every individual case."[23]

---

[21] The pertinent references are: Clément Juglar, *Des crises commerciales et de leur retour périodique en France, en Angleterre et aux États-Unis* (Paris: Guillaumin et Cie, 1862) ; Joseph Kitchin, "Cycles and Trends in Economic Factors," *Review of Economic Statistics*, v (January 1923), pp. 10–16; Charles A. R. Wardwell, *An Investigation of Economic Data for Major Cycles* (Philadelphia: privately printed, 1927) ; Simon S. Kuznets, *Secular Movements in Production and Prices* (Boston and New York: Houghton Mifflin Co., 1930).

[22] It is not, of course, beyond the bounds of conceivable possibility that these various findings could somehow be reconciled. But the probability that these writers can *all* be correct would seem rather small. Cf. Wardwell, *op. cit.*, p. 83, fn. 5, "it will be seen upon comparison of the two sets of results how far is the present study from confirming Mr. Kitchin's suggestions."

[23] The discussions of the preceding paragraphs have been confined to consideration

(3) Last of all, it may be stressed that before we enter upon an attempt to develop a theoretical explanation for the flow of economic events, we need to know *what it is that we are trying to explain.* It makes a great deal of difference with respect to our theoretical explanation, for example, whether the expressions "secular trend" and "cyclical variations" are essentially arbitrary in their application — representing little more than a *façon de parler* — or correspond to lines of causal influence which really are inherent in the course of economic change, and which can be rather definitely distinguished and delineated. And it makes a great deal of difference with respect to the diagnosis, prognosis, and prescription in a given economic situation whether economic life is marked by a single wave-like form of fluctuation, or by two or more such movements each (though doubtless related to the other or others) having its own individuality and possessing its own particular theoretical counterpart. The reader may test the validity of these assertions by comparing carefully the historical survey for the United States over the era preceding the first World War, as presented, respectively, by the compilers of the *Financial Review* of the *Commercial and Financial Chronicle* (writing currently), by Alexander Dana Noyes in his *Forty Years of American Finance,* by O. M. W. Sprague in his *History of Crises under the National Banking System,* by Wesley C. Mitchell in the "Annals of Business" of his 1913 *Business Cycles,* by Warren M. Persons in the "Statistical and Chronological Records of Business" of his *Forecasting Business Cycles,* and by Joseph A. Schumpeter in the "Historical Outline" of his *Business Cycles.*

## THE PRESENT VOLUME

The present volume is intended as a contribution toward the fulfillment of the broad general program of attack upon the problem of time-series decomposition which has been set forth on preceding pages. The remaining chapters of this book are devoted to an elaborate analysis of an extensive and significant body of data. As is more fully stated below, our basic material consists of

---

of variations in opinion upon the "intermediate cycles," or "secondary trends." All of this is not to mention the lack of unanimity regarding (1) the "long waves" of Kondratieff and others; (2) particular cycles for individual industries and the like — e.g., the building cycles of Riggleman, Newman, Long, and others — or the re-investment cycles of Einarsen.

significant economic series pertaining to the United States; our interval of study, the period from the close of the Civil War to the outbreak of the World War in 1914.

In Part Two of this volume, we make a thoroughgoing search for these same "consistencies and uniformities of behavior" to which we have so often referred — we look, that is, for patterns of fluctuation in time series. We first examine a group of thirteen economic series, selected on the basis of fundamental importance, continuity, and homogeneity; following this, we give our attention to certain supplementary bodies of data — those for production, for employment, for commodity prices, and for a group of miscellaneous series.

Guided by the results of the pattern analyses of Part Two, we turn in Part Three to the task of effecting the explicit statistical decomposition of a group of leading time series. We first develop a Fundamental Proposition regarding the nature of secular and cyclical movements and their relation to each other. Then we devise two independent methods for the decomposition of this group of economic series. Finally, we present our array of results in collected graphic form

# PART TWO

## THE SEARCH FOR PATTERNS OF FLUCTUATION IN ECONOMIC TIME SERIES

# CHAPTER III

## THE STANDARD PATTERN FOR THE THIRTEEN IMPORTANT
## ECONOMIC SERIES: QUARTERLY DATA

As is indicated at the conclusion of the preceding chapter, we turn in Part Two of this volume to an extensive analysis of significant time series for the United States over the pre-war interval 1866–1914.[1] And we begin this analysis in the present chapter by examining a group of economic series, chosen on the basis of fundamental importance, continuity, and homogeneity, as is more fully set forth below.

### The Selection of Material

The material selected for the statistical analysis of this chapter is limited to data pertaining to the United States and readily obtainable, monthly or quarterly, in substantially complete form over the period 1866–1914. Among such data, there is a further restriction to important basic unadjusted series, setting aside any found to be inflexible or erratic. This latter statement may now be amplified.

Only important basic series are included. This means the exclusion of series pertaining to individual commodities, individual securities, and the like.

Where two or more series exhibit, with reference to the purposes at hand, a marked degree of similarity, only one is included. Thus, among possible series of commercial-paper rates, the continuous set of figures for prime paper in New York City, compiled by the Harvard University Committee on Economic Research, is employed; for industrial stock prices, the Axe-Houghton index, 1883–1914, and the Clement-Burgess index, 1866–82 (published in the *Annalist*) are chosen; bank clearings for seven selected

---

[1] This chapter reproduces (with certain additions — notably the section on "Absolute versus Relative Fluctuations") the substance of an article by the present writer, published under the title "The Pattern of Short-Time Fluctuation in Economic Series, 1866–1914," in the *Review of Economic Statistics*, xvi (December 15, 1934), pp. 248–255, and xvii (November 1935), pp. 139–142.

cities, 1875–1914, supplemented by Philadelphia clearings, 1866–75, are used to represent the volume of check transactions.[2]

Only unadjusted series (except as regards correction for seasonal variation, as is more fully set forth below) are included. This means the rejection of series secured by some systematic process of manipulation — for example, by "elimination of secular trend," or by the taking of ratios (e.g., of bank loans to deposits). Exclusions of this sort are quite necessary, since (as is indicated in Chapter II) it is our wish to leave at the end of the investigation no just ground for a charge that the results were, *or even might have been,* created by manipulation of the data. Further, with respect to many types of statistical adjustment it will be preferable to let the assembled results of the preliminary statistical survey furnish a guide in determining precisely what sort of adjustment will be most serviceable.

Finally, highly inflexible series such as the capital and surplus of the New York City Clearing-House banks, and extremely erratic series such as the rate on call loans in New York City are rejected.

## THE ADEQUACY AND RELIABILITY OF THE DATA

Our choice of material has been greatly restricted by availability of data. This material is from several points of view unsatisfactory. With respect to adequacy of coverage, it is distressing to compare our short list of thirteen series (cf. Chart 1)[3] with the

[2] In view of the criterion developed in this paragraph, question may be raised as to the propriety of including in the analysis two commodity-price series and two stock-price series (see curves 8 and 9, and 5 and 6 on Chart 1). The author feels these inclusions to be altogether justifiable. For both pairs, there is sufficient contrast between the movements of the two series to give each a definite individuality (cf. the chart). Furthermore, the economic and statistical significance of a sensitive commodity-price index is decidedly different from that of a general wholesale price index, as Professor Warren M. Persons and Miss Eunice S. Coyle have been at pains to point out [see their article, "A Commodity Price Index of Business Cycles," *Review of Economic Statistics*, III (1921), pp. 353–369]; and the railroad and industrial stock-price indexes have reference to two distinct and important elements in our economic life over this period. It may be added that dropping one commodity-price and one stock-price series would not materially alter the final results.

[3] The captions of Chart 1 give brief designations for the thirteen individual series (we shall speak of *thirteen* individual series, since series 1b — Philadelphia clearings — is to be used only for the purposes of backward extension from 1875 of series 1a — clearings, seven selected cities). More extended designations of the several series, together with statements as to sources of data, are presented in Appendix III-A.

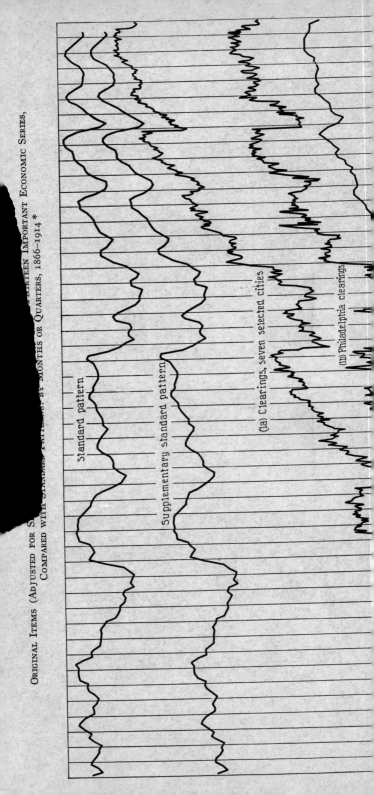

ORIGINAL ITEMS (ADJUSTED FOR S̶ FOURTEEN IMPORTANT ECONOMIC SERIES,
COMPARED WITH STANDARD PATTERNS, BY MONTHS OR QUARTERS, 1866–1914*

Standard pattern

Supplementary standard pattern

(1a) Clearings, seven selected cities

(1b) Philadelphia clearings

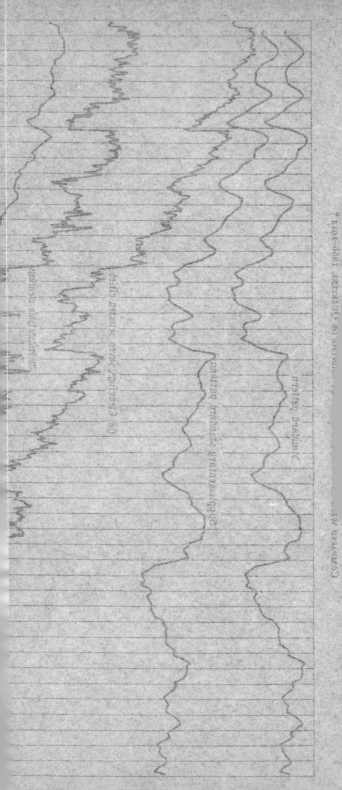

Important Transport ...uson... Economic Series

* CHANGES IN QUANTITIES 1830–1914 *

United Kingdom

Augmented standard pattern

Daily Average Series, combined (B)

Railroad Capita series (D)

COMPARED WITH

Original Yearly Capitation for...

array of data which one might ideally desire for the purpose at hand; we have here, for example, no measure of employment, of the physical volume of production, of either the dollar volume or the physical volume of construction, of business profits.

With reference to the accuracy and reliability of the various individual series, it may be said that each of them — for example, the series of bank clearings for seven selected cities, constructed by the present author — is open to criticism with respect to one or more of the following criteria of homogeneity: technical excellence of construction; perfection of measurement of the phenomenon which the series purports to represent; reliability of sampling; comparability over the period covered.

Attention may also be called to the fact that this list, embracing only thirteen series, affords a comparatively small number of cases for the sort of statistical analysis which we shall apply to these data in the course of the investigation described in Part Two. But clearly, for the purpose at hand the comprehensiveness of the data would not in any true sense be increased by inclusion of series for individual commodities or securities, series which are essentially duplicates, series obtained by various combinations of statistical manipulation, or erratic and inflexible series. By such inclusions, the value of the *basic* analysis would, in fact, be lessened rather than enhanced.[4] Possibly, by extensive and careful research a few important series might be added, but the expense involved would be greater than the probable gains would justify.

These various limitations and defects in the basic data must be frankly faced, and there is no desire to conceal or to minimize them. Nevertheless, each of the thirteen series represents, directly or indirectly, a highly important element in the economic structure. Furthermore, the fact that there are significant and clearly marked consistencies of behavior among these important series, as will shortly be shown, suggests that in the various composite patterns which are presently to be derived from these data we shall have first approximations to concrete representations of the effects produced by certain groups of important causal forces — forces which have operated more or less generally within the economic system. And, finally, the evidence afforded by these thirteen series fortunately does not have to stand alone. Numerous addi-

---

[4] Many of the series here rejected will, of course, be useful for supplementary analysis.

tional monthly or quarterly series are obtainable for appreciable parts of the period under consideration, as well as a great mass of annual data. With the information derived from the analysis of these bodies of material we can test and supplement the generalizations based upon study of the thirteen series.

There is, however, urgent need from the very beginning of the investigation for some long, continuous basic patterns which can be used as backgrounds against which to compare this supplementary material. Without such basic patterns difficulty will arise in fitting various segments of statistical data — pertaining perhaps to comparatively short time intervals, and therefore awkward to handle if taken individually — into their proper places in the general scheme; and further difficulty will appear in seeing the full implications of the fluctuations in the annual series, since in such series much significant detail (which might appear if monthly or quarterly data were obtainable) is concealed.

## Seasonal Variations

In the statistical analysis of the data for the thirteen important series, 1866–1914, we hold in mind throughout one guiding principle, frequently enunciated upon these pages: this analysis should be so performed as to lead to complete conviction in the end that the results portray only relationships inherent in the original figures; ground should not be left for the suspicion that these results even *might have been* in whole or in part created by some process of adjustment or manipulation.

Our plan of action does, however, permit and even definitely call for one type of adjustment: the correction for seasonal variation. This appears altogether justified, for we have in general sufficient knowledge of the causes producing seasonal fluctuations, and a sufficient body of statistical technique, to make at least reasonably satisfactory seasonal allowances possible for most economic series.[5] It will in the end be wholly clear, even upon superficial examination of the evidence, that the results of the statistical analysis presented could not conceivably have been produced by the seasonal adjustments which have been applied, but that on the contrary these adjustments have materially assisted by clari-

---

[5] Further, in measuring seasonal variation, as contrasted with other types of fluctuation in time series, we have the special advantage that the movement has a period of fixed and known length.

fying the picture and allowing other tendencies to stand out in clear relief.

Of the thirteen series included in the present investigation, eight exhibit distinct seasonal variations of such magnitude as more or less seriously to obscure the other short-run fluctuations of the series.[6] For none of these eight series is it possible to employ over the period 1866–1914 a uniform set of seasonal indexes; in each case, a changing or shifting seasonal movement appears, usually progressive. Simple seasonal variations are measured by the Persons median-link-relative method.[7] The progressive seasonals are measured by the link-relative method developed some years ago by Professor W. L. Crum,[8] modified only in that the lines in the various link-relative diagrams are fitted free-hand, rather than by the use of mathematical functions (which presents difficulties, in view of the numerous irregular items present). The statistical problems involved in the measurement of the changing seasonals are difficult and tedious of solution. The various seasonal corrections are worked out with care; and, while of course nothing approaching perfection of measurement can be claimed, the author feels confident that any residual errors of measurement are not important enough appreciably to distort the series, or to interfere with the subsequent analysis. It is believed that significant contribution has here been made to the historical information regarding the form of seasonal fluctuations over this extended pre-war interval, and also to the body of experience with the technical problems relating to the measurement of seasonal tendencies over long periods.

The seasonal indexes for the several series are presented in Table 3. The adjustment for seasonal variation is accomplished in each case by division of the original item by the appropriate seasonal index.

[6] The exceptions are the two wholesale commodity-price indexes, the two security-price indexes, and the bond-price index — all of which show no appreciable seasonal movement.

[7] A description of this method may conveniently be found in W. L. Crum, A. C. Patton, and A. R. Tebbutt, *Introduction to Economic Statistics* (New York and London: McGraw-Hill Book Company, Inc., 1938), pp. 330–342.

[8] See his article, "Progressive Variation in Seasonality," *Journal of the American Statistical Association*, xx (March 1925), pp. 48–64.

## THE GENERAL PLAN OF ANALYSIS

The various series having been subjected to seasonal adjustment, where required, the material is ready to be used in the search for "consistencies and uniformities of behavior." It is first necessary, however, to decide upon the nature of the procedure by which this search is to be conducted. As is set forth in the preceding chapter, it is immediately clear that an investigation such as this, which undertakes to examine the subject by the genetic method — *ab initio* — cannot begin with the application of the conventional methods of trend-cycle separation, involving the fitting of secular trends and the computation of cyclical deviations therefrom, for employment of such methods at the outset would involve begging the very question under consideration, namely: "How *should* the statistical decomposition of time series be performed?" [9]

Manifestly, in any statistical study which is at all extensive, limitations of time and expense prevent investigation of all conceivable combinations of types of relationship. At the very beginning, a vital question presents itself: one is forced to select those lines of attack which hold out the greatest promise of yielding helpful and significant results. In the present case, we decide to commence our statistical analysis of the data with a search for relationships of the simplest sort; [10] among these, we give first consideration to period-to-period (e.g., quarter-to-quarter, year-to-year) changes.

## ABSOLUTE VERSUS RELATIVE FLUCTUATIONS

This general statement immediately brings into the foreground a second question: in our search for "consistencies and uniformities of behavior," should we fix attention upon *absolute* or upon *relative* fluctuations? Investigators in the field of time-series analysis have for the most part attached primary significance to

[9] And this is by no means a fanciful objection. The possibilities for deriving, in the case of a given economic series, a wide variety of diverse "cyclical" pictures through employment of various trend lines are very real and very great. See, for example, the secular trends fitted to pig-iron production and the corresponding average lengths of "cycle," assembled and compared in the preceding chapter.

[10] This decision does not, of course, preclude application of more complex types of procedure at subsequent stages of the investigation. In fact, statistical analysis by more elaborate methods definitely constitutes a later step in the program.

## TABLE 3

INDEXES OF SEASONAL VARIATION FOR IMPORTANT ECONOMIC SERIES: QUARTERLY AND MONTHLY *

(*Average for the year = 100*)

| Series | Time intervals† (a) Based upon | (b) Used for | Quarterly indexes First quarter | Second quarter | Third quarter | Fourth quarter |
|---|---|---|---|---|---|---|
| Railroad earnings ...... | 1866–76 | 1866–76‡ | | | | |
| | | 1866 | 83.0 | 93.5 | 113.8 | 109.9 |
| | | 1876 | 78.5 | 105.1 | 104.9 | 111.3 |
| | 1877–87 | 1877–87‡ | | | | |
| | | 1877 | 82.6 | 97.2 | 105.9 | 114.5 |
| | | 1887 | 89.2 | 95.9 | 105.3 | 109.4 |
| | 1887–93 | 1887–93‡ | | | | |
| | | 1887 | 89.2 | 95.9 | 105.3 | 109.4 |
| | | 1893 | 91.0 | 94.0 | 105.8 | 109.4 |
| | 1894–1902 | 1894–1902‡ | | | | |
| | | 1894 | 90.3 | 91.8 | 103.7 | 114.2 |
| | | 1902 | 94.0 | 97.0 | 102.8 | 105.8 |
| | 1902–14 | 1902–14‡ | | | | |
| | | 1902 | 94.0 | 97.0 | 102.8 | 105.8 |
| | | 1914 | 91.4 | 96.5 | 105.8 | 106.1 |
| Immigration‖ .......... | 1856–68 | 1856–68‡ | | | | |
| | | 1856 | 36 | 147 | 128 | 90 |
| | | 1868 | 52 | 160 | 109 | 78 |
| | 1869–96 | 1869–96‡ | | | | |
| | | 1869 | 46 | 173 | 108 | 72 |
| | | 1896 | 72 | 1.. | 82 | 73 |

For all footnotes, see end of table.

## TABLE 3 (Continued)

| Series | Time intervals† (a) Based upon | (b) Used for | Monthly indexes | | | | | | | | | | | |
|---|---|---|---|---|---|---|---|---|---|---|---|---|---|---|
| | | | Jan. | Feb. | Mar. | Apr. | May | June | July | Aug. | Sept. | Oct. | Nov. | Dec. |
| Immigration‖ ......... | 1892–1903 | 1892–1903‡ | | | | | | | | | | | | |
| | | 1892 | 40 | 58 | 126 | 190 | 209 | 114 | 88 | 74 | 92 | 90 | 66 | 54 |
| | | 1903 | 52 | 67 | 145 | 173 | 174 | 120 | 76 | 70 | 80 | 86 | 83 | 76 |
| | 1903–14 | 1903–14‡ | | | | | | | | | | | | |
| | | 1903 | 52 | 67 | 145 | 173 | 174 | 120 | 76 | 70 | 80 | 86 | 83 | 76 |
| | | 1914 | 56 | 68 | 147 | 140 | 132 | 113 | 84 | 84 | 93 | 98 | 96 | 88 |
| Outside clearings:§ | | | | | | | | | | | | | | |
| Seven selected cities .. | 1875–1902 | 1875–1902‡ | | | | | | | | | | | | |
| | | 1875 | 103.4 | 85.9 | 94.7 | 95.5 | 100.3 | 98.0 | 98.0 | 96.4 | 101.0 | 113.6 | 105.4 | 107.1 |
| | | 1902 | 104.6 | 90.0 | 100.6 | 102.5 | 105.3 | 102.8 | 100.3 | 92.1 | 92.0 | 104.8 | 100.0 | 105.3 |
| | 1903–13 | 1903–14 | 106 | 90 | 103 | 100 | 99 | 100 | 101 | 94 | 94 | 106 | 101 | 106 |
| Philadelphia ......... | 1858–68 | 1858–68 | 104 | 92 | 103 | 109 | 110 | 93 | 94 | 88 | 94 | 110 | 105 | 100 |
| | 1869–78 | 1869–78 | 108 | 91 | 105 | 106 | 105 | 100 | 101 | 90 | 95 | 106 | 92 | 101 |
| | 1875–1902 | 1879–1902 | 107 | 90 | 100 | 102 | 101 | 102 | 101 | 92 | 94 | 106 | 100 | 105 |
| | 1903–13 | 1903–14 | 109 | 88 | 100 | 101 | 103 | 104 | 102 | 91 | 91 | 104 | 100 | 107 |
| Imports** ......... | 1867–77 | 1866–77 | 94 | 101 | 119 | 113 | 112 | 103 | 100 | 106 | 99 | 96 | 83 | 75 |
| | 1878–1901‡ | 1878–1901‡ | | | | | | | | | | | | |
| | | 1878 | 92.5 | 92.9 | 109.2 | 106.6 | 101.7 | 104.4 | 102.9 | 103.3 | 97.7 | 100.2 | 93.8 | 94.5 |
| | | 1901 | 101.0 | 100.0 | 118.3 | 107.7 | 103.5 | 97.5 | 96.6 | 93.8 | 89.2 | 100.0 | 94.2 | 98.9 |
| | 1903–13 | 1902–14 | 103 | 100 | 109 | 101 | 97 | 96 | 93 | 98 | 96 | 101 | 102 | 105 |

| | Period | Period / Year | | | | | | | | | | | | |
|---|---|---|---|---|---|---|---|---|---|---|---|---|---|---|
| New York clearings†† | 1866–80 | 1866–80 | 108 | 92 | 107 | 108 | 109 | 97 | 88 | 84 | 93 | 110 | 103 | 100 |
| | 1881–1902 | 1881–1902 | 112 | 97 | 103 | 101 | 106 | 96 | 89 | 87 | 90 | 107 | 103 | 110 |
| | 1903–16 | 1903–14 | 115 | 90 | 101 | 101 | 100 | 96 | 97 | 91 | 90 | 109 | 103 | 108 |
| Commercial-paper rates†† | 1866–73 | 1866–73 | 104.1 | 99.3 | 103.2 | 106.9 | 91.3 | 82.0 | 85.4 | 89.1 | 98.9 | 110.9 | 118.0 | 111.4 |
| | 1874–89 | 1874–89 | 104.4 | 95.1 | 97.6 | 97.7 | 89.0 | 85.6 | 85.7 | 98.6 | 110.2 | 113.6 | 110.3 | 112.1 |
| | 1890–1916 | 1890–1914 | 97.0 | 92.4 | 96.1 | 94.4 | 91.9 | 89.2 | 95.4 | 103.3 | 110.5 | 111.8 | 108.6 | 110.0 |
| Exports | 1866–75 | 1866–75‡ | | | | | | | | | | | | |
| | | 1866 | 114.4 | 121.9 | 131.3 | 114.5 | 99.3 | 85.7 | 73.7 | 72.3 | 69.3 | 89.1 | 108.6 | 120.3 |
| | | 1875 | 117.8 | 109.0 | 116.0 | 100.4 | 92.1 | 87.0 | 80.8 | 78.6 | 79.0 | 101.2 | 113.9 | 124.2 |
| | 1876–80 | 1876–80‡ | | | | | | | | | | | | |
| | | 1876 | 110.3 | 103.5 | 111.8 | 96.6 | 89.9 | 87.0 | 81.5 | 86.4 | 88.6 | 101.8 | 114.9 | 127.1 |
| | | 1880 | 108.9 | 98.2 | 104.5 | 91.2 | 85.2 | 86.3 | 86.5 | 91.0 | 94.0 | 109.2 | 117.0 | 129.0 |
| | 1880–85 | 1880–85‡ | | | | | | | | | | | | |
| | | 1880 | 108.9 | 98.2 | 104.5 | 91.2 | 85.2 | 86.3 | 86.5 | 91.0 | 94.0 | 109.2 | 117.0 | 129.0 |
| | | 1885 | 110.9 | 95.7 | 100.8 | 88.0 | 82.9 | 81.5 | 82.4 | 85.9 | 88.5 | 124.1 | 125.8 | 134.3 |
| | 1885–1900 | 1885–1900‡ | | | | | | | | | | | | |
| | | 1885 | 110.9 | 95.7 | 100.8 | 88.0 | 82.9 | 81.5 | 82.4 | 85.9 | 88.5 | 124.1 | 125.8 | 134.3 |
| | | 1900 | 109.8 | 92.5 | 98.4 | 90.0 | 86.7 | 81.6 | 79.5 | 85.4 | 101.8 | 126.3 | 121.9 | 127.0 |
| | 1900–14 | 1900–14‡ | | | | | | | | | | | | |
| | | 1900 | 109.8 | 92.5 | 98.4 | 90.0 | 86.7 | 81.6 | 79.5 | 85.4 | 101.8 | 126.3 | 121.9 | 127.0 |
| | | 1914 | 110.0 | 93.4 | 96.2 | 90.3 | 86.4 | 83.8 | 76.2 | 83.0 | 102.0 | 127.2 | 123.2 | 128.1 |
| Loans of New York banks | 1866–75 | 1866–75 | 98.8 | 101.0 | 100.2 | 98.3 | 100.8 | 101.9 | 102.2 | 101.6 | 99.1 | 100.4 | 98.2 | 97.8 |
| | 1875–85 | 1876–84 | 99.7 | 102.0 | 101.1 | 99.0 | 98.9 | 100.0 | 100.3 | 100.6 | 100.4 | 100.6 | 99.6 | 99.3 |
| | 1885–94 | 1885–93 | 98.4 | 101.6 | 102.3 | 101.4 | 100.1 | 100.8 | 100.1 | 99.1 | 99.4 | 98.7 | 98.7 | 98.0 |
| | 1894–1914 | 1894–1914 | 97.7 | 100.8 | 100.8 | 100.4 | 100.5 | 101.1 | 101.6 | 100.6 | 97.7 | 97.7 | 98.4 | 96.8 |

For all footnotes, see next page.

TABLE 3 (Continued)

* In general, these seasonal indexes have been developed by the present writer; exceptions are noted below. The indexes are ordinary, simple seasonals unless indicated as progressive.

† Indexes are *based upon* data for interval (*a*), and are used *as representative of seasonal variation* for interval (*b*).

‡ Progressive seasonal variation; indexes are given for the first and last years of period. These figures are in most cases computed to tenths, in order to facilitate estimation of indexes for intermediate years (which are secured by straight-line interpolation); the progressive indexes are not, however, significant beyond the nearest whole per cent.

¶ For immigration, monthly data are available only since July 1892; in the process of seasonal adjustment, the break between the quarterly and monthly seasonals is made at the middle of 1892.

§ These seasonal indexes — except those for Philadelphia, 1858–68 and 1869–78, which were computed for the purposes of the present study — are taken from an earlier study by the present writer. For sources, see Appendix III-A.

** These seasonal indexes have been computed by the present writer, except those based upon 1903–13, which are taken by permission from the research files of the *Review of Economic Statistics*.

†† These seasonal indexes have been taken from articles in the *Review of Economic Statistics* by Professor W. L. Crum and Miss Ada L. Matthews. For sources, see Appendix III-A.

relative movements, as opposed to absolute, though usually without indicating any formal analytical basis for their choice. We may well pause at this point to consider whether the prevailing practice is well advised.[11]

## INFORMAL GRAPHIC EXAMINATION OF DATA; THE CONCEPT OF DISPERSION-RATIO CONSISTENCY

In the first place, informal graphic examination of economic time series seems definitely to support the view that consistencies and uniformities of behavior present themselves much more clearly in comparisons of relative fluctuations than in comparisons of absolute fluctuations. The matter may be put somewhat more technically by saying that in the course of graphic intercomparisons of economic time series we find a much closer approach to *consistency of dispersion ratio* [12] in fluctuations exhibited by time-series charts drawn with *logarithmic* vertical scale (suitable for the exhibition of relative fluctuations) than in the corresponding fluctuations for charts drawn with *arithmetic* vertical scale (suitable for the exhibition of absolute fluctuations).

To illustrate the concept of consistency of dispersion ratio, we may compare the movements of, for example, the two series, imports and outside clearings of seven selected cities (seasonally adjusted in each case), over the pre-war interval for which both are available, 1875–1914. If we fix our attention upon relative fluctuations, we find for these two series a high degree of consistency in dispersion ratio, well maintained over the period. Throughout, the short-run fluctuations of imports are of greater intensity than the corresponding fluctuations of outside clearings, and the ratio of intensity of fluctuation, roughly estimated graphically as $1\frac{1}{4} \div 1$, shows fairly close approach to uniformity over

---

[11] The word "absolute" is used with a different force here than in Chapter I. By "absolute fluctuations" we here mean differences in the successive values of the series expressed in terms of the original unit (e.g., tons, bushels, dollars); by "relative fluctuations" we mean ratios of change between successive items. Thus, if the items of a series are 785 tons, 910 tons, 692 tons, etc., the successive measures of absolute fluctuation — in technical terms, the "first differences" — are $+125$ tons, $-218$ tons, etc.; and the successive measures of relative fluctuation — the "link relatives" — are $\frac{910}{785} = 116$ per cent, $\frac{692}{910} = 76$ per cent, etc.

[12] We shall shortly define this expression technically. For the present, we shall employ the concept non-technically, referring to rough judgments made upon the basis of graphic examination of the data.

the period; this consistency can be well brought out by comparison of the graphs of the two series drawn with logarithmic vertical scales (cf. Chart 1).[13] If, on the other hand, we should fix attention upon absolute fluctuations, plotting the series with arithmetic vertical scales, we should find definite and systematic divergence from consistency in dispersion ratio: the intensity of fluctuation would be found to increase much more rapidly over time for outside clearings than for imports.

We may now extend our graphic observations to include all of our list of thirteen important economic series, as previously selected, over the period 1866–1914. Fixing attention upon *relative* fluctuations and looking at the data plotted with logarithmic vertical scales (cf. again Chart 1), we can indeed see a considerable degree of consistency in dispersion ratio, in the sense developed in the preceding paragraph, among the various series compared one with another. And, specifically, we are unable to discern any general tendency over time for divergence to appear among the series in this respect; we see, on the contrary, that dispersion-ratio consistency is well maintained for the whole array of series, as we pass from left to right across the chart. It further happens to be true (though this additional fact is in no way essential to the argument) that there is no marked general tendency over time, in the case of any of the thirteen series, toward either increase or decrease in the amplitude of fluctuation.

If now, turning our attention to *absolute* fluctuations, we examine the same thirteen series plotted with arithmetic vertical scales,[14] pronounced departure from dispersion-ratio consistency unmistakably appears. And, specifically with relation to broad general tendencies over time, it may be noted that for three series

[13] The difference in average intensity of fluctuation, just referred to, has been roughly compensated for in Chart 1 by drawing the imports curve on a more compressed scale than that for outside clearings.

[14] The chart of the series plotted with arithmetic vertical scales has not been reproduced. The implications of this chart (as set forth in the accompanying text) are, however, quite clear. Even without the chart, these conclusions can be seen to follow from a consideration of the findings regarding relative fluctuations, as developed in the preceding paragraph of the text, taken in conjunction with the fact of wide divergence among the general "long-run drifts" of the series (cf. the section, later in this chapter, entitled "Adjustment for Differences in Average Level," and also the geometric averages in the table of Appendix III–A).

(Attention may also be called to the arithmetic-scale charts of original items for various economic series presented in the *Review of Economic Statistics*, 1 (January and April 1919), pp. 64–103 and 162–181, *passim*).

— railroad earnings, outside clearings, and loans of New York banks — the intensity of absolute fluctuation increases very rapidly as we pass from left to right across the chart; for certain other series — imports, exports, railroad stock prices, industrial stock prices, bond prices — the same situation exists, the increase being a little less rapid; for the series immigration and New York clearings, progressive increase in intensity of fluctuation is clearly discernible, though not pronounced; and for the remaining three series — wholesale commodity prices, sensitive commodity prices, commercial-paper rates — the general tendency of amplitudes seems to be toward a slight, but barely perceptible, decrease in intensity of fluctuation.

Our graphic tests for the thirteen important economic series pertaining to the United States, 1866–1914, have, then, led very definitely to the conclusion that for this body of data consistency of dispersion ratio approaches much more nearly to realization with respect to relative fluctuations (as revealed by charts drawn with logarithmic vertical scale) than with respect to absolute fluctuations (as revealed by charts drawn with arithmetic vertical scale). And it seems almost certain that this conclusion would be broadly substantiated if the process of graphic examination were extended to cover other bodies of materials — for various series, geographical areas, and time intervals. Such observations as the present writer has made, over a long period, of charted economic data lead him irresistibly to this conclusion, and doubtless it would be substantiated by the experience of other analysts.

Before leaving the matter of graphic examination, one point must be emphasized. The findings based upon graphic examination of the data, such as have just been discussed, are in no way dependent upon the choice of particular logarithmic scales (or arithmetic scales) for the several series which may be under comparison in any given case, for in all such examinations attention is specifically directed to *consistency over time* in dispersion ratios, and this cannot be affected by differences in the plotting scales selected for the various series.

### THE DISPERSION INDEXES

Nevertheless, conclusions based upon inspection of charted data are not completely satisfying as to cogency and definiteness. We may very well, then, supplement our investigations based upon

informal graphic examination for the thirteen important economic
series, over the pre-war period, by *analytical* treatment of the
data. We begin with an analysis of quarterly data.[15]  In accordance with an earlier general methodological decision, set forth on
a preceding page, we fix attention upon period-to-period changes.
And, specifically, we compute for each of the thirteen series (seasonally-adjusted, where such adjustment is required) two sets of
figures: (1) quarterly *link relatives* — measures of period-to-
period relative change — and (2) quarterly *first differences* —
measures of period-to-period absolute change.[16]

Before proceeding with our analytical work, we may pause
briefly for graphic examination of these newly computed series.
They give, when plotted and assembled on two charts — one for
link relatives and one for first differences [17] — definite confirmation of the findings earlier reached through inspection of the
charts of actual items.  Once more, consistency of dispersion ratio
for the short-time fluctuations of the thirteen series is shown to
come very much closer to realization for relative than for absolute
movements.  That is to say, the thirteen link-relative series exhibit a fairly high degree of consistency in dispersion ratio; the
array of first-difference series, on the other hand, reveals pronounced and systematic divergence with respect to dispersion
ratio.

We turn now to the construction of *dispersion indexes* for the
several individual series, giving first attention to dispersion indexes for relative fluctuations. We first must establish, within our
interval of study, sub-periods for measurement of dispersions.
Since our purpose at this point is merely to observe broad general
tendencies, the exact arrangement of these sub-periods is not a
matter of crucial importance. We select decades as affording us a
sufficient number of sub-periods to make possible the discovery

[15] We set aside monthly data as too much affected by minor irregularities and
perturbations; in any case, not all of the series are available in monthly form over
the entire period.

[16] Cf. fn. 11 in this chapter. As to the convention for dating of the link relatives
(an analogous practice is followed for the first differences), see p. 89.

[17] These two charts have not been reproduced. So far as the relative fluctuations
are concerned, however, the main conclusions can easily be read from Chart 3. The
link-relative series of Chart 3 have, to be sure, been put through certain adjustment
operations (as described later in this chapter), but these operations do not in any
way affect the comparisons in which we are now interested — the study over time
of constancy in dispersion *ratios*.

of such general tendencies as may be present, and at the same time containing enough items (forty, in each case) to render our dispersion constants for sub-periods statistically reliable. We set up, then, the four sub-periods 1871–80, 1881–90, 1891–1900, and 1901–10. For each of the thirteen series, we compute four quartile deviations of link relatives, pertaining, respectively, to the four sub-periods just named.[18] In the case of the series exports, for example, the dispersion measures — quartile deviations of quarterly link relatives — are as follows:

| 1871–80 | 1881–90 | 1891–1900 | 1901–10 |
|---------|---------|-----------|---------|
| 6.12 per cent | 5.38 per cent | 6.12 per cent | 5.75 per cent |

Such quartile deviations we take as our measures of degree of dispersion in short-run fluctuation, upon a relative basis, for the several series over the various sub-periods.[19]

We may reduce each of the thirteen sets of dispersion measures (pertaining, respectively, to the thirteen important economic series) to indexes, dividing through in each instance by the average of the four sub-period dispersion measures as the base figure, or 100 per cent. Thus, for the series exports, to continue the illustration, we compute the average of the four quartile deviations set forth in the above tabulation, as follows:

¼(6.12 per cent + 5.38 per cent + 6.12 per cent + 5.75 per cent) = 5.84 per cent,

and then divide through by this average, obtaining as indexes:

| 1871–80 | 1881–90 | 1891–1900 | 1901–10 |
|---------|---------|-----------|---------|
| 105 | 92 | 105 | 98 |

The indexes thus secured for the thirteen link-relative series we may designate as the *dispersion indexes for relative fluctuations*.

[18] For the series commercial-paper rates, we make one adjustment before proceeding to the calculation of the quartile deviations. The dispersion of the link relatives for commercial-paper rates is abnormally high in the sub-period 1891–1900, and it is quite obvious that this abnormality is accounted for by the presence of certain extremely high or low link relatives pertaining to times of political, military, diplomatic, or economic disturbance. We accordingly adjust by omitting these extreme link relatives from the calculation of the quartile deviation for the sub-period 1891–1900. (A similar adjustment is later made in the computation of quartile deviations for first differences.)

[19] With respect to the reasons for the choice of the quartile deviation here, as opposed to other possible dispersion measures, see the extended discussion in a later part of this chapter.

Operating in altogether similar fashion upon the first differences, we arrive, correspondingly, at thirteen sets of indexes which may be designated as the *dispersion indexes for absolute fluctuations*. In the case of the series exports, for example, dispersion indexes for absolute fluctuations are obtained as indicated in the following tabulation:

| 1871–80 | 1881–90 | 1891–1900 | 1901–10 |
|---------|---------|-----------|---------|
| 64      | 69      | 108       | 159     |

### THE MULTIPLE FREQUENCY TABLES

We now construct two multiple frequency tables — one relating to indexes for relative fluctuations, the other to indexes for absolute fluctuations. The multiple frequency table for relative fluctuations has four columns, pertaining to the four sub-periods 1871–80, 1881–90, 1891–1900, and 1901–10, respectively; each column contains thirteen tally marks, indicating, respectively, the magnitude of the thirteen dispersion indexes of relative fluctuation for the sub-period in question, plotted along the vertical scale. The multiple frequency table for absolute fluctuations is constructed in precisely analogous fashion, substituting, of course, the indexes of absolute fluctuation for the indexes of relative fluctuation.[20]

These two multiple frequency tables are well suited to serve as the basis for comparison, contrasting relative and absolute fluctuations, of the degree of consistency in dispersion ratio (as above defined). More specifically, if, within a multiple frequency table such as one of these, we find that in every column all the tally marks coincide, thus indicating precise agreement in the movements over time of the dispersion indexes for the constituent series, we may say that we have a case of perfect consistency in dispersion ratio among the series; if there is departure from precise coincidence of tally marks in the several columns, then we may take the scatter or variability of the tally marks (measuring in each column from some indicator of central tendency — e.g., the arithmetic mean of that vertical array) as a measure of the degree of inconsistency in dispersion ratio among the constituent series.

Upon even casual inspection, the scatter or variability of the

---

[20] The two multiple frequency tables (not reproduced) are both drawn up with arithmetic vertical scale. The possibility of using the logarithmic vertical scale for these tables will be considered shortly.

several columns of tally marks in the multiple frequency table for relative fluctuations is seen to be markedly less than that in the corresponding columns of the multiple frequency table for absolute fluctuations, thus indicating a much higher degree of consistency in dispersion ratio for the former case. It is desirable to confirm this finding, based upon visual comparison, by analytical treatment of the data.

We give first attention to the multiple frequency table for relative fluctuations. We begin our analysis of this table by calculating the means [21] of the four vertical arrays. These means — since they are computed as arithmetic averages of the dispersion indexes of the thirteen individual constituent series, for the several sub-periods, respectively — may be referred to collectively as constituting the *general dispersion index*. The numerical values obtained for the general dispersion index are as tabulated below:

| 1871–80 | 1881–90 | 1891–1900 | 1901–10 |
|---------|---------|-----------|---------|
| 110     | 81      | 107       | 102     |

(This index is shown graphically in the lower right-hand corner of Chart 2.) Except for the second sub-period, 1881–90 — where there is a moderate drop — the general dispersion index does not depart a great deal from constancy. That is to say, except for this second period our thirteen important economic series exhibit no general tendency toward variation, as between sub-periods, with respect to amplitude of short-run relative fluctuation (cf. once more Chart 1).

#### STUDY OF VARIANCE FOR THE MULTIPLE FREQUENCY TABLES

We come back now to our multiple frequency table for relative fluctuations, with a view to giving it somewhat broader consideration. It would appear particularly pertinent and important to study the *variances* within this table.[22]

---

[21] Some other measure of central tendency — e.g., the median — might be employed in place of the mean. However, it can be foreseen that the final results of our analysis would in no essential respect be altered by such a substitution, and the use of the mean simplifies the variance analysis, to follow.

[22] Variance analysis has to do with the comparison of dispersion measures for entities which are thought of as in some way related, or which are being contrasted; specifically, the form of dispersion measure employed is the *variance*, or square of the standard deviation. For elementary discussions, see G. Udny Yule and M. G. Kendall, *An Introduction to the Theory of Statistics* (London: Charles Griffin & Company, Ltd., 1937), pp. 444 ff.; or Frederick C. Mills, *Statistical Methods Applied*

The arithmetical work will be facilitated somewhat if we shift the figures from percentages to decimal fractions. Thus, the general dispersion index — set down just above as 110, 81, 107, 102 — is rewritten 1.10, 0.81, 1.07, 1.02: the dispersion index for the series exports — which reads 105, 92, 105, 98 — is rewritten 1.05, 0.92, 1.05, 0.98; and so on, for the dispersion indexes of the other individual series.

We first calculate the variance [23] for the multiple frequency table as a whole, taking into account the scatter of the whole group of fifty-two dispersion indexes about the general mean (such mean, of course, being unity); this variance comes out 0.0688. Now, speaking broadly, we may think of this total variance of 0.0688 as being capable of separation into two elements — first, the scatter or variability in the multiple frequency table reflecting certain general tendencies as to dispersion behavior, operating more or less broadly upon the whole group of thirteen selected series; and, second, the scatter or variability related to peculiar or individualistic characteristics in the dispersion behavior of the several constituent series.[24] For a numerical measure of the in-

---

*to Economics and Business* (New York: Henry Holt and Company, 1938), pp. 490 ff. For more elaborate treatment, refer to the works of R. A. Fisher.

There is difference of opinion among statisticians as to the interpretation and helpfulness of mathematical probability calculations when applied to economic time series. In the accompanying text, the emphasis has been laid upon general non-technical analysis. For the benefit of those interested in formal tests of significance, however, it may be said that, judged by conventional tests, the two variances 0.1169 and 0.0560 differ significantly (also, incidentally, the variance between array means — 0.0128 — is significant, and thus additional evidence is furnished as to the validity of the general dispersion index). Similar statements can be made for the corresponding variances in the "logarithmic handling," referred to below. In applying these tests, the variances are, of course, "corrected" to take proper account of degrees of freedom.

[23] The variances referred to in this paragraph of the text are squares of standard deviations, or else are derived in some simple fashion from a group of such squares. The variance 0.0688 is the square of the standard deviation of the fifty-two dispersion indexes from their general mean (unity). The variance 0.0128 is the squared standard deviation of the four items of the general dispersion index — 1.10, 0.81, 1.07, 1.02, respectively. The variance 0.0560 is the arithmetic average of the four variances for the respective columns of the multiple frequency table, such variances (squares of standard deviations for the respective vertical arrays) being as follows:

| 1871–80 | 1881–90 | 1891–1900 | 1901–10 |
|---------|---------|-----------|---------|
| 0.0420  | 0.0388  | 0.1052    | 0.0379  |

As is indicated in the accompanying text, the figure 0.0560 is also capable of description as the variance pertaining to the deviations of the fifty-two individual tally marks, each measured as a departure from the appropriate array mean.

[24] This sentence is not to be taken as indicating approval for a general practice

tensity of the first of these scatters — that connected with general tendencies as to dispersion behavior — we may employ the variance of the four array means (such array means having already been calculated, as set forth above, and designated collectively as constituting our general dispersion index); this variance comes out 0.0128. The intensity of the second scatter — that connected with the individualistic characteristics in dispersion behavior of constituent series — we may indicate numerically by calculating the variance pertaining to the deviations of the fifty-two individual tally marks, each measured as a departure from the appropriate array mean; such variance comes out 0.0560.

Since this latter variance possesses (as we have seen above) the intrinsic property of increasing progressively in magnitude as the dispersion indexes for the constituent series depart more and more from coincidence, we may appropriately designate it as a *coefficient of dispersion inconsistency*. And, since in the case at hand this measure has been applied to dispersion indexes pertaining to relative fluctuations, we may refer specifically to the variance of 0.0560 as the coefficient of dispersion inconsistency for relative fluctuations.

We may now compare this figure of 0.0560, the coefficient of dispersion inconsistency for relative fluctuations, with a corresponding figure (computed in entirely analogous fashion from the multiple frequency table for absolute fluctuations) of 0.1169 for the coefficient of dispersion inconsistency for absolute fluctuations. The second coefficient is more than twice the first. The coefficient of dispersion inconsistency is thus markedly lower for relative than for absolute fluctuations.

It may, however, at this point be objected that this comparison of coefficients is open to doubt, upon certain methodological

---

of making naïve and mechanical transitions from measures of variance to evaluation in numerical terms of the comparative intensity attaching to various lines of causal influence. The present writer most emphatically would not support any such undiscriminating attitude toward variance coefficients (whether in connection with correlation problems, or elsewhere). All that it is desired to suggest here is that *for the case at hand*, taking into account all the attendant circumstances — notably the presence among the thirteen series of a considerable degree of resemblance as regards dispersion behavior, along with tendencies (clearly discernible upon even casual graphic examination of the data) towards general correspondence in form of short-run fluctuation — we are fairly well entitled to regard the interpretation put upon the variance measures in the text above as constituting at least a good rough approximation to the truth.

grounds. More specifically, we recall that when previously we set up the two multiple frequency tables — for relative and absolute fluctuations, respectively — we arbitrarily chose to employ the *arithmetic* vertical scale, rather than the *logarithmic*. Is it not conceivable that the comparative size of the two coefficients of dispersion inconsistency — 0.0560 and 0.1169 — results merely from this arbitrary decision in favor of arithmetic, as opposed to logarithmic, handling of the vertical measurements?

This question can readily be answered. We repeat our computations, using the *geometric* average for the four sub-periods (rather than the arithmetic) as the base figure for the dispersion indexes of the several individual series, and then drawing up two new multiple frequency tables — one for absolute, and one for relative fluctuations, as before — this time plotting not the indexes themselves, but their *logarithms*. (We use natural, rather than ordinary, logarithms, with a view to facilitating detailed quantitative comparisons of results with those of the earlier computations.) Carrying through variance analysis for these new multiple frequency tables, we finally obtain 0.0541 and 0.1160 as coefficients of dispersion inconsistency for relative and absolute fluctuations, respectively, the ratio of the second of these to the first being $\dfrac{0.1160}{0.0541} = 2.14$.[25] It will be seen that these results correspond very closely to those obtained in the earlier calculations (coefficients 0.0560 and 0.1169, respectively, with a ratio $\dfrac{0.1169}{0.0560} = 2.09$).

The other results of the new variance analysis also check up quite closely with those of the earlier computation. The newly computed general dispersion index shows movements practically identical with those of the old. For the multiple frequency table of relative fluctuations, the variances — employing (a) arithmetic and (b) logarithmic handling, respectively, of the vertical scales — are as follows:

|  | (a) | (b) |
|---|---|---|
| Variance about general mean ............ | 0.0688 | 0.0685 |
| Variance of array means ................ | 0.0128 | 0.0144 |
| Variance of scatter about array means .... | 0.0560 | 0.0541 |

[25] If we substitute ordinary for natural logarithms, thus obtaining 0.01020 and 0.02188, respectively, for the two coefficients, the ratio (which is the essential point in the comparison) is of course not altered.

### CONCLUSION WITH RESPECT TO RELATIVE VERSUS ABSOLUTE FLUCTUATIONS

Now that this methodological doubt has been resolved, we may say that our analytical investigation of quarterly data for the thirteen important economic series has definitely established that the coefficient of dispersion inconsistency is markedly lower for relative than for absolute fluctuations. This finding is confirmed by a similar study carried out with reference to *annual* data for the thirteen series. It does not seem feasible to extend this kind of analysis further for the body of statistical material at hand; that is to say, when we come to averages for periods longer than annual — e.g., two-year, three-year, etc. — the number of time intervals within the period of study, 1866–1914, becomes too small for clear-cut sub-period analysis.

Our analytical investigations have thus completely and emphatically confirmed the findings of preliminary graphic examination: for this group of important economic series pertaining to the United States over the pre-war period 1866–1914, consistency of behavior as regards dispersion ratios among the series has been demonstrated to be much more highly marked for relative than for absolute fluctuations.[26] And it therefore definitely appears more expedient, in our general search for "consistencies and uniformities," to direct attention to relative, rather than absolute, fluctuations — to work, that is, with link relatives, as opposed to first differences.

### THE CLOSE CORRESPONDENCE BETWEEN SIZE OF ORIGINAL ITEM AND INTENSITY OF ABSOLUTE SHORT-RUN FLUCTUATION

Before we enter upon the main line of computation, however, we may pause to give digressionary consideration to one significant phase of the dispersion behavior in the group of thirteen important series. Our various graphic and analytical findings, taken as a whole, suggest a certain hypothesis: *viz.*, that the variations over time in the degree of dispersion of absolute fluctuations for the several series are closely associated with variations in the absolute size of the original items of such series.

---

[26] The writer has little doubt that this proposition is capable of much wider extension — to other bodies of statistical material for the United States, to other time periods, and to other countries.

We now proceed to put this matter to more formal test. For each of the thirteen series we take the dispersion index for absolute fluctuations, as previously computed, and divide through by the general dispersion index, with a view to eliminating (at least, approximately) the influence of those general forces which have affected the dispersion behavior of the group of thirteen series taken as a whole,[27] and thus permitting the peculiar and individualistic dispersion characteristics of the several series to stand out in clear relief. In the case of the series exports, for example, the calculations relating to the dispersion index of absolute fluctuation for the series itself, the general dispersion index, and the quotient of these, respectively, yield numerical results as tabulated below:

|  | 1871–80 | 1881–90 | 1891–1900 | 1901–10 |
|---|---|---|---|---|
| (a) Dispersion index of absolute fluctuation for exports | 64 | 69 | 108 | 159 |
| (b) General dispersion index | 110 | 81 | 107 | 102 |
| (c) Quotient = (a) ÷ (b) | 58 | 85 | 101 | 156 |

The thirteen series of quotients resulting from this operation have been plotted as full lines upon thirteen sections, respectively, of Chart 2.[28]

We next compute, for each of the thirteen series, relatives which are proportional to the *average size of original item* in each sub-period. In the case of exports, for example, the average size of original item (calculated on the basis of quarterly totals) comes out as indicated in the tabulation presented below:

| 1871–80 | 1881–90 | 1891–1900 | 1901–10 |
|---|---|---|---|
| $206.0 millions | $254.6 millions | $351.6 millions | $548.6 millions |

Reducing these to relatives, with the average for the four periods ($340.2 millions) as the base, or 100 per cent, we obtain the following set of results.

| 1871–80 | 1881–90 | 1891–1900 | 1901–10 |
|---|---|---|---|
| 61 | 75 | 103 | 161 |

Relatives such as these for all thirteen series are plotted as dotted lines upon the several sections of Chart 2.

[27] Upon this point, see the discussion in an earlier part of this section relating to the statistical measurement of variances within the multiple frequency table.

[28] Chart 2 also shows, in the lower right-hand corner, the graph of the general dispersion index.

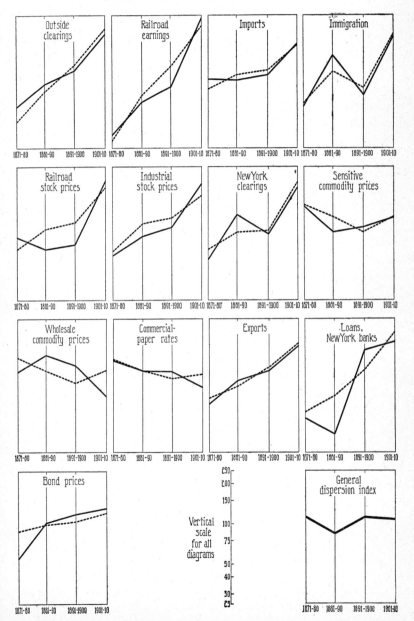

## CHART 2

Comparison, for Each of Thirteen Important Economic Series,
of (1) Dispersion Index for Absolute Fluctuations,
Divided by General Dispersion Index (————),
and (2) Average Size of Original Item (- - - -):
by Decades, 1871–1910 *

*(Base: average for the four periods = 100)*

Outside clearings

Railroad earnings

Imports

Immigration

Railroad stock prices

Industrial stock prices

New York clearings

Sensitive commodity prices

Wholesale commodity prices

Commercial-paper rates

Exports

Loans, New York banks

Bond prices

Vertical scale for all diagrams

250
200
150
100
75
50
40
30
25

General dispersion index

\* Also, in the lower right-hand corner of the chart, the general dispersion index.
Uniform logarithmic vertical scales.

If now we survey Chart 2 generally, we see that the correspondence between the full and dotted lines is on the whole a very close one. For certain series — outside clearings, imports, immigration, exports, commercial-paper rates — the two lines come very near to coincidence. For certain other series — railroad earnings, industrial stock prices, New York clearings, sensitive commodity prices — the correlation is quite high. And even in those cases where there are differences as to detailed configuration of the two lines, the curves track together in their general tendencies. It is important to note that the generally high correspondence between the full and dotted lines upon Chart 2 does not in any significant degree result from the process of dividing through by the general dispersion index. On another chart — similar to Chart 2 in all respects except that for each series the relatives for average size of original item are compared simply with the corresponding dispersion index for absolute fluctuations, without the application of any adjustment by the general dispersion index — the correlations are almost equally high; and indeed this second chart presents very much the same appearance as does Chart 2, the only difference to impress the eye being that upon the new chart the full line is in each instance moderately lower (by about one-eighth of an inch for the scale on which Chart 2 is here presented) in the second sub-period.

Through the investigations the results of which are epitomized in Chart 2, we have thus established a quite basic proposition of great significance, considered as a contribution to the general body of knowledge concerning the essential nature of time-series variations: *for our group of important economic series, pertaining to the United States, 1866–1914, the general long-run tendencies as to the degree of dispersion of short-run absolute fluctuation (and more especially, those elements of this dispersion which may be ascribed to peculiar and individualistic dispersion behavior of the several series) are closely associated, series by series, with the long-run variations in size of original item.*[29] The point might be put in mathematical terminology by saying that for our present body of data intensity of absolute short-run fluctuation tends, over time, to be a function (and, specifically, a simple function of

---

[29] Here, as upon an earlier page, it seems to the present writer highly probable that the proposition enunciated in the text is capable of much wider extension — to other time periods, countries, and bodies of statistical data.

the form $y = kx$) of the size of original item. With respect to the intensity of short-run *relative* fluctuation, no tendency toward any functional relationship has revealed itself; on the contrary, our observations have indicated very definitely the absence of any systematic relationship between size of original item and degree of dispersion of short-run relative fluctuation.

#### FURTHER GENERAL METHODOLOGICAL CONSIDERATIONS

We return now to our main line of analytical procedure. We have so far decided to begin our statistical treatment of the data for the thirteen important economic series by a search for relationships of the simplest sort — to give first consideration to period-to-period changes. We have further decided (upon the basis of the extended analytical investigation described at length in the preceding section) to fix attention upon relative, as opposed to absolute, fluctuations — to work with link relatives, rather than first differences. Even yet, however, a range of possibilities remains. We may, that is, deal with link relatives of various periods — commencing with quarterly data, thence proceeding to annual, and so on. And it seems highly desirable to investigate a number of these possibilities, for the various sets of link relatives may well be expected to yield supplementary information. We may reasonably anticipate that the several link-relative analyses will afford an opportunity for oscillating movements of various lengths (if indeed these truly exist) to demonstrate their reality and to show something of their concrete form.

The link relatives of various periods will, accordingly, be examined and subjected to statistical treatment. We begin with the quarterly link relatives,[30] already computed as described in the preceding section (the original items of the series, it will be remembered, have first been adjusted for seasonal variation where such adjustment is required). In the dating of link relatives, we shall follow in this book the convention of giving each link relative the date of the *second* of the two time periods involved: thus, the quarterly link relative for $\dfrac{1866\text{–}\text{II}}{1866\text{–}\text{I}}$ is dated 1866–II, and so on. The interval of computation of the quarterly link relatives is in general 1866–II to 1914–II, thus omitting from the calculation

---

[30] As regards *monthly* link relatives, cf. fn. 15 in this chapter.

the last half of the year 1914, when the movements of many economic series were violently affected by the outbreak of the World War.

We now desire to intercompare the movements of the quarterly link relatives for the thirteen series, with a view to discovering such "consistencies and uniformities of behavior" as may be present. We begin with preliminary graphic examination. We at once are able to discern a considerable degree of congruence among the link-relative series as regards form of short-time fluctuation. But we also find that our attempts at comparison are interfered with in various ways: specifically, we are hindered (1) by differences among the series with respect to average level of fluctuation; (2) by wide divergence among the series with respect to amplitude of short-run variation; (3) by time lags in the movements of the series; (4) by individualistic peculiarities of particular series. We now give attention to these difficulties, each in turn, as is set forth in the remaining sections of this chapter.[31]

## ADJUSTMENT FOR DIFFERENCES IN AVERAGE LEVEL

As has just been pointed out, our attempts at intercomparison of the short-run fluctuations of the various link-relative series are interfered with somewhat by differences in their average level over our period of study, 1866–1914. Such differences obviously are traceable to the presence in the original series of long-time drifts, upward or downward (cf. Chart 1). In order to reduce the influence of this disturbing element — which may be characterized as one producing mild distortion, from the point of view of studying short-run variations — we express the link relatives for each series as deviations from the average link relative for that series.[32]

No one, of course, would expect this procedure, in any realistic sense, to "eliminate secular trend" for any of the various series (unless perhaps by the merest chance). We must in fact expressly repudiate the notion that any such elimination has been accomplished. Indeed, we go much further: in accordance with an early general methodological decision,[33] we at this stage of our investi-

---

[31] Certain technical details regarding individual series and procedure are given in Appendix III–B.

[32] The geometric average, which seems most appropriate when dealing with these relative changes, is employed.

[33] Cf. Chapter II.

gation deny ourselves *even the concepts* "secular trend" and "cyclical variations"; we refuse at this time to admit these expressions to our working vocabulary.

There may, however, be readers who will feel that "corrections for secular trend" have nevertheless been made by implication, and that (since such corrections would be in general patently inappropriate)[34] the final results of our present line of analysis will to this extent be open to question. This criticism does not seem to the present writer to be well taken. The procedure here employed, while it unfortunately cannot be expected completely to eliminate the distortion in short-time fluctuation occasioned by the long-time drifts in the original series, nevertheless does on the whole very materially reduce such distortion.[35] We shall, however, later in this chapter return to consideration of this possible criticism.

We might, of course, appreciably "improve" the results by splitting each of the link-relative series into sections and computing separate averages for each section — by taking judicial notice, so to speak, of such well-known facts as, for example, the observation that the long-time movement of wholesale commodity prices shows a break around 1896 (cf. Chart 1). But, since our announced intention has been, from the very beginning of the present investigation, to avoid any methods which might be open even to the suspicion of question-begging, it is imperative to maintain here a simple and consistent procedure.[36]

## ADJUSTMENT FOR VARIATION IN AMPLITUDE

The several series of link relatives expressed as deviations from average, secured as just described, exhibit — as indeed might be expected in the light of theoretical considerations and the results

---

[34] This procedure could bring about precise "elimination of secular influences" only in the unlikely case that the trend should be a compound-interest curve coinciding with or paralleling a geometrical progression connecting the first and the last original items in the calculation interval (cf. the movements of the original-item series in Chart 1).

[35] The argument embodied in this sentence is put more explicitly by the statement of fn. 44 in this chapter, below.

[36] When the statistical analyses of Part Two have been completed and their findings are available to assist in the selection of methodology for further investigation, it may be possible to employ more complex and more effective methods for dealing with the distortion produced by the long-time drifts of the original items. We shall return to this question in Chapter XIV.

of previous statistical studies by various writers — wide divergencies in amplitude of fluctuation. The causal forces operating upon these series clearly have produced short-time movements of highly varying intensity. Since our primary interest here lies in the *form*, as opposed to the magnitude, of short-run fluctuation, we may well eliminate differences in average amplitude of fluctuation by dividing each series of link relatives through by some appropriate measure of its dispersion.

The standard deviation has the disadvantage (because of the squaring process inherent in its calculation) of being subject to distortion by even moderately extreme items; furthermore, for the simple type of analysis which we are planning to carry out in Part Two of our investigation there appears to be no theoretical consideration leading to the choice of the standard deviation as dispersion measure. The average deviation can be computed with facility for time series of the sort with which we shall have to deal; and it corresponds in a very simple and direct way to the notion of "average degree of dispersion," thus admitting of an easy, non-technical explanation. As for the quartile deviation, in our broad link-relative investigation most of the series will be relatively short — being annual or less frequent, and thus consisting of some fifty items or less — and for such series the magnitude of the quartile deviation (like that of the median) may be somewhat arbitrary, depending capriciously upon the location of certain items which happen to occupy a crucial position. All things taken into account, the average deviation seems preferable, and we shall plan in general to use it as our dispersion measure throughout the present study.

The situation immediately at hand, however, is exceptional in that the series are quarterly and thus comprise in each instance almost two hundred items; the position of the quartiles, therefore, is not likely to be governed by accidental circumstances. Furthermore, these series, relating to successive comparisons of brief, three-month intervals, are in every instance subject to numerous extreme irregularities of short-run behavior — irregularities which would inevitably bring about serious distortion in the measure of dispersion afforded by the average deviation (not to speak of the standard deviation). For the particular case of the *quarterly* link-relative study, then, we shall by exception resort to the use of the quartile deviation as dispersion measure.

# CHART 3

## LINK RELATIVES FOR THIRTEEN IMPORTANT ECONOMIC SERIES — DEVIATIONS FROM AVERAGE IN QUARTILE-DEVIATION UNITS — COMPARED WITH THE LINK-RELATIVE STANDARD PATTERN: BY QUARTERS, 1866–1914

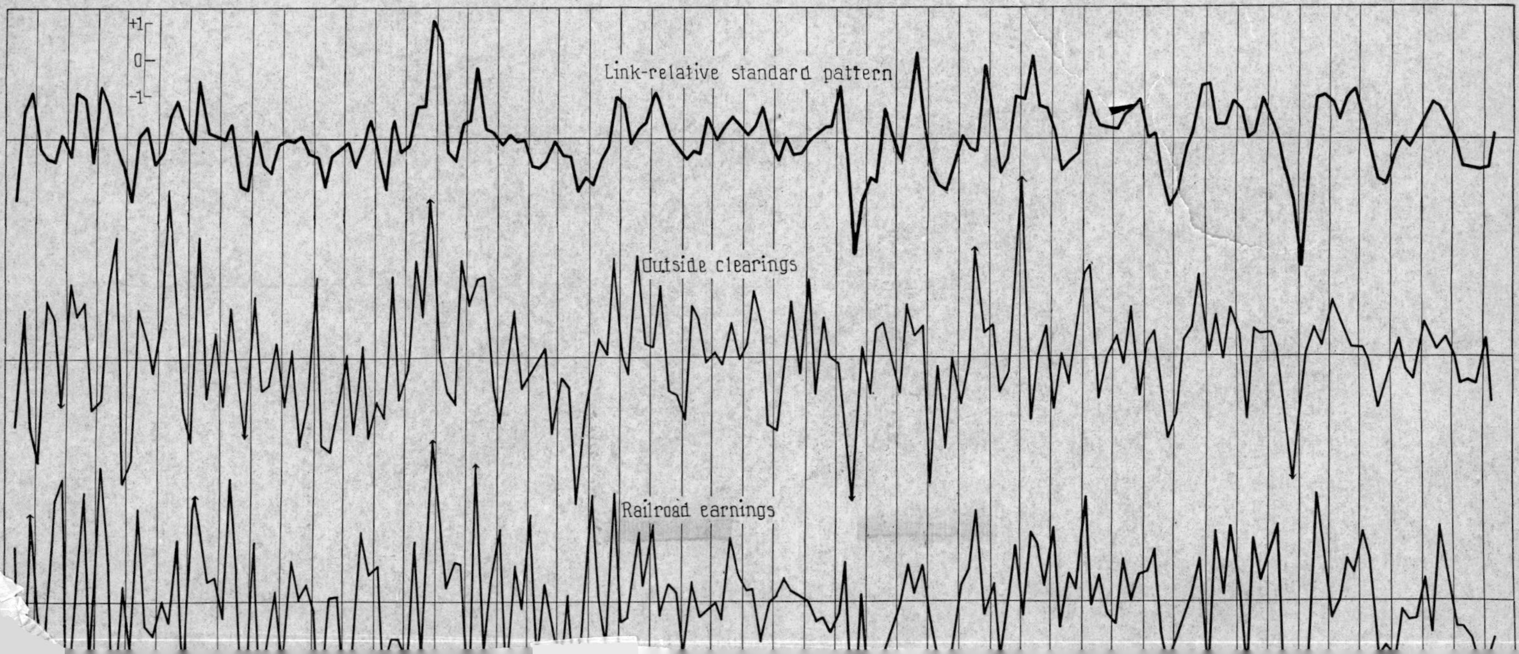

Link-relative standard pattern

Outside clearings

Railroad earnings

CHART 3

We compute, then, the thirteen quartile deviations,[37] and then divide through each series of link relatives (such link relatives first having been adjusted for differences in average level, as described in the preceding section) by its quartile deviation. The resulting series, which we shall designate as "link relatives, deviations from average in quartile-deviation units," are presented in Chart 3.[38] It will be seen that differences in average intensity of fluctuation among the series have been eliminated.

It may be pointed out parenthetically that this process of reduction to quartile-deviation units could not possibly "create" fluctuations of any particular type or pattern, for the procedure in no way alters the *shape* of the variations in the series; it alters only their intensity. The process could not have produced the general concurrence of movement readily observable among the series of Chart 3; in fact, in so far as the series failed to show correspondence, the procedure would merely bring out this failure of correspondence more vividly.

## ADJUSTMENT FOR LAGS

The individual series of Chart 3 exhibit on the whole close correspondence in their major fluctuations, but with definitely discernible lags. We may begin study of these lags with a careful graphic examination of the figures. There are four series whose movements are in the main consistently concurrent, with high correlation as to general contour.[39] These four series are outside clearings, imports, immigration, and railroad earnings — which may be designated briefly as "the four volume series," since each

---

[37] These quartile deviations are tabulated in Appendix III–A.

[38] The first curve of Chart 3 should be disregarded for the time being.

In Chart 3, inaugurating a practice which will in general be followed for comparisons of this sort throughout the present volume, each curve is plotted with reference to its own base line (indicated here in each case by a light horizontal line through the curve), and a scale is shown at the top in the upper left-hand corner of the chart, with a view to facilitating graphic estimates of the numerical magnitude of the several items.

In order to keep the height of Chart 3 within manageable limits, it has been necessary to cut off certain irregular extreme points of the curve. Such irregularities have been in each instance designated by arrows upon the curve, pointing upward or downward, as the case may be.

[39] For all of the possible pairs which can be formed from these series, superiority of the concurrent correlation over those for lags in either direction — whether tested by graphic comparison, by the Pearsonian correlation coefficient, or by the special method alluded to below and described in Appendix III–C — is definitely marked.

directly or indirectly reflects some aspect of short-time change in the volume of business activity. The average of these four sets of link relatives may conveniently be employed as the basic series for the measurement of lags.

Continuing the graphic examination of the data, we find another group of series (industrial stock prices, railroad stock prices, and New York clearings) which may be referred to as "the three speculative series," and which show among themselves close concurrence of movement. The average of the link-relative series for this group exhibits, with respect to the basic series, high correlation and a precedence averaging one quarter.

Wholesale commodity prices move, on the whole, concurrently with the basic series, but with considerable inconsistency as to timing of movement; a similar statement may be made regarding sensitive commodity prices. The series for exports presents nothing better, for any lead or lag, than a moderate correlation with the basic series; the closest approach to correspondence appears when exports are lagged one quarter.

Three series — commercial-paper rates, bond prices, and loans of New York banks — show both a lagging and a leading correlation with the basic series. The "best correlations" are those indicated in the following tabulation:

|  | Lagging | Leading |
|---|---|---|
| Commercial-paper rates (taken positively) | One quarter | |
| Commercial-paper rates (taken negatively) | | Five quarters |
| Bond prices (taken negatively) .......... | Two quarters | |
| Bond prices (taken positively) ........... | | Three quarters |
| Loans of New York banks (taken negatively) ............................ | Two quarters | |
| Loans of New York banks (taken positively) ............................ | | Four quarters |

The lagging correlation is appreciably superior to the leading for commercial-paper rates, and slightly better for bond prices and loans of New York banks. Accordingly, for these three series we adopt the lagging correlations.[40]

[40] Since for the two series, bond prices and loans of New York banks, there is so little to choose between the lagging and leading correlations, we shall plan to make at a later stage of the investigation an experimental calculation by substituting, in the computation of the "link-relative standard pattern" (see the next section), the positive (leading) correlations in place of the negative (lagging) correlations for these two series. Anticipating the results, we may say here that no significant changes appear.

It seems desirable to confirm these conclusions, reached through graphic examination of the data, by formal statistical tests. Such statistical tests (described in detail in Appendix III–C) yield results which in every case agree with those just obtained by graphic intercomparison.

### The Common Pattern of Movement in the Link-Relative Series

Careful examination of the thirteen individual series of Chart 3 with allowance for the lags just measured indicates that, ignoring irregularities and fixing attention upon the general contour of fluctuation, these series exhibit a remarkable degree of correspondence. This correspondence, to be sure, is by no means perfect. For the last three series on the chart — exports, loans of New York banks, and bond prices — the correlation with the general tendencies is not consistently good, and the other series show occasional divergencies in fundamental movement. Nevertheless, taking the array of curves as a whole, a basic pattern of fluctuation is clearly discernible, definitely tracing itself through the irregularities and idiosyncrasies of particular series.

A convenient way to make a decisive test for the existence of this pattern is to construct a multiple frequency table of the figures in quartile-deviation units. In this table, we set up a column for each quarter, 1866–II to 1914–II. In each column, there are thirteen entries, representing the appropriate link-relative items for the several series. In making these entries, the item for each lagging (or leading) series is shifted a sufficient number of quarters to compensate for its average lag (or lead), as previously measured. The object of this shifting is to lessen the blurring of the general contour of fluctuation occasioned by differences in the time order of movement of the various series.[41]

Examination of the multiple frequency table reveals a tendency for the items to form clusters in the several columns — to be concentrated in clearly-marked "zones of distribution" which stand out from one another very distinctly. The table as a whole presents to the eye a vivid picture of a common wave movement, alternately advancing and receding, among the constituent series.

It is not feasible to reproduce here the elaborate multiple fre-

---

[41] The items for the two series, bond prices and loans of New York banks, are, of course, entered inverted (see text, just above).

quency table. In view of this, resort is had to a device often convenient in cases of this kind — the employment of "partition values" (quartiles, deciles, percentiles) to indicate the general characteristics of a frequency distribution.[42] The upper part of Chart 4 shows the quartiles derived from the successive columns of the multiple frequency table. The close approach to parallelism among the three quartiles, taken in conjunction with the presence of most clearly distinct "zones of distribution" for the successive columns of the multiple frequency table, affords decisive evidence as to the presence of a common pattern of movement among the series.[43]

### The Link-Relative Standard Pattern

In order to secure a concrete representation of this basic pattern, the average of the seven middle items — the group lying within the first and third quartiles — is computed for each column of the multiple frequency table.[44] The "link-relative standard pattern" thus obtained is plotted on Chart 4, and also as the top curve of Chart 3. The comparative smoothness of the curve is surprising, considering the intrinsic severity of the link-relative test for concurrence of agreement among economic series.

If now we carefully compare each individual series of Chart 3 with this link-relative standard pattern, once more ignoring

[42] For examples of effective uses of this device, see Wesley C. Mitchell, *Index Numbers of Wholesale Prices in the United States and Foreign Countries* (U.S.B.L.S. Bulletin No. 284), chart opposite p. 14; and Arthur F. Burns, *Production Trends in the United States since 1870* (New York: National Bureau of Economic Research, Inc., 1934), pp. 182 ff.

[43] The evidence is indeed so decisive that it seems superfluous to appeal to formal tests of significance.

[44] It is at this point that the argument of p. 91, above — to the effect that our process of reducing the link-relative series to deviations from average and thus eliminating differences in average level of fluctuation, while it unfortunately cannot be expected completely to eliminate the distortion in short-time fluctuation occasioned by the long-time drifts in the original series, nevertheless does on the whole very materially reduce such distortion — can be made more specific. We may now say that, had we failed to make some adjustment for average level, the influence of the disturbing element would at this stage of our work show itself in a certain degree of blurring in the measurement of central tendency for the various columns of the multiple frequency table of link-relative items; but, through application to the several link-relative series of our correction for differences in average level of fluctuation, the effects of this disturbing influence (though of course not entirely removed) have been very materially lessened, and our measurements of central tendency in the multiple frequency table have correspondingly been made more nearly precise.

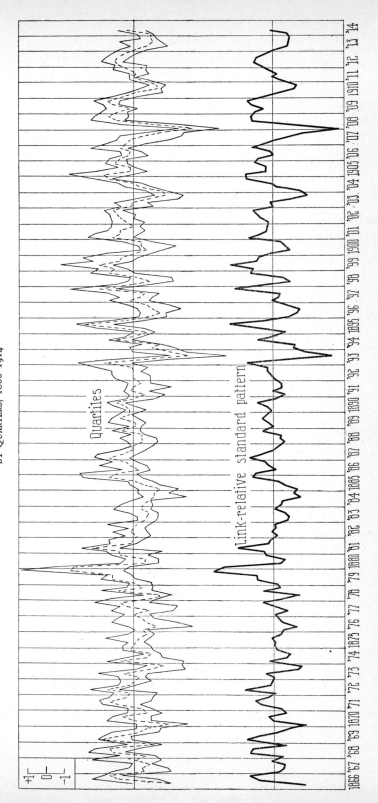

CHART 4

QUARTILES FROM MULTIPLE FREQUENCY TABLE OF LINK RELATIVES —
DEVIATIONS FROM AVERAGE IN QUARTILE-DEVIATION UNITS —
COMPARED WITH LINK-RELATIVE STANDARD PATTERN:
BY QUARTERS, 1866–1914

Quartiles

Link-relative standard pattern

irregularities and fixing attention upon the major movements of the series, we observe the correspondence to be on the whole a remarkable one; the individual curves in general show close conformity to the standard pattern in their general contour and even with respect to many minor movements.[45] These comparisons not only afford further convincing evidence as to the existence of a common pattern of movement, but also demonstrate beyond question that our link-relative standard pattern faithfully reflects characteristics which are inherent in the constituent data.

### THE STANDARD PATTERN FOR ORIGINAL ITEMS

In order to obtain a representation of this basic pattern of fluctuation in such form as to admit comparison with the *original items* of the individual series, we must build up a chain series derived from the link-relative standard pattern. As a preliminary to this chaining, a conversion constant is required, to be used in transforming the link-relative standard pattern from quartile-deviation units to percentages. Strictly, we should make thirteen separate conversions — one for the purposes of comparison with each of the thirteen series of original items. Since, however, it is the general contour of fluctuation which is of interest rather than the amplitude, a compromise figure will suffice.[46] This compromise figure we may obtain by a process bearing some analogy to the procedure followed in deriving the link-relative pattern itself. Briefly, we array in order of magnitude the quartile deviations for the thirteen individual series (shown in the last column of the table in Appendix III–A), and then take the average of the middle seven items. The resulting figure (3.78) is our conversion constant.

We turn now to the process of conversion and chaining. The exact procedure is as follows. The various items of the link-relative standard pattern are multiplied by 3.78, the conversion constant just obtained, and the resulting products are then increased by 100, thus transforming the series from quartile-deviation units to percentages, 1866–II to 1914–II. These percentages

---

[45] Here again, we must record that for the last three series on the chart the correlation with the basic movement is not consistently maintained throughout the period.

[46] Variations in the conversion constant can, of course, bring about differences in shape of fluctuation, as well as in amplitude, but for the cases at hand these differences in shape are minor and unimportant.

are next chained by successive multiplication, taking 1866–1 as base, or 100, to obtain the standard pattern pertaining to the original items. Of course, the starting point of the chain series is purely arbitrary and the absolute value of the items has no significance.

The standard pattern for original items obtained by this process of conversion and chaining — referred to in the remainder of this chapter simply as "standard pattern" — is plotted at the top of Chart 1, in conjunction with the original series. If now we make the comparisons thus invited, not forgetting to allow for lags and leads as previously discussed, we see that the short-time oscillations in this standard pattern may be clearly traced [47] — sometimes, to be sure, exaggerated or minimized; occasionally distorted by irregularities — in the movements of the original series.[48] While this graphic comparison affords striking confirmation of the previously stated conclusions, it is nevertheless true that our conviction as to the presence of a common pattern of movement rests fundamentally upon the cumulation of evidence furnished by the general concurrence of fluctuation appearing in the display of link-relative series (Chart 3); the presence of clear-cut "zones of distribution" in the multiple frequency table; the close approach to parallelism among the quartiles, taken in conjunction with the narrowness of the "band" between the first and third quartiles (Chart 4); and the remarkable correspondence in basic movement revealed by the comparison of the link-relative standard pattern with the array of individual series (Chart 3).

## THE SUPPLEMENTARY STANDARD PATTERN

In connection with the reduction of link relatives to "deviations from average" (as set forth in a preceding section of this chapter, "Adjustment for Differences in Average Level"), a possible objection — that this process in effect amounted to "elimination of secular trend" by a method palpably inadequate — was dismissed, on seemingly sufficient grounds. In order, however, that question

---

[47] Attention may be called to the fact that the series railroad earnings conforms closely, in its short-time fluctuations, to the standard pattern. This close correspondence is partially concealed by the compressed scale which, because of the exigencies of charting, it has been necessary to employ for this series on Chart 1.

[48] Still once more, we must note that for exports, loans of New York banks, and bond prices, the correlation with the general pattern of short-run fluctuation is not consistently maintained over the time interval.

regarding this methodological point should cast no doubt upon the validity of our findings, we make a supplementary experimental calculation.

This calculation begins with the computation of a "supplementary link-relative standard pattern," in which no attempt is made at reduction of the influence of differences in average level of the link-relative series — the calculation is based, in other words, simply upon "deviation from 100" rather than upon "deviation from average." Using the same methods of conversion and chaining as before, a "supplementary standard pattern" for comparison with the original items is derived. This supplementary series shows short-run fluctuations almost identical with those of the standard pattern itself,[49] but superimposed, so to speak, upon a gradually rising long-run drift (compare the first two curves of Chart 1).

[49] Here and there, minor differences in short-run movement appear. Comparison of the multiple frequency tables for the two cases suggests that these differences are, to a considerable degree at least, ascribable to the blurring of measurement of central tendency in the multiple frequency table for the supplementary standard pattern case (cf. fn. 44 in this chapter).

# CHAPTER IV

## THE STANDARD PATTERN FOR THE THIRTEEN IMPORTANT
## ECONOMIC SERIES: ANNUAL DATA

IN ACCORDANCE with a decision, indicated on a preceding page, to test the application of our link-relative procedure to the thirteen important economic series for periods of various lengths, successively, we turn next to the consideration of annual data, having in mind particularly to discover whether there can be discerned in such data a pattern (or possibly patterns) of different sort from that revealed by the quarterly data analyzed as described in the preceding chapter.

In general, our fundamental material is identical with that employed in the quarterly study (cf. Appendix III–A). In two cases, however — outside clearings and railroad earnings — though the series basically remains the same as before, we are able to substitute a continuous set of figures from a new source in place of the "spliced" series employed for the quarterly analysis. Details regarding these two series are given in Appendix IV–A.

A preliminary operation of the statistical analysis for the annual study consists, of course, in striking annual averages of those of the thirteen series for which annual figures are not supplied in the original source. The annual data, like the quarterly, extend over the interval 1866–1914. With respect to the year 1914, however, a special adjustment is made: having in mind that many economic series show highly disturbed fluctuations as a result of the outbreak of the World War in the summer of 1914, we may wisely eliminate data for the last half of 1914 from the analysis. We accomplish this in each case by employing, instead of the average for the calendar year 1914, the average of the figures (seasonally adjusted where such adjustment is appropriate) for the first two quarters of 1914. We shall plan, so far as may be feasible, to follow this practice more or less generally in dealing with annual data throughout the investigations described in the present volume; and this policy with reference to the 1914 items should be kept in mind in examining and interpreting the various charts appearing on the pages which are to follow.

## The Annual Link-Relative Analysis

The procedure which we shall employ in the analysis of the annual data follows closely that previously used in the quarterly study. It is consequently unnecessary for us to enter here upon extended consideration of methodological questions. (For a discussion at length of the methodological issues, see the two preceding chapters. Certain minor technical details regarding the statistical procedure in the annual case are given in Appendix IV–B.) The first step in our analysis is, of course, the computation of link relatives by years, 1867–1914, for each of the thirteen series.[1] Next, with a view to adjusting the several series of link relatives for differences in average level of fluctuation, we divide each such series through by its geometric average.[2] (These geometric averages are tabulated in Appendix IV–C.)

The thirteen series of annual link relatives, expressed as deviations from average, exhibit, as in the quarterly analysis, wide variations with respect to amplitude of fluctuation. And, as before, we divide each series through by a measure of its dispersion, in order to eliminate differences in average amplitude of fluctuation among the various series. The absence of highly extreme items enables us to employ here the average deviation as a dispersion measure (rather than the quartile deviation, as in the quarterly case), in accordance with an earlier general methodological decision set forth in Chapter III (in the section entitled "Adjustment for Variation in Amplitude"). Our reasons for this decision, as there indicated, would seem to be cogent. Nevertheless, we shall plan shortly to make certain experimental computations,[3] with a view to removing any possible doubt as to whether this shift in methodology, between the quarterly and annual studies, could in any essential way have affected our results.

We now compute the average deviations for the thirteen series

---

[1] We are following, as the reader will remember, the convention of giving each link relative the date of the later of the two time intervals involved. Thus, for each series the first annual link relative $\left( \dfrac{1867}{1866} \right)$ is dated 1867, and so on.

[2] For discussion of the rationale of this procedure, see the preceding chapter.

[3] As described in a later section of this chapter.

(tabulated in Appendix IV–C), and then divide through each series of link relatives — previously adjusted for differences in average level of fluctuation, as described just above — by its average deviation. The resulting series, designated as "link relatives, deviations from average in average-deviation units" (Chart 5), give — as in the quarterly analysis (cf. Chart 3) — an impression of general correspondence in major fluctuations.

We turn, as before, to the investigation of lags among the series. Graphic examination (cf. Chart 5) indicates that there are four series (outside clearings, imports, immigration, and railroad earnings) which show fairly good intercorrelation and seem to move in general concurrently. These observations suggest that we may take the average of these four series as basic for the measurement of lags. We thus have arrived at the same form of basic series, "the average of the four volume series," as was employed previously in the quarterly case. It is strongly to be emphasized, however, that our selection here is independent. Bearing in mind that the principal object in applying the link-relative procedure to periods of successively increasing length is to discover whether *new* patterns will emerge, *essentially different* from the pattern discovered through the use of quarterly data, we can see at once the impropriety which would be involved in allowing our choice of basic series for lag measurements in the annual investigation to be dictated by the results of the quarterly analysis. We adopt "the average of the four volume series" here, not because such average was previously used in the quarterly case, but because its employment is indicated through independent consideration.

Taking, then, "the average of the four volume series" as basic for the measurement of lags, each of the thirteen individual series of Chart 5 is compared with it, in order to discover, for the period 1867–1914 as a whole, whether the "best correlation" in each case is positive or negative, and the amount of lag or lead pertaining to such "best correlation." These measurements are made, as in the quarterly analysis, by graphic intercomparison supplemented and verified through statistical tests.[4] For all series except three, the best correlations are found to be positive, with "zero lag" (concurrent). The three exceptional series — loans of New York banks, bond prices, and exports — show in each case both a lag-

---

[4] As to the nature of these statistical tests, see Appendix IV–B.

CHART 5

LINK RELATIVES FOR THIRTEEN IMPORTANT ECONOMIC SERIES —
DEVIATIONS FROM AVERAGE IN AVERAGE-DEVIATION UNITS —
COMPARED WITH LINK-RELATIVE STANDARD PATTERNS:
BY YEARS, 1867–1914 *

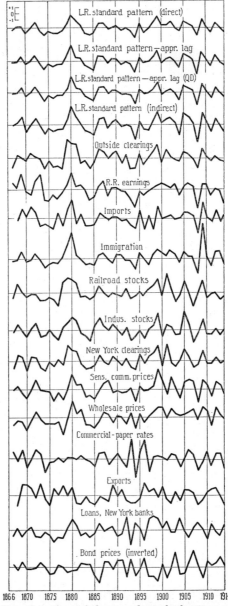

* For explanation of captions of the several standard-pattern curves, see accompanying text.

ging and a leading correlation with the basic series. The "best correlations" are as follows:

| | Lagging | Leading |
|---|---|---|
| Loans of New York banks (taken negatively) | One year | |
| Loans of New York banks (taken positively) | | One year |
| Bond prices (taken negatively) | One year | |
| Bond prices (taken positively) | | One year |
| Exports (taken negatively) | Three years | |
| Exports (taken positively) | | Two years |

For loans of New York banks, the leading correlation is definitely superior to the lagging; for bond prices the lagging correlation is slightly better; for exports, both leading and lagging correlations are poor, but the leading correlation is, upon technical test, a trifle higher.

The measurement of lags for the annual series having been completed, we may (postponing for a time the comparison of these measurements with those of the quarterly study) proceed to examine the annual curves with a view to seeing whether any general pattern of movement can be discerned. The conclusions here run closely parallel with those previously reached in the quarterly analysis. The correlations among the thirteen individual series of Chart 5 are, to be sure, by no means perfect. All of the series exhibit individual peculiarities of behavior and, as earlier, the correlations with the general tendencies shown by the three series, bond prices, loans of New York banks, and exports, are not consistently good. Nevertheless, here as in the quarterly case, a basic pattern of fluctuation is clearly present, definitely tracing itself through the irregularities and idiosyncrasies of particular series. The multiple frequency table of annual link relatives, arranged by years, 1867–1914, exhibits most clearly-marked clustering — "zones of distribution" — in the several columns, and a definite picture of common wave movement. The "partition-values" test reveals close approach to parallelism among the quartiles.[5] This parallelism, taken in conjunction with the very distinct "zones of distribution" in the multiple frequency table, affords decisive evidence of a general pattern of movement.[6]

The presence of this general pattern of movement having thus

---

[5] The multiple frequency table and the "partition-values" chart have not been reproduced, but their general features can be inferred from Chart 5.

[6] Compare the conclusions of the quarterly link-relative investigation in Chapter III.

been established for the annual series, it is now appropriate to derive the annual link-relative standard pattern. As for the quarterly case, the process is to average the group of items lying within the first and third quartiles — "the middle seven" — of each column in the multiple frequency table. The resulting series is shown as the top curve of Chart 5, and may be designated as "link-relative standard pattern (direct)." [7] If now we compare the individual series of Chart 5 with this curve, we find further convincing evidence that a common pattern of movement truly exists, and that the annual link-relative standard pattern faithfully reflects characteristics which are implicit in the constituent data.

### COMPARISON WITH RESULTS OF THE PRECEDING CHAPTER

Do we have, in this wave-like picture of general fluctuation for the annual link relatives, the manifestations of a *new* pattern of movement inherent in the original figures from which these link relatives were computed — new, that is, in the sense that it is distinct from the standard pattern previously derived from quarterly data? It is to be emphasized that at this point we refer specifically, not to the *quarterly link-relative standard pattern* of Chart 3, but to the *quarterly standard pattern proper* of Chart 1, which was, it will be recalled, built up as a chain series through successive multiplication applied to the items of the quarterly link-relative series,[8] thus transforming the basic quarterly link-relative pattern into such form as to admit direct and simple comparison with the original items of the several constituent series (see pages 98–99, above, and also contrast Chart 1, opposite page 66, with Chart 3, opposite page 92).

We may obtain a basis for a decisive answer to our question by the following procedure: we take the quarterly standard pattern shown at the top of Chart 1 (that is, the *chain series* just referred to, comparable with original items of constituent series), strike annual averages of this chain series, compute the link relatives of these annual averages, and finally reduce such link relatives to average-deviation units. The resulting annual series — designated, for obvious reasons, as "link-relative standard pattern

---

[7] The force of the designation "direct" will appear shortly.

[8] Such items being first multiplied by a "conversion constant," and increased by 100 per cent, as previously explained.

(*indirect*)" — is shown as the fourth curve on Chart 5. Comparison of the two pertinent lines, the first and fourth curves of the chart, gives us immediately an unmistakable answer to our question. The two series approach very near to coincidence.[9] Clearly, we have not through our annual analysis developed a new pattern; we have merely in effect derived the old pattern over again, following a different route, so to speak, but arriving at the same destination.

The essential identity of the two patterns may (as has doubtless already occurred to the reader) be shown in another way, somewhat simpler and more straightforward. In this alternative procedure, we take our annual link-relative standard pattern as derived from annual data by the *direct* process, and transform it into a chain series through application of the process of successive multiplication.[10] This chain series — "standard pattern proper derived from annual data" — is in such form as readily to permit comparison of fluctuations with the corresponding quarterly chain series — i.e., the standard pattern proper derived from quarterly data, described in the preceding chapter and presented as the first curve upon Chart 1.

For convenience of examination, these two chain series have been plotted in conjunction on Chart 6 (the first two lines). The essential likeness of movement is immediately apparent. A more precise test, however, is afforded by the comparison of our chain series derived directly from annual data (the second curve of Chart 6, marked "Y"), with the *annual averages* of the quarterly chain series (the fifth curve, marked "Y–Q").[11] The two series exhibit close correspondence in the details of their fluctuations.

The results of the comparison of chain series, then, reënforce

---

[9] And, indeed, the minor divergencies which do appear (as in 1867–69) are, as will shortly be set forth, explainable on minor technical grounds.

[10] The procedure here is quite analogous to that previously employed in the quarterly analysis of the preceding chapter. The items of the annual link-relative series are first multiplied by the conversion constant 8.82 per cent (8.82 per cent is the average of the seven middle average deviations in the array of average deviations for the thirteen series, arranged in order of size) and then increased by 100 per cent, thus transforming the series from average-deviation units to percentages, 1867–1914. These percentages are then chained by successive multiplication, taking 1866 as base, or 100, to obtain the annual standard pattern proper. Here, as before, the starting point is purely arbitrary, and the absolute value of the items has no significance.

[11] The third and fourth curves of Chart 6 should be disregarded for the time being.

the conclusion earlier reached through comparison of link-relative series: through our investigation based upon annual data, we have in essence simply rederived the pattern of short-time movement previously yielded by our quarterly analysis. We have not as yet succeeded in discovering any new pattern of fluctuation. We shall nevertheless continue our search, going on to deal with periods of greater length than one year. First, however, we shall pause briefly to consider certain methodological questions pertaining to our annual standard pattern.

### A Slight Modification and Improvement in the Annual Standard Pattern: the "Appropriate-Lag" Computation

We revert now to a matter which was temporarily set aside at an earlier stage of the analysis described in this chapter: the comparison of the *lag measurements* obtained in the quarterly and annual studies, respectively. Knowing now that it is the same pattern of short-time fluctuation which manifests itself in the two analyses, we have fairly a right to expect that the two sets of lag measurements should be consistent. If we review and bring into conjunction our summary statements concerning the lag measurements in the quarterly analysis (Chapter III, in the section entitled "Adjustment for Lags") and in the annual analysis (earlier in this chapter), we note, in the first place, that "the average of the four volume series" is in both cases employed as a basis for the measurement of lags and leads. Further, bearing in mind that in the annual study lags and leads were measured only to the nearest year, we find that the two sets of results are almost completely consistent with each other.

For the most part, positive correlation accompanied by concurrence ("the four volume series" and the two commodity-price series) or one quarter lead ("the three speculative series") or one quarter lag (commercial-paper rates) in the quarterly study is cognate with positive correlation and concurrence in the annual study — as close a correspondence as is possible with annual lag measurements accurate only to the nearest year. We may fairly count also the series bond prices — for which the quarterly "best correlation" is negative with two quarters lag, and the annual "best correlation" is negative with one year lag — as a case of congruence. For loans of New York banks, in the quarterly analysis the negative correlation with two quarters lag is superior,

# CHART 6

STANDARD PATTERN FOR THIRTEEN IMPORTANT ECONOMIC SERIES —
CHAIN SERIES DERIVED BY (1) DIRECT, AND (2) INDIRECT METHODS:
1866–1914 *

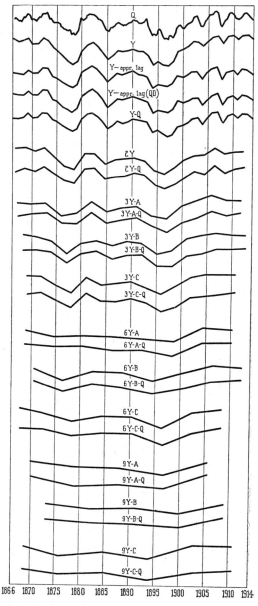

* Uniform logarithmic vertical scales. For explanation of captions, see text, accompanying, and also Chapter V.

but only slightly so, to the positive correlation with four quarters lead; in the annual analysis, the positive correlation, since it happens to work out integrally in years, naturally has a better chance to exhibit itself. Only one case remains, then, which is really anomalous. That is the series exports, where the quarterly reading is positive correlation with one quarter lag, as compared to positive correlation with two years lead for the annual. The explanation lies in the fact that for this particular series the intrinsic correlation with the basic series is in any case poor, and consequently indications of "best correlation" obtained by formal arithmetical tests are likely to vary capriciously, depending upon the particular form such test may take.

We conclude, then, that the lag measurements in the annual analysis are consistent with those of the quarterly analysis. The annual lag measurements, however, being expressed only to the nearest year, are for a number of constituent series necessarily somewhat less reliable than the quarterly. The deduction follows, as an obvious corollary, that the picture of the annual link-relative pattern of fluctuation, as presented by the curve derived directly from annual data (the top line of Chart 5), must suffer some slight degree of malformation from this cause. All these considerations suggest that we can effect a moderate improvement in the measurement of the annual link-relative pattern by making a small modification in our procedure, availing ourselves of the more reliable lag measurements furnished by the quarterly analysis.[12]

A suitable technique can readily be devised. For those six series classified as "concurrent" in the quarterly lag measurements, we retain calendar-year figures in our modified annual analysis; for the other seven series, we make appropriate shifts in the dating of the items. To illustrate, for the series industrial stock prices, which has a lead of one quarter in the quarterly schema, we take the average of October 1865 to September 1866, inclusive, as the annual item for 1866, and so on throughout the period 1866–1914; for the series commercial-paper rates, which has a lag of one quarter, we take the average of April 1866 to March 1867, inclusive, as the annual item for 1866, and so on throughout the period.

Through the adoption of this device, we make more nearly

---

[12] It must be pointed out that the adoption of this line of attack, though entirely appropriate now, would most clearly have been logically improper at the time of

precise allowance for the lags among the constituent series. The remaining steps are obvious: starting with the thirteen annual series (shifted, where required, to the "appropriate-lag" basis, as just explained), we compute link relatives, make adjustments for differences in average level and in average amplitude among the series, set up the multiple frequency table, and finally derive our modified link-relative pattern. This new pattern (presented as the second curve on Chart 5) we designate as "link-relative standard pattern (direct) on the appropriate-lag basis."[13]

Comparing with the corresponding pattern previously secured by the straightforward procedure (the first curve of Chart 5), we see that, as we had anticipated, only minor modifications have been accomplished. Careful examination of the chart, however, reveals that at several points (e.g., 1867–68, 1896–97, 1900–01) the new curve exhibits clear superiority over its predecessor as regards congruence with the "link-relative standard pattern (indirect)," which appears as the fourth curve on the chart.

We may go on now to apply to our new link-relative pattern the process of conversion to a percentage basis followed by successive multiplication, and thus to derive a new *chain series* — standard pattern proper — presented as the third curve ("Y — appr. lag") on Chart 6. Comparing this with the second and fifth curves of the chart, we see that our refinement in procedure has produced only minor alterations in the annual chain series, but nevertheless has at certain points brought it into closer conformity to the annual averages of the quarterly standard pattern ("Y–Q").

Through application of the "appropriate-lag" methodology we have thus been able to derive slightly improved annual patterns.[14] Whenever hereafter in Part Two of our investigation we shall have occasion to employ representations of the annual link-relative standard pattern, or of the annual standard pattern proper, we shall have resort to these improved series.

---

the *original derivation* of the link-relative standard pattern from annual data, for then it had not been demonstrated that the quarterly and annual patterns were manifestations of the same intrinsic short-run form of fluctuation.

[13] Abbreviated on the chart to "L.R. standard pattern — appr. lag."

[14] We also extend this improvement to the quarterly case, by deriving a slightly modified quarterly standard pattern: this derivation is accomplished by superimposing the quarterly fluctuations of the standard pattern of Chapter III upon the annual movements of the "appropriate-lag" standard pattern just obtained. (This new quarterly series may be seen as the fourth curve of Chart 32, in Chapter XIV, below.)

### A METHODOLOGICAL EXPERIMENT: QUARTILE-DEVIATION UNITS VERSUS AVERAGE-DEVIATION UNITS

We return now to a certain methodological point referred to on an earlier page. In passing from the quarterly analysis of Chapter III to the annual analysis of the present chapter, we have made one shift in procedure: we have substituted the average deviation for the quartile deviation as a measure of dispersion. Though this shift was made for reasons which seemed entirely cogent (as set forth in the earlier pages of this chapter), nevertheless it appears desirable to carry out certain experimental computations, with a view to removing any possible doubt as to whether the change in methodology could have any essential bearing upon our results.

The test computation is simple. We merely recompute the "link-relative standard pattern (direct) on the appropriate-lag basis," substituting the quartile deviation for the average deviation as dispersion measure. The result of this substitution is to leave the link-relative pattern virtually unchanged, except for an almost uniformly consistent difference in amplitude of fluctuation (corresponding closely to theoretical expectation, taking into account the properties of the average and quartile deviations). With suitable adjustment of vertical scale to allow for such difference in amplitude,[15] the curve on the quartile-deviation basis (third line on Chart 5) is almost precisely identical with that on the average-deviation basis (second line on the chart). And the corresponding comparison of chain series (the third and fourth curves of Chart 6) yields a consistent reading: the two chain series are very closely similar.[16]

Our conclusion is unmistakably clear. The transition in methodology involved in substituting the average deviation for the quartile deviation is responsible for no significant alteration in our results.

[15] The vertical scale for the curve in quartile-deviation units on Chart 5 has been reduced in the ratio 0.85, corresponding to the relation of quartile deviation to average deviation for the normal curve $\left( \dfrac{0.6745}{0.7979} \right)$. It is not meant to imply that we are here necessarily dealing with distributions which closely approach normality; as is well known, the ratio holds approximately for other distributions so long as they do not differ markedly from the normal form.

[16] For the chain series, no adjustment of scale is required (cf. the preceding footnote), for the difference in amplitude of the link-relative series is automatically removed in the process of conversion to percentage basis.

# CHAPTER V

## THE STANDARD PATTERN FOR THE THIRTEEN IMPORTANT ECONOMIC SERIES: DATA FOR LONGER PERIODS

WE CONTINUE the pattern analysis for the thirteen important economic series by turning to the investigation of link relatives pertaining to periods longer than one year. Since our methods are, with but minor modifications, those developed in the two preceding chapters, only very brief description of the statistical procedure need be given here (certain technical details are presented in Appendix V–A).

### TWO-YEAR PERIODS

The investigation by two-year periods closely parallels, both in methods and in results, that of the annual case. We take, for each of the thirteen series, two-year averages — 1866–67, 1868–69, 1870–71, ......, 1912–13. We then compute link relatives —
$$\frac{1868-69}{1866-67} \quad \frac{1870-71}{1868-69} \quad \cdots\cdots\cdots, \quad \frac{1912-13}{1910-11}. \quad \text{From these, employ-}$$
ing methods corresponding to those of the annual analysis,[1] we derive the link-relative standard pattern (the first curve of Chart 7) and the standard pattern proper (the sixth curve, "2 Y", of Chart 6). The correlations (as revealed in the array of curves of Chart 7, in the multiple frequency table, and in the chart of quartile "partition values") are almost as good as those in the annual case.[2] And here again, our graphic comparisons, whether for link relatives (the first two curves on Chart 7), or for chain

---

[1] That is, the annual analysis by the "straightforward" procedure, as described in the earlier pages of Chapter IV. It did not seem worth while here to carry out an "appropriate-lag" computation (cf. the description of this computation, as set forth in the later pages of Chapter IV), taking into account the slight alteration of results produced by this modification of procedure in the annual case, as well as the consideration that exactness of lag measurement presumably becomes even less important as we go on to analyses for still longer periods.

[2] With regard to the convention for the dating of the items of Chart 7, and the other charts of this chapter, see Appendix V–A. In this chapter, as in Chapter IV, the multiple frequency tables for the several cases, and the corresponding charts of quartile "partition values," have not been reproduced.

CHART 7

LINK RELATIVES FOR THIRTEEN IMPORTANT ECONOMIC SERIES —
DEVIATIONS FROM AVERAGE IN AVERAGE-DEVIATION UNITS —
COMPARED WITH LINK-RELATIVE STANDARD PATTERNS:
BY TWO-YEAR PERIODS WITHIN THE INTERVAL 1866–1914

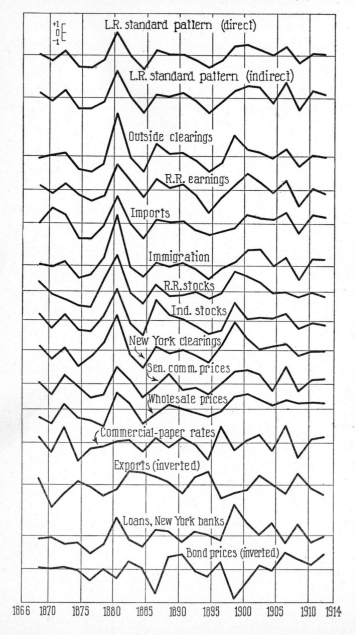

series (the curves labelled "2 Y" and "2 Y–Q", respectively, on Chart 6),[3] clearly indicate that we have done nothing more than to rederive the pattern of movement originally revealed by analysis of the quarterly data. We have not as yet succeeded in discovering any new pattern of fluctuation in the movements of the thirteen important economic series.

## THREE-YEAR PERIODS

In the investigation of the three-year case, we begin by taking averages of original items for the respective intervals 1866–68, 1869–71, 1872–74, . . . . . . . ., 1911–13; and we then compute the link relatives for $\dfrac{1869–71}{1866–68}$, $\dfrac{1872–74}{1869–71}$, . . . . . . . ., $\dfrac{1911–13}{1908–10}$.
These data we shall refer to as the "3 Y–A" series (the force of the symbol "A" will shortly appear). Once more, we find generally high correlation indicated by the chart of link relatives in average-deviation units (Chart 8, Part A),[4] as well as in the multiple-frequency table and the chart of quartile "partition values"; and once more our comparisons, whether on the basis of link relatives (Chart 8, Part A) or of chain series (Chart 6),[5] definitely indicate mere rederivation of the pattern originally obtained from quarterly data: there is no indication, nor even suggestion, of a new pattern of movement.

It may, however, at this point very well be objected that our conclusions regarding three-year data cannot yet be regarded as definitely established. Three years is a sufficiently long time

---

[3] On Chart 7, the first curve — captioned "L.R. standard pattern (direct)" — is, as the title implies, derived directly from the link relatives of two-year averages; and the second curve — captioned "L.R. standard pattern (indirect)" — is obtained by first taking two-year averages of the chain series derived in Chapter III from quarterly data, computing link relatives of such averages, and then reducing these link relatives to average-deviation units.

On Chart 6, the curve marked "2 Y" represents the chain series obtained by applying successive multiplication to the items of the link-relative standard pattern derived directly from data for two-year periods; and the curve marked "2 Y–Q" represents the two-year averages of the chain series derived in Chapter III from quarterly data.

[4] We are obliged, as in previous analyses, to enter a reservation regarding the three series bond prices, loans of New York banks, and exports, where the correlation with the general movement is not high.

[5] Specifically, attention should be directed to the first two curves of Chart 8, Part A, and to the two curves marked "3 Y–A" and "3 Y–A–Q", respectively, on Chart 6.

# CHART 8

Part A

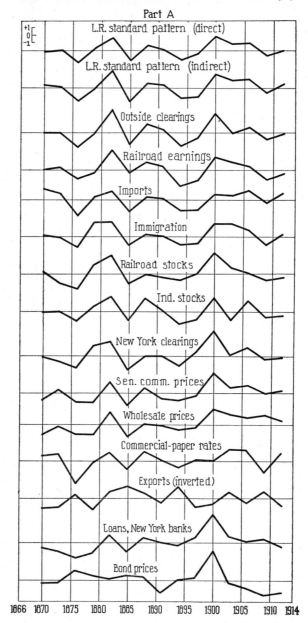

# CHART 8

LINK RELATIVES FOR THIRTEEN IMPORTANT ECONOMIC SERIES —
DEVIATIONS FROM AVERAGE IN AVERAGE-DEVIATION UNITS —
COMPARED WITH LINK-RELATIVE STANDARD PATTERNS:
BY THREE-YEAR PERIODS WITHIN THE INTERVAL 1866–1914 (*Continued*)

Part B

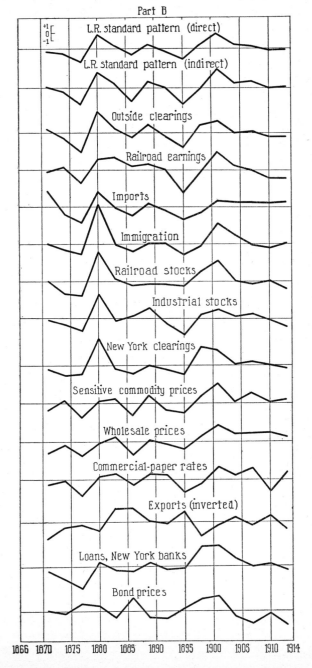

# CHART 8

Part C

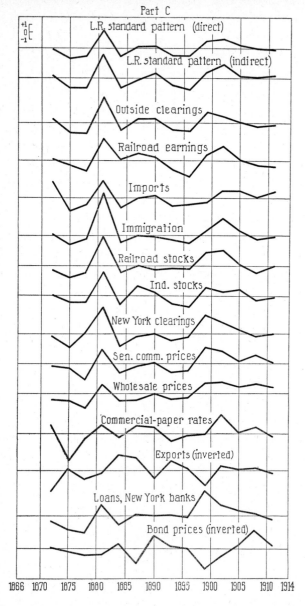

L.R. standard pattern (direct)

L.R. standard pattern (indirect)

Outside clearings

Railroad earnings

Imports

Immigration

Railroad stocks

Ind. stocks

New York clearings

Sen. comm. prices

Wholesale prices

Commercial-paper rates

Exports (inverted)

Loans, New York banks

Bond prices (inverted)

1866 1870 1875 1880 1885 1890 1895 1900 1905 1910 1914

interval to make it possible that one should, either by deliberate design or by chance, "gerrymander" the boundary lines of the periods, so to speak, in such way that results unrepresentative of the true characteristics of the body of data under examination should be obtained.

To guard against the possibility of misleading conclusions from this source, we proceed to secure two other series of three-year averages — designated as the "3 Y–B" series and the "3 Y–C" series, respectively — shifting successively the boundary dates of the time intervals to begin with 1867 and 1868, respectively, as opposed to 1866 for the "3 Y–A" series. We then compute the link-relative series and carry out complete pattern analyses for the "3 Y–B" and "3 Y–C" data.[6] The results naturally, on account of the shifting of boundary lines of time intervals, yield pictures differing in outward form from those secured in the "3 Y–A" case, but the intrinsic significance of the results remains unaltered, and the essential conclusions are confirmed. The general structural correlation of the array of series is still high; the "3 Y–B" and "3 Y–C" patterns are quite consistent with those derived by the quarterly approach; we fail to discover indication of any new pattern.

## SIX-YEAR PERIODS

We turn next to investigation by six-year periods. Here, as in the three-year analysis, it seems wise to set up three sets of averages, varying systematically the delimitation lines of the time intervals. In the present case, the boundary dates are shifted by increments of two years as we pass from the "6 Y–A" averages to the "6 Y–B" averages, and from the "6 Y–B" averages to the "6 Y–C" averages, respectively.[7]

Some difficulties now begin to appear regarding our statistical methodology and, relatedly, the trustworthiness of our results. With so few items in our time series, we are clearly not in a position to measure lags with anything approaching precision; the reliability of the dispersion measures is somewhat in question; and we may have some misgivings as to the dependability of the indications of correlation. These difficulties with respect to sta-

---

[6] See Parts B and C of Chart 8; also compare, on Chart 6, the two pairs of curves marked "3 Y–B" and "3 Y–B–Q", "3 Y–C" and "3 Y–C–Q", respectively.

[7] For details, see Appendix V–A.

# CHART 9

### LINK RELATIVES FOR THIRTEEN IMPORTANT ECONOMIC SERIES — DEVIATIONS FROM AVERAGE IN AVERAGE-DEVIATION UNITS — COMPARED WITH LINK-RELATIVE STANDARD PATTERNS: BY SIX-YEAR PERIODS WITHIN THE INTERVAL 1866–1914

#### Part A

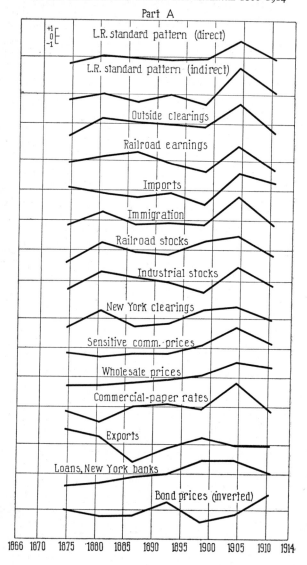

L.R. standard pattern (direct)

L.R. standard pattern (indirect)

Outside clearings

Railroad earnings

Imports

Immigration

Railroad stocks

Industrial stocks

New York clearings

Sensitive comm.·prices

Wholesale prices

Commercial-paper rates

Exports

Loans, New York banks

Bond prices (inverted)

1866  1870  1875  1880  1885  1890  1895  1900  1905  1910  1914

# CHART 9

LINK RELATIVES FOR THIRTEEN IMPORTANT ECONOMIC SERIES —
DEVIATIONS FROM AVERAGE IN AVERAGE-DEVIATION UNITS —
COMPARED WITH LINK-RELATIVE STANDARD PATTERNS:
BY SIX-YEAR PERIODS WITHIN THE INTERVAL 1866–1914 (*Continued*)

Part B

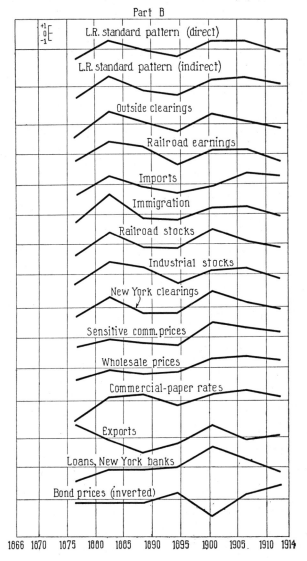

L.R. standard pattern (direct)

L.R. standard pattern (indirect)

Outside clearings

Railroad earnings

Imports

Immigration

Railroad stocks

Industrial stocks

New York clearings

Sensitive comm. prices

Wholesale prices

Commercial-paper rates

Exports

Loans, New York banks

Bond prices (inverted)

1866  1870   1875   1880   1885   1890   1895   1900   1905.   1910  1914

CHART 9

LINK RELATIVES FOR THIRTEEN IMPORTANT ECONOMIC SERIES —
DEVIATIONS FROM AVERAGE IN AVERAGE-DEVIATION UNITS —
COMPARED WITH LINK-RELATIVE STANDARD PATTERNS:
BY SIX-YEAR PERIODS WITHIN THE INTERVAL 1866–1914 (*Continued*)

Part C

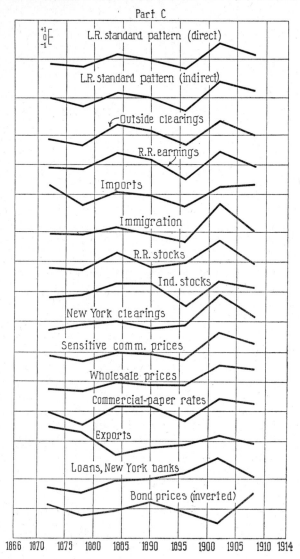

tistical methodology unquestionably confront us. Nevertheless, examination of the successive steps in the computation, and of the final results, leads rather convincingly to the conclusion that these results, though admittedly suffering some blurring of precision due to the methodological difficulties just mentioned, are rather definite in their indications. For each of the three multiple frequency tables of link relatives in average-deviation units, the "zones of distribution" stand out most clearly, and the "partition values" — quartiles — exhibit very close approach to parallelism; the presence of a general pattern of movement is in each case unmistakably indicated (cf. Chart 9).

Making our usual comparisons of "direct" and "indirect" link-relative patterns (the first two curves on Chart 9, Parts A, B, and C, respectively), and of the corresponding chain series (the three pairs of curves "6 Y–A" and "6 Y–A–Q", "6 Y–B" and "6 Y–B–Q", and "6 Y–C" and "6 Y–C–Q", respectively, of Chart 6) we see that the basic pattern of fluctuation first discerned in the quarterly analysis persists in practically unmodified form. Notwithstanding, if now we go back and examine carefully the details of Chart 9, we perceive that at last *some new element is beginning to enter the situation. The cohesiveness which has, so to speak, held the movements of the curves together is commencing to lessen. Some force, some influence, is beginning to disjoin them from their mutual attachment.* We do not stop now to consider what may be the nature of this force, or what name should be applied to its manifestations. We merely record the fact that this disjoining influence has manifested itself, and proceed, in the hope that the next step will throw more light upon the matter.

## NINE-YEAR PERIODS

In the investigation by nine-year periods, we once more set up a tripartite arrangement for the delimitation dates of time intervals. The nine-year averages ("9 Y–A", "9 Y–B", "9 Y–C") are shifted successively three years with respect to such delimitation dates.[8]

Methodological difficulties, which had begun to put in their appearance in connection with the six-year averages, now become pronounced. There can, of course, be no thought here of attempting to measure lags; even the decision as to whether a given series is to enter the calculation as positive or negative — in direct or in

---

[8] For details, see Appendix V–A.

# CHART 10

### Link Relatives for Thirteen Important Economic Series — Deviations from Average in Average-Deviation Units — Compared with Link-Relative Standard Patterns: by Nine–Year Periods within the Interval 1866–1914

## Part A

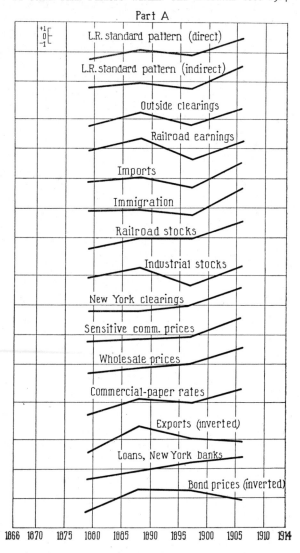

# CHART 10

Link Relatives for Thirteen Important Economic Series —
Deviations from Average in Average-Deviation Units —
Compared with Link-Relative Standard Patterns:
by Nine–Year Periods within the Interval 1866–1914 (*Continued*)

## Part B

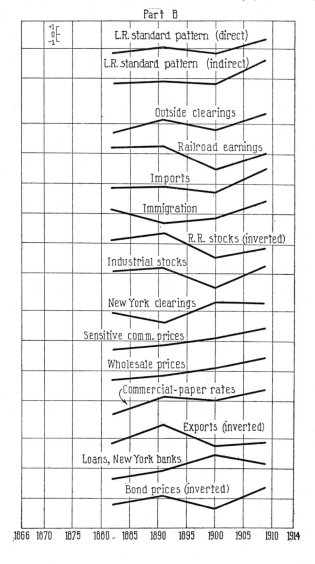

L.R. standard pattern (direct)

L.R. standard pattern (indirect)

Outside clearings

Railroad earnings

Imports

Immigration

R. R. stocks (inverted)

Industrial stocks

New York clearings

Sensitive comm. prices

Wholesale prices

Commercial-paper rates

Exports (inverted)

Loans, New York banks

Bond prices (inverted)

1866 1870 1875 1880 1885 1890 1895 1900 1905 1910 1914

# CHART 10

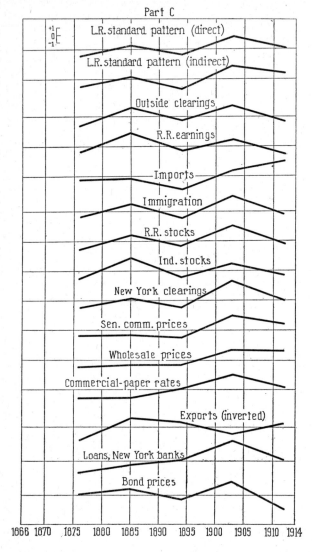

Part C

inverted form — has to rest in each case on the scanty and often somewhat ambiguous evidence furnished by a few pairs of link relatives, and there are certain suggestions of capriciousness in the results.[9] Further, in view of the extreme brevity of the series, it is highly questionable how much intrinsic significance can be attached to the dispersion measures. Still further, the dependability of any correlations which may be discovered is certainly very much impaired.

Even setting aside the doubts which these methodological considerations raise, and fixing attention without prejudice upon the results, we see that the indications have become much less clear than they were in the six-year case. The tendency toward intercorrelation among the series, though still operating, has plainly been decidedly weakened (compare Chart 10 with Charts 8 and 9); the "zones of distribution" in the multiple frequency tables are much less clearly marked; appreciably less close approach to parallelism appears among the quartile "partition values."

Another piece of evidence that the correlations are becoming weakened is afforded by the appearance of the three nine-year link-relative standard patterns (see the top curve, in each case, of Parts A, B, and C of Chart 10). The link-relative patterns are losing that wave-like character which they had exhibited in earlier analyses, and appear to be degenerating rapidly toward straight lines, or at least toward lines with very little fluctuation and very mild curvature.

In so far as a pattern of movement does still remain in the nine-year results, it is altogether consistent with the patterns previously derived from quarterly data. Our usual comparisons — both those for link-relative series (Chart 10) and those for chain series (Chart 6) clearly indicate this.[10]

Though, as we have just seen, similarity of appearance between the patterns derived by the "direct" and "indirect" methods still persists in our graphic comparisons, we have nevertheless now reached a point in our investigation where the situation has essentially changed. We indeed have already observed, in our examination of the six-year case, the first suggestions of this change. But

[9] The series railroad stock prices, the correlations for which have up to this point been clearly positive in their indications, must here, on the basis of the available evidence, be entered positively for "9 Y–A" and "9 Y–C", and *negatively* for "9 Y–B".

[10] Specifically, attention is directed to the first two curves on Parts A, B, and C, respectively, of Chart 10, and to the three pairs of curves "9 Y–A" and "9 Y–A–Q", "9 Y–B" and "9 Y–B–Q", "9 Y–C" and "9 Y–C–Q", of Chart 6.

now it has become definitely apparent. The intercorrelation in the structure of our array of series, though by no means obliterated, has been essentially weakened. The truth of this statement is apparent when we make comparisons even with the six-year case, and becomes unmistakably clear if we make comparisons with the earlier cases — three-year, two-year, annual, or quarterly.

When we have reached the nine-year analysis, then, the suggestion of a disintegrating influence upon our array of curves, overcoming their coherence — which first came to attention in the six-year analysis — has now become a definite and unquestionable indication. The evidence is now very strong that some disrupting force, or complex of forces, is operating upon the array of series, pushing them away from one another, driving them apart. Without attempting to consider the nature of this influence, we may record that in our nine-year analysis we have arrived at the point where our original basic pattern, derived from quarterly data, has become greatly weakened, and no clear-cut new pattern has appeared, though evidence of some underlying disjoining influence has clearly presented itself.

It would seem that we have carried the application of our link-relative technique as far as is worth while, for this body of data. To go on, say with twelve-year averages, would hardly be profitable. The number of periods would be so small as almost completely to destroy the validity of the statistical technique, and in any case we could scarcely hope to draw helpful conclusions from the results.

If the process of pattern investigation by our method is to be carried out with reference to link relatives pertaining to periods appreciably longer than those which have entered into our formal analysis here, resort must be had to an essentially different body of material: series extending, let us say, over a century or more. The investigation of such a body of data — data presumably from necessity international in scope — by our link-relative technique would be a very interesting study, and might be expected to yield results of considerable significance, especially when compared with the findings of N. D. Kondratieff and others.[11]

[11] With reference to Kondratieff's work, see his article, "Die langen Wellen der Konjunktur," *Archiv für Sozialwissenschaft und Sozialpolitik*, LVI (1926), pp. 573–609. Note also the English translation (in abridged form) by W. Stolper, "The Long Waves in Economic Life," *Review of Economic Statistics*, XVII (November 1935), pp. 105–115.

# CHAPTER VI

## THE PATTERN INVESTIGATION FOR THE THIRTEEN IMPORTANT ECONOMIC SERIES: CONCLUSIONS

WE MAY now undertake to set forth the conclusions of our pattern investigation for the thirteen important economic series.

(1) A general method of attack has been set up, capable of wide applicability in the search for "consistencies and uniformities of behavior" among time series. This procedure is designed to discover and to represent such common patterns of movement as may be inherent in the data. The method is not, of course, intended to be employed blindly or mechanically. The critical examination of the multiple frequency table of link relatives, together with the study of "partition values" — e.g., quartiles — is an essential part of the method. Furthermore, within a particular group of series we may be able to discover no significant common tendencies; or we may find two or more divergent patterns within the structure.

(2) In the chapters which have preceded, we have considered the application of the method to a group of thirteen important economic series, over the period 1866–1914. In the first step of this investigation — the examination of link relatives based upon quarterly data — the presence of a common pattern of short-run fluctuation tracing itself through the irregularities and peculiarities of the individual series was definitely demonstrated, and a standard pattern representing this basic movement was derived (cf. Chart 1).

The derivation of this pattern is of very great significance, for the reason that it affords *analytical* demonstration of the presence in the data of a smooth, wave-like fluctuation of particular form. Our standard pattern could not possibly, in any essential respect, have been created by the methodology. We have employed a simple procedure, and have avoided question-begging assumptions. It has been shown, quite cogently, that the movements pictured in our standard pattern are inherent in the statistical material.

(3) After the investigation based upon quarterly data had yielded us this standard pattern of fluctuation, we extended our analysis to successively longer time intervals. Our anticipation that we might thus discover other patterns distinct from that first derived — differing from it in timing and presumably also in contour and intensity — was unfulfilled. As we proceeded, the basic pattern which we had first discovered was maintained, without appreciable modification; and, though we extended our investigation until the application of the methodology reached almost the point of technical breakdown, we failed to obtain evidence of the presence of an additional distinct pattern of fluctuation in the data. *Within the limits of possible analysis set by the boundary lines of our half-century of time and the availability of statistical material meeting our criteria of length, continuity, and importance, we have found analytical evidence of the presence of one, and only one, definite pattern of fluctuation.*

We may pause here to consider the significance of the analytical work leading to this conclusion. This work, equally with that involved earlier in the derivation of the quarterly standard pattern itself, possesses decided importance. We have through this work taken a step which is an indispensable prerequisite, necessary to be satisfied before we can properly undertake later the task of developing more powerful and effective modes of attack upon the specific problem of decomposing our time series. This indispensability must be emphasized. Though we may have felt at times a certain sense of futility as we passed successively through the several stages of the investigation (as described in the two preceding chapters), repeatedly setting forth the conclusion that "we have not as yet succeeded in discovering any new pattern of fluctuation," this was nevertheless an essential part of the conclusive demonstration, and affords no occasion for quoting *magno conatu magnas nugas*. Without making any attempt to anticipate the nature of the methodology which may be involved, it is clear that the question whether there is more than one pattern of fluctuation inherent in the data has to be settled analytically as fully as possible before it is permissible for us to proceed to the development of more complex methodological machinery for application to these data. As we develop such machinery, in Part Three, the force of the observation just made will become unescapably apparent.

(4) The striking correspondence among the main movements of the link relatives for the thirteen important series (cf. the various link-relative charts in Chapters III, IV, and V) — together with the appearance of sharply defined "zones of distribution" in the multiple frequency tables, and of close approach to parallelism of the quartiles in the "partition-values" charts — strongly suggests that certain causal impulses have operated during our selected time interval with an appreciable approach to uniformity over at least a considerable part of the economic system. But the conclusion is not inevitable that the standard pattern represents the effect of a *completely unified* set of causal forces. While our pattern investigation has failed to produce analytical evidence in favor of the hypothesis of, let us say, the coexistence of "major-cycle" and "minor-cycle" impulses, the results are nevertheless not necessarily incompatible with this hypothesis, or others of like nature. Conceivably, our standard pattern may be essentially [1] a composite, reflecting the joint effect of two (or even more than two) such sets of causal impulses — somewhat related perhaps, but nevertheless each having a definite individuality of its own, and each possessing its own theoretical counterpart.

(5) In connection with the interpretation of the standard pattern, still another matter deserves careful consideration. Letting our minds go back to the investigations described in the concluding sections of the preceding chapter, we recall that, first in the six-year case and then more definitely in the nine-year case, a new element began to impress itself upon us. The intercorrelations within the structure of the array of series were becoming essentially weaker. The cohesion which had, so to speak, bound the movements of the curves together was clearly commencing to lessen. Some force, we concluded, was beginning to disjoin the curves from their mutual attachment.

What now can we say as to the nature of this force? Is it simple, or complex? If we are dealing with a complex of forces, can the effect they have here produced in our pattern investigation be regarded as "accidental," in the sense that there is not even an approach to a unifying element? Or, is it true, as some would doubtless urge, that what we encounter here is simply a residuum of "secular influence"? More specifically, can it be that there is

---

[1] The qualifying word "essentially" is inserted here, primarily with reference to the point discussed in the immediately following paragraphs.

in operation in our array of series a system of long-run "secular tendencies," possibly interrelated causally, and that their effect shows itself in those peculiar disturbances which we have observed in the six-year and nine-year cases? Or, to consider still another possibility, may it be that these disturbances are but the manifestations of, let us say, the "Kondratieff wave," with all that is implied by giving this designation?

It would be patently inappropriate, at this point in our investigation, to undertake to set forth even tentative answers to these questions, for we have yet to develop analytical evidence sufficient to give cogency to such answers;[2] indeed, at this stage of our genetic analysis we cannot properly allow ourselves even the concepts "secular trend" and "cyclical variations," and must refuse to admit the terms to our vocabulary.[3]

We may, however, note now that it is of decided significance to have established *analytically*, without the employment of any preliminary question-begging assumptions, *the presence of some force, or complex of forces, of a comparatively long-run sort, which is operating upon our array of series, gradually destroying their cohesiveness and driving them away from one another.* And the investigation into the nature of this disintegrating force, simple or complex as it may be, is plainly a task calling for attention as soon as we are able to turn to it. But other tasks have a prior claim upon our efforts: we are under obligation first to broaden the scope of our preliminary analysis of economic material by examination into certain additional bodies of data.

(6) The methods which have so far been developed obviously do not accomplish the statistical decomposition of the various time series examined, and it should be clear from the statements which have been made in the preceding sections of this chapter that there is no thought of making any such claim for them. Nevertheless, the results — even if our statistical analysis were to be carried no further — should be of material assistance in dealing with the problem of time-series decomposition. The original series and

---

[2] With respect to the Kondratieff hypothesis, however, it must be pointed out here that our results are at least *consistent with* such hypothesis. The chain series for the standard pattern (see Chart 6) suggests — especially clearly in the six-year and nine-year cases — a break in movement, an upward swing, around the turn of the century. It will be remembered that the "third Kondratieff wave" begins about 1890–96. (For references, see fn. 11 in Chapter V.)

[3] Cf. the discussion of this point in Chapter II.

standard patterns presented in Chart 1 (and the various other charts of the three preceding chapters), together with the generalizations which may be derived therefrom, make it possible to set up a method of attack the results of which shall at least have the merit of representing a unified and consistent theoretical interpretation of the general picture shown by this assemblage of curves — a procedure far superior to that of studying the series one at a time. Further, with reference to isolated problems involving time-series analysis, the standard patterns which have here been presented furnish, as was suggested on an earlier page, a background against which to compare the particular material under examination in a given case and thus enable the investigator to fit segments of statistical data, otherwise perhaps awkward to handle, into their proper places in the general scheme.

But, as has already been indicated, it would be palpably inappropriate for us — having in mind our announced program for treatment of the problem by the genetic method, *ab initio* (as is set forth in Chapter II) — to proceed now with any attempt at statistical decomposition of the time series. We have, and it would appear wisely, given our first attention to the development of a long, continuous fundamental pattern, based upon a group of series satisfying certain necessary criteria. But now, with this foundation work completed, we must turn to the investigation of certain important bodies of supplementary material available for our period — notably those on production and employment. The discussion of these investigations will occupy the chapters immediately following.

# CHAPTER VII

## THE PATTERN OF PRODUCTION: LINK–RELATIVE APPROACH

Now THAT our study of the pattern of fluctuation for the thirteen important economic series is completed, we turn, as originally contemplated, to the examination of bodies of supplementary data. We give attention first to *production* — the economic field possessing for our time period the most comprehensive body of readily available statistical material.

In investigating the pattern of production, we shall attack along two different lines. First, we shall take the *link-relative approach*, starting with the array of available individual series and attempting to see whether there can be discerned in this array any pattern of fluctuation permeating, so to speak, the production structure, or at least certain portions of that structure. We shall then employ the *fixed-base approach*, dealing with index numbers of production and endeavoring to discover what systematic elements of behavior are present. To what extent the two approaches will show correspondence of results, we need not now attempt to forecast. We turn to the link-relative approach.

### THE LIST OF SERIES

So far as the first step involved in applying the link-relative approach to production data is concerned — the setting up of a list of series to be included in the analysis — there is fortunately available a systematic list of continuous annual production series, drawn up by Professor Arthur F. Burns with reference to the period since 1870.[1] Though this listing was made with a some-

---

[1] Arthur F. Burns, *Production Trends in the United States since 1870* (New York: National Bureau of Economic Research, Inc., 1934), pp. 12–13. For this outstanding work the present writer, though not concurring in all conclusions, has the most sincere admiration, and heartily seconds the praise given in the review by Professor W. L. Crum, *Quarterly Journal of Economics*, XLVIII (August 1934), pp. 742–748. By permission of the National Bureau of Economic Research, we have availed ourselves of Professor Burns' convenient tabulations of basic data for 1870 onward (*op. cit.*, pp. 284–304). Backward extension of series over the years 1866–69 has been performed by the present writer.

what different end in view than ours here,[2] it is nevertheless wholly suited to our present needs.

Indeed, in an important respect this list — quite aside from the intrinsic merits which it possesses — is definitely superior to one which we might draw up for the specific purposes of the present study: the use of the Burns list is a bar to a "methodology bias" which might otherwise be introduced in our selection of basic data. To put the matter more specifically, obviously one of our main objectives is to compare the pattern (or patterns) of fluctuation in production series with the standard pattern previously derived for the thirteen important economic series. Now, since this objective manifestly will be in mind from the very beginning of the present investigation, we might in drawing up for ourselves a schedule of production series tend (perhaps altogether unconsciously) toward bias in the selection of data, in the direction of producing an appearance of greater correspondence between the two sets of results than the facts intrinsically justify. The employment of a listing set up wholly independently by another investigator happily avoids this danger, and thus will lend confidence to our conclusions, particularly as to the validity of any systematic relationships which may be found to exist.

Certain questions may be raised regarding Professor Burns' list. First, among his 104 series a certain amount of duplication appears, though such duplication is by no means very far reaching. Professor Burns discusses this matter at some length.[3] In the course of a statement indicating in detail the nature and extent of this duplication, he makes the point that such overlapping as does exist "suggests that the production data lack qualitative homogeneity." He further indicates that "differences in the industrial dimension of the series result, in part, from practical exigencies which imposed limitations on the use of such materials as are available, but mainly, from the nature, that is, the quantity and quality, of the data which have come down to us." And he finally concludes, "the heterogeneity of the underlying data is in a sense intellectually unsatisfactory; but the inelegancies in the list of series could not be wholly eliminated or even appreciably reduced

[2] Professor Burns was mainly concerned with the secular movements in production series, while our primary emphasis in this chapter is upon the short-run fluctuations in the structure of production.

[3] Burns, *Production Trends*, pp. 15–16.

without discarding a large portion of the usable statistical records of production." This conclusion seems in all respects well taken, whether applied to Professor Burns' study of secular trends or to our present investigation of patterns of fluctuation.

A second question pertains to production series not extending back to 1885, which are omitted from Professor Burns' list. So far as the present study is concerned, it must be remembered that we cover only the period up to 1914; the new production series available over any large part of the interval 1885–1914 are not very numerous. The inclusion, in the link-relative analysis, of such additional series as might be secured could not in any essential degree alter the conclusions (as will be apparent beyond question when the findings of this chapter are completely before us), and in fact would perhaps render them less useful by making their interpretation more uncertain.[4]

With respect to the general scope of the production data, to turn to another point, it is of course immediately obvious that, though Professor Burns' list is fairly exhaustive of continuous series available during the period since 1870–85, there are nevertheless numerous inadequacies in the coverage of the data. As he points out, "a large portion of the field of 'service' production is completely unrepresented; . . . there are glaring gaps even in the field of 'commodity' production"; and "clearly the production series . . . fall far short of a comprehensive coverage of the area of national production."[5] Nevertheless, in spite of these unavoidable deficiencies, the range of the production series is extensive and, within certain limitations, rather broad. The data would seem altogether adequate for the discovery of any patterns of fluctuation which may have been generally pervasive in the field of production over the period 1866–1914.

### General Methodological Considerations

Since one of the principal objects of the investigation described in this chapter is to arrive at a comparison of the pattern (or patterns) of movement for production data with the standard pattern previously derived for the thirteen important economic series, we naturally desire to make the methodology as nearly identical with

[4] In the fixed-base approach, developed in the next chapter, the problem as to new industries and new data is somewhat different.

[5] Burns, *Production Trends*, p. 17. Cf. in general, section III of his chapter 1, pp. 17–22.

that earlier employed as may be possible. But complete identity of procedure is out of the question. Considerations of time and expense definitely preclude the unmodified application of the meticulous and thoroughgoing analysis earlier applied to the link relatives for the thirteen series — the calculation for each individual series of the average link relative for the period, the expression of the several items of each link-relative series as deviations from such average, the development of a measure of dispersion for each series, the careful measurement of lags for all the series in units of a quarter-year both by graphic methods and by formal calculation, the derivation for each series separately of items upon a "standard-unit" basis.[6] It was very much worth while to carry out fully this elaborate procedure for the thirteen important economic series, in order that the representation of the fundamental basic pattern might possess all the significance and trustworthiness possible. But quite certainly the application of this procedure in rigorous and unmodified form to each of the 104 individual production series is not, taking account of the time and expense involved, practically possible.

The choice lies between, on the one hand, modifying the procedure in the direction of making it materially less time-consuming and expensive, and, on the other, abandoning the whole attempt to measure in any comprehensive way the pattern (or patterns) of fluctuation for production series. The decision is clear: the advantages of having developed and ready at hand such comprehensive measures are too great to be foregone, especially in view of the fact that (as will presently be set forth) graphic inspection of the basic data and careful consideration of the possibilities with respect to alteration of the procedure lead to the conclusion that modification in the direction of simplification, and such material reduction of expense as to bring the project into the realm of practical possibilities, can be accomplished without sacrificing the essential soundness of the procedure, or the essential accuracy of the results. While the impossibility of retaining the full procedure is naturally to be regretted, we nevertheless may feel the assurance that nothing really vital to our main purpose has been lost through the adoption of necessary modifications.

Of the expedients to keep the expenditure of time and money within reasonable bounds, the most important is (a) that con-

[6] Cf. the discussion of Chapters III and IV.

nected with the abandonment of the attempt to measure the "average amplitude of short-run fluctuation" for each individual series. Other expedients are: (b) giving up the effort to measure the "average level of fluctuation" for each link-relative series separately, and (c) substituting the simpler median link relative for the "average of the middle group of link relatives" in deriving the pattern of fluctuation from the multiple frequency table. Only "(a)" above would appear to require extended comment.

### The Procedure for Measurement and Elimination of Differences in Amplitude of Fluctuation

We first consider the problem of the measurement and elimination of differences in amplitude of fluctuation. Instead of applying the tedious and highly expensive procedure which would be involved in calculating for each of the 104 production series individually a statistical measure of the dispersion of its fluctuations (by taking, let us say, the average deviation of its link relatives over our selected time interval) and then reducing each such series to (say) average-deviation units by dividing its successive items through by this dispersion measure, we shall have resort to a substitute method. We shall plan to allocate the series to groups — endeavoring to obtain within each group as high a degree of economic (and, relatedly, statistical) homogeneity as is possible consistently with the necessity of keeping each of the groups large enough to insure statistical significance of the results — and then, after the pattern of fluctuation for each group has been derived, in terms of percentages, to reduce these *composite series* to average-deviation units.

We set up groups for analysis as follows:[7]

> Agriculture.
> Mining.
> Manufacture, goods destined for capital equipment.
> Manufacture, goods destined for human consumption.
> Transportation and trade combined.

This selection calls for some comment. On both statistical and economic grounds, the subdivision of the manufacture group seems desirable. The number of series (45) is sufficient to admit of two

---

[7] Because of paucity of data, the fisheries group, with only three series, and the construction group, with only two, are obviously unsuited for pattern analysis.

sub-groups, each possessing statistical significance. And such dichotomies as "producers' goods vs. consumers' goods," "durable goods vs. non-durable goods," "goods destined for capital equipment vs. goods destined for human consumption," [8] have played a leading rôle in the theoretical analysis of economic fluctuations.[9] From among these dichotomies, we for the purposes of the statistical investigations now at hand choose the third, "goods destined for capital equipment vs. goods destined for human consumption," as involving us least in difficulties of definition and classification of series.

The consolidation of the two groups designated by Professor Burns as "transportation" and "trade," respectively, seems desirable. This is true in the first place, because the number of series falling within each of the two classifications, taken by itself, is so small as to render of questionable statistical significance the results which might be obtained in a pattern study.[10] Moreover, as Burns himself suggests, the allocation of series between the two groups is to a considerable extent arbitrary, and probably unavoidably so. He points out that "the series 'postage stamps' and 'postal money orders' are placed in the transportation division, on the view that the postal service is a communication industry. The series 'railway freight' is placed under trade, and 'railway ton-miles' under transportation, on the view that the actual volume of goods shipped is symptomatic of trade activity, and that a compound series of freight and distance is the real measure of the service rendered by the freight branch of the railway transportation industry. The series 'coastal trade' is placed under transportation, on the view that coastal shipping is a distinct branch of the transportation category. But plausible grounds could be advanced for assigning some of the series placed in the transportation category to the trade category, and vice versa." [11] And Burns, in fact, found it desirable to combine the two in most of his tabulations and computations.

---

[8] Cf. Frederick C. Mills, *Economic Tendencies in the United States* (New York: National Bureau of Economic Research, Inc., in coöperation with Committee on Recent Economic Changes, 1932), *passim*, especially p. 21.

[9] Cf. Gottfried von Haberler, *Prosperity and Depression* (Geneva: League of Nations, 1939), *passim* (note subject index, pp. 463–473, under such headings as "producers' goods," "consumers' goods," "acceleration principle").

[10] This is particularly pertinent with reference to the earlier years 1866–80.

[11] Burns, *Production Trends*, p. 11, fn. 5.

Of course, to turn to still another point, in speaking of economic homogeneity within each of the several groups (as we have above), we are employing the term "homogeneity" in a sense which is highly relative. But, on the other hand, production in our various groups is manifestly affected by fundamentally different conditions. The following statement from Dr. Edmund E. Day's monograph on the physical volume of production, relative to the subdivisions agriculture, mining, and manufacture, is pertinent in this connection.[12]

"In agriculture, the round of the seasons and the vagaries of climatic change — of rainfall, temperature, wind — play a commanding part in determining the outcome of the farmer's productive efforts. There is an element of the fortuitous in agriculture which is hardly equaled in other lines of activity. Furthermore, agriculture is peculiar in that the unchanging and unchangeable period of production is the year. In mining and manufacture, interest may attach to monthly data of output. In agriculture, while we may have monthly *estimates* of output, the output in question is always of the crop year.

"Mining in turn is peculiar in that production normally involves an exhaustion of the deposit from which the current output is drawn. Agriculture may involve an exhaustion of the soil, but does not ordinarily if scientifically conducted.

"Manufacture differs from both mining and agriculture in being much less immediately bound by natural limiting forces, and in being indefinitely expansible in most lines except as agriculture and mining themselves afford only limited amounts of material for fabrication and equipment. Manufacture, furthermore, as contrasted with agriculture, shares with mining, a sensitiveness to general business conditions. Marked variations of output may occur within a single year; in fact, within much shorter periods. Seasonal variation and cyclical movements may be expected to appear in the physical output of mine and mill."

Nevertheless, a considerable amount of heterogeneity still remains within each of the groups. What we have accomplished by

[12] Edmund E. Day, *An Index of the Physical Volume of Production* (Cambridge: Harvard University Committee on Economic Research, 1921), p. 2. This monograph is a reprint of certain articles with the general title, "An Index of the Physical Volume of Production," *Review of Economic Statistics*, II (September, October, November, and December 1920), pp. 246–259, 287–299, 309–337, 361–367, and III (January 1921), pp. 19–23.

our classification is to attain as high a degree of intra-group economic homogeneity as is practically possible, in view of the limitations set by the amount of physical volume data available for the period.[13]

We give consideration now to the question of *statistical* homogeneity within each of the groups, as regards relative amplitude of short-run fluctuation. This is clearly an important, and in some respects crucial, matter, for upon it hangs to a considerable extent our judgment as to the probable reliability of the results which we shall later obtain. The pertinent question is whether by our alteration of procedure we are going to bring it about that a comparatively few series having large amplitude of fluctuation shall dominate the picture of the pattern of short-time movement presently to be derived.

Examination of the charts for the 104 series (drawn with logarithmic vertical scale) indicates, in the first place, the presence of clear differences among our five groups, each taken as a whole, with respect to amplitude of short-time fluctuation. The appearance of these differences gives additional support to the earlier decision (based mainly on economic considerations) to divide the groups as we have.

Our graphic inspection further indicates that within each group a considerable degree of statistical homogeneity exists as regards amplitude of short-run movement. If we were, within each of our groups, formally to compute for each of the several individual series of that group some appropriate measure of dispersion (e.g., the average deviation of the link relatives) and then set up a

---

[13] Numerous detailed questions might, of course, be raised regarding the grouping of the various series. The locations of the exact division lines between agriculture and manufacture, and between mining and manufacture, are not beyond dispute (see Burns, *Production Trends*, p. 11, fn. 5; and also Day, *An Index of the Physical Volume of Production*, p. 28). The two construction series might possibly be attached to the manufacture group; see, however, an argument with contrary implications by William H. Newman, in his monograph, "The Building Industry and Business Cycles," *Journal of Business of the University of Chicago*, VIII, No. 3 (July 1935), Part 2, Studies in Business Administration, v, No. 4, pp. 52–53. Fisheries might plausibly be joined with agriculture, on the ground that both relate to organic raw materials; on the whole, however, a greater approach to homogeneity is attained by avoiding such a combination.

None of the various possible alternatives of grouping which the considerations of this footnote bring to attention is of substantial importance, with reference to the purposes now at hand. No such alternative grouping could in any appreciable way affect the results or conclusions of this chapter.

*frequency distribution of these dispersion measures,* such frequency distribution would for each group tend roughly to approach the form of a normal curve. To be sure, a few extreme cases would appear at the "tails" of the distribution, but the bulk of the items would be concentrated fairly symmetrically around a central value. If, however, we were to extend this idea and set up a composite frequency distribution for the dispersion measures of all groups combined — the whole 104 series — the result would unquestionably be a *multimodal* distribution, clearly suggesting heterogeneity of material. These considerations, also, give strong confirmation to our previous decision regarding the division of the series into groups.

Nevertheless, within each of the five groups appreciable variation appears with respect to amplitude of fluctuation. Is it then possible that the picture of the pattern of fluctuation, which we shall shortly derive by the application of our modified procedure, will be controlled in each case by a few widely-swinging series, and thus fail truly to represent the inherent characteristics of the whole array of series embraced within the group? Our graphic examination of the material indicates conclusively that this cannot occur, for two reasons, either of which is by itself sufficient.

In the first place, the variations within each group as to amplitude of short-run fluctuation are not large enough to permit such a result. With the exception of a few extreme series, insufficient in number materially to influence the results,[14] it is true for each group that the differences in degree, as regards amplitude of fluctuation, are not sufficiently great to constitute differences in kind. Upon the basis of this finding alone, then, we may say that there is no possibility in any of the groups for a few widely-swinging series to dominate the results.

But the graphic examination gives us another reason why we need not fear that such domination will occur. For each of the four non-agricultural groups — mining; manufacture, goods destined for capital equipment; manufacture, goods destined for human consumption; transportation and trade combined — we are able to discern, even without resorting to formal analysis, tracing through all the peculiarities and eccentricities of the individual series of the group something which may fairly be called a

[14] Especially as our link-relative method, employed in these pattern studies, has very great power to reduce the effect of extreme variations.

common pattern of group movement.[15] And, which is the essential point, this appearance of a common pattern shows no tendency in any of these groups to be confined to a *particular sector* of our suppositional frequency distribution of amplitude measurements. In each instance, those series which appear to correlate most closely with the roughly discerned group pattern are scattered more or less regularly throughout this suppositional array of series arranged in order of dispersion amplitude.

For the agriculture group, the graphic examination leaves us in some doubt as to whether or not there is anything which can be properly called a general pattern of movement. We are obliged to reserve judgment upon this question until at a later time we have before us the multiple frequency table of link relatives. However, so far as the problem now at hand is concerned, inspection of the charts definitely indicates that we need fear no tendency, when later we come to formal computation, for the more widely moving series to dominate the results.

In sum, then, the graphic survey of the data gives confirmation to our earlier decisions as to the division of the series into economic groups. And, more broadly, it permits us to proceed to formal analysis with confidence that the principal modification of procedure made necessary by considerations of time and expense — calculating amplitude measures for a few group patterns only, in place of computing them for the series individually — will not bring about any material loss of precision or fall in significance of the results to be obtained in such formal analysis. The point which has formed the central theme of this section is, however, of such crucial importance that we shall return to it at a later stage of the investigation.[16]

## IS THE LOGARITHMIC PARABOLA ADEQUATE FOR REPRESENTATION OF LONG-RUN TENDENCIES IN INDIVIDUAL PRODUCTION SERIES?

In connection with the preliminary survey of production data we enter incidentally upon a topic which has such important implications as to justify us in digressing temporarily from our

[15] Further, the patterns for these several non-agricultural groups, so far as we are able to make them out by this elementary mode of investigation, bear rather close general resemblance to one another. To avoid digressing from the present theme, however, we postpone consideration of this matter.

[16] See the section headed "Tests of the Composite Pattern of the Structure of Production," toward the close of this chapter.

present main theme. In the course of graphic examination of the individual production series, certain observations have been made which are worthy of most careful attention.[17]

As might be expected in view of the large body of evidence already available in various published studies, scarcely a single production series, out of the whole array of 104, traces over the pre-war years anything at all like a compound-interest movement; almost all exhibit definite retardation in rate of growth. *But we further find that very few indeed of the 104 series exhibit in their long-run tendencies an indication of even rough approximation to a constant rate of retardation in growth over the pre-war period, 1866–1914.* The logarithmic parabola,

$$(\log y = a + bt + ct^2),$$

is almost always a very poor fit.

It is to be emphasized that this conclusion, regarding non-constancy of the retardation rate for the various individual industries, relates not merely to *oscillatory* movements in retardation rates (the discovery of which in the course of our graphic examination was indeed to be anticipated, taking into account our general knowledge as to the character of economic fluctuations), *but also — and more particularly — to general, gradual long-run tendencies of retardation rates, extending over the entire period of analysis.*

A word of explanation may be inserted here as to the significance of certain technical terms. The logarithmic parabola is a curve exhibiting constancy in rate of *acceleration*, or of *retardation*, as the case may be. However, we may well confine ourselves here to the case where retardation is present, since this is of principal interest in the study of long-time movements for individual production series.

We show, in Table 4, a brief example which will serve to indicate the significance of the logarithmic parabola for a series exhibiting retardation. In this illustrative case, the tabulation of annual rate of growth begins with 5 per cent, and the constant annual rate of retardation is 0.2 per cent. This may be put more

[17] The reader may find it of interest to compare the conclusions stated here with those arrived at, through different modes of approach, by Professor Burns in his study of retardation in the growth of industries (*Production Trends*, ch. iv), and by Dr. Kuznets (in his *Secular Movements in Production and Prices*).

## TABLE 4

### LOGARITHMIC PARABOLA: ILLUSTRATIVE CASE

#### Assumed Data

| Year | Original item for production series (in, say, tons) | Annual ratio of growth |
|------|------|------|
| 1951 | 100,000 | |
| 1952 | 105,000 | 1.0500 |
| 1953 | 110,029 | 1.0479 = 1.0500 × 0.998 |
| 1954 | 115,069 | 1.0458 = 1.0479 × 0.998 |
| 1955 | 120,098 | 1.0437 = 1.0458 × 0.998 |
| 1956 | 125,096 | 1.0416 = 1.0437 × 0.998 |

#### Logarithmic Work

| Year | Logarithm of original item | First difference of logarithm (= logarithm of ratio of growth) | Second difference of logarithm (= logarithm of retardation ratio) | Third difference of logarithm |
|------|------|------|------|------|
| 1951 | 5.000000 | .... | .... | .... |
| 1952 | 5.021189 | 0.021189 | .... | .... |
| 1953 | 5.041508 | 0.020319 | −0.000870 | .... |
| 1954 | 5.060957 | 0.019449 | −0.000870 | 0.000000 |
| 1955 | 5.079536 | 0.018579 | −0.000870 | 0.000000 |
| 1956 | 5.097245 | 0.017709 | −0.000870 | 0.000000 |

The equation is of the form

$$\log y = a + bt + ct^2;$$

the first derivative decreases over time, the second derivative is a constant, and the third derivative is zero. If, following the usage which is observed for the writing of such equations in this volume, we take the origin at the center of the time interval (in the present "six-year" period, midway between "1953" and "1954"), the equation becomes

$$\log y = 5.051341 + 0.019449t - 0.000435t^2.$$

With this placing of the origin, $a$ is the logarithm of the central ordinate

(here, $a = 5.051341 = \log 112{,}550$);

$b$ is the logarithm of the ratio of growth at the center of the period

(here, $b = 0.019449 = \log 1.0458$);

$2c$ is the logarithm of the constant retardation ratio

(here $2c = -0.000435 \times 2 = -0.000870$ [or $9.999130 - 10$] $= \log 0.998$).

Compare the values given in the table above.

For the purposes of the present non-technical discussion, we have presented the explanation in the accompanying text in terms of finite differences. The mathematical reader will know how to translate the explanation for this simple example into the language of the differential calculus.

explicitly. If we transform these numerical values, 5 per cent and 0.2 per cent, into decimal fractions, we have 0.05 and 0.002, respectively. Or, throwing these decimal fractions into the form of *ratios*, we have 1.05 (1 + 0.05) and 0.998 (1 − 0.002), respectively.

These figures signify that the annual ratio of growth for the series decreases over time in a systematic way. Specifically, the first annual ratio of growth is (by hypothesis) 1.05; the second is 1.05 x 0.998, or 1.0479; the third is 1.0479 x 0.998, or 1.0458; and so on (cf. the upper part of Table 4). The series thus exhibits a declining annual rate of growth, but the annual rate of retardation is constant.[18]

The reader, if unfamiliar with the logarithmic-parabola equation, will find it helpful to plot the "logarithms of original items" of Table 4 (or, what comes to the same thing, plot the "original items" of Table 4 with logarithmic vertical scale), and study the movements of the resulting curve in conjunction with the discussion in the text, just above.[19]

Our graphic study of the 104 individual production series definitely indicates (to repeat) that in anything resembling a proper equation for representation of long-run tendencies of individual industries constancy of retardation rate cannot be assumed. In more technical language, we cannot assume constancy in the second derivative of the logarithmic equation (perhaps not even in the third derivative, for certain series).

This reference to derivatives in a logarithmic equation suggests the study of *logarithmic differences* — the successive differences of logarithms of original items for individual production series

[18] Strictly, we should refer to 0.002 as "the annual rate of retardation in the annual *ratio* of growth." For the sake of brevity, however, we shall in general hereafter refer simply to "annual retardation rate" or "annual rate of retardation"; indeed we shall often omit even the word "annual" where not necessary for the sense. And we shall use the expression "retardation in growth" (or, sometimes merely "retardation") to designate *relative* movements — that is, to denote "retardation in *ratio* of growth."

[19] On a chart of *logarithms of original items* (or, alternatively, a chart of original items drawn with logarithmic vertical scale), a constant rate of growth results in an upward-sloping straight line, and upon any given logarithmic scale the larger the rate of growth, the steeper the slope of the line; retardation in ratio of growth manifests itself in curvature away from a straight-line movement — the line, that is, is convex upward — and upon any given logarithmic scale the more rapid the rate of retardation in growth, the greater is the curvature.

(cf. the logarithmic work of Table 4). If for the 104 series we calculate such differences and examine them in graphic form,[20] we find that in general the first differences show, in their long-run tendencies, very definitely a curvilinear rather than a straight-line movement, as is illustrated in Chart 11, Part A, for three fairly typical cases — zinc production, steel production, and freight ton-miles.[21] Such curvilinear tendencies in the first differences ($d'$) clearly indicate departure from constancy in the retardation rate for individual production series.[22]

Another conspicuous feature of the several sets of curves for logarithmic differences (cf. again Chart 11, Part A) is the presence in the first differences of wave-like swings which suggest a very rough approach to periodicity, accompanied by swings in the *second* differences whose contour is rather similar to those of the first differences, but which deviate as to timing in a somewhat systematic way. The short-run movements of the second differences tend to precede those of the first differences by a time interval which may, very roughly and without any pretense to mathematical precision in use of language, be described as one-quarter of the (variable) period of wave-like fluctuation in the first differences. These characteristics unquestionably have a certain analogy with the well-known relationship between the sine curve and its derivative.

If, for a particular individual production series, we (by fitting a straight line to the logarithmic first differences) give graphic representation to the concept of growth accompanied by a constant rate of retardation, and then (by taking deviations from this fitted straight line) eliminate from these first differences the average rate of growth and the average rate of retardation, we in general obtain such lines as the three wavy curves marked "$d'$-devs."

---

[20] On a chart of *logarithmic first differences* a constant rate of growth manifests itself in a horizontal line, and a constant rate of retardation in a downward-sloping straight line.

[21] As compared with the curves for zinc production, the curves for steel production are drawn with less expanded vertical scale, and the curves for freight ton-miles with more expanded vertical scale.

[22] Theoretically, one might expect that, correspondingly, departure from general horizontal drift would in each case be discernible in the curve of *second* differences; the manifestations of such tendencies, however, are comparatively small in magnitude for production series, and our attempts to observe or to measure them are seriously interfered with by short-run oscillations, rhythmic or irregular, in the second differences (cf. the $d''$ curves of Chart 11, Part A).

## CHART 11

*(In Part A, a straight line is in each case fitted to the first differences, and for the second differences the horizontal line stands at zero)*

### Part A

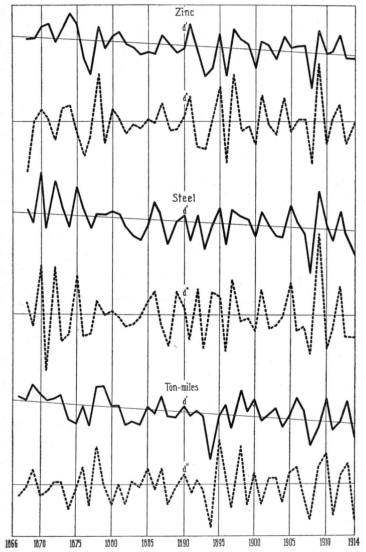

* As to scales, see fn. 21, p. 147. For explanation of captions, see accompanying text.

CHART 11

*(In Part B, the first differences are in each case expressed as deviations from straight line, and the second differences are adjusted for amplitude and timing; for each of the three series, the first differences are plotted below the second differences in such manner as to exhibit the systematic alteration over time in the "band" between the two curves — such "band" first steadily widening and then gradually narrowing as one proceeds from left to right across the chart)*

Part B

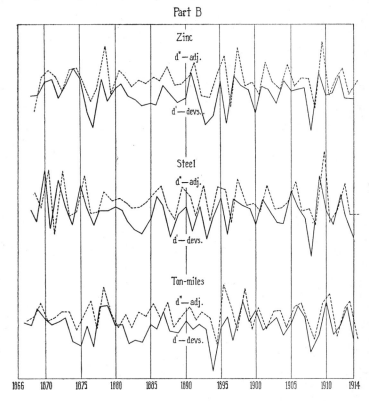

on Chart 11, Part B. If now in each case we redraw the curve of second differences adjusting the vertical scale so as to produce a mathematically appropriate correspondence in amplitude of fluctuation with the new curve of "first-difference deviations," derived as just described, and also shifting the time scale to make proper mathematical compensation for the average difference in timing between the two curves — thus obtaining such lines as the three series designated "*d″*-adj." on Chart 11, Part B — we find in general that, even after allowing for the fact that the timing-lag involved is variable rather than constant, the fluctuations of the two curves show in each case distinct departure from parallel movement (cf. the chart).[23] Comparing the curves, bearing in mind the variability of lag, we are easily able to discern that the space between them, as we pass in order of time across the chart, suffers alteration in some systematic way. For example, in each of the three illustrative cases of Chart 11, Part B, this "band" steadily widens over the first part of the period, and then gradually narrows. In phenomena of this sort we have the most unmistakable evidence that the rate of retardation for individual production series in general exhibits clear departure from constancy in long-run movement.

The essential point in the mathematical background for this analysis is the consideration that, if the logarithms of first differences (*d′*) for a particular series conform closely to the equation

$$d' = C_1 t^2 + C_2 t + C_3 + A' \sin \frac{t}{p} 2\pi,$$

then the logarithmic second differences (*d″*) will conform closely to the equation

$$d'' = 2\,C_1 t + C_2 + A'' \sin\left(\frac{t}{p}\,2\pi + \frac{\pi}{2}\right),$$

where the ratio $\dfrac{A''}{A'}$ is determinable, given the value of $p$ ($p$ is the length of the period).

---

[23] The amplitude adjustment is made by changing the plotting scale for the second differences in the ratio

$$\frac{\text{Average deviation of first differences (deviations from straight line)}}{\text{Average deviation of second differences}}.$$

For the three cases at hand — zinc production, steel production, and freight ton-miles — such adjustment ratios are 0.665, 0.612, 0.678, respectively.

With respect to the time-scale adjustment, we note that for the three series now under consideration the "average length of period" for the short-run swings of the various curves is approximately four years, and accordingly we take one-fourth of this figure, or one year, as a sufficiently accurate indication of the distance the second-difference curve should be shifted along the horizontal scale (attempts at formal calculation will yield results ranging from ten to fourteen months, depending upon the precise criterion adopted for marking off the individual "swings"; obviously, from the point of view of our present observations, there is no necessity to strive meticulously for precision).

For the production series now under consideration the "length of period" is palpably far from uniform (even within a given series), and the mathematical relationships above indicated do not, of course, hold rigidly between the first and second logarithmic differences. Nevertheless, certain essential features do appear: as is illustrated in Chart 11, there is in each case a considerable degree of similarity between the curves of first and second differences as to contour of the short-run "swings"; there is in each instance a lag, variable in time length to be sure, but notwithstanding conforming fairly well on the whole to one-quarter of the (variable) period; and there is an appreciable curvature [24] in the long-run movements of the first differences, such curvature being capable of easy discernment upon observation of the systematic changes which occur over time in the width of the band between two such curves as any of the pairs of Chart 11, Part B.

The results of our analytical work with first and second logarithmic differences yield indications which are quite definite, and which have implications of the greatest importance. *The suggestion is very strong that the long-time tendencies of individual production series are much less simple than has commonly been supposed. Our tests with the first and second differences of logarithms for individual production series suggest that such tendencies do not take, even approximately, the form of a constant rate of retardation, and consequently are not capable of adequate representation by the logarithmic parabola fitted to the original items.*[25]

In this connection, there is one point which it is desired particularly to emphasize. The matter, in fact, is so important that we may perhaps be permitted for the moment to exempt ourselves from our self-imposed interdiction upon the use of the term "secular trend" [26] (and this is really not a lapse of "principle," for the present section of Chapter VII is digressionary, and we shall

---

[24] That is to say, such movements are clearly curvilinear for most of the 104 series. It may very well be that some more complicated curve than the parabola (*applied to the logarithmic first differences*) is necessary in order adequately to describe them; we make no attempt to pursue this point further here.

[25] And in general probably not by the logistic curve, the Gompertz curve, or the normal-curve integral, fitted to the original items.

[26] Cf. the discussion of this point in Chapter II.

abide strictly by the interdiction throughout the whole of the main line of argument in Part Two of this volume). The point here stressed is that the proposition set forth in the preceding paragraph, regarding the lack of simplicity in long-time tendencies for production series pertaining to individual industries, cannot be dismissed as being merely an aspect of the distinction between "primary secular trends" and "secondary secular trends" (supposing such to exist; the writer must for the present take a purely agnostic position). Acquiescing in this *façon de parler*, we may say that the clear inadequacy of the logarithmic parabola for the description of the long-time tendencies of individual production series (such tendencies having been shown, in the study at hand, for example, to extend persistently over at least some fifty years) cannot be cured by bringing in, to amplify the description, "secondary trends" — at least not as such "secondary trends" have so far been conceived of by investigators in the field of time-series analysis, as being wave-like with periods averaging something like ten, fifteen, twenty years. On the contrary, for series of the sort now under consideration, it is clearly the "*primary* trend" itself which is inadequately described by the logarithmic parabola. For such series, we certainly cannot properly think of the "primary trend" as possessing anything resembling a constant rate of retardation in growth.

Our tests have pertained to the pre-war period 1866–1914 only. Now (as is developed more fully on a later page of this chapter) if we bring the war years (1914–18) and the earlier post-war years (1919–29) into the picture — not to speak of the period of the great depression — our findings appear to hold *a fortiori*; that is to say, still greater difficulty attaches in general to employing a logarithmic parabola for an individual production series over (say) the period 1866–1929 than over the period 1866–1914.

This matter of the representation of long-time tendencies in individual production series, here touched upon in a very general way as part of a digression, obviously deserves much more extended development. It is hoped to give this topic more thoroughgoing treatment in a later publication. For the present, we bring this digression to a close, and return to our main theme — the development of the production pattern (or patterns) by the link-relative approach.

### The Problem of Lags among the Individual Series

Resuming now our main line of analysis, we observe that still other methodological questions require attention before we can begin the formal process of computation. One of these has to do with lags among the various individual series. On several grounds we should anticipate that such lags would appear: partly because of lags intrinsic in the economic phenomena which are involved; partly because in many cases the statistical measurement is not coincident in time with the phenomenon being measured (e.g., building permits); partly for the purely technical reason that in certain cases the figures are reported upon a fiscal-year, as opposed to calendar-year, basis.

However, the fact that prior to 1914 production data are with very few exceptions available only annually (or for less frequent time-intervals) sharply limits the possibility for deriving statistical measurements of lags among the 104 series. There is decided lack of flexibility: in the arrangement of our multiple frequency tables the choice lies between entering the items for a particular series as concurrent, or shifting them by an integral number of years.

Once more, we may have recourse to graphic examination of the data. Looking first at the four non-agricultural groups — mining; manufacture, destined for capital equipment; manufacture, destined for human consumption; transportation and trade combined — we find that within each group there indeed is, among those series which on the whole exhibit conformity to the general group movement, something more than a suggestion of the presence in the background of lags and leads. In no case, however, does such lag or lead appear to approach a full twelve-month period, or even seem great enough to make us estimate that the concurrent correlation would not, under formal arithmetical test, come out the higher. And as regards such individualistic and eccentric series as are present in each group, our graphic survey does not suggest that any intrinsic ground exists for giving any of them lags or leads with respect to the general group movement; formal computing tests here might well, in fact, lead to fallacious conclusions, and to more or less absurd shifting of items in the multiple frequency tables in conformity to specious "best lags" based upon accidental correlations.

In the agriculture group, it will be remembered, our earlier graphic scrutiny failed to yield definite evidence of the presence of a common pattern of fluctuation. And now, without making anything resembling a completely exhaustive test of all possible combinations of arrangement, the conclusion seems fairly valid that not much, if anything, in the way of systematic lag can be established within the array of series, and that on the whole we would do well not to complicate the multiple frequency tables by introducing lag and lead shiftings.

The general conclusion of the graphic survey of the production material with respect to lag, then, is that we shall not plan to set up any system of adjustments for lags or leads. It may incidentally be pointed out that, in any case, the expense of applying formal computing tests in an attempt to determine statistically in each instance the "best lag" for the whole list of 104 series would involve so great an amount of work as to make the cost practically prohibitive. Even setting aside the question of expense, however, it appears clear that nothing essential is to be gained by attempting to establish lag and lead adjustments — at any rate, not for this aspect of the investigation into production data.[27]

At this point the suggestion might be made that we should, before starting the main computations, do some preliminary work upon the individual series: try to shift the fiscal-year series to a calendar-year basis, for example, or more ambitiously try to allow for differences between the formal and the intrinsic dating of statistical series (e.g., with respect to series on "consumption of materials" employed to represent production). As regards the specific problem now at hand, however, such suggestions do not seem well-advised. Adjustments of this sort would at the present stage of the study have to rest upon a foundation which could at best be described as insecure; and, what is much more vital, these doubtful adjustments would leave the door open for suspicion that the final results (and specifically, any correlations or relationships found, e.g., with the standard pattern for thirteen series) carried

---

[27] Later, after we have derived our basic production patterns and have studied their relationships with certain of our other results (e.g., the standard pattern for the thirteen series, the fixed-base pattern for production, the pattern of employment), and perhaps have brought other bodies of information into the analysis, we may be in a position to derive some valid conclusions regarding the lags in production.

a "methodology bias" — that in the course of the numerous adjustments the investigator had consciously or unconsciously impressed into the material his preconceptions as to what relationships *ought* to appear. It seems better, *in the particular situation at hand,*[28] to endure a small degree of blurring in the results and a certain minor annoyance in their interpretation, than for the sake of doubtful gain from rather questionable slight adjustments to prejudice the credibility of these results by throwing them open to even the suspicion that they may have been distorted by preliminary question-begging assumptions.

Still another possible general suggestion with reference to the lag problem would be that all series showing deviation of dating from a strict calendar-year basis should be dropped from the analysis. Only brief consideration, however, is required to convince us that to carry out this idea literally would mean the elimination of most of the list, for in few cases can the *economic activity* which the statistical series purports to measure be fairly regarded as confined strictly to twelve-month calendar-year periods. And even to proceed only so far as to remove those series which are formally designated as "fiscal-year" would mean the exclusion of an appreciable part of the statistical evidence. It is clearly preferable to put up with a certain amount of blurring of results rather than to weaken so appreciably the factual basis of our conclusions — especially as the criterion for exclusion would in any case rest on formal, rather than intrinsic, grounds. It does, however, seem desirable to exclude from the analysis a few series which *shift* from a fiscal-year to a calendar-year basis during the period of study, 1866–1914, and also one series for which the data are not completely continuous.[29]

---

[28] This statement, as is emphasized in the text, is made with reference to a particular situation, and is not, of course, to be taken as blanket condemnation of all attempts to improve basic data by preliminary adjustment. And, in fact, at later stages of the present writer's investigation of physical production such preliminary adjustment is resorted to, wherever the probabilities appear to favor real gain therefrom.

[29] The series with shifting temporal basis, just referred to, are as follows: No. 32, phosphate rock; No. 51, jute imports; No. 54, manila-hemp imports; No. 55, minor-fibre imports; No. 61, sisal imports; No. 63, superphosphate; No. 69, tobacco and snuff (cf. Burns, *Production Trends*, pp. 12–13, and his Appendix B, pp. 326–346). It will be observed incidentally that the principal effect of these exclusions is to prevent undue influence being given to the relatively unimportant minor-fibres series.

The non-continuous series referred to is No. 75, roofing slate, which has a gap at 1890 (cf. Burns, *Production Trends*, pp. 12–13, especially fn. 6).

## The Break at about 1880 with Respect to Quantity of Data Available

Still another problem of procedure remains to be settled before we are prepared to embark upon the formal process of computation. The list of production series shows a rather abrupt break, in the neighborhood of 1880, with respect to the quantity of data available. In fact, as we go backward in time, about one-third the series obtainable in 1885 have disappeared from the list by the time the year 1880 has been passed.

This sharp break in the quantity of data raises a serious methodological question. Shall we apply the statistical analysis to the full list from approximately 1880 onward, and to the more restricted list prior to 1880? Or, shall we hold the application of the statistical procedure to a uniform (but very much limited) list of series — those obtainable over all of the interval 1866–1914?

Careful consideration leads us to reject the latter alternative. Its adoption would mean reducing the coverage of the investigation by about one-third, involving the omission of many important series. Moreover, such omissions would apply to an interval of some thirty-five years, 1880–1914 — constituting almost three-quarters of the total period of our investigation, and embracing an epoch during which the quantity and reliability of data for fields other than production steadily increase and consequently opportunities for accurate comparisons with such non-production data constantly become greater. A still further consideration is that the adoption of the more restricted list for the entire period 1866–1914 would, in each of the several groups, decrease the number of tally marks in the various columns of the multiple frequency table to such an extent as materially to reduce the reliability of the results, even looking at the matter from a purely technical point of view. All in all, it does not seem desirable to sacrifice the advantages connected with having the longer list of production series over the important period 1880–1914 for the sake of possessing a uniform, but much inferior, list over a somewhat longer interval.

Our decision, then, is that we shall base the link-relative analysis upon the complete list, 1880–1914, utilizing the shorter, restricted list for the purpose of extending the analysis back, as

well as may be, over the earlier interval 1866–80. This arrangement, while apparently the best that can be made, has the disadvantage that some doubt attaches to the comparability of data
and results as between the two sections, 1880–1914 and 1866–80.
This defect, however, is not so serious as might at first glance
appear. Graphic inspection of the original items for the production
series strongly suggests, for every one of our several groups, that
over the later period, 1880–1914, the smaller sample will give
results which are generally similar to those yielded by the complete
list (though presumably less dependable in detail). This indication, which we later confirm by direct calculation (as will shortly
be set forth), makes it defensible to join the two sets of median
link relatives in each group — those for the complete list, 1881–
1914, and those for the restricted list, 1867–80 — to form a continuous series. While the indication of rather close general
correspondence between the two sets of results over the long
interval 1880–1914 gives a measure of confidence in the joined
series, we must of course keep in mind the lack of precise comparability which exists between the two sections, 1866–80 and
1880–1914; we must not impute too great accuracy to the measurements for the earlier period, which are based upon more severely
limited evidence; and we are, of course, not at liberty to assume
that the complete list — supposing data to be available [30] for the
backward extension — would exhibit exactly the same statistical
characteristics over the years 1866–80 as actually appear for the
restricted list.

The lack of full comparability between the two sections 1880–
1914 and 1866–80, resulting from deficiencies in the quantity of
available statistical data which are largely unremediable, is to be
regretted. But our decision as to procedure gives a comparatively
firm statistical basis for the analysis of the important thirty-five
year period 1880–1914, and, taking account of the fact that results
from the two "samples" overlap as well as they do, enables us to
draw at least broad general conclusions with respect to the entire
interval 1866–1914.

[30] Available, that is, in so far as the industries were in existence — and nearly
all of them were.

## The Patterns of Fluctuation for the Several Groups

Now that our preliminary survey of methodological questions is completed, we are ready to inaugurate the formal process of calculation.

### THE LINK-RELATIVE FREQUENCY TABLES

We begin by computing, for each of the individual production series, the annual link relatives over the period 1867–1914.[31] Next, for each group these link relatives are thrown into the form of a multiple frequency table (each such table, of course, containing one column of tally marks for each of the years 1867–1914). In drawing up the multiple frequency tables, the items for the series of the "restricted list" (i.e., those having data extending over the entire interval 1866–1914) are for convenience entered in a distinctive color.

The multiple frequency tables verify and make more definite the earlier tentative conclusions based upon graphic examination of the data. For each of the four non-agricultural groups — mining; manufacture, destined for capital equipment; manufacture, destined for human consumption; transportation and trade combined — a definite pattern of group movement is present.[32] To be sure, this tendency does not within any one of the four groups go so far as to approach complete concurrence among the constituents. There is evidence of irregularity and of individualistic eccentric behavior for particular series. But the "zones of distribution" are most clearly marked in the multiple frequency tables, and in each instance close approach to parallelism of movement appears in the "partition-values" test.[33] Certainly, in each of these four groups we may properly proceed to develop a general group pattern.

For the agriculture group, the story is somewhat different. The multiple frequency table of link relatives does show a number

---

[31] Or over such part of this period as availability of data permits.

In the dating of the link relatives we follow the convention, previously established, of giving each link relative the date of the *later* of the two years involved in the comparison; thus the link relative for $\dfrac{1867}{1866}$ is dated 1867, and so on.

[32] And, incidentally, setting aside differences in amplitude of fluctuation, general similarity of short-run pattern can be discerned among these four groups.

[33] Cf. the corresponding discussion in Chapter III.

of fairly general tendencies of movement — e.g., the years 1871, 1876, 1900, and 1913 — and some tendency toward parallelism of movement appears in the "partition values" (quartiles). But, in general, "zones of distribution" in the tally marks of the multiple frequency table stand out much less clearly than for the non-agricultural groups, and the tendency toward parallelism in the "partition values" is appreciably less definite. Further, we can easily foresee that not many of the link-relative series for individual commodities will show any great resemblance to a computed link-relative group pattern. While we shall formally develop a group pattern for agriculture, we must present it with a warning that it is not to be thought of as highly representative of the individual components.

We proceed, then, in each of the five groups, to the derivation of the group pattern. The first step is in each case to calculate successively, year by year, 1867–1914, the medians in the multiple frequency table of link relatives. In accordance with an earlier methodological decision, we take the medians pertaining to the "complete list," 1881–1914, and to the "restricted list," 1867–1880, joining these two sets of medians to form a continuous series. In addition, we carry out for each group a special test computation, with a view to comparison of results for the "complete list" and the "restricted list," over the interval 1881–1914. The results definitely confirm the previous conclusion, based upon graphic examination of the individual series, that over this period the smaller sample gives for each group a picture generally similar to that yielded by the full list, though presumably less dependable in detail.

### AMPLITUDE OF SHORT-RUN FLUCTUATION

We now secure measures of the amplitude of short-run fluctuation for the several group link-relative series. Specifically, we compute in each case the average deviation of the annual median link relatives. These average deviations are tabulated in Table 5. Notable are the contrasts in amplitude between manufacture, destined for capital equipment, and manufacture, destined for human consumption; the comparatively moderate amplitudes for agriculture and mining; and the low amplitude for transportation and trade.

Following the calculation of these dispersion measures, we proceed to eliminate differences in average amplitude among the median link-relative series for the five groups, dividing each such series through by its average deviation.[34] The resulting series in average-deviation units are presented as the lower five curves of Chart 12. (For the time being, the upper five curves of Chart 12

TABLE 5

THE STRUCTURE OF PRODUCTION (LINK-RELATIVE APPROACH)
AMPLITUDE OF SHORT-RUN FLUCTUATION

*(Unit: one per cent)*

| Series | Average deviation of median link relatives |
|---|---|
| Manufacture, destined for capital equipment .......... | 8.16 |
| Manufacture, destined for human consumption ....... | 5.05 |
| Manufacture, all ................................. | 5.68 |
| Mining ............................................. | 3.95 |
| Transportation and trade combined ................. | 2.66 |
| Agriculture ........................................ | 4.45 |
| All non-agricultural series* ........................ | 3.51 |

* See the section, later in this chapter, entitled "The Composite Pattern."

should be ignored. The downward-sloping lines, drawn through each link-relative curve, will be discussed shortly.)

We may now examine and intercompare the curves for the five groups, with reference to certain of their characteristics.

#### AVERAGE RATE OF GROWTH

We begin this examination by obtaining, for each of the five group patterns, measures of average annual rate of growth (Table 6). We secure the measure, in each case, by determining the average level, over our period of analysis, of the series of median link-relatives for the group, derived as described on page 159. Although, as is more fully developed in the accompanying footnote, the method here employed [35] can yield only approximate

[34] The reader will observe that at this point a divergence appears with respect to order of procedure, contrasted with that of Chapter III: there, the discussion of differences in average level of fluctuation came ahead of the consideration of variations in average amplitude of fluctuation; here, the order is reversed. This transposition facilitates the exposition of the present case in certain respects, and at the same time has no consequential effect upon the intrinsic significance of the results.

[35] Specifically, the procedure in each case is to take the central ordinate of the straight line (i.e., the height of the line at the center of the time interval) fitted,

CHART 12

PATTERN OF THE STRUCTURE OF PRODUCTION (LINK–RELATIVE APPROACH) —
LINK RELATIVES IN AVERAGE–DEVIATION UNITS:
BY YEARS, 1867–1914 *

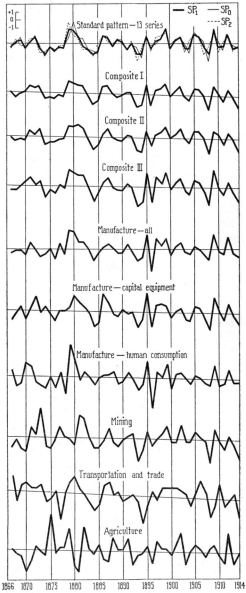

* Link-relative standard pattern for the thirteen important economic series is
shown at top of chart, for comparison. For explanation of the captions, see the
accompanying text, especially pp. 168, 169, 171–172.

results, there are reasons for regarding the measures of average annual rate of growth obtained in the present chapter as good approximations. Certainly, they possess accuracy ample for the purposes of the analytical use which we propose to make of them, and they are sufficiently reliable for rough general comparisons.

Our results (see Table 6) show average annual rates of growth appreciably higher than those indicated by Professor Burns' findings, as set forth on pages 50–62 of *Production Trends*. We may obtain a rough contrast by setting the figures in our Table 6 against medians derived from the tables on his pages 55, 57, 58–60, and 61 (we have in each case used the figures in the next-to-last column of the table, captioned "average annual rate of growth, in period covered" — and, in order to obtain as close a comparison as possible, have rearranged the items to conform to our classification system). The two sets of measurements are, of course, by no means fully comparable from the point of view of methodology involved, for the methods in the two studies follow differing pathways, and in addition there are certain variations as to details of procedure.

Nevertheless, it seems fairly certain that the divergence of re-

---

over our period of analysis (omitting the year 1914), to the logarithms of the median link relatives, find the antilogarithm of this ordinate — expressed as a percentage — and subtract 100 per cent. This process is, of course, equivalent to finding the geometric average of the median link relatives — once more, expressed as a percentage — and subtracting 100 per cent. (The reason for fitting a straight line to the logarithms is that we wish to measure not only average rate of growth, but also average rate of retardation; cf. Table 4, earlier in this chapter, and the accompanying discussion, and also see fns. 37 and 38, just below.) For purposes of plotting the central ordinate upon Chart 12, we reduce to average-deviation units through division by the appropriate average deviation.

To illustrate, for the mining group the central ordinate of the straight line fitted to the logarithms of the median link relatives is 0.03101; the antilogarithm of this is 1.074, or 107.4 per cent; the indicated average annual rate of growth is thus 7.4 per cent (cf. Table 6); this rate reduced to average-deviation units is 7.4 per cent divided by 3.95 per cent (cf. Table 5), or 1.87 units (on Chart 12). To determine the position of the horizontal zero line for mining on Chart 12, measure downward 1.87 units from the ordinate for the central year — 1890 — using scale at top of chart.

The method which we employ here for estimating average annual rate of growth is not in general a highly reliable one, inasmuch as the measure is open to distortion by eccentric behavior of the items in the terminal years of the time interval. We might, by a more tedious procedure (described in fn. 38, just below), obtain results possessing a closer approach to precision. However, for the specific cases under consideration in this chapter, graphic inspection of the material indicates that the computed measures of average rate of growth do not suffer any appreciable distortion, and can be taken as amply adequate for our purposes.

sults is in the main not to be ascribed to methodological factors, but is rather to be accounted for by the consideration that our study stops at the year 1914, while Professor Burns' investigation includes also the war and post-war years (through 1929).[36] With

## TABLE 6

THE STRUCTURE OF PRODUCTION (LINK-RELATIVE APPROACH)
AVERAGE ANNUAL RATE OF GROWTH

*(Unit: one per cent)*

| Series | Average annual rate of growth |
|---|---|
| Manufacture, destined for capital equipment .......... | 8.3 |
| Manufacture, destined for human consumption ........ | 6.0 |
| Manufacture, all ................................... | 7.0 |
| Mining ............................................. | 7.4 |
| Transportation and trade combined .................. | 5.9 |
| Agriculture ........................................ | 3.2 |
| All non-agricultural series* ........................ | 6.7 |

\* See the section, later in this chapter, entitled "The Composite Pattern."

retardation in rate of growth predominantly present for the individual industries included in the two investigations, it is to be expected that a lower average annual rate of growth should emerge in the study embracing the longer time interval. The question at once comes to mind whether the differences between the two studies as to indications of average rate of growth are to be ascribed merely to the continuance of pre-war rates of retardation for the several individual industries into the post-war years 1915–29, or have some further significance. We shall return to this question shortly.

### AVERAGE RATE OF RETARDATION

If we examine the curves for the various production groups on the lower half of Chart 12, we can see at once that in every case there is an appreciable downward slope in the link-relative series — a definite indication of retardation in rate of growth.[37] These

[36] It is true that our study begins four years earlier (1866 as opposed to 1870), but this is not enough to compensate for the disparity at the other end of the period.

[37] The reading of retardation indications from a chart of *link relatives* follows, for all practical purposes, the same principles as are involved in corresponding reading from a chart of *logarithmic first differences* (see fn. 20 in this chapter).

indications are so clear that it is desirable to give them statistical expression. We accordingly compute, for each group pattern, the average annual rate of retardation over the period, obtaining results as shown in Table 7. While, as is more fully set forth in the accompanying footnote,[38] we can regard our results only as approximations and must be careful not to impute too much precision to them, nevertheless our measurements of average annual rate of retardation (like those of average annual rate of growth) are quite adequate for the analytical employment which we sub-

---

To be sure, on a chart of link relatives a curve depicting a constant rate of retardation in growth will — for technical reasons, because of the logarithmic equation involved — depart from strict rectilinearity, but this departure will ordinarily for economic data be so slight as to be quite imperceptible upon the chart, and consequently the curve may without sensible error be thought of as a straight line (cf. the downward-sloping lines upon Chart 12).

[38] The procedure in each of the five cases is to take the annual slope of the straight line fitted to the logarithms of the median link relatives, find the antilogarithm of this slope — expressed as a percentage — and then subtract it from 100 per cent. For purposes of plotting upon Chart 12, we reduce the successive ordinates to average-deviation units through division by the appropriate average deviation.

Thus, for the mining group the annual slope of the straight line fitted to the logarithms of the median link relatives is −0.00026 (or, in the ordinary convention, 9.99974−10); the antilogarithm is 0.99940, or 99.940 per cent; taking the difference between this figure and 100 per cent, we obtain 0.060 per cent as the indicated average annual rate of retardation (cf. Table 7); we reduce the successive ordinates to average-deviation units through division by 3.95 per cent (cf. Table 5), and plot (Chart 12).

More nearly precise results (not only for average rate of retardation, but also for average rate of growth) could be obtained by resort to a more tedious method of derivation: we might in each instance form a cumulative annual series through successive addition of the logarithms of the median link relatives, and then fit a parabola

$$(y' = a + bt + ct^2, \text{ where } y' = \log y)$$

to this cumulative series. From the constants of this equation (cf. the note at the bottom of Table 4, earlier in this chapter, and also the accompanying text discussion) — specifically, by taking the antilogarithms of $b$ and $2c$, respectively, each expressed as a percentage and reduced by 100 per cent — we could obtain improved measures of average annual rate of growth and average annual rate of retardation, respectively. (Experiments which the present writer has conducted indicate that, for retardation in particular, more reliable measurements can be obtained — though with much more time and effort — by employing the method of cumulation and fitting of a parabola to logarithms than by dealing directly with the link relatives. This is so because eccentric behavior of the link relatives at the extremities of the series may distort somewhat the slope of lines fitted to them, or to their logarithms.) However, since we plan to use our present results only for purposes of drawing certain very broad, general conclusions, it seems sufficient to use here the simple procedure of fitting directly to the median link relatives.

sequently make of them, and they are also useful for purposes of certain broad, general comparisons.

The rates of retardation shown in Table 7, for each of the major groups — manufacture, mining, transportation and trade, agriculture — and for all non-agricultural series, are appreciably lower

TABLE 7

THE STRUCTURE OF PRODUCTION (LINK-RELATIVE APPROACH)
AVERAGE ANNUAL RATE OF RETARDATION

(*Unit: one per cent*)

| Series | Average annual rate of retardation |
|---|---|
| Manufacture, destined for capital equipment .......... | 0.128 |
| Manufacture, destined for human consumption ....... | 0.076 |
| Manufacture, all ................................. | 0.099 |
| Mining ........................................... | 0.060 |
| Transportation and trade combined ................. | 0.058 |
| Agriculture ...................................... | 0.032 |
| All non-agricultural series* ...................... | 0.065 |

\* See the section, later in this chapter, entitled "The Composite Pattern."

than those indicated by Professor Burns' results, as presented in *Production Trends*. A rough comparison may be accomplished by contrasting the figures in our Table 7 with estimated medians derived from appropriate columns of the table on his page 109. For purposes of this comparison his percentage rates, which are in terms of retardation *per decade*, must be reduced to our basis of retardation rates *per year*. This may be accomplished with sufficient accuracy simply by dividing his figures by ten.[39] It may quite properly be objected that Professor Burns' tabulations for retardation rates are derived from a somewhat more extended list of constituent series than ours (since his list includes certain "noncontinuous" series, bringing the total number of series up to 142); but if his tables are recast to conform to our grouping system and list of constituents, the conclusions just set forth are not altered.

We must not, of course, impute too much precision to these comparisons, for the technical methods in the two studies follow different pathways, and further (as has already been indicated)

[39] We also drop his minus signs, since in our terminology we deem the word "retardation" sufficient to indicate the essentially negative nature of the alteration over time in rate of growth.

our procedure is such as to yield only approximate results. Nevertheless, the differences between our retardation measures and those of Professor Burns are so large and so consistently present among the groups as strongly to suggest that, for the contituent industries of the two studies, the predominant general tendency *is not simply for the pre-war retardation rate to continue into the post-war years 1915–29, but rather is for the retardation to become more severe in these later years.*

The immediate significance of this conclusion lies in the additional force which it gives to our objection (set forth earlier in this chapter) to the use of the logarithmic parabola for production series pertaining to individual industries. *In the evidence afforded by the comparisons just presented, we have still further indication that for representation of long-run tendencies of such series over extended periods we cannot properly assume even approximate long-run constancy of the retardation rate.* These comparisons suggest that if we were to extend our study of logarithmic first differences of individual production series into the post-war era, after 1914, we should find (even omitting the depression years from 1930 onward) curvilinear tendencies *stronger* than those we previously observed when confining ourselves to the pre-war interval 1866–1914.

Our results for average rate of growth and average rate of retardation may readily be given graphic expression. The downward-sloping lines drawn through the several curves of Chart 12 give a representation in each case of average rate of growth (the average level) and of average rate of retardation (the slope).[40]

The measures for growth and retardation pertaining to the *structure of production*, derived in this chapter, should not, of course, be confused with measures pertaining to the *total volume of production* for a particular economic field, such as might be derived from a properly weighted index number (cf. the results of the next chapter).

## THE COMPOSITE PATTERN

With the aid afforded by the amplitude adjustments and the "growth-retardation" lines, we are able effectively to compare the

---

[40] On Chart 12, such representations have been reduced to the basis of "average-deviation units," as explained in preceding footnotes. (See also fn. 37, just above.)

short-time fluctuations of the several groups (cf. the lower five curves of Chart 12). We see that, as indeed our preliminary graphic examination of the original data had enabled us to fore-cast, the four non-agricultural groups exhibit a high degree of correspondence as to the general form of short-run movement.

The correspondence is in general less good for the earlier inter-val 1867–80, where the list of production series available for each of the four groups is as we have seen somewhat restricted and the "sample" available is presumably less representative. Further, over the whole period 1867–1914 each of the four curves has its own individualistic peculiarities. These are doubtless in part inherent, in part due to defects of basic figures, in part ascribable to technical factors connected with the form of statistical report-ing of economic data. In particular, the curves show certain dif-ferences and inconsistencies with respect to timing of movement. These, in their turn, may be attributed in part to real lags in the economic phenomena which the statistics attempt to portray, in part to deficiencies of the statistical material, in part to technical causes (e.g., the presence of fiscal-year series).

Taking all elements into account, however, we may say that a high degree of intrinsic correspondence appears among the four non-agricultural groups as regards the fundamental form of short-time fluctuation. The curve for the agriculture group, on the other hand, pursues a course of its own, and traces out short-run move-ments which have little similarity to those for the non-agricultural curves.[41]

Our results, taken in conjunction with our previous extended methodological observations, clearly indicate that *for the United States over the pre-war period 1866–1914 a well-defined pattern of short-time fluctuation is generally pervasive throughout the structure of the nation's industrial and commercial life.* It is im-portant to emphasize that this conclusion does not rest merely upon a comparison of certain curves in Chart 12; the conclusion rests also upon the findings of our graphic survey of the individual production series, upon the emergence of most clearly marked "zones of distribution" in the multiple frequency tables, and upon

---

[41] This is not to say, of course, that there may not be *relationships* between the agricultural group and the non-agricultural groups, but only to indicate that such relationships do not express themselves in simple correlations in form of movement — as do the relationships among the non-agricultural groups.

the appearance of close approach to parallelism in the "partition-values" charts. It is on the basis of this extended and elaborate analysis that we set forth our present conclusion.

The general correspondence in form of short-time fluctuation among the non-agricultural groups suggests the development of a composite series. This suggestion we may very readily carry out, by averaging the items of the four constituent groups, year by year, 1867–1914. This average series is plotted near the top of Chart 12, labelled "Composite I." It may be described as the "link-relative pattern of short-time fluctuation in the structure of industrial and commercial production." The purpose in assigning such a cumbersome title is to distinguish this series from another composite link-relative pattern (quite different in derivation) to be presented in the next chapter, based upon production *indexes*. In view of the pervasiveness of the present pattern throughout the array of individual production series, the expression "structure of production" appears in any case altogether appropriate.

The composite curve just derived presumably delineates more clearly than any of its constituents this fundamental pattern of non-agricultural production. And, while doubtless at certain points precision in detail is lacking, because of the limitations of the basic statistical material, we may nevertheless fairly say that this curve gives an essentially correct picture of the intrinsic phenomenon which it is intended to represent. And, further, this picture portrays something very real: pulsations in economic activity — far-reaching and pervasive in the nation's industrial and commercial life — over the half-century from the close of the Civil War to the outbreak of the World War in 1914.

## Comparison with the Standard Pattern for Thirteen Series

We may now appropriately compare our link-relative pattern for the structure of industrial and commercial production with the link-relative standard pattern for the thirteen important economic series, as developed in earlier chapters.[42] A technical obstacle, however, must first be surmounted. We shall want to consider lags, and the production curve is derivable in annual form only. We may meet the difficulty by setting up the link-relative standard

---

[42] Specifically, we turn to the annual link-relative standard pattern for the thirteen series, derived directly from annual data and on the "appropriate-lag" basis, as described in the latter part of Chapter IV.

pattern for the thirteen series not merely upon a calendar-year basis ("SP$_0$" at the top of Chart 12),[43] but also on other bases. We derive this pattern moved forward one quarter ("SP$_1$" on the chart),[44] and moved forward two quarters ("SP$_2$" on the chart); also, going in the other direction, we derive the pattern moved backward one quarter ("SP$_{-1}$") and moved backward two quarters ("SP$_{-2}$").[45]

Aided by the array of "SP" series, we may compare the composite link-relative production pattern with the link-relative pattern for the thirteen series. The "best correlation" manifestly is that with "SP$_1$"; i.e., on the whole the tendency is for the pattern of the thirteen series to move about one quarter later than the production pattern. We are not at liberty, however, to put upon this fact the simple interpretation that pulsations running through the structure of industrial and commercial production tend on the average over our selected time interval to occur about three months in advance of corresponding pulsations in (let us say) "the average of the four volume series" — outside clearings, imports, immigration, and railroad earnings — which, it will be remembered, constituted the basis for lag measurements in the construction of the standard pattern for the thirteen series.[46] The lag which appears between the two patterns may have some intrinsic economic significance,[47] but probably this lag has its origin, in part at least, in the limitations of the basic production material or in technical factors (e.g., the inclusion of a considerable number of fiscal-year series).

We may now intercompare the link-relative standard pattern

[43] Here the link-relative item dated 1867 pertains to $\dfrac{1867\text{–I to }1867\text{–IV}}{1866\text{–I to }1866\text{–IV}}$; and so on.

[44] That is, the link-relative item dated 1867 pertains to $\dfrac{1867\text{–II to }1868\text{–I}}{1866\text{–II to }1867\text{–I}}$. and so on.

[45] "SP$_{-1}$" and "SP$_{-2}$" have not been reproduced. "SP$_{-2}$" is, of course, the same as "SP$_2$", but shifted one year.

[46] Cf. the discussion of this point in Chapters III and IV.

[47] Plausible arguments can be made out for this view with respect at least to outside clearings ("the lag in payments"), and to immigration (the "pull" of business conditions in the United States). As regards the lag in immigration, see Harry Jerome, *Migration and Business Cycles* (New York: National Bureau of Economic Research, Inc., 1926), pp. 91–95, 153, 208–209. And, in general, differences in timing of the "price element" and the "volume element" for certain series of the standard pattern may have some bearing upon the lag.

for the thirteen series (taking specifically on Chart 12 the proper curve for "best lag," "SP₁") and the composite link-relative pattern for the structure of industrial and commercial production (the curve labelled "Composite I" on the chart). Setting aside certain small discrepancies (occurring for the most part in the earlier years, when the statistical basis, for both curves, is less good than for the rest of the period),[48] the correlation is truly remarkable. This correlation is all the more noteworthy when one considers that: (1) it appears in spite of numerous defects of the basic constituent series for each pattern; (2) the two patterns are derived from wholly distinct lists of series; and (3) even the *lists* were set up by independent investigators, each in entire ignorance of the other's work.[49]

### TESTS OF THE COMPOSITE PATTERN OF THE STRUCTURE OF PRODUCTION

The striking correlation which is revealed when the composite pattern for the structure of industrial and commercial production is compared with the earlier-computed pattern for the thirteen series imposes upon us certain responsibilities. After such notable correlation has been found, it is all the more imperative that we should test our composite production curve as thoroughly as we can, in order to assure ourselves that the close correspondence does not have its origin, partially at least, in some turn or twist of the procedure. We accordingly apply several tests to the results.

#### THE FIRST TEST, RELATING TO THE MANUFACTURE GROUP

The first test relates to a very simple question. In our computations we have split manufacture into two groups — "goods des-

---

[48] The discrepancy which may be observed in the chart for the year 1914 is technical in origin. In setting up the standard pattern for the thirteen series, we avoided the use of data for the last half of the year 1914 (see p. 101), and thus prevented the pattern from being affected by the irregular fluctuations occasioned by the outbreak of the World War. (Specifically with reference to "SP₁", the application of this principle means that the curve is based on the second quarter of 1914, at least for the "concurrent" series among its constituents. Cf. fn. 44, p. 169, just above, with pp. 108–111 in Chapter IV.) For the production pattern, no such arrangement is possible, inasmuch as in general monthly or quarterly figures are unobtainable. Hence we are obliged simply to employ the annual data, which predominantly pertain to calendar years.

[49] [The present author's selection of thirteen series for the standard-pattern

tined for capital equipment" and "goods destined for human consumption." This differentiation seemed then (and seems now) wholly justified, on the basis of adequate economic and statistical analysis. Nevertheless, in order to resolve any possible doubt it is desirable to determine by experiment what modification of result would appear if manufacture were taken as a single group instead of being divided into two. The answer is definite. Handling manufacture as a single group and recalculating the composite pattern for the structure of commercial and industrial production, we get the curve on Chart 12 marked "Composite II," and we see at once (comparing with "Composite I") that the alterations in result are quite minor.[50]

### THE SECOND TEST: THE "ALL-INCLUSIVE" COMPUTATION

We now reconsider the methodology somewhat more broadly. It comes to mind that, though the basic list of individual production series has indeed been taken from another writer and hence may be regarded as unprejudiced by preconceptions, nevertheless from time to time a certain amount of discretionary judgment has entered decisions as to procedure — the choice of the particular general system of grouping employed, as opposed to possible alternatives; the decision to drop certain series from the analysis; and so on.

To be sure, we have endeavored to make these decisions in good faith, and reasons, apparently cogent, have been set forth in support of each choice of procedure. Nevertheless, it seems highly desirable, especially in view of the remarkably high correspondence between the production pattern and the standard pattern earlier derived for the thirteen selected series, to remove even the suspicion of "methodology bias" [51] in the selection and classification of the material.

Accordingly, we proceed to calculate an "all-inclusive" pattern of the structure of industrial and commercial production, not affected by these various methodological decisions. This new pattern is based upon *all* of the non-agricultural production series in

---

computation of Chapters III and IV was made before Professor Burns' *Production Trends* appeared.]

[50] The link-relative pattern for manufacture, handled as a single group, is shown as the fifth curve on Chart 12.

[51] With respect to the general expression "methodology bias," see p. 135, above.

the basic list,[52] and the series are not divided into groups. The proposed procedure (if indeed the arguments regarding methods of the earlier sections of this chapter possess any soundness) is logically much inferior to that we have chosen to employ in arriving at our "Composite I." We nevertheless apply this new procedure, in order to satisfy ourselves still further that our composite pattern does not carry a "methodology bias." The results are altogether clear in their indications. The "all-inclusive" pattern ("Composite III" on Chart 12)[53] differs in only minor detail from that earlier derived ("Composite I").

### THE THIRD TEST: THE "AMPLITUDE-GROUP" EXPERIMENT

In our preliminary survey of methodological matters, one question was regarded as of fundamental, and indeed even crucial, importance. This question was, it will be recalled, whether our principal expense-saving modification of procedure — the elimination within each group of the formal arithmetical derivation of dispersion measures for the several individual series, and the substitution therefor of a "blanket" measurement pertaining to the group pattern — would impair the representativeness of the final results, by bringing it about that a comparatively few series with wide amplitude should dominate.

To be sure, our preliminary graphic examination of the data (as described in the earlier pages of this chapter) afforded definite evidence that such domination would not occur. The point involved is of such importance, however, that it seems desirable to remove any possible remaining doubt by applying a formal statistical test.[54] To test the validity of our final pattern for the structure of production, we take the complete list of pertinent series,[55] and regroup them upon a new principle.

The first step in regrouping is to array the series in order of amplitude of short-run fluctuation. This can readily be accomplished with adequate accuracy, so far as our present purpose is concerned, without any extended resort to formal calculation. We

---

[52] That is, the series numbered 24 to 104, inclusive, in the Burns list (cf. Burns, *Production Trends*, pp. 12–13).

[53] The amplitude, growth, and retardation constants for this composite are shown in Tables 5, 6, and 7, respectively.

[54] Limitations of data make it impracticable to extend this test back of the year 1880.

[55] That is, the series marked 24 to 104, inclusive, in the Burns list.

simply set up an approximate order, based on graphic inspection of the charts drawn with logarithmic vertical scale,[56] and employ computation only in a few doubtful cases which for our purposes are border line.[57] We next separate the series into groups according to dispersion amplitude, first dividing them into halves. That is, we take the series of the "upper half" (those possessing the greater amplitude of dispersion) and the series of the "lower half" (those possessing the lesser amplitude of dispersion), and then for each of these two groups we derive the "link-relative pattern in average-deviation units" — thus eliminating the difference in amplitude of fluctuation (see the curves marked "UH" and "LH", respectively, on Chart 13). Next, by averaging these two series we obtain the "composite pattern for halves" (the curve marked "Ave. H" on Chart 13). We then supplement these computations for "halves" by analogous computations for "thirds" and for "quarters" (cf. the chart).[58] For purposes of comparison, we put at the top of the chart the pattern for the thirteen series ("SP$_0$", "SP$_1$", "SP$_2$"), and the composite production pattern ("Composite I").

We observe, in the first place, that the three composites based upon "halves," "thirds," and "quarters," respectively (labelled "Ave. H", "Ave. T", and "Ave. Q", respectively, upon the chart) exhibit, as might be anticipated, almost perfect agreement with one another and with the composite derived from combination of economic groups ("Composite I"), and in consequence show high correlation with the pattern for thirteen series (specifically, with "SP$_1$"). But principal interest and significance attaches to the lower nine curves of Chart 13. Each of these pertains to a selected sector of the array of production series arranged with reference

[56] Specifically, the object in this graphic inspection is to sort the series in the order which they would have if arranged according to the magnitude of the average deviations of their link relatives over the period of analysis (beginning, that is, with 1881, for the sake of uniformity).

[57] As will shortly appear, the pertinent border lines here are the quartiles, and the boundaries which separate the series into three equal parts.

[58] The various amplitude measures may be of interest. The average deviations of median link relatives for the group patterns, 1881–1913, are as follows (unit, one per cent):

| Halves | | Thirds | | Quarters | |
|---|---|---|---|---|---|
| Upper ("UH") | 7.74 | Uppermost ("UT") | 9.59 | Uppermost ("UQ") | 11.36 |
| Lower ("LH") | 2.76 | Middle ("MT") | 4.05 | Third ("TQ") | 7.39 |
| | | Lowest ("LT") | 2.54 | Second ("SQ") | 3.90 |
| | | | | Lowest ("LQ") | 2.17 |

# CHART 13

PATTERN OF THE STRUCTURE OF INDUSTRIAL AND COMMERCIAL PRODUCTION —
LINK RELATIVES IN AVERAGE-DEVIATION UNITS
FOR "HALVES," "THIRDS," AND "QUARTERS":
BY YEARS, 1881–1914 *

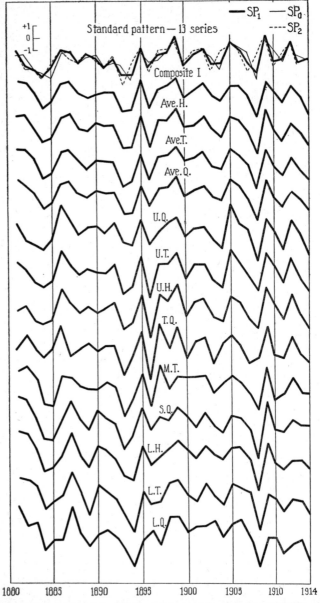

* Link-relative patterns for thirteen series and for "Composite I" also shown.
See accompanying text, and also fns. 43 and 44 on p. 169.

to amplitude of fluctuation. The plan of Chart 13 is to place the nine curves in order according to the sector of such array to which they pertain. As we go down the chart through the nine curves, the composition of the pattern undergoes progressive change. Indeed, the two curves "UH" and "LH" are entirely independent of each other as to composition, as are the three curves "UT", "MT", and "LT", and the four curves "UQ", "SQ", "TQ", and "LQ". In spite of this progressive tendency to change in composition, the fundamental pattern is very well maintained.[59]

We have obtained in Chart 13 a very striking picture. It would be difficult to find a more dramatic way of exhibiting the general pervasiveness of our short-time production pattern. And clearly, since this pattern has been found to persist through all the amplitude groupings, it has been shown beyond possible doubt that the delineation of short-run pattern furnished by "Composite I" is not dominated by a relatively few high-amplitude series, but on the contrary is highly representative of the entire array.

We have in this chapter demonstrated that over our period of analysis a well-defined pattern of short-time fluctuation is generally pervasive throughout the structure of the nation's industrial and commercial life. We have developed a composite curve to portray this pattern in the structure of production, and we have found a remarkably close correspondence between this new pattern and that previously derived, as described in Chapters III and IV, for the thirteen important economic series. In this connection, we have incidentally given some attention to the matter of "methodology bias." Further, we have presented extensive evidence for the view that the long-time tendencies of production series for individual industries are by no means simple; specifically, that such long-time tendencies are clearly not capable of even approximate representation by the logarithmic parabola.

[59] Detailed differences, to be sure, appear as we go down the chart through the nine curves. Most conspicuous are certain systematic shifts in timing. These variations in timing are probably due mainly to technical factors (e.g., a preponderance of fiscal-year series in certain sectors of the array of series).

# CHAPTER VIII

## THE PATTERN OF PRODUCTION: FIXED-BASE APPROACH

IN THE PRECEDING CHAPTER, we considered the field of production with particular reference to its structure, employing the *link-relative approach*. We now turn to an examination of production data by the *fixed-base approach*, involving the use of index numbers.

The investigations to be described in the present chapter form in a sense a part of a larger study of physical production in the United States over the period 1860–1914 which the present writer has carried out. This larger study constitutes the general subject of another volume, which it is hoped to publish in the near future. Inasmuch as the publication of this later volume is contemplated, we shall not in the present volume attempt to give any detailed description of the procedure employed, nor shall we present here any extended discussion of the theoretical and practical problems involved in the methodology for the derivation of index numbers of production, or consider in any thoroughgoing way the bearing of the nature and limitations of production data upon the interpretation and significance of our statistical findings. And we shall not undertake to set forth here any elaborate presentation of numerical results in tabular or graphic form, nor to discuss these results at length.

In this chapter, then, we shall for the most part give only short summary statements of the statistical procedure, and shall deal rather briefly with the theoretical and practical methodological issues just alluded to. And, so far as presentation and discussion of numerical results are concerned, we are in general obliged to confine ourselves to those features which are particularly pertinent to the task immediately before us — the search for patterns of fluctuation in pre-war economic series.

We now make a survey, with special reference to the problem at hand, of certain of the major groups into which production is conventionally divided in statistical literature.

## Manufacture

Upon undertaking the measurement of changes over time in total production for the field of manufacture, one immediately encounters the theoretical and practical difficulties of index-number construction to which reference has just been made. On the theoretical side, such problems as the following emerge:[1] the application of the definition of "production" to manufacturing operations, which characteristically are divided into stages;[2] the selection of a proper mathematical formula for giving concrete numerical expression to the definition as thus applied; the determination of policy regarding the handling of new industries; the decisions as to the weighting basis, such as those with respect to the value-added principle, to fixed as opposed to variable weights, and so on; the avoidance of technical (type and weight) bias.[3]

On the practical side, also, numerous difficulties present themselves, arising from the limitations of available data upon the volume of production in the field of manufacture. We may briefly allude to some of these difficulties, considering them with particular attention to our chosen pre-war time interval of study, 1866–1914.

One group of problems has its origin in deficiency as to time coverage, or as to continuity, for numerous individual production series. Some series are obtainable over only a part of the pre-war industrial life of the branch of manufacture to which they pertain (e.g., series indicative of stone, clay, and glass production; gold

---

[1] It is to be noted that, antecedent to these specific questions, there are certain more general, philosophical issues. Cf. an article by the present writer: Edwin Frickey, "Some Aspects of the Problem of Measuring Historical Changes in the Physical Volume of Production," in the volume entitled *Explorations in Economics: Notes and Essays Contributed in Honor of F. W. Taussig* (New York and London: McGraw-Hill Book Co., Inc., 1936), pp. 477–486. See also the article by Professor Arthur F. Burns, "The Measurement of the Physical Volume of Production," *Quarterly Journal of Economics*, XLIV (February 1930), pp. 242–262; and his *Production Trends in the United States since 1870* (New York: National Bureau of Economic Research, Inc., 1934), pp. 5–10, 253–281.

[2] Incidentally the question arises as to the choice between the concepts of manufacturing production in the more general, etymological sense and in the sense of factory production.

[3] In connection with the problem of technical bias, reference may be made to an article by the present writer: Edwin Frickey, "The Theory of Index-Number Bias," *Review of Economic Statistics*, XIX (November 1937), pp. 161–173. The theory is there explicitly developed for price index numbers, but can very readily be adapted to quantity indexes by a simple interchange of symbols.

and silver consumption). Others extend over the entire interval of study, but are available only discontinuously (e.g., lumber and paper production). Still others suffer from the defects of both incomplete temporal coverage and discontinuity (e.g., production of leather, of boots and shoes, and of certain chemicals).

Further, many lines of production are represented only indirectly in the existing data upon production. Such indirect representation most often occurs through the use of "materials-consumed" data (e.g., the so-called "consumption" series for cotton and wool, and for pig iron and the non-ferrous metals; the import series for coffee, cocoa, and rubber) as denotative of the volume of production. Numerous difficulties arise in this connection, notably those pertaining to changes in stocks — ordinarily allowed for imperfectly, if at all, in the statistical records — and the use of reclaimed materials (e.g., steel scrap) in industrial processes.

Still other influences operate to bring about lack of essential continuity and comparability over time for individual manufacture series. The *unit of measurement* ordinarily falls short of possessing full intrinsic temporal homogeneity — perhaps because of alterations in quality of materials or products, or variations in degree of fabrication; or as a result of changes in the extent of industrial or commercial utilization of by-products; or on account of defects peculiar to the particular statistical series.

To this catalogue of theoretical and practical difficulties we must subjoin another range of problems, which may be classified under one or the other of these two rubrics, according to the point of view from which they are attacked — the problems, that is, which emerge because of the inadequacy of coverage, in the economic field of manufacture, by the available statistical material (such inadequacies being particularly conspicuous with respect to moderately-fabricated and highly-fabricated goods). We may, depending upon our approach, think of these deficiencies as pertaining, on the one hand, to the "theoretical" problem of sampling in index-number construction, or, on the other, to the "practical" problem involved in setting up a system of imputed weighting for the particular case under consideration.

Our survey of the theoretical and practical difficulties connected with the measurement over time of changes in the volume of manufacturing production has by no means been exhaustive, but it is sufficiently comprehensive to establish the conviction that in the development of a production index for this economic field we must exercise the greatest discrimination in the methodological decisions, and the greatest care and diligence in the handling of the body of imperfect basic materials. And, of course, the attainment of anything approaching perfection in such measurements is quite out of the question. Some theoretical difficulties are logically unsurmountable; some limitations of basic production data are irremediable, even by the utmost ingenuity and effort. Notwithstanding, two things would seem clear. (1) Much can be done to raise the quality of statistical results, and the accuracy of interpretation of these results, by intelligent effort in the construction of manufacturing index numbers and by employment of a discriminating critical attitude in the interpretation of such index numbers, especially with reference to specific purposes of application of the statistical findings. (2) Granted that to certain questions our statistical measurements can give no simple and direct answer (e.g., the question as to average annual rate of growth of manufacturing production over a given period), nevertheless, if every possible amount of discrimination, care, and diligence be exercised (as is suggested just above), a great measure of truth can be secured — we may obtain, in fact, a degree of accuracy fully adequate for many specific purposes.

## THE DAY-PERSONS INDEX

The only published index number of manufacturing production in the United States covering our pre-war interval of study is the Day-Persons index.[4] This series, as is more fully set forth in the accompanying footnote, was derived by Professor Warren M. Persons, taking the index developed by Dr. Edmund E. Day and

[4] The various series referred to in this chapter as the Day-Persons indexes are those presented by Professor Warren M. Persons in his book, *Forecasting Business Cycles* (New York: John Wiley & Sons, Inc., 1931), pp. 169–177. Professor Persons derived these series by taking the indexes developed by Dr. Edmund E. Day in his monograph, *An Index of the Physical Volume of Production* (for complete references, see fn. 12, p. 140, above), and making calculations to extend them back to 1860 (1863 for manufacture).

On one phase of Dr. Day's study — the "census-year" investigation for manufacture (cf. the monograph, pp. 30–34) — he was assisted by Professor Persons and Miss Eunice S. Coyle. In developing the indexes as presented in *Forecasting Business Cycles*, Professor Persons was assisted by Mr. A. S. McLeod and Mr. Herbert Harvey. For more detailed statements regarding the formation of the indexes, see Persons and Day, *loc. cit.*

extending it back to 1863. The series thus obtained is shown, for the period 1863–1914, as the fifth curve on Chart 14.[5]

We may now examine this series, with special reference to our interval of study, 1866–1914, and our particular objective — the search for patterns of fluctuation in economic data. So far as the period covered by Dr. Day's index is concerned (1899 onward), it must be said at once that his monograph is outstanding as regards the fullness of presentation, not only of results, but also of basic material and statistical procedure. Some thirty-five folio pages are devoted to such presentation for the field of manufacture. The source and nature of the individual constituent series are discussed at length and methodological questions are given consideration. The list of component series is virtually uniform throughout the period.[6] Without undertaking at this time to present an exhaustive survey of all questions involved relating to fundamental data and methodology, it would seem that in the construction of this index a great deal of discrimination and effort has been exerted, with a view to securing as high a degree as possible of comparability and continuity over time — qualities highly important from the point of view of the present investigation of pattern movements in economic series.

Turning now to consider as a whole the index presented by Professor Persons, we note that it is a "spliced" series. Four sections — pertaining to 1863–67, 1867–74, 1875–99, and 1899–1914, respectively — have been joined, on the basis of ratios for overlapping data. The number of constituent series varies among the sections, being six, twelve, twenty-one, and thirty, respectively. The weighting systems also vary, as among the four sections. Further, there is divergence as to the mathematical formula employed: the aggregative is used during 1863–99, and the geometric average for 1899 onward.

These variations as regards basic data and statistical procedure are bound to cause some misgiving. However, we must be careful not to exaggerate the importance of these departures from

---

[5] Chart 14 is drawn with logarithmic vertical scale. The logarithmic scales for the various curves are identical, but the base lines have been separated for convenience in comparison of form of fluctuation. The smooth, thin dotted lines drawn through certain of the curves of Chart 14 should be ignored for the present, since they do not enter the discussion until a much later stage of the analysis (cf. Chapters XIII, XIV, and XV, below).

[6] Certain series are available for census years only.

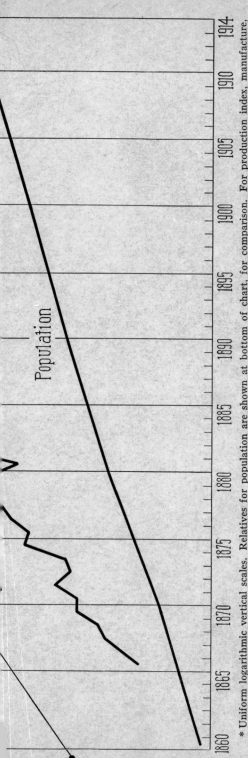

Population

* Uniform logarithmic vertical scales. Relatives for population are shown at bottom of chart, for comparison. For production index, manufacture, transportation and communication, and employment, quarterly estimates are also shown for selected periods. For forestry, only census-year figures are available prior to 1904. For explanation of the captions, see the accompanying text, and also Chapter IX. The smooth, thin dotted lines drawn through certain of the curves will be discussed in Chapters XIII, XIV, and XV.

uniformity in the construction of the index. We cannot be sure, without extended analysis, just how much effect is exerted by the changes in the weighting system. But one may question whether, within the short fifteen-year period from 1899 to 1914, the shift to the geometric average causes the course of the index to be markedly different from what it would have been if calculated with an aggregative properly constructed to avoid technical bias. The variations in the index with respect to the list of constituent series are admittedly to be regarded more seriously; yet so far as our period of study, 1866–1914, is concerned (excepting only the initial year 1866), the index embraces uninterruptedly some eleven important industries.[7] There are thus present important elements making for continuity.

It is in passing only fair to point out that Professor Persons, in developing his index of manufacturing production, desired the series primarily for use in connection with his chronological survey of the "Records of Business," [8] and for this purpose the matter of precise long-run comparability was by no means so important as in the present investigation. We may quote the last paragraph of the chapter in which the series is developed. "In presenting the indexes of manufactures, 1863–1899, it is realized that the data are not all that could be desired, but it is believed that a fair measure of the growth and annual fluctuations of total manufacture has been obtained. Upon further investigation it may be possible to enlarge the scope of the data and to attain more precise annual measurements." [9]

It would seem suitable, then, after recording our appreciation of Professor Persons' pioneer work [10] in this field, to proceed with the "further investigation" suggested by the passage quoted, having in mind "to enlarge the scope of the data and to attain more precise annual measurements," as well as long-run comparisons possessing as high a degree of homogeneity as possible.

[7] Cf. Persons, *Forecasting Business Cycles*, pp. 177 and 175–176, and Day, *An Index of the Physical Volume of Production*, Table XXI, pp. 47–48.

[8] Cf. Persons, *Forecasting Business Cycles*, pp. 88–168.

[9] Persons, *Forecasting Business Cycles*, p. 177.

[10] A full list of the pioneer endeavors initiated through the exercise of Professor Persons' fertile imagination, and developed through his resourcefulness and ingenuity, would indeed be an extended one.

### THE NEW INDEX

In accordance with the decision just announced, we set ourselves to the tedious task of developing a new index of manufacturing production over the long interval extending from the Civil War to the World War,[11] with the purpose (as indicated) of securing as high a degree of intrinsic continuity and comparability over time as possible. The construction of the index involves an elaborate and extended analysis, including intensive examination (and, so far as feasible, improvement) of basic data, careful consideration of a variety of methodological issues, and a long-extended series of computations. Detailed presentation of discussions concerning procedure, and of results, for this new index must await the publication of the later volume, devoted to production in the United States over pre-war years, to which reference has previously been made. We can give here only a brief statement indicating in summary fashion certain leading features of this piece of analysis.

In the construction of the new index of manufacturing production, serious attempt is made to grapple with the various theoretical and practical difficulties to which allusion is made earlier in this chapter and, so far as may be, to resolve the attendant problems. On the theoretical side, the application of the definition of "production" to manufacturing operations is given attention. Then, reviewing various possible mathematical formulae in the light of such application, the arithmetic mean of relatives (which, as is well known, is under certain simple conditions equivalent to the aggregative) is chosen as the most suitable. With respect to weighting, after careful consideration of the possibilities fixed weights, derived on the "value-added" principle, are employed.

Attention is given to the problem of avoiding technical (type and weight) bias. Simple logical considerations, as well as more complex mathematical analysis, suggest that the base period and weighting period should here be identical. Theoretically, the employment of "compromise base" and "compromise weighting-period" would seem to be indicated.[12] The use of "compromise weights," however, is in the present case impracticable, because

---

[11] The period of analysis is 1860–1914. Over the years 1860–66, however, no great precision can be claimed for the year-to-year movements of the index.

[12] See the article, "The Theory of Index-Number Bias," by the present writer, to which reference is made just above. Cf. also Warren M. Persons, *The Construction of Index Numbers* (Cambridge: Houghton Mifflin Company, 1928), pp. 36–44.

of lack of adequate pertinent data in the earlier years. The best available substitute is a set of weights pertaining to some period intermediate between the terminal dates of the computation interval chosen with a view to obtaining relative weights approximating reasonably well those of the desired "compromise-weight" system. The practical choice lies between the two census years 1889 and 1899. On purely theoretical grounds the year 1889 should probably be given the preference, as it is situated nearer the center of the computation interval, and it seems likely that many of the long-run economic tendencies pertinent to our weighting problem were at least roughly continuous over this interval. Since, however, the 1899 Census is the first to furnish weighting data in the detail required for our present purposes, this year is selected.[13] The final decision, then, is to compute the index with 1899 as base and 1899 weights.

The weighting system is examined from still other points of view, and various systems of cross-classification are investigated. Finally, a sort of rudimentary *tableau économique* is drawn up for the year 1899; the study of this table is from many points of view highly instructive.[14]

Turning now to the "practical" side, we first make a survey of the individual series, attempting to extend and improve them. On the basis of intensive analysis, revised figures are set up for a number of industries. In several cases, research makes possible the backward extension, at least in approximate form, of series formerly available only for the later part of the period. Such extensions are particularly to be desired, since we wish to have the list of series as comprehensive as possible, and at the same time want to avoid breaks in continuity which may seriously interfere with the homogeneity over time of our measurements.

Careful consideration is given to the complex problem as to the

---

[13] In setting up the weights, careful attention is given to the consideration that "value-added" weights pertaining to a particular year (especially a year of rather rapid change in business activity, such as 1899) are subject to possible distortion, owing to the operation of dynamic forces which materially affect various price margins. We take care to scrutinize the weights indicated by the data for 1899 in the light of available information for preceding and following census years, and to investigate apparent anomalies. In only one case does modification of the 1899 weights seem called for: the "value-added" weight for pig-iron production in 1899 is markedly out of line with that for preceding and following census years and is, accordingly, reduced.

[14] Further discussion of the various aspects of the weighting problem must be postponed to the later volume on production.

best policy regarding utilization of the incomplete and the discontinuous production data to which reference has previously been made. The decision is that, in view of the importance of preserving continuity over time, we should refuse admission to series not extending over all (or nearly all) of the period of analysis — except in cases, such as that of automobile production, where the new series represents the emergence of a new industry. Data for series which are available over the entire period, but only discontinuously, are by means of a certain methodological device brought into the index, with a view to avoiding distortions of long-run movements which might otherwise have been occasioned.

These various theoretical and practical issues, as well as certain others of which limitation of space forbids mention here, have been given extended and careful attention. There is, of course, no thought of suggesting that all problems have been solved, or that we have here arrived at statistical measurements which are from all points of view unimpeachable. As has been indicated, there are some theoretical difficulties which are logically unsurmountable, and there are some limitations of basic statistical material which are irremediable, even by the utmost ingenuity and effort. Nevertheless, it would appear that we may properly claim for our new index of manufacture some degree of merit, relative to that which lies within the realm of practically achievable possibility — especially as regards the qualities of continuity and comparability over time which are crucial with reference to the purposes of our present investigation into the patterns of movement inherent in economic data.

Our new annual index of manufacturing production, 1860–1914, is shown as the fourth curve on Chart 14.[15] It will be seen that, setting aside certain differences in detail of movement at particular points, the short-run fluctuations of this new index correspond rather closely to those of the Day-Persons index. In so far as long-run characteristics can be determined by graphic inspection of the two curves (which are drawn with logarithmic vertical scale), it would appear that the new index exhibits a slightly lower average annual rate of growth than the old; and that retardation in growth, clearly discernible in the Day-Persons

---

[15] The smooth dotted line drawn through the curve should be ignored, since it does not enter the analysis until a much later stage (cf. Chapters XIII, XIV, and XV, below).

index, is present to a very minor degree, if at all, in the new index.[16]

For the period 1904–I to 1914–II, quarterly figures as well as annual are shown for the manufacture index on Chart 14. These quarterly figures have been presented in order that the picture of rather rapid fluctuation in these more recent years may be seen more clearly. The quarterly items represent estimated quarterly indexes of manufacturing production adjusted for seasonal variation. These estimates are secured by superimposing, upon the annual manufacture index, the form of short-run movement exhibited by quarterly pig-iron production adjusted for seasonal variation, with due regard to differences in average amplitude of (annual) fluctuation of the two series.[17]

## TRANSPORTATION AND COMMUNICATION

So far as is known to the present writer, no attempt has ever been made to construct an index of production over our period of study, 1866–1914, for the important group transportation and communication.[18] The advantages in having at hand, for the purposes of our pattern investigation, a production index pertaining to this highly significant branch of economic activity are so great that it seems urgently desirable to undertake the task — though it be most intricate and toilsome — of constructing such an index.

For the present case, as for that of the new manufacture index, detailed presentation and discussion of basic data, methods, and results must be postponed to a later volume. We are obliged to confine ourselves here to a brief consideration of certain outstanding aspects of the analysis.

In the derivation of the transportation and communication index we encounter various theoretical and practical problems. These

[16] Throughout this chapter, and in the rest of the book, we shall use the expression "retardation in growth" (or, sometimes, merely "retardation") to designate *relative* movements — more technically, to denote "retardation in *ratio* of growth" — as is developed and illustrated in the preceding chapter (cf. Table 4, and the accompanying discussion). In particular, for explanation of the reading of growth and retardation indications from charts with logarithmic vertical scale, see fn. 19 in Chapter VII.

[17] As to the high correlation, over this period, between the short-run movements of pig-iron production and total manufacture, see Day, *op. cit.*, p. 62.

[18] Professor Walter W. Stewart, in his article, "An Index Number of Production," *American Economic Review*, XI (March 1921), pp. 57–69, published an index for transportation, but this index began with 1890 and embraced railroad traffic only.

problems in a general way correspond to those met in the construction of the manufacture index, but naturally take a somewhat different form, because of variations between the two cases with respect to the nature of the economic activities involved and the characteristics of the available statistical material.

For the transportation and communication index, theoretical and practical difficulties are in many respects closely interconnected. For example, the theoretical question, "What is the unit of measurement for 'value added by transportation service'?" is tied up with the practical decision regarding the choice between tonnage and ton-miles to represent the volume of railroad freight service; the theoretical question of the proper basis for weighting is closely intertwined with the practical problem of developing a suitable system of weights from such pertinent data as exist. As for the manufacture index, the formula used is the arithmetic mean of relatives, the base date is 1899, and 1899 weights are employed.

Because of the predominant importance of steam railroads, we may very well give first attention to the derivation of a production index for the sub-group steam-railroad transportation. For the period beginning with 1890, we are able readily to secure basic data — on tonnage, ton-miles, passengers, passenger-miles — substantially complete as to coverage.[19] The situation with respect to obtainable fundamental material before 1890, however, is more difficult. As we go backward from that year, the proportionate coverage of the available "aggregate" series becomes progressively less. Quite clearly, the only satisfactory solution lies in the construction of new basic series, over the three decades prior to 1890, developed with special attention to homogeneity and representativeness of sampling.

The procedure for deriving such series involves, in the first place, the setting up of a suitable "sample list" of railroad systems. We carry out a careful study of the extensive data of the United States Census pertaining to these earlier decades. We make an especial effort to secure something approximating equal proportionate representation for various geographical sections. Specifically, we endeavor to secure a coverage of about fifty per cent for each geographical group of the 1880 Census. We attempt

---

[19] For these years, we make use of the series of *Poor's Manual of Railroads in the United States*, and of the Interstate Commerce Commission.

to obtain, at the same time, some approach to equitable distribution from the point of view of economic grouping.

With the establishment of the list of railroad systems, our work has barely begun. We must next perform the tedious task of searching through the various volumes of *Poor's Manual of Railroads in the United States*, the Census records, and the annual reports of individual roads. This work is rendered extremely intricate, as well as laborious, by the necessity for aiming at *actual*, as opposed to *formal*, homogeneity. The history of the roads — especially as to consolidations, acquisitions, extensions — must be studied with care. Constant vigilance must be exercised to avoid being led astray by the "surface appearance of things" in tabulations of figures. Methods of adjustment must be worked out for application to cases of perplexing breaks in material. The tasks is not merely to assemble arrays of items pertaining to corporations of particular name, but rather to assure *real continuity* with respect to certain *economic entities*.[20]

We thus build up four continuous annual series, pertaining to tonnage, ton-miles, passengers, and passenger-miles, respectively. These series are from practical necessity based upon data for the larger railroad systems. This fact naturally raises the question of sampling by size of road. Can the movements of these series be taken as representative of fluctuations in activity for the whole industry? Thoroughgoing examination into this question — referring to the year-to-year changes appearing in other series [21] which, though less homogeneous from the long-range point of view, are much more comprehensive, and include a very great many small railroads — yields an affirmative answer to this question.

Our series of aggregates would seem now to possess a high degree of homogeneity, but still another problem confronts us. A further possible source of error must be considered: granted that our picture may be an excellent one as regards the form of short-run movement, it may still give an incorrect impression in a respect which is decidedly vital. Quite possibly, that is, our series

---

[20] Cf. the work of Professor Arthur H. Cole, described in his article, "A Monthly Index of Railroad Earnings, 1866–1914," *Review of Economic Statistics*, xviii (February 1936), pp. 31–41.

[21] The series of *Poor's Manual of Railroads in the United States*, and of the United States Census.

may have a gradual bias over time: the proportionate size of the sample may exhibit progressive change, and our series may little by little drift away from a true representation. To avoid error from this source, we compare our annual series at certain points against comprehensive "cross-section" estimates, and make suitable corrections for "drifts" in the sampling proportion. We thus obtain our final series for use in the investigation of the volume of steam-railroad transportation.

Although we devote the major part of our attention to the steam railroads, we must also consider numerous questions and perplexities relating to the other series of the transportation and communication group — those pertaining to traffic other than steam railroad, to postal activity, to communication by telephone and telegraph. Limitation of space, however, makes it impossible to give in the present volume a discussion of these problems.

For transportation and communication, as for manufacture, it may be said that we have given extended attention to the theoretical and practical problems connected with the construction of the index number. And while, as before, there can be no thought of suggesting that the statistical measurements finally arrived at are from all points of view unimpeachable, nevertheless we may perhaps once more fairly claim a high degree of merit, relative to that which is practically possible — especially with regard to the qualities of continuity and comparability over time, so important for our present pattern investigation.

The newly-derived annual index of production for the transportation and communication group, 1860–1914, is presented on Chart 14.[22] Here, as for the manufacture index, estimated quarterly figures are shown for the period 1904–I to 1914–II. The method of derivation of these quarterly indexes is the same as that for manufacture, except that in the present case the short-run movements of quarterly railroad earnings adjusted for seasonal variation constitute the basis of the estimates.

### TRADE

For trade, as for manufacture and for transportation and communication, we shall here make no attempt to set forth any thor-

---

[22] The indexes for 1860–65 are not so reliable as those for subsequent years. The smooth, thin dotted line drawn through the curve, 1860–1914, should be ignored for the present.

oughgoing treatment of the issues and problems connected with the formation and critical evaluation of an index over our pre-war period of investigation. We shall restrict ourselves to brief consideration of certain points which are particularly significant for our special purpose of pattern analysis.

Over our time interval of study, 1866–1914, the only index which can be regarded as in any sense comprehensive with reference to the volume of trade is deflated bank clearings. We may turn attention at once to the series developed in the Federal Reserve Bank of New York under the direction of Mr. Carl Snyder. Mr. Snyder obtained this series by deflating annual "bank clearings outside New York City," employing his revised index of the general price level as a deflator.[23]

In considering the index of trade for the pre-war period afforded by this deflated-clearings series, the first question to come to mind relates to the deflating procedure. Inasmuch as the general validity of the statistical process of deflation, as well as its specific application to the particular case of bank transactions, has been critically examined by another writer,[24] we need not enter here into any extended discussion of the issues involved. Having in mind, however, that the *weighting* of the deflating index is in general held to be a matter of vital importance, we may undertake certain experimental calculations pertaining to such weighting for the series immediately at hand.

We note that Mr. Snyder's revised index of the general price level has six constituents, as follows: (1) wholesale prices, (2) cost of living, (3) wages, (4) security prices, (5) urban realty

---

[23] The "bank clearings outside New York City" cover, for the years 1880–1914, all reporting centers except New York City. The figures back of 1880 were estimated by Mr. Snyder, such estimates being based upon the year-to-year movements of the totals for six cities. The index of the general price level, used as a deflator, is a weighted average of six constituent groups, as is more fully set forth in the text below. This index, and the corresponding deflated-clearing series, constitute revisions of those originally presented by Mr. Snyder in his articles, "A New Index of the General Price Level," *Journal of the American Statistical Association*, XIX (June 1924), pp. 189–195; and "A New Clearings Index of Business for Fifty Years," *ibid*. (September 1924), pp. 329–335. The revised series were furnished to the present writer by Mr. H. V. Roelse of the Federal Reserve Bank of New York, who has also supplied detailed information regarding the make-up of the index of general price level.

[24] Professor W. L. Crum, in the article, "Deflated Dollar-Value Series as Measures of Business," presented by Professor Crum and Mr. Snyder in the *Review of Economic Statistics*, VIII (April 1926), pp. 85–100.

values, (6) rents. We may now ask ourselves the question, "To what extent is the weighting of these constituents crucial — crucial, that is, as regards the form of the final curve of deflated clearings?" Our experimental computations are designed to put this question to very severe test. We take each of the six constituents in turn, and use that constituent *alone* as the deflator. In other words, we assume successively six *very bad* weighting systems — assigning in each case, so to speak, to the particular constituent in question a weight of 100, and to all of the others a weight of zero.

The six "deflated" series resulting from these calculations, 1866–1914, together with the deflated clearings proper — that is, clearings deflated by the general price index — are shown on Chart 15, the curves being plotted with uniform logarithmic vertical scale. This graphic comparison indicates definitely that the six experimental series differ from one another, and from the Snyder series, mainly with respect to three characteristics: (1) the average rate of growth over the period; (2) the average rate of retardation in growth over the period; (3) the average amplitude of short-run fluctuation over the period.[25]

These experimental tests are cogent in their indications. However, they do not, of course, by any means dispose of all the difficulties connected with the statistical deflation of pre-war bank clearings. Certain questions still remain — e.g., as to the validity of the six constituent price index numbers themselves, considering each in turn; as to the divergencies over time in regards to "regi-

---

[25] See, again, fn. 19 in Chapter VII, for explanation of the reading of growth and retardation indications from original-item charts with logarithmic vertical scale.

The one anomalous case in Chart 15 is that of the series deflated by security prices, which exhibits, not retardation, but acceleration, in relative growth. Obviously, security prices, taken alone, would make a bad deflator for pre-war bank clearings outside New York City. However, the weight of security prices in the Snyder pre-war index of the general price level is comparatively small (less than 10 per cent) ; and the intrinsic importance of security sales, as opposed to ordinary business transactions, cannot at any time within our pre-war period of analysis have been high for bank clearings *outside* New York City. Furthermore, the fact that of the six experimental series, one (having a comparatively small weight) shows to a moderate extent the algebraically positive quality of acceleration in growth, as opposed to the algebraically negative quality of retardation exhibited in marked degree by the other five series, does not in any way effect the mathematical validity of the conclusions derived from the present piece of analysis.

It must be noted that for the series deflated by security prices, the short-run fluctuations, also, are somewhat out of line — particularly in the later years of the period (cf. the chart).

## CHART 15

### Snyder's Bank Clearings Outside New York City Deflated by Index of General Price Level, and by Various Other Price Indexes: by Years, 1866–1914 *

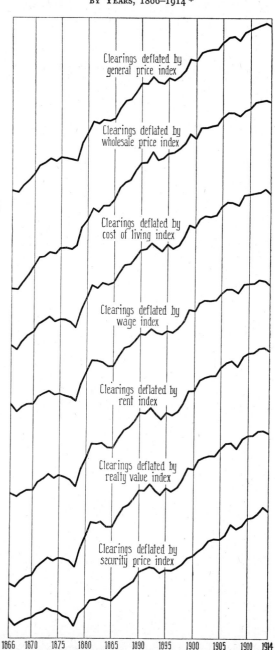

Clearings deflated by
general price index

Clearings deflated by
wholesale price index

Clearings deflated by
cost of living index

Clearings deflated by
wage index

Clearings deflated by
rent index

Clearings deflated by
realty value index

Clearings deflated by
security price index

1866  1870  1875  1880  1885  1890  1895  1900  1905  1910  1914

* Uniform logarithmic vertical scales.

men" versus "usage" in the weighting system; as to elements unrepresented in the deflating index.[26] We may perhaps fairly summarize our conclusions as follows: the test computations suggest (though they by no means fully prove) that for the particular case at hand, and *for the pre-war period 1866–1914*,[27] the limitations of the deflation process largely [28] exhaust themselves in affecting the average rate of growth, the average rate of retardation, and the average amplitude of fluctuation.

Even granting, however, the validity of the deflation process as applied in the present case, still other difficulties and perplexities remain. The series for "outside bank clearings" is certainly affected by the marked increase which took place over the pre-war years in the number of reporting centers. Furthermore, pre-war clearings — even for a series pertaining to a fixed list of cities — unquestionably are materially affected by the growth in the employment of checks (as opposed to paper and metallic money) for media of exchange.[29]

Any serious attempt at resolution of the issues involved in the range of questions just brought to attention must require certain intricate analyses, as well as judgments concerning particular matters of fact with reference to which the available evidence is far from satisfactory. It is not possible to undertake here anything in the nature of a thoroughgoing examination into these issues. We must content ourselves with a few simple, and by no means completely conclusive, statistical comparisons.

Let us now on Chart 14 — which, it will be remembered, is

[26] Cf. the article by Professor Crum to which reference is made in a preceding footnote.

[27] It is to be emphasized that our argument from the curves of Chart 15, and our present findings, are advanced for the *pre-war period 1866–1914* only. If we were to extend the period of reference to include the years subsequent to 1914, precision in weighting of constituents of the general price index would certainly become a matter of fundamental importance, and the argument set forth above, based upon the series of Chart 15, could no longer be sustained.

[28] The insertion of this qualifying adverb seems to be called for, in view of certain specific anomalies of behavior presented by the curve for the series as deflated by the general price index — e.g., in 1911 the curve does not drop below the average of the two adjacent years, while almost without exception other indicators of the volume of industrial and commercial production show a definite dip in that year (cf. Chart 14).

[29] A complete discussion would involve the consideration of still other points — e.g., the increase (sometimes interrupted by consolidations) in the number of banks attached to the several clearing-house associations.

drawn with uniform logarithmic vertical scales — compare the curve for the deflated-clearings series (captioned "trade" on the chart) with the curves pertaining to non-agricultural production. Without attempting anything more than a broad general appraisal, we may say that differences between the deflated-clearings curve and the non-agricultural production curves of Chart 14 appear (employing language used above in another connection) mainly with respect to three characteristics: (1) the average rate of growth over the period; (2) the average rate of retardation in growth over the period; (3) the average amplitude of short-run fluctuation over the period. With reference to the present comparisons, however, it must be emphasized that this summary conclusion is to be regarded only as a rough generalization. Even on the basis of the simple graphic comparison, we can discern at numerous points detailed variations in the behavior of the curves, and quite possibly more elaborate analysis would indicate further significant reservations to our broad general conclusions.[30]

Another point may at this juncture be considered parenthetically. The question naturally arises whether the series "total outside bank clearings," as reported in the original compilations, may not — on account of its rapidly changing composition, accompanying the growth throughout the pre-war years 1866–1914 in the number of reporting clearing-house centers — exhibit some heterogeneity over time as regards its *short-run* fluctuations. We may in this connection compare the "total outside bank clearings" with certain aggregate outside-clearings series based upon fixed lists of cities — e.g., the series for seven selected cities, 1875–1914, developed by the present writer some years ago;[31] or another set of totals more recently compiled for six cities, 1866–1914.[32] If we make such comparisons, we find that — though, as might be expected, divergence appears in long-run tendencies — there is close correspondence in short-time movements. Manifestly, then, the progressive change in the list of constituent cities has not essen-

---

[30] The judgments based upon examination of Chart 14, may (if we permit ourselves to anticipate some later work) be verified by examination of the link-relative curves of Chart 16, which by a different route lead to similar findings.

[31] See article by this writer: Edwin Frickey, "Bank Clearings Outside New York City, 1875–1914," *Review of Economic Statistics*, VII (October 1925), pp. 252–262.

[32] Cf. Appendix IV–A.

tially affected the comparability over time of *short-run* fluctuations for the series "total outside bank clearings."

In fine, then, we may say that we have attempted here no thoroughgoing or extensive examination into the validity of the deflated-clearings series. Such simple analyses as we have made, however, suggest (though, of course, they by no means completely demonstrate) that, *for the pre-war period 1866–1914*, such defects as are present largely exhaust themselves in affecting the average rate of growth, the average rate of retardation, and the average amplitude of short-run fluctuation exhibited by the series deflated by the index of general price level. As has already been indicated, this conclusion must be regarded as a broad generalization, presented subject to certain reservations which have been set forth above.

## OTHER GROUPS

We show indexes for certain other groups on Chart 14. The series for mining is the Day-Persons index.[33] The index for manufacture and mining combined has been computed by the present writer, averaging the Day-Persons indexes of manufacture and mining, with weights of 7 and 1, respectively.[34] The curve for forestry is based upon the United States Census series of total lumber produced;[35] figures are available for census years only prior to 1904. The series for agriculture (which embraces crops only) is the revised index developed by the Bureau of Agricultural Economics of the United States Department of Agriculture, and presented by Mr. C. M. Purves, in a publication of the Bureau.[36] We show also, for purposes of comparison with the various production indexes, a curve representing the growth of population, 1860–1914.

The two curves near the top of the chart, labelled "production index," and " 'check production index,' " respectively, will be discussed later in this chapter. The employment index (the first curve on the chart) will be described in the next chapter.

[33] See fn. 4 in this chapter.

[34] Cf. Persons, *Forecasting Business Cycles*, p. 174.

[35] See *A National Plan for American Forestry* (73d Congress, 1st session, Senate Document No. 12, Vol. I), pp. 247–248. [Report of the Forest Service of the Agricultural Department on the Forest Problem of the United States.]

[36] *The Agricultural Situation*, January 1, 1935, pp. 2–4.

Certain important economic groups are not represented on Chart 14. For construction, while several investigators have developed statistical measures of production in the sub-group urban building, no comprehensive index relating to the group as a whole is available over our period. As for "services production" (except as embraced within "transportation and communication" and "trade," already considered), there are, of course, no indexes, and indeed this field in general fails of coverage by usable basic statistical data.[37]

### The Link-Relative Patterns for Production-Group Index Numbers

We may now proceed to the derivation of link-relative patterns for the various production-group index numbers which we have calculated or collected, as follows:

> Manufacture (our new index)
> Manufacture (Day-Persons)
> Mining (Day-Persons)
> Manufacture and mining combined (Day-Persons)
> Transportation and communication (our new index)
> Trade (deflated "outside bank clearings")
> Forestry
> Agriculture (crops)

Since here we deal in each case with a single series, the procedure is very simple. We begin by taking link relatives for each of the indexes just listed. The period of the link relatives is 1867–1914,[38] except for forestry, where (owing to paucity of annual data) the link-relative computations are restricted to the interval 1905–14.

---

[37] For the fisheries group, a series of total yield of all fisheries is available beginning 1880, but since the data are "estimates based on intermittent statistical canvasses by regions" (Burns, *Production Trends*, p. 330), it does not seem that the series possesses sufficient continuity, especially with respect to short-run movements, to make its inclusion in the pattern analysis desirable.

[38] We follow, here and subsequently in this chapter, our usual convention for the dating of the link relatives: that is, we give each link relative the date of the *later* of the two years involved; thus, the link relative for $\dfrac{1867}{1866}$ is dated 1867, and so on.

## AMPLITUDE OF SHORT-RUN FLUCTUATION

We next obtain measures of the amplitude of short-run fluctuation for the link-relative series pertaining to the several production-group index numbers. We calculate, that is, for each such series the average deviation, over our period of analysis, of the link relatives. These average deviations are shown in Table 8.

TABLE 8

Production Indexes (Fixed-Base Approach)
Amplitude of Short-Run Fluctuation

(*Unit: one per cent*)

| Index | Average deviation of link relatives |
|---|---|
| Manufacture (our new index) ...................... | 6.17 |
| Manufacture (Day-Persons) ........................ | 7.05 |
| Mining (Day-Persons) ............................. | 5.82 |
| Manufacture and mining combined (Day-Persons) ..... | 6.79 |
| Transportation and communication (our new index) ... | 3.56 |
| Trade (deflated "outside bank clearings") ............ | 6.09 |
| Forestry ......................................... | 3.77* |
| Agriculture (crops) ................................ | 8.12 |
| Production index .................................. | 5.33 |
| "Check production index" .......................... | 5.57 |

* Based on data beginning with 1904, when annual figures are first available.

Following the calculation of the dispersion measures, we proceed to eliminate differences in amplitude of short-run fluctuation among the link-relative series for the several production-group index numbers, dividing each series through by its average deviation. The resulting series in average-deviation units are presented as the eight lower curves of Chart 16. (For the time being, the three upper curves of Chart 16 should be ignored. The thin downward-sloping or horizontal lines, drawn through the various curves, will be explained shortly.)

We may now examine and intercompare the curves for our eight groups, with reference to certain of their characteristics.

## AVERAGE RATE OF GROWTH

We begin this examination by deriving, for each of the eight production-group index numbers, measures of the average annual

# CHART 16

### Pattern of Production Indexes (Fixed-Base Approach) — Link Relatives in Average-Deviation Units: by Years, 1867–1914 *

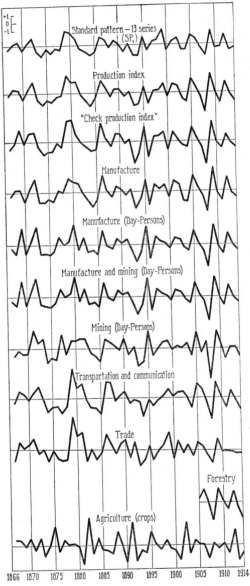

* Link-relative standard pattern for the thirteen important economic series ("SP₁" — cf. fn. 44 in Chapter VII) is shown at top of chart, for comparison. For explanation of captions, see the accompanying text.

rate of growth. These measures are presented in Table 9 (cf. also Chart 14).[39] We see that our new manufacture index (as indeed preliminary graphic inspection had already enabled us to discern) has an average annual rate of growth slightly less than that of the Day-Persons manufacture index. Our new index for transporta-

TABLE 9

PRODUCTION INDEXES (FIXED-BASE APPROACH)
AVERAGE ANNUAL RATE OF GROWTH

(*Unit: one per cent*)

| Index | Average annual rate of growth |
|---|---|
| Manufacture (our new index) ..................... | 4.8 |
| Manufacture (Day-Persons) ...................... | 5.1 |
| Mining (Day-Persons) ........................... | 7.3 |
| Manufacture and mining combined (Day-Persons) ..... | 5.3 |
| Transportation and communication (our new index) ... | 5.8 |
| Trade (deflated "outside bank clearings") ............ | 5.8 |
| Forestry ....................................... | −0.6* |
| Agriculture (crops) ............................. | 2.7 |
| Production index .............................. | 5.3 |
| "Check production index" ....................... | 5.5 |

* Based on data beginning with 1904, when annual figures are first available.

tion and communication exhibits very rapid growth, exceeded in this tabulation only by that of the Day-Persons mining index. Contrasting our results with those of Professor Burns,[40] we note that for each of the four cases where direct comparison is feasible — Day-Persons manufacture, mining, crops, and deflated clearings — the rates of growth shown in our Table 9 are appreciably greater than those listed in his table. This divergence in results is to be expected, however, taking into account that our measurements pertain to the pre-war period only (ending at 1914), while

[39] Of the two general lines of procedure for measuring average annual rate of growth and average annual rate of retardation described in fns. 35 and 38 of Chapter VII — (1) fitting of a straight line to the logarithms of the link relatives and observing its central ordinate and slope; and (2) cumulating the logarithms of the link relatives, fitting a parabola to the items of this cumulated series, and then observing the constants of its equation — we here employ the latter, more precise method. (For further statement, see the two footnotes just referred to.) As regards the graphic reading of growth and retardation, see fns. 19, 20, and 37 in Chapter VII.

[40] *Production Trends*, p. 263.

Professor Burns' calculation interval extends through the war and post-war years, to 1929 or 1930, and that in all four cases the index numbers are subject to retardation in rate of growth.[41]

We cannot undertake here any extended comment upon the results presented in Table 9. We must, however, enter one emphatic caveat: the reader should not suppose that these average annual rates of growth pertaining to the several *index numbers* can be taken as veritably representing the corresponding average annual rates of growth for the respective *economic entities* which the index numbers attempt to represent. On the contrary — quite aside from any question of technical (type and weight) bias — definite grounds exist for suspecting the presence of growth biases in the various indexes. These growth biases have their origin for the most part in the limitations of available production data; however, there are also certain *logical* issues which are involved in the question of growth bias.[42] It is not possible to discuss this topic further here.

### AVERAGE RATE OF RETARDATION

Most of the curves of Chart 16 give evidence of the presence of retardation in rate of growth for the corresponding index numbers, such evidence taking the form of a downward slope in the link-relative series. The retardation measures are presented in Table 10.[43] The indication of retardation in rate of growth for the index number — whether obtained from examination of Table 10, or from study of the slopes of the lines fitted to the link-relative series — is clear for agriculture (crops), trade (deflated clearings), Day-Persons mining, Day-Persons manufacture, and Day-Persons manufacture and mining combined. In the new index for transportation and communication only very slight retardation appears. For our new manufacture index there is no perceivable indication either of retardation or of acceleration over the period in rate of growth; we accordingly take the average rate of retardation as zero.

We may once more contrast our results with those of Professor

[41] It is true that our period begins four years earlier (1866 as contrasted with 1870), but this can hardly be an important factor in the comparison.

[42] See the article by the present writer to which reference is made in fn. 1 of this chapter. Cf. also Burns, *Production Trends*, pp. 258–259, 268–269.

[43] As to method, see fn. 38 in Chapter VII and the references therein contained. See also fn. 39, just above, in this chapter.

Burns.[44] There are, as previously, four cases where comparison is feasible — Day-Persons manufacture, mining, crops, and deflated clearings. For Day-Persons manufacture and for crops, the Burns retardation rates, pertaining to an interval ending in 1930,

TABLE 10

PRODUCTION INDEXES (FIXED-BASE APPROACH)
AVERAGE ANNUAL RATE OF RETARDATION

*(Unit: one per cent)*

| Index | Average annual rate of retardation |
|---|---|
| Manufacture (our new index) ...................... | 0.000 |
| Manufacture (Day-Persons) ........................ | 0.071 |
| Mining (Day-Persons) ............................. | 0.064 |
| Manufacture and mining combined (Day-Persons) ..... | 0.070 |
| Transportation and communication (our new index) ... | 0.015 |
| Trade (deflated "outside bank clearings") ............. | 0.096 |
| Forestry ......................................... | * |
| Agriculture (crops) ................................ | 0.108 |
| Production index .................................. | 0.007 |
| "Check production index" ......................... | 0.083 |

* Annual data inadequate for measurement.

are somewhat lower than ours, pertaining to an interval ending in 1914; [45] but it is probable that these differences in rates would largely disappear if Burns' calculation interval were extended to cover the decade of the nineteen-thirties. For mining, Burns' retardation rate is appreciably higher than ours — as indeed might be expected, in view of the rather abrupt slackening of the rate of advance in mining after 1914–17. Only the deflated-clearings series is really anomalous (possibly because of the limitations of the deflation process): here the discrepancy between Burns' rate and ours is very marked.

For the retardation measures, as for the measures of growth, it is not possible to enter here upon any extended discussion of the results. But, as before, we must set forth an emphatic caveat. With reference to retardation also, it is important to stress the distinction between statistical properties of the *index number* and those

[44] *Production Trends*, p. 274. Here, as in Chapter VII, we divide his figures by ten — to put them approximately upon an annual basis — and drop the minus signs.
[45] Here, as for growth, the fact that our period begins four years earlier (1866 as opposed to 1870) can hardly have any important bearing on the comparisons.

of the corresponding *economic entity*. Because of the deficiencies of available production data, as well as unavoidable logical limitations of methodology, these two retardations may diverge. Over our pre-war period of analysis, 1866–1914, it is practically certain that forestry and mining actually underwent retardation in rate of growth. Probably retardation also occurred in crop production. For the other groups, the matter is more doubtful. It is likely that the retardation for the trade index has its origin, very largely at least, in the method of derivation of the series. The slight suggestion of retardation for the transportation and communication index is of very uncertain significance. The indication of retardation for the Day-Persons manufacture index results, in a considerable degree at least, from certain technical factors involved in its construction; our new manufacture index, in which special effort is made so far as possible to obtain continuity, shows no indication at all of retardation. The precise conclusion for manufacture is uncertain, but retardation, if present over our pre-war period, could hardly have been great; it is indeed conceivable that for manufacture there was even some degree of acceleration in rate of growth.[46]

The smooth thin lines drawn through the various production link-relative curves of Chart 16 graphically represent the average rate of growth (the average level) and average rate of retardation (slope).[47]

### THE FORM OF SHORT-RUN FLUCTUATION

Assisted by the "growth-retardation lines," we are now able to compare the form of short-run fluctuation for the link-relative series pertaining to the several production-group index numbers (see Chart 16). We first observe that the pattern of short-time fluctuation for agriculture, here as in the link-relative approach, exhibits decided individuality of behavior; little resemblance ap-

---

[46] Compare the conclusions of Professor Burns in *Production Trends*, pp. 275–279.

[47] For purposes of graphing these lines, the successive ordinates have been reduced to average-deviation units through division by the respective average deviations of Table 8. For forestry, where the annual data are inadequate for measurement of retardation, we have simply drawn in a horizontal line, indicative of average rate of growth. (As to position of zero lines, see fn. 35, p. 162.)

Technically, because of the logarithmic method of derivation, the lines (unless horizontal) depart from strict rectilinearity, but this departure is in each case so slight as to be imperceptible on the chart and they may for practical purposes be thought of as straight lines.

pears between the curve for the agriculture group index on Chart 16 and those for the other group indexes.

Among the non-agricultural groups, however, we find that — setting aside differences in average rate of growth and average rate of retardation, and fixing attention upon the form of short-time fluctuation — the correspondence of the link-relative curves is in general very close. The curves for the two manufacture indexes, in spite of differences in method of construction, show notable approach to congruity. The curves for the indexes of mining and of transportation and communication are in general similar in movement to those for manufacture. The curve for the trade index correlates well with those for the non-agricultural groups, though possessed occasionally of individualistic irregularity. The curve for the forestry index, over its brief period, also conforms well.

### A New Index Number of Industrial and Commercial Production

The close correspondence in form of short-time fluctuation throughout the pre-war years 1866–1914 which appears among the curves for the non-agricultural production groups of Chart 16 indicates that we may quite properly speak in terms of a *general pattern* of short-run movement for industrial and commercial production over these years, and suggests that we should undertake the derivation of a suitable index number to represent the course of such production.

#### THE MODE OF ATTACK

It is immediately evident that for the period 1866–1914 we cannot hope to obtain the desired index number through the straightforward process of building up a composite by combination of series representing various components of this broad economic entity. The lacunae in the statistical material are too numerous and too serious to make this line of approach feasible.

We have resort, then, to a different mode of attack. We endeavor to find "points of observation," so to speak, upon which to stand and review the passage of economic activity. But, specifically, in applying this plan of procedure to our pre-war period of analysis, which of the available indicators of the course of production (discussed in the earlier part of this chapter) shall we choose? The answer seems clear: among the indexes previously considered, the most suitable for the ends now in view are the new index of manufacture and the new index of transportation and communication. These two indexes were constructed with special attention to the qualities of continuity and comparability over time — qualities highly important, as we have so often indicated, for the purposes of pattern analysis.

Furthermore, from the economic point of view the selection of the two fields — manufacture, and transportation and communication — appears appropriate with reference to the observation of the flow of industrial and commercial production. As regards manufacture, it is true that practically all the elements connected with industrial and commercial production pass through the manufacturing process, and so we are able to set up a "checking station" at this part of the economic system. The following remarks by Dr. Edmund E. Day — though made specifically with respect to the concept, "the national real income" — are pertinent here. "So far as the national real income is embodied in goods, the most important single barometer of changes in the size of the income is the physical volume of output in manufacture. This follows from the fact that the great bulk of modern articles of consumption pass at one stage or another through factory processes. Even our foodstuffs — our flour, meat, sugar, coffee — emerge in finished form from industrial plants. Only a few commodities — fresh vegetables and fruits, milk, household coal — are not regarded as in any way manufactured. The production of all others — the bulk of our food, our clothing, our shelter — involves manufacture." [48] Likewise, the formation of producers' capital goods is closely interconnected with the manufacturing process. It is also true that, by and large, the elements connected with industrial and commercial production pass through the nation's widespread system of transportation and communication, and consequently we are here again enabled to set up a "checking station" for observation of the flow of economic activity.

We make the new index, then, by averaging, yearly, 1860–1914, our indexes for manufacture and for transportation and communication, derived as described on preceding pages. Since,

---

[48] Edmund E. Day, "The Measurement of Variations in the National Real Income," *Quarterly Publication of the American Statistical Association*, xvii (March 1921), pp. 553–554.

all things considered, there seems little ground for discrimination between these two indexes with regard to intrinsic merit as indicators of the economic entity in which we are here interested, we assign them equal weight. For the purposes at hand, the choice of form of average is not of any essential importance. We select the geometric average, for the reason that we thus make it possible to simplify somewhat certain technical comparisons connected with measurements of relative growth and retardation (which are, of course, worked out on a geometrical-progression basis); however, had the arithmetic average been employed instead, the results — except for very slight alteration in the indicated rates of growth and retardation — would have been virtually the same.

### THE NEW INDEX AND ITS LINK-RELATIVE PATTERN

Our new annual index of industrial and commercial production, 1860–1914, is shown as the second curve on Chart 14.[49] Frequently hereafter we shall for the sake of brevity designate this series simply as "production index."

For the period 1889–I to 1914–II we show on Chart 14, in addition to the annual items of the production index, estimated quarterly items adjusted for seasonal variation. These quarterly estimates are obtained by superimposing, upon the annual production index, the form of *short-run* movement exhibited by our quarterly employment index adjusted for seasonal variation, with proper regard for differences in amplitude of fluctuation of the two series.[50] It is recognized, of course, that these quarterly figures for the production index must be regarded merely as approximations; there are many reasons (of which limitations of space forbid discussion here) for anticipating lack of full agreement between the short-run fluctuations of employment and production indexes. Nevertheless — taking into account the statistical comparisons to be presented in the next chapter, especially the very close correspondence between the *annual* link-relative patterns of the employment and production indexes — it is believed that the estimate afforded by the quarterly items for the production index, plotted on Chart 16, is reasonably dependable, at least for purposes of broad, general analysis.

---

[49] The indexes for 1860–65 are not so reliable as those for subsequent years. The smooth, thin dotted line drawn through the curve should be ignored for the present, as it does not enter the analysis until a much later stage.

[50] The employment index will be described in the next chapter.

Returning now to the annual production index, we apply the link-relative procedure to this series, the results being shown in Tables 8, 9, and 10, and in Chart 16. It will be seen that the production index exhibits a rather high average annual rate of growth (5.3 per cent), and a very slight average annual rate of retardation (0.007 per cent). In this connection, however, we must call attention to what is said above as to the contrast between growth and retardation in the *index number* and in the *economic entity*. We are not at liberty to assume that the rate of growth shown by our production index veritably represents that of industrial and commercial production. And the available evidence does not enable us to say that there was any retardation in rate of growth for industrial and commercial production over this pre-war period; it is quite conceivable that there was even some degree of acceleration.

The link-relative pattern for the production index (Chart 16) exhibits — as would be expected, in view of the correlations earlier observed in the array of curves of the chart — a high degree of similarity to the link-relative patterns of its two constituent series — manufacture, and transportation and communication — and generally close correspondence with the other non-agricultural patterns.

A CHAIN SERIES, WITH AVERAGE RATE OF GROWTH AND AVERAGE RATE OF RETARDATION ELIMINATED

In the course of deriving the link-relative pattern for the production index, we have found indication that such long-run tendencies as are present in this index over our pre-war period of analysis mainly exhaust themselves in a rather high average annual rate of growth, accompanied by very slight but nevertheless perceptible retardation in growth. The same statement can be made with reference to the two constituent series — the new index for manufacture, and the new index for transportation and communication — except that for the new manufacture index, as has already been indicated, there is no perceivable indication of either retardation or acceleration over the period in growth, and the average rate of retardation is, therefore, taken as zero.

These findings suggest that it may be of interest to set up, for the production index and also for each of its two constituents, a *chain series* with average rate of growth and average rate of retardation eliminated. Such series may readily be formed. In each case, we take deviations from the smooth "growth-retardation line" (cf. Chart 16). We then transform these deviations into a chain series by methods already familiar through our earlier work with the standard pattern for the thirteen series.[51] That is to say, we multiply each deviation, just obtained, by the pertinent dispersion measure (average deviation) and add 100 per cent; the resulting figures are then chained by successive multiplication (using 1866 as a preliminary arbitrary base). We thus obtain in preliminary form a chain series, capable of ready comparison with the original items of Chart 14. We here add one further step: we shift the base of the chain series, so that the average for the entire period 1866–1914 shall be 100 per cent.

The resulting chain series, with average rate of growth and average rate of retardation eliminated, are shown on Chart 17.[52] It will be seen that the three series now under consideration (cf. the first, third, and fourth curves on the chart) exhibit a high degree of correspondence in their form of fluctuation. In addition to the annual figures for the period 1866–1914, Chart 17 also presents quarterly figures (on a seasonally-corrected basis) for the production index, 1889–1 to 1914–11, and for the indexes of manufacture and of transportation and communication, respectively, 1904–1 to 1914–11; these quarterly figures are derived from the quarterly estimates for the several indexes, obtained as described on earlier pages.

### Comparisons with Results of Preceding Analyses

We may now revert to the link-relative patterns for production indexes, in order to make certain comparisons with the results of earlier analyses. We begin by bringing into conjunction (on Chart 18) the curves pertinent for a comparison of the link-relative patterns of the present chapter, resting upon *production indexes*, and those of the preceding chapter, derived from a study of the *structure of production*. Looking at Chart 18, we see for industrial and commercial production as a whole (the first two curves) a correspondence which is surprisingly close, especially in view of the differences in procedure, and to some extent in basic data, between the two cases. Generally high correlation, with

---

[51] See Chapter III, pp. 98–99, and Chapter IV, pp. 107, 111.

[52] The curve " 'check production index' " on Chart 17 will be explained later in this chapter; the curve for employment will be described in the next chapter.

CHART II

INDEXES OF PRODUCTION AND EMPLOYMENT,
WITH AVERAGE RATE OF GROWTH AND AVERAGE RATE OF RETARDATION ELIMINATED:
BY YEARS AND QUARTERS, 1866–1914 *

(*Average for 1866–1914 = 100*) †

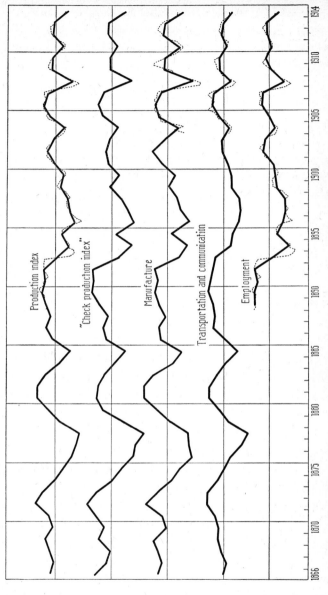

* Uniform logarithmic vertical scales. For the manufacture index and the employment index, the average rate of retardation is taken as zero. Quarterly figures are adjusted for seasonal variation.
† For employment, average for 1889–1914 = 100.

occasional detailed divergence, appears in each of the non-agricultural group comparisons. For the pair of curves pertaining to agriculture, only a fair correlation can be made out.[53]

We turn next to a comparison of the link-relative pattern for the production index, derived as previously described in this chapter, with the annual link-relative standard pattern for the thirteen important economic series, developed in Chapter IV. We show this latter link-relative pattern as the top curve of Chart 16; we present it, not upon a calendar-year basis, but upon the basis of years moved forward one quarter ("SP$_1$"), since in general this arrangement as to timing is best suited for comparison with the production-index curve.[54]

Examining carefully the first two curves of Chart 16, we see that — setting aside the manifestations of average rate of growth and average rate of retardation in the production index, as embodied in the thin downward-sloping line drawn through the second curve [55] — the correspondence between the link-relative patterns for the thirteen important economic series and for the production index, respectively, is most remarkable; the two curves trace out short-run fluctuations which are not far from being identical. This closeness of agreement is all the more impressive when we remember that the two patterns are based upon entirely distinct lists of series.[56]

## THE "CHECK PRODUCTION INDEX"

The notable correspondence just observed on Chart 16 between the curves for the standard pattern and the production index has one aspect which lays upon us a special obligation. The standard pattern was earlier constructed by the present writer. Then, when the subject of production index numbers was taken up, it seemed requisite that this same writer should develop a new measure of the course of industrial and commercial production. All this was,

---

[53] The curve on Chart 18 captioned "average of (a) transportation and communication, and (b) trade" is obtained by taking a simple arithmetic average of the link relatives in average-deviation units for the two constituent series.

[54] Cf., in Chapter VII, fn. 44 and the accompanying text discussion.

[55] The thin horizontal line drawn through the first curve represents simply the zero line of the standard pattern for thirteen series.

[56] The curve for the standard pattern also shows high correlation with the curves for the various non-agricultural group indexes on Chart 16, though here more differences in detail of movement appear.

# CHART 18

COMPARISON OF RESULTS, PATTERN OF PRODUCTION INDEXES (———)
AND PATTERN OF THE STRUCTURE OF PRODUCTION (═══) —
LINK RELATIVES IN AVERAGE-DEVIATION UNITS:
BY YEARS, 1867–1914

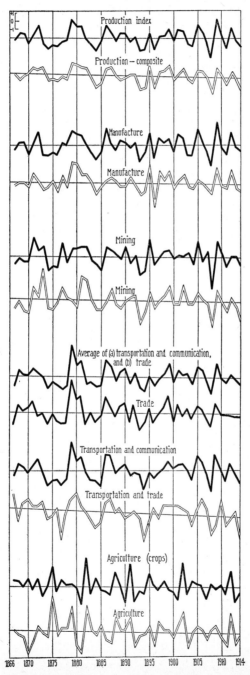

under the circumstances, quite unavoidable; but we are left in the position that the standard pattern and the production index have been constructed by the same person. This cannot help in some degree prejudicing the conclusions. In the production index, especially, the exercise of discretionary judgment has had repeatedly to enter: decisions have had to be made regarding a multitude of matters — the establishment of estimates where exact facts were unknown; the designation for inclusion, or the rejection, of particular series; the formal basis of weighting; the philosophy of imputation for missing elements; and so on. Here as in an earlier case (cf. the opening pages of Chapter VII) the investigator — even with the very best of intentions — might well, in the course of making a great range of discretionary judgments, altogether unconsciously impress into the somewhat plastic mass of material confronting him certain preconceptions as to what the results *ought* to show. Once more, in other words, we encounter the danger of a *methodology bias*.

It seems, therefore, in the highest degree desirable to set up for the production index some "*control*" series. More specifically, we wish to form a "check production index," based entirely upon indicators of the volume of industrial and commercial production which have been constructed independently by *other analysts*, such index to be used throughout the entire course of our investigation as a "control," as a check upon the validity of the various conclusions reached. We shall in this way guard against the possibility that we might be led astray through some unconscious "methodology bias" in the development of our own production index.

With respect to constituents for the proposed index, our survey, earlier in this chapter, of available long-range indicators of the course of industrial and commercial production over our pre-war period of analysis indicates two, and only two, possibilities: (1) the Day-Persons index for manufacture, and (2) the index of trade afforded by the Snyder deflated clearings. We form the "check production index," then, by striking unweighted averages by years of these two constituents, each being first shifted to the base 1899.[57]

We carry out for the "check production index" the various

---

[57] Cf. the discussion above of the construction of the production index itself. Here, as before, we employ the geometric average. For the period 1863–65, when

operations previously performed for the production index itself. The several statistical constants connected with the link-relative analysis are shown in Tables 8, 9, and 10. We see that the "check production index" exhibits an average annual rate of growth not greatly different from that of the production index (5.5 per cent, as compared with 5.3 per cent); the average annual retardation rate, however, is markedly higher (0.083 per cent, as contrasted with 0.007 per cent). This higher retardation rate for the "check production index" is doubtless to be accounted for by certain technical factors in its derivation.

We further see that — whether we compare the original items (Chart 14), or the link-relative patterns (Chart 16), or the chain series with average rate of growth and average rate of retardation eliminated (Chart 17) — the form of short-run movement for the "check production index" is closely similar to that for the production index, with only minor divergencies at particular points. It is clear that at least with respect to the conclusions of the present chapter we have, through the development of this "control" series, effectively guarded against the possibility of "methodology bias."

The results of the investigations described in this chapter give still further confirmation to the validity of the original standard pattern for the thirteen series, developed in Chapters III and IV, as an indicator of a general pattern of short-run fluctuation widely permeating the economic system of the United States over our selected pre-war time interval. *And these results further suggest that in the short-time movements of our index of industrial and commercial production we have a clear delineation of this general, pervasive pattern.*

---

the Snyder series is unavailable, we estimate the movement of the combined index on the basis of the year-to-year fluctuations of the other constituent.

# CHAPTER IX

## THE PATTERN OF EMPLOYMENT

IN THIS CHAPTER we supplement our examination of production statistics, described in Chapters VII and VIII, by a study of employment data. In two respects, however, the present analysis is more restricted than that just presented for manufacture. First, continuous usable employment data are obtainable only beginning with the year 1889. Secondly, while it is possible to secure a great mass of detailed figures pertaining to employment in individual industries over the years prior to 1914, the amount of labor required to put the data into shape for further use in analysis such as that of Chapter VII is so great as to be virtually prohibitive: it is impossible, therefore, to carry out for employment anything analogous to the study by the link-relative approach for production; we can here use only the fixed-base approach, involving the use of employment index numbers.

The investigations to be described in this chapter form a part of a larger study of the volume of pre-war employment which the present writer has conducted. This larger study constitutes the general subject of a monograph, which the author hopes to publish in the near future. Inasmuch as the publication of this monograph is contemplated, we shall here, as in the case of production, limit ourselves to summary statements regarding statistical procedure, shall refer only very briefly to the theoretical and practical issues which are involved, and shall confine ourselves in the presentation of results to those features which are particularly pertinent to the immediate task of pattern analysis.

We shall in this chapter deal mainly with employment in manufacture (the field where statistical data upon employment are relatively most abundant and most readily usable), with brief attention to other branches of economic activity.

### INDEXES FOR INDIVIDUAL STATES

#### ANNUAL INDEXES

Within the pre-war period 1866–1914, we find four states for which there are available data upon manufacturing employment

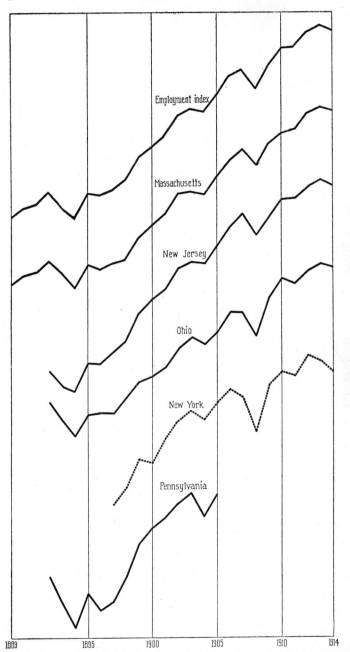

* Uniform logarithmic vertical scales. The series for New York is estimated by use of *unemployment* data.

sufficiently comprehensive and continuous to make possible the calculation of annual indexes. These states, and the periods of possible calculation, are as follows: Massachusetts, 1889–1914; New Jersey, 1892–1914; Ohio, 1892–1914; Pennsylvania, 1892–1905. Indexes for these four states are presented in Chart 19. The index for Massachusetts rests upon a series developed by Dr. William A. Berridge.[1] The index for New Jersey is that constructed by Professor Harry Jerome,[2] with slight revision, and extension back to 1892. The indexes for Ohio and Pennsylvania have been developed by the present writer, going to the original records of the respective state Bureaus of Statistics,[3] critically examining the data thus secured, and making extended calculations based upon them. The derivation of the Ohio index, in particular, was an extremely laborious task. So far as is known to the present writer, no analytical treatment upon any extended scale of the employment data for these two states over the years prior to 1914 has ever previously been carried out.[4] The basis for drawing conclusions regarding pre-war movements in the volume of employment has thus been appreciably broadened.

In addition to the four indexes based upon employment data, we show also on Chart 19 a curve (drawn as a dotted line to indicate that its statistical derivation is different from that of the others) relating to the state of New York, 1897–1914. This New York series has been estimated by use of *unemployment* figures of the Bureau of Statistics and the Industrial Commission of New York, together with data of the United States Census.

## QUARTERLY INDEXES

We show, on Chart 20, pre-war quarterly indexes based upon data for manufacturing employment. Here the situation as to available series is less satisfactory than in the annual case. The index for Massachusetts, to be sure, is obtainable upon a quarterly

---

[1] This series is taken by permission of Dr. Berridge from his "Employment and the Business Cycle" (1922), a thesis deposited in the Widener Library of Harvard University.

[2] See his *Migration and Business Cycles* (New York: National Bureau of Economic Research, Inc., 1926), pp. 73–74.

[3] For Ohio, the Bureau of Labor Statistics; for Pennsylvania, the Bureau of Industrial Statistics.

[4] The methods and results of the investigation into Ohio and Pennsylvania data will be presented in the later monograph to which reference is made above.

CHART 20

INDEXES OF EMPLOYMENT, ADJUSTED FOR SEASONAL VARIATION —
GENERAL INDEX, AND SERIES FOR INDIVIDUAL STATES:
BY QUARTERS, 1889–1914 *

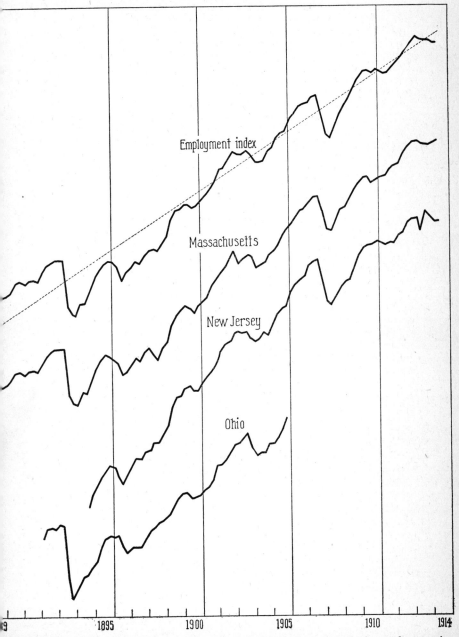

Employment index

Massachusetts

New Jersey

Ohio

99    1895    1900    1905    1910    1914

* Uniform logarithmic vertical scales.  The thin dotted line drawn through the employment in-
x will be explained in Chapter XV.

basis over the entire period 1889–1914. For New Jersey, quarterly figures can be developed from the middle of 1894 onward. For Ohio, quarterly figures can be secured only for the years 1892–1905. The Pennsylvania records give annual data only.

We take, then, the three available series,[5] compute seasonal indexes, and adjust for seasonal variation. The resulting quarterly adjusted series are presented as the lower three curves of Chart 20.[6]

We proceed now to pattern analysis for the annual index numbers pertaining to the five states — Massachusetts, New Jersey, Ohio, New York, and Pennsylvania — respectively. In each case, we compute the link relatives and reduce them to average-deviation units, obtaining the five link-relative patterns for individual states plotted on Chart 21. These link-relative series exhibit certain detailed differences in contour, but broadly indicate close correspondence of short-run movement.

### A New Index of Manufacturing Employment

The high correlation in form of short-time fluctuation which appears among the curves for state employment indexes in Chart 21 suggests that we should undertake the derivation of a general index of manufacturing employment for the years 1889–1914. We give attention first to the problem of constructing an *annual* index.

Care must be taken here if we are to preserve those qualities of continuity and comparability over time which are so important, especially with reference to our present purposes of pattern analysis. While the five state indexes show broad similarity as to form of short-run fluctuation, even cursory examination of Charts 19, 20, and 21 reveals that they exhibit divergence with respect to such fundamental properties as average amplitude of short-run fluctuation, average rate of growth, and average rate of retarda-

---

[5] For Massachusetts and New Jersey, we use series based upon the Berridge and Jerome figures, respectively; the Ohio series is that developed by the present writer.

[6] Charts 19 and 20 are each drawn with uniform logarithmic vertical scales. All series have been reduced to the base 1899. The top curve in each case (captioned "employment index") will be discussed shortly. For the series of Chart 20 it is possible to obtain monthly indexes also. These monthly indexes, together with corresponding measures of seasonal variation, will be presented in the later monograph upon pre-war employment.

## CHART 21

### THE PATTERN OF EMPLOYMENT INDEXES —
### LINK RELATIVES IN AVERAGE-DEVIATION UNITS:
### BY YEARS, 1890–1914

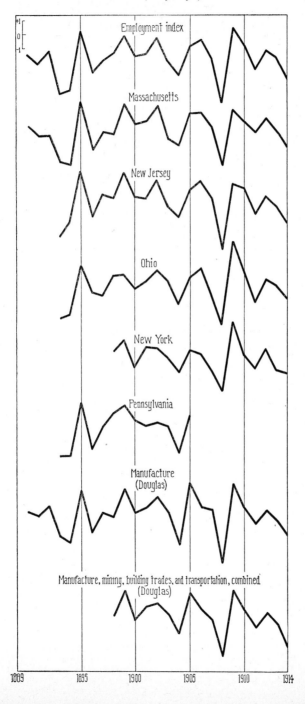

tion.[7] In view of this, it manifestly would be highly improper to form our general index by "splicing" together fragmentary sections with variable composition; such a procedure would be almost certain to result in distortion of long-run movement, as well as in lack of comparability over time in the amplitude of short-run fluctuation.

Taking these considerations into account, it seems best to base the general index, for the period 1892–1914, upon the series for the three states — Massachusetts, New Jersey, and Ohio — which furnish data continuously over the interval;[8] we reserve the Pennsylvania series (as well as the New York series estimated from *unemployment* data) for purposes of confirmation. For the three years 1889–91, it is necessary to base the movements of the general index upon the year-to-year fluctuations of the Massachusetts series alone. Even here, however, the important matter of long-run comparability is not forgotten: the extension of the index back to 1889 is not made by simple "splicing," but rather by a procedure which takes into account any important divergence, as regards certain fundamental properties enumerated just above, between the Massachusetts series and the average for three states.

Our new annual index of manufacturing employment, 1889–1914 — which, for the sake of brevity, will frequently be referred to hereafter simply as the "employment index" — is shown as the top curve of Chart 19. As will be seen, this index faithfully reflects the characteristics of its three constituent series, and the series for Pennsylvania and New York afford general confirmation as to form of short-run fluctuation.

We turn next to the problem of developing the *quarterly* index of manufacturing employment. Here, in view of the lacunae in our basic data, it appears best to utilize the items of the annual index already developed as a set of supporting columns, so to speak, to which the frailer quarterly measurements are attached. We obtain the quarterly index through superimposition, upon the annual index, of the form of short-run fluctuation indicated by the

---

[7] With respect to the reading of these properties of growth and retardation from charts with logarithmic vertical scale, see fn. 19 in Chapter VII. See also Table 4, and the accompanying text discussion.

[8] In view of the fact that the 1913 item for New Jersey is markedly affected by the great silk strike of that year, the 1912–13 and 1913–14 movements of the general index are estimated on the basis of the year-to-year fluctuations of the Massachusetts and Ohio data.

available quarterly constituents — more specifically, by the following quarterly items, seasonally adjusted in all cases: those for Massachusetts, 1889–I to 1891–IV; for the average of Massachusetts and Ohio, 1892–I to 1894–II; for the average of Massachusetts, New Jersey, and Ohio, 1894–III to 1905–IV; and for the average of Massachusetts and New Jersey, 1906–I to 1914–II (except in the year 1913, when the New Jersey series was severely disturbed by the great silk strike, and Massachusetts data alone are used).

Our new quarterly index of manufacturing employment adjusted for seasonal variation, 1889–I to 1914–II, is shown as the first curve of Chart 20.[9] This index, also, will often be referred to simply as the "employment index."

With respect to the new annual and monthly employment indexes, as with respect to the production index, there is no thought of suggesting that all difficulties have been overcome, or that we have obtained statistical measurements which are from all points of view unimpeachable. Once more we must point to the existence of certain theoretical problems which are logically unsurmountable, and of limitations of basic statistical data which are irremediable, even by the utmost ingenuity and effort. Here, as before, we must grant that to certain questions our statistical measurements can give no simple and direct answer (e.g., the question as to the average rate of growth over a given period). But, as previously, it would appear that we may fairly claim for our new index some degree of merit, relative to that which is practically possible — especially with regard to the qualities of continuity and comparability over time, so important for the progress of the present investigation of the pattern of movement inherent in economic data.

## THE LINK-RELATIVE PATTERN FOR THE NEW INDEX

We now apply the usual link-relative procedure to the annual employment index, the resulting series of link relatives in average-deviation units being shown at the top of Chart 21. The new employment index has an average annual rate of growth, over our period of analysis, of 3.81 per cent.[10] There is no clear indication

---

[9] The smooth, thin dotted line drawn through the curve should be ignored for the time being, since it does not enter the developments of this volume until a much later stage of the analysis (cf. Chapter XV).

[10] This figure was obtained through application to the logarithmically-plotted

of retardation (or of acceleration) in rate of growth, and the retardation rate, accordingly, is provisionally taken as zero.[11] We must, however, call attention here, as in the case of production, to the distinction between growth and retardation of the *index number* and the corresponding properties of the *economic entity*. We are not at liberty to assume that the situation as to long-run growth and retardation presented by our employment index over the prewar years 1889–1914 veritably represents that for commercial and industrial employment, or even that for employment in manufacturing industries alone. Our index is subject to various long-run biases, ascribable in part to limitations of sampling, in part to other causes.[12]

The link-relative pattern for the employment index (Chart 21) exhibits — as we should anticipate, in view of the correlations previously discovered — close similarity of movement with its three constituents (the series for Massachusetts, New Jersey, and Ohio), and also corresponds quite well, over the periods for which they are available, with the fragmentary series for Pennsylvania and New York.

At the bottom of Chart 21 we present link-relative patterns for two employment series derived from data developed by Professor Paul H. Douglas.[13] The first of these two link-relative patterns relates to Professor Douglas' totals for manufacturing employment, 1889–1914, and — setting aside certain minor divergencies — shows close correspondence of short-run fluctuation with the link-relative series of our own employment index. Especial interest, however, attaches to the second link-relative pattern curve

---

data of the "minimum-absolute-sum" criterion (cf. the discussion of this criterion in Chapter I, in the section entitled "A Problem in Statistical Description").

[11] This tentative conclusion is later confirmed by the analytical work of Part Three; cf., fn. 31 in Chapter XIII, fn. 27 in Chapter XIV, and fn. 2 in Chapter XV. (See, however, the next footnote in this chapter.)

[12] It is not possible, within the limits of the present volume, to enter into discussion of these biases. With respect to the "zero retardation rate" in our employment index, 1889–1914 — referred to just above — it should be borne in mind that the statement is set forth for this particular index number, with its particular implicit *sampling*. It is doubtful whether manufacturing employment for the United States as a whole exhibited constancy in rate of growth over the interval 1889–1914; the data of the United States Census upon manufacturing employment suggest that, for the period *1899–1914* at any rate, retardation in growth was present.

[13] The basic data are taken from his *Real Wages in the United States* (Boston and New York: Houghton Mifflin Co., 1930), pp. 440, 460.

based upon Douglas data, which is derived from Professor Douglas' figures on employment in manufacturing, transportation, building trades, and mining, combined, 1897–1914. The general similarity of this pattern to our own (compare the top and bottom curves of Chart 21) suggests that our series, though it relates specifically to manufacturing employment, may be taken as broadly denotative, so far as *short-run* fluctuations are concerned, for commercial and industrial employment as a whole.

### COMPARISONS

On Chart 14, in Chapter VIII, our new employment index is plotted in conjunction with the production index. It will be seen that the employment index differs from the production index in exhibiting a less rapid average rate of growth and in failing to present any clear indication, over the period, of retardation in growth. As to short-run fluctuations, however, the two series show marked similarity (compare the two annual indexes, 1889–1914),[14] though with some differences in amplitude of fluctuation.

On Chart 22, in the next chapter, the annual link-relative pattern for the employment index may be compared with corresponding patterns previously derived — the link-relative patterns for the thirteen important economic series (Chapters III and IV), for the structure of industrial and commercial production (Chapter VII), and for the production index (Chapter VIII).[15] The showing of the chart is so clear that comment is hardly necessary: the link-relative pattern for employment, over the twenty-five years for which the index is available, exhibits a remarkably high degree of correlation with the other patterns previously developed.

We may, finally, return to Chart 17, where certain *chain series*, adjusted for average rate of growth and average rate of retardation, are presented. Upon this chart we may compare the chain series for the employment and production indexes, respectively (cf. the top and bottom curves of the chart). The chain series for the employment index is analogous in its method of calculation to that for the production index; the employment index, however, is

---

[14] The *annual* items of the two series have been derived altogether independently; the movements of the *quarterly* items, however, are not independent, since the quarterly employment index is used in estimating the intra-yearly fluctuations of the production index (cf. p. 204.)

[15] The remaining series of Chart 22 — the link-relative pattern for wholesale commodity prices — will be discussed in the next chapter.

adjusted for average rate of growth only, since the average rate of retardation has provisionally been taken as zero.[16] On Chart 17, the close similarity between the configuration of short-run movement for the production and employment indexes, as revealed by the *annual* items, is even more clearly discernible than in Chart 14.[17]

The results of our various comparisons, just set forth, afford additional confirmation of the validity of the standard pattern for the thirteen series, developed in Chapters III and IV, and give added significance to the patterns of short-run fluctuation for the structure of production and for production indexes, respectively, which were derived in the two preceding chapters.

[16] Cf. pp. 219–220, just above, especially fns. 11 and 12.

[17] Cf. a preceding footnote with respect to the lack of independence between the intra-yearly (*quarterly*) fluctuations of the two indexes. As is there indicated, however, the *annual* indexes of production and employment are entirely independent in their derivation.

# CHAPTER X

## OTHER PATTERNS: COMMODITY-PRICE INDEXES; THE STRUCTURE OF COMMODITY PRICES; MISCELLANEOUS SERIES

### COMMODITY-PRICE INDEXES

THE SHORT-RUN movements of composite series for wholesale commodity prices — index numbers — show over the period 1866–1914 general conformity to the standard pattern for the thirteen important economic series, as well as to the patterns for production and employment which we have developed in previous chapters. This conformity is somewhat closer for the various "sensitive price indexes" — e.g., Warren M. Persons' "ten-commodity index," Joseph L. Snider's "cyclical index," Carl Snyder's "index for fourteen basic commodities," Bradstreet's index — than it is for those series which are more nearly capable of description as "indexes of the general wholesale price level."

When the link-relatives of the wholesale price indexes available over our period (adjusted for average level and for amplitude of short-run fluctuation according to the methods of Chapter IV) are compared graphically with the link-relative standard pattern for thirteen series, the impression, as has already been suggested, is of generally close correspondence (though with some irregularity as to timing). One significant difference does, however, appear: until about the middle of the eighteen-nineties the link-relative curves for the commodity-price indexes tend to move on a level somewhat lower than the link-relative pattern curve for the thirteen series; then a rather abrupt change takes place and thereafter, up to the end of our period of analysis, the opposite situation prevails. This fact may be brought out through contrast of the top and bottom curves of Chart 22, which compare (1) the annual link-relative standard pattern for thirteen series, and (2) a composite link-relative pattern for commodity-price indexes, derived by averaging the annual link relatives in average-deviation units for (a) wholesale commodity prices and (b) sensitive commodity prices.[1] The findings of graphic comparisons may be confirmed

[1] The link-relative series for the two constituents — wholesale commodity prices,

by formal calculations. For the earlier period 1867–96, the link-relative pattern pertaining to commodity-price indexes fluctuates on a level averaging one-quarter of a unit *lower* than the corresponding level for the standard pattern of the thirteen series; for the later period 1897–1914, the level of fluctuation for the commodity-price pattern averages two-fifths of a unit *higher* than that for the standard pattern of the thirteen series: there is thus a shift in comparative average level of fluctuation of the two series, as between the first and second time intervals, of almost two-thirds of a unit. These conclusions relating to *link-relative* series, arrived at by graphic comparisons and confirmed by formal calculations, suggest that the long-run tendencies of the *original items* for commodity-price indexes over the pre-war period 1866–1914 take the form of gradual drifts, first downward to the middle-nineties, then upward.

## The Structure of Commodity Prices

It manifestly would be highly desirable to make an extended investigation into the pattern (or patterns) of movement within the structure of commodity prices, comparable in scope with the extended study, presented in Chapter VII, previously carried out for the structure of production. (*And it would be desirable to relate these two studies rather intimately to each other, for thus we might have greater hope of reaching cogent conclusions.*)

No practical possibility appears, however, of including within the present investigation such a study of commodity-price structure. For our time period, the difficulties in the way of a thoroughgoing study of the pattern of structure in commodity prices are most decidedly greater than those involved in a corresponding study for volume of production. The difference in degree is so great as to constitute a difference in kind. The commodity-price data are not confined to annual series, wide in scope and already conveniently assembled, as is true in the main for the production case; on the contrary, it would be necessary — even after making all possible use of existing collections of basic commodity-price

---

and sensitive commodity prices — are developed in Chapter IV, and presented graphically on Chart 5. As is indicated in the text above, and easily apparent from examination of Chart 22, the timing-relationship between the link-relative curve pertaining to the thirteen series and that pertaining to commodity-price indexes is variable, but on the whole the concurrent correlation (using "SP₀") is definitely superior.

## CHART 22

### Comparison of Various Patterns of Short-Run Fluctuation in Economic Series — Link Relatives in Average-Deviation Units: by Years, 1867–1914 *

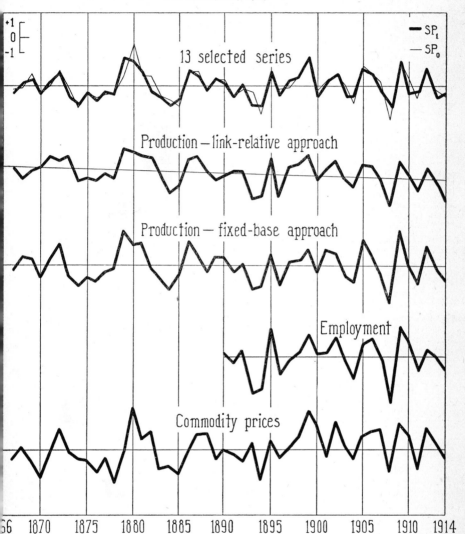

* All series are *link-relative* patterns. The curves captioned "13 selected series" pertain to the standard pattern for the thirteen important economic series, derived as described in Chapters III and IV — specifically, that developed on the "appropriate-lag" basis (for explanation of the symbols $SP_1$" and "$SP_0$" see fns. 43 and 44 in Chapter VII). The curve captioned "production — link-relative approach" is the pattern of short-run fluctuation in the structure of industrial and commercial production, derived as described in Chapter VII — specifically, the series "Composite I." The curve captioned "production — fixed-base approach" pertains to the production index of Chapter VIII. The curve captioned "employment" pertains to the employment index of Chapter IX. The curve captioned "commodity prices" is obtained as described in Chapter X.

material — to gather the prices for a number of series in daily, weekly, or monthly form; to work out for such series some process of averaging leading to (say) monthly and annual items; to perform for the array of available price series generally certain adjustments with a view to securing as high a degree of homogeneity as might be; to construct seasonal indexes for those series (by no means few) which possess seasonal movements; to compute seasonally-adjusted figures for such series. All of this would be required before the formal process of pattern analysis could even be inaugurated; indeed, to make a pattern investigation for the commodity-price structure would demand a large-scale statistical study in itself.

Though we cannot, therefore, undertake here an extended study of the commodity-price structure over the pre-war interval 1866–1914, it is possible to set forth certain broad conclusions suggested by graphic examination of a large number of individual price series.[2]

(1) If we were in fact to make a comprehensive pattern study for wholesale commodity prices over our period, the emerging pattern would be similar to those we have already derived for the thirteen important economic series and for production and employment.

(2) The pattern for commodity prices would not be so definitely delineated, however, as those for the other cases: more divergence would be apparent — more scatter in the multiple frequency tables, less clarity in the "zones of distribution."

(3) In such a commodity-price pattern study, the conformity to the general price pattern would be less good for commodities of agricultural origin than for commodities of non-agricultural origin.

(4) More individualistic or eccentric tendencies would appear for particular commodities or groups of commodities (even setting aside the field of agriculture) than in the production case.

(5) We should find — again in contrast to production series — numerous inflexible series, such inflexibility persisting for short or long periods.

(6) The commodity-price structure would exhibit less consistency with respect to timing — lags and leads — than we have discovered in the production structure.

(7) The commodity-price structure would reveal much less

[2] Cf. the conclusions for production series, in Chapter VII.

consistency over time in the "dispersion ratios" of short-time fluctuation (see, in the early pages of Chapter III, the discussion of "Absolute versus Relative Fluctuations") than was present for the thirteen series, for production, or for employment. What is had in mind here is that the individual commodities exhibit for prices, in contrast particularly with production, a considerable degree of capriciousness with respect to the relative intensity of short-time movements. A particular commodity may show, for example, a tremendous price swing in 1899–1901, or in 1910–12, and scarcely move at all in 1907–09, while the price swings of another commodity exhibit comparative amplitude movements more in accord with those of industrial production and trade. These inconsistencies, taken in conjunction with those noted above as regards timing, indicate that the impact of the forces of depression and recovery upon the price structure is far from consistent from one time interval to another. Evidently, some variation exists either in the forces themselves or in the routes along which they travel.

Our tentative conclusion, then, is that the general pattern of fluctuation in the commodity-price structure would — like the composite commodity-price index numbers referred to earlier in this chapter — give confirmation to the patterns already derived for the thirteen important economic series, for the structure of production, for production indexes, and for employment. It is certain, however, that there are divergencies and variations within the price structure which are highly significant and which deserve much more thoroughgoing study than we can give them here.

## Miscellaneous Series

There are a number of economic series which, on the one hand, do not measure up to the qualifications for admission to the standard pattern as set forth in Chapter III, and, on the other, do not fall in any of the categories — production, employment, commodity prices — previously treated. These are such series as, for example, Dun's and Bradstreet's number and liabilities of business failures, the number of shares traded on the New York stock exchange, numerous banking and money-market series, dividend payments. Graphic study of these miscellaneous series, either in their original form (adjusted for seasonal variation where required) or on the basis of link relatives, clearly indicates that the general tendency among them is to confirm the standard pattern for thirteen series and those other patterns which we have found to be closely correlated with the standard pattern. That is to say, if one were to make up a "special standard pattern" based upon these miscellaneous series, such special pattern would tend to move closely with the original standard pattern for the thirteen series, and the conformity of individual series, as indicated by the multiple frequency table and "partition values," would be almost equally good.

# CHAPTER XI

## CONCLUSIONS OF PART TWO

WE ARE NOW in a position to reëxamine the conclusions earlier reached as a result of the first section of our pattern analysis — relating to the basic group of thirteen important economic series, and set forth in Chapter VI — with a view to seeing what we have added to these conclusions.

(1) We have further applied our pattern analysis, extensively, to various bodies of statistical material pertaining to important phases of economic activity. Specifically, we have investigated the pattern of the structure of production within major production groups — manufacture, mining, transportation and trade, agriculture — as well as for industrial and commercial production generally (the link-relative approach, Chapter VII). We have also examined the pattern movements of production indexes for various major groups and for industrial and commercial production as a whole (the fixed-base approach, Chapter VIII). We have investigated the pattern of employment indexes (Chapter IX). We have considered the pattern movement for wholesale price indexes; and we have given some attention to the pattern of the commodity-price structure (Chapter X). Finally, we have studied a group of miscellaneous series, with a view to discerning their pattern tendencies (Chapter X).

The results of these various pattern analyses exhibited in general a high degree of similarity. In one important field, however, unmistakable divergence appeared. Production for the agriculture group, whether investigated by the fixed-base approach or the link-relative approach, was found to pursue an individualistic course.[1] The agricultural production patterns traced out short-time fluctuations bearing little resemblance to those for the other major production groups. The causal relationships between the agricultural and non-agricultural groups certainly did not express themselves in the form of any simple correlation.

---

[1] Agricultural prices should in all probability also be added to the list of non-conforming elements.

Setting aside the field of agriculture, which plainly presents a special case, the results of the various pattern analyses show most striking tendencies to correspondence in form of short-time fluctuation. The leading features of this correspondence are well brought out by Chart 22, in the preceding chapter, on which are assembled link-relative pattern curves for the thirteen important economic series, for the structure of industrial and commercial production (link-relative approach), for the index number of industrial and commercial production (fixed-based approach), for the index number of employment, and for a composite formed from index numbers of wholesale commodity prices.[2]

On the basis of the analytical work described in the four preceding chapters, we are able now to state in much broader terms than in Chapter VI our conclusion regarding the pattern of short-run movement. We are now able to assert that, *for the United States over the half-century from the close of the Civil War to the outbreak of the World War in 1914, there is a clearly-defined pattern of short-run fluctuation which permeates the whole structure of the nation's industrial and commercial life.*[3]

At the cost of repetition, we may call attention once more to the importance which attaches to the derivation of our standard pattern of short-run fluctuation — an importance greatly heightened by the demonstration of the widespread appearance of this pattern, as set forth in the preceding four chapters. The derivation of this pattern is significant, because it affords *analytical* demonstration of the presence in the economic life of the United States over our chosen time interval of a smooth, wave-like fluctuation of particular form. Once more, we point out that this pattern could not possibly, in any essential respect, have been created by the methodology. Our procedure has been simple, and has been checked at many stages to avoid "methodology bias." The results cannot represent the effects of question-begging assumptions impressed into the data. It has been shown, and it would seem

---

[2] A pattern curve for the "miscellaneous series" (Chapter X), if derived and added to the chart, would also show high correlation in form of short-run movement.

[3] Of course, "to permeate" should not be interpreted as signifying "to be universally present in totally unmodified form." We may anticipate, for example, that when at a later time we come to examine the production and price structures in still more detail, we shall find numerous deviations — cases of individualistic and eccentric behavior.

altogether cogently, that the movements pictured in our standard pattern are inherent in the statistical material and, more fundamentally, in the economic phenomena which these series represent.

This demonstration as to the existence of a pattern of short-run movement, pervasive within the geographical and temporal limits of the investigation, is further important because it furnishes, as will very soon become apparent, the *first foundation stone* for the analytical work of Part Three of this volume — the development of methodology for the statistical decomposition of our time series.

( 2 ) In Chapter VI we stated the conclusion, having in mind the standard pattern for the thirteen important economic series, that *within the limits of possible analysis set by the boundary lines of our half-century of time, we had thus far found analytical evidence of the presence of one, and only one, definite pattern of fluctuation.* We now should extend this conclusion to cover also various additional patterns (setting aside, however, the field of agriculture) — the production patterns by the two approaches, the pattern of employment indexes, the pattern of commodity-price indexes, and the pattern for miscellaneous series. Apparently, such divergence as appears for the patterns of non-agricultural production and employment, when contrasted with the basic standard pattern for the thirteen series, can mainly be accounted for in each case by a rather rapid average rate of growth, accompanied by moderate or negligible retardation, in production or employment.[4] There does not seem to be any room here for the appearance of a second, distinctive, pattern of fluctuation.[5] As regards the pattern of commodity prices, the situation is somewhat similar. To be sure, it is hardly appropriate in this connection to speak in terms of growth and retardation. But, as will be recalled,

[4] It is not implied that these long-run tendencies necessarily involve in any instance a *constant* rate of retardation in growth; whether or not that can be justly claimed remains to be seen. Here we assert only that the statistical evidence indicates that over our period of analysis the long-run tendencies for the production and employment patterns appear to involve either a constant (perhaps even zero) or a gradually-changing rate of retardation.

[5] It is, of course, quite conceivable that if we had the perspective afforded by a study based upon a longer time interval, say a century or more, we should see these long-range tendencies as part of a system of very long undulatory movements (e.g., "Kondratieff waves"). In fact, as we shall see when the appropriate statistical evidence is assembled in a later chapter, the results are at any rate consistent with such a hypothesis. For the present, it may be pointed out that the statement in the text above (as will be carefully noted) is made with references to *the limits of possible analysis set by the boundary lines of our fifty-year time interval.*

we found that divergence of the commodity-price pattern from the basic thirteen-series standard pattern took the form of substantially parallel movements in the link-relative chart, with a rather abrupt shift in comparative level of fluctuation just before the turn of the century (cf., in the preceding chapter, the second paragraph, and also Chart 22). Here again, there does not seem to be any opportunity for the emergence, within the limits of our chosen time interval, of any second, distinctive pattern of movement, in addition to the basic pattern already discovered.[6] And with respect to the group of "miscellaneous series" of Chapter X, careful study of these series suggests that if we were explicitly to carry through a complete pattern analysis for them, we should accomplish nothing more than essentially to duplicate the results of the study for the thirteen selected series.[7]

Definite importance attaches to the analytical work leading to the conclusion that, within the limits set by the temporal and geographical scope of the investigation, we have found analytical evidence of the presence of one, and only one, pattern of fluctuation in the fabric of the nation's industrial and commercial life. The performance of this work was an indispensable prerequisite, which had to be satisfied before we were at liberty to proceed with the task before us in Part Three of this volume — the setting up of methodology for the statistical decomposition of our time series. In fact, we are here dealing with the *second foundation stone* for this later methodological development.

[6] Once more, it is necessary to say that with a more extended temporal and geographical basis of investigation the long-run tendencies might quite conceivably turn out to be the manifestations of very long wave movements. Palpably, the long-run tendencies that we have observed — particularly the shift of mutual position in the link-relative chart just before the turn of the century — would fit into the Kondratieff system.

[7] We must be careful, of course, not to overstate the scope of the conclusion regarding the presence of one, and only one, definite pattern of fluctuation. It applies to the results (setting aside those pertaining to the agriculture group) of the various pattern studies which we have carried out — for the thirteen series, for production by the two approaches, for employment, for commodity prices, and for the "miscellaneous series." When we come to examine the economic structure more closely, we may very well find at particular points — as, say, for the prices or production of certain individual commodities — evidence of forms of fluctuation supplementing or superseding the basic standard pattern. For example, in one sub-group of the construction industry — the volume of urban building — the evidence is highly convincing (even making all allowance for limitations of statistical data and methods) that over a century at least clear wave-like movements have taken place of a sort quite different from those indicated by our standard pattern.

(3) It may be well to indicate, even again at the cost of a certain amount of repetition of expository material presented in Chapter VI, that — while our findings, and our observations upon the successive steps by which they were obtained, suggest most strongly that certain causal impulses operated very extensively, with a considerable approach to uniformity, upon the nation's economic system over the selected time interval — the conclusion is not inevitable that the results of the pattern analysis represent the effect of a *completely unified* set of causal forces. Conceivably, the general form of pattern movement which we have found so pervasive may be essentially [8] a *composite*, reflecting the joint effect of two or more sets of causal impulses, possibly somewhat related, but each possessing nevertheless its own individuality and its own theoretical counterpart.

(4) In the conclusions pertaining to the pattern study for the thirteen basic series, as set forth in Chapter VI, it was recited that definite statistical indication had been found (in the course of the extended investigation of link relatives of various periods) relating to the presence of some force, or complex of forces, of a comparatively long-run sort, which was steadily weakening the mutual attachment of the fluctuations of the constituent economic series, as link relatives of successively longer periods were brought into the analysis. We did not at that point attempt to inquire into the nature of this disjoining force or complex, or to decide what name should be given to its manifestations. We did, however, note that it was of decided importance to have established *analytically*, without the employment of any preliminary question-begging assumptions, *the presence, in our array of series, of certain long-run tendencies which were gradually over the course of time overcoming the cohesiveness of these series and driving them away from one another.*

We have since discovered additional evidence which broadens materially the scope of this significant conclusion. In the various production and employment patterns, we found clear indication of long-run tendencies of the sort we have been discussing; here the tendencies appeared to express themselves in terms of rather

---

[8] The qualifying word "essentially" is necessary here (as in Chapter VI), because of the complication that our various patterns contain in each case at least a "residuum" of long-time tendency, as is more fully set forth in subsequent paragraphs.

high average rates of growth, accompanied by moderate or negligible retardation. Again, in connection with wholesale commodity-price indexes we obtained suggestions of long-run tendencies which, so far as our simple tentative analysis enabled us to judge, took the form of gradual drifts in price movements, first downward to the middle-nineties, then upward.

All these various indications are definite, in the sense that the evidence for their reality is fairly conclusive. But the indications fail in clear delineation; they lack precision. One of the tasks lying immediately before us, as we prepare now to enter upon the work of Part Three of our general study, is to examine these tendencies and to invest their statistical measurement and representation with a much greater approach to clarity and exactitude. As we proceed with this task we shall quickly perceive that our preliminary findings regarding the presence of certain long-run tendencies in the data, set forth in earlier chapters and summarized in the preceding paragraphs, constitute the *third foundation stone* for the analytical work connected with the development of methodology for the statistical decomposition of our time series.

(5) After the completion of the pattern study for the thirteen important economic series, it was suggested (in Chapter VI) that while most certainly we had not yet accomplished the statistical decomposition of the various time series examined, the results nevertheless — even supposing that the statistical analysis was not to be extended to the development and utilization of more complex and powerful methods — could be of material assistance in dealing with the problems of time-series decomposition. It could even then fairly be claimed that our findings made possible the setting up of a method of attack which should at least have the merit of representing a unified and consistent theoretical interpretation of the general picture presented by the statistical array of results — a procedure far superior to that of studying the series one at a time — and, further, it could fairly be urged that, with reference to isolated problems involving time-series analysis, the standard pattern and the other results furnished a background against which to compare any particular material under examination, and thus enable the investigator to fit segments of statistical data, otherwise perhaps awkward to handle, into their proper places in the general scheme.

Now — inasmuch as we have broadened the scope of the array

of statistical results by bringing in curves and supplementary lines of general tendency pertaining to such fundamental aspects of economic activity as production, employment, and prices — we are in a position to make these claims *a fortiori*. But we shall not stand content with that which has been accomplished. We shall now proceed, in Part Three of our general study, with a more ambitious endeavor — an attempt to reach at least a good first approximation to the truth as regards the statistical decomposition of certain leading time series.

(6) However successful we may be in this undertaking, we shall still need to keep in mind that the complete solution of the problem of time-series analysis can never be attained by statistical procedure alone, no matter how extensive or ingenious. We shall be obliged in the end to call theoretical and historical investigation to our aid.

# PART THREE

## THE STATISTICAL DECOMPOSITION OF
## LEADING TIME SERIES

# CHAPTER XII

## AN INVESTIGATION INTO THE ESSENTIAL NATURE OF
## TIME–SERIES VARIATIONS

IN PART TWO of this volume we have studied a great body of material — the more significant series of economic statistics for the United States over our chosen period of analysis, 1866–1914. The work already performed has been prolonged and toilsome. Now we enter upon another long and tedious task, as we prepare to move toward more ambitious goals. And this task will be long and tedious precisely because of our very great anxiety to establish our conclusions *analytically*, step by step as we proceed. We shall endeavor to free ourselves from influence of preconceptions, to state no conclusion until cogent evidence for its acceptance has been developed.

Of the findings of Part Two, set forth in the preceding chapter, there are three which are (as was indicated) of fundamental importance with respect to the work now before us. (1) We established that for the United States over the pre-war interval 1866–1914 there was a clearly-defined pattern of short-run fluctuation permeating the whole structure of the nation's industrial and commercial life. (2) After an extended pattern investigation — into the structure of industrial and commercial production as well as production indexes for the major non-agricultural groups, into employment indexes, into the data on commodity prices, and into a group of miscellaneous series — we were able to find analytical evidence of the presence of one, and only one, such pattern of fluctuation. (3) We did, however, discover throughout all these various pattern investigations clear indication of the existence of long-run disjoining tendencies in our array of economic series, gradually over the course of time overcoming the cohesiveness which the general pervasiveness of the standard pattern of short-time fluctuation had given them, and driving them away from one another.

Once more, the indispensability of these basic conclusions must be emphasized. These findings form a necessary prerequisite for the development of the methodology which we shall set up as we undertake the task of decomposing our time series. As will readily be recognized in the course of our progress, the application of this methodology would be unjustified and clearly open to challenge if we lacked the foundation afforded by the findings of our earlier analyses.

## The First Step: The Study by Sub-Periods

We come now to take the first step in the direct attack upon the problem of the statistical decomposition of our time series. What body of statistical material shall we select for this purpose? Our minds naturally run first to the original standard pattern based upon the thirteen series, derived as described in Chapters III and IV. We next think of the several components of this pattern — all fundamental, important economic series, and for the most part showing close correspondence with one another and with the standard pattern in form of short-time movement. We recall, however, that there were three of the thirteen series (loans of New York banks, bond prices, exports) regarding which there was much less clarity than in the other ten cases as to the precise nature of the relationship; certain ambiguities appeared relating to the interpretation of the statistical evidence (e.g., the uncertainty whether these series logically should be thought of as leading or lagging the general movement). Inasmuch as we are now preparing to initiate analytical work of a sort which we have never previously undertaken (more specifically, we are preparing to attack by the genetic method, *ab initio*, the problem of explicit time-series decomposition) it seems decidedly wiser not to attempt to deal, in this pioneer endeavor, with the doubtful or ambiguous cases. Accordingly, we shall for the present eliminate from consideration the three series named, and give attention to the other ten. It may be pointed out in passing that in this, the first methodological decision of the new phase of our general investigation, we illustrate the statement just above that the findings of the preceding phase constitute an indispensable prerequisite for the new work. Without the conclusions of the earlier part of the study to guide us, the present decision to include certain series and to exclude others would appear to be founded upon caprice, rather than upon analysis.

As we scan the list of ten series which, together with the standard pattern itself, we have set down for inclusion in the present investigation, we see that these are indeed important series, all relating to significant manifestations of economic activity.[1] The list is not, of course, so extended as we should like to have it. Some of the deficiencies are irremediable, but two of the most serious lacunae we now can fill, one completely and the other in part. On the basis of extended investigations described in Chapters VIII and IX, respectively, we are able to add to the list our new production index for the entire period 1866–1914, and our new employment index for the interval 1889–1914.

The original standard pattern and the twelve individual series just selected — ten from the standard-pattern study, and the production and employment indexes — will constitute the basic statistical material for the initial investigation into the essential nature of time-series variations, upon which we now enter.

We know, as a result of the foundation work in Part Two, that elements of short-run and of long-run movement are present in our statistical series. But our knowledge as to the nature of these two types of elements, and especially as to the relationship between them, is very far indeed from being precise. We wish now to study the series more carefully, more in detail, from the point of view of this general question. It seems desirable, then, to break the interval 1866–1914 into sub-periods for intensive study. Numerous possible criteria might be adopted as a basis for setting up a schedule of such sub-periods. In order to make it wholly clear that the conclusions later to be reached are not dependent upon the selection of a particular criterion for the arrangement of sub-periods, we shall perform a number of experiments, employing in them, successively, various systems for subdividing the time interval 1866–1914.

Even though (as will shortly be shown) the choice of criterion for delimiting the sub-periods is in no sense determinative with respect to the broad conclusions presently to be drawn, it nevertheless seems desirable, in our initial experiment, to adopt a procedure which shall have as few elements of arbitrary choice as possible, and shall employ as logical a basis as is available — available, that is, taking into account the stage of progress, as regards definiteness of conclusions, to which our investigations

[1] Cf. the discussion of this point in the opening pages of Chapter III.

have so far carried us. As we look back over the earlier work, it appears that in the light of present knowledge the best guide for sub-period separation is that afforded by certain analysis which was incidentally applied, as described in the latter part of Chapter VIII, to the index of the physical volume of industrial and commercial production. Specifically, we presented on Chart 17 a chain series for this index with average rate of growth and average rate of retardation eliminated. Palpably, it would be quite improper, at this stage, to use the chain series for purposes of close reasoning or precise analysis; say, for example, to employ it as a basis for marking off the exact limiting dates between "areas of prosperity" and "areas of depression." [2] But the series will suffice for the general, preliminary study by sub-periods which we now propose to make — more especially since (as will later be demonstrated by numerous experiments) the criterion selected for marking off such sub-periods is not in any sense a decisive factor with respect to the broad conclusions which are finally drawn.

Looking now at this chain series for the production index, as shown by the first curve of Chart 17 (and taking into account also what we know of the movements of the index in the years immediately preceding 1866),[3] we can count seven distinct swings about the horizontal base line — that is, seven cases where the curve starts from a point below the base line, rises to a point above the base line, and then recedes to a point below the base line.[4] This reading is confirmed by the other curves of Chart 17: by the "check production index"; by the two constituents of the production index (the manufacture index, and the index for transportation and communication); and, over the years 1889–1914, by the employment index.[5]

[2] The tentative analysis in Chapter VIII suggested that the long-run tendencies of the production index expressed themselves over the period 1866–1914 mainly in terms of a rather high average annual rate of growth, together with very slight retardation. *But* there has as yet been no demonstration that it is proper to take this rate of retardation *as essentially constant* (and that, of course, is the implicit assumption involved in the derivation of the chain series for the production index, as presented on Chart 17).

[3] See Chart 14.

[4] The first such swing, 1862–78, is incomplete on Chart 17, but may be read off in full on Chart 14; the last swing, 1911–14, may be incomplete also in the sense that we do not know just how far the depression of 1914 would have gone had there been no World War.

[5] Suggestion might be made that in the selection of boundary dates for the sub-periods we should consider the possibility of taking, not the dates of the low

We proceed now to lay off such periods for our first experiment, as follows: (1) 1866–78, (2) 1878–85, (3) 1885–96, (4) 1896–1904, (5) 1904–08, (6) 1908–11, (7) 1911–14.[6]

We next locate the turning points of 1878, 1885, 1896, 1904, 1908, and 1911 more carefully, in terms of quarters of a year, using the quarterly estimates of the production index (supplemented by the standard pattern for thirteen series)[7] as a guide from 1889 on, and employing the standard pattern prior to 1889. These more carefully defined turning points are: 1878–II, 1885–III, 1896–III, 1904–III, 1908–II, 1911–III.[8]

Having located these turning points on the production-index curve of Chart 17 and on the standard pattern, we next mark off the corresponding points on the charts of quarterly original items for the various individual series entering the present analysis.[9] Here and there, a minor detailed question comes up as to the exact location of the "corresponding point," but in general the short-run configuration of the several series in the vicinity of a given turning point is so similar as to leave little doubt as to the proper selec-

---

points (or of the high points) for the wave-like swings, but rather certain intermediate dates, i.e., those at which some approach to "normal points" of general economic equilibrium might be expected to appear — cf. the discussion of Professor Joseph A. Schumpeter in his recent *Business Cycles* (New York and London: McGraw-Hill Book Company, Inc., 1939), pp. 70–71, 138, 156. It would seem, however, that at this stage of our genetic investigation we are debarred from the employment of this approach, for we can scarcely utilize it without essentially begging the basic questions which we have undertaken to study. We must accept a possible loss in logical preferability as to criterion for sub-period delimitation in order to avoid the charge of begging the question.

It appears capable of demonstration, however, that if — given proper directions for marking off the required "intermediate" points — we should apply such directions and carry through an investigation along the lines of that connected with Chart 23, but with the new boundary dates substituted, the conclusions suggested by Chart 23 would be wholly maintained.

[6] The first period is necessarily incomplete, since the standard pattern and certain of its constituents do not extend back of 1866.

[7] Specifically, the standard pattern (both annual and quarterly) used in the investigations of the present chapter is that developed on the "appropriate-lag" basis, as described in the later pages of Chapter IV, and presented in the first and fourth curves of Chart 32, in Chapter XIV.

[8] We here use the expression "turning point" to denote the low point *from* which the upturn takes place — e.g., in the first case the nadir is at 1878–II, and the advance therefrom begins in 1878–III.

[9] The series are adjusted for seasonal variation where such adjustment is required. As to original sources, etc., see Appendix III–A, except for outside clearings and railroad earnings (see Appendix XII–A), and production and employment (see Chapters VIII and IX, respectively).

tion. The few doubtful decisions made are in no way of importance as regards the final conclusions.

Our position now is this: one of the basic foundations for the present analysis is (as indicated in the preceding chapter) the finding that certain long-run tendencies are present in our assembly of fundamental statistical series, gradually over the course of time overcoming that cohesiveness which these series possess by virtue of the pervasiveness of the standard pattern, and driving the series away from one another; we wish, therefore, to make within each of the seven sub-periods an intensive investigation of the behavior of the array of twelve selected series. More specifically, we wish to study, in each sub-period, the form of short-run fluctuation for the series, and see as clearly as possible how that form is affected by the long-run tendencies earlier demonstrated to exist.

This statement of purpose suggests that attention first be given to amplitude of short-run fluctuation within each sub-period, for otherwise we cannot hope effectively to make comparisons among the several series with respect to *form* (as opposed to intensity) of short-run movement. In accordance with a general methodological decision, established after careful weighing of the possibilities at the very beginning of our study,[10] we employ the average deviation as the type of dispersion measure. But how shall we apply the average deviation to the present data? If we take deviations from a horizontal line for each series, we are exposing the dispersion measures to possible distortion by those long-run tendencies which our earlier analysis has demonstrated to be present in the array of series. If instead we take deviations in each case from a sloping or curved line, we shall be putting ourselves into the position of begging the very question which is under investigation. To meet these difficulties, a promising expedient suggests itself: to take the average deviation of the *link relatives*, which (especially over such short intervals as our sub-periods) is not open to significant distortion by gradual long-time tendencies. But here new dangers replace the old. If the period of the link relatives is too long, the number of items entering the sub-group dispersion analysis may become so small as to put in question the statistical significance of the result; if the period of

[10] Cf. Chapter III, in the section entitled "Adjustment for Variation in Amplitude."

the link relatives is too short, the calculated dispersion measures are subject to serious distortion by irregular fluctuations in the data. Taking all these considerations into account, the best working solution seems to be to apply the average deviation to the annual link relatives for the sub-periods up to 1904, and to the quarterly link relatives for the shorter swings occurring during 1904–14.[11]

Equipped with these dispersion measures, we are prepared to draw up, for each sub-period, a set of charts — one for the standard pattern, and one for each of the twelve individual series. For convenience, we draw the charts on separate slips of translucent paper. Since we are directing attention primarily toward the investigation of relative, rather than absolute, movements,[12] we draw the charts with logarithmic vertical scales. In order that we may be in position to make effective intercomparisons of short-run movements (as well as of possible disturbance of such movements by long-run tendencies), we, in drawing the charts for each sub-period, employ for the several series logarithmic scales inversely proportional to the dispersion measures, thus graphically eliminating differences in average intensity of short-run movement over the sub-period.

When these various charts are assembled by sub-periods, the most conspicuous feature which they exhibit (aside from the close general correspondence among the series in form of short-time movement, which of course is to be expected, in view of the results of our previous analyses) is the emergence within each sub-period of distinct differences among the series with respect to general direction of movement. In each sub-period something resembling a gradation appears, from series showing steep upward slopes to other series whose general tendency is roughly horizontal, and

---

[11] Experiment suggests that the indications of comparative intensity of short-run fluctuation among the series, yielded by use of annual and quarterly link relatives, respectively, are in general substantially the same.

Further, it is found that the use of the *average deviation of logarithms* (which, in the light of our emphasis on the logarithmic method of treatment, might seem more logical) would yield indications of comparative amplitude among the series almost precisely identical with those obtained through use of the simple average deviation.

[12] This is in accordance with a general methodological decision, made at the outset of our study, on the basis of an extended analytical investigation presented in Chapter III (see the section on "Absolute versus Relative Fluctuations," early in that chapter).

perhaps thence to still others that definitely track downward. This observation suggests that for each sub-period we arrange the curves in the order of their slopes, as discerned in the array of charts. Such arrangement can be made with sufficient accuracy for our purposes by simple inspection; formal computation is unnecessary.

One further adjustment seems desirable. We know from our preceding work as well as from even cursory examination of the present charts, that lags and leads appear among the short-time movements of the several series, and that these lags and leads exhibit some variability over time. We accordingly measure, in each of the sub-periods, the average lag (or lead) of each series, taking the production index as basic for the purpose and making the lag and lead measurements with reference to the link relatives.[13] We now make small adjustments, moving the series backward or forward sufficiently to compensate for the average lag or lead of the particular case. We must not, of course, impute too much significance or importance to lag and lead measurements for these relatively brief periods, but by this latest adjustment intercomparisons of series are slightly facilitated. The matter is in any case of no great consequence in the present connection, for the lags and leads are small (ordinarily not more than one or two quarters) and the adjustment of the series (or the failure to adjust) could not possibly affect any of the broad conclusions we shall later draw.

### The Fundamental Proposition

The various graphs, arranged and adjusted as above described, are shown in collected form on Chart 23.[14] Examination of this

---

[13] Over the interval during which the production index is available only annually, the testing for lags and leads is accomplished by contrasting various sets of annual totals (twelve-month totals ending with March, June, September, and December, respectively) for the given series with the calendar-year data of the production index.

Practically identical systems of lag and lead relationships are obtained, substituting the standard pattern for the production index as basic series. There is, however, an almost constant difference of one-quarter of a year in the two sets of results, consistent with the lag previously found (cf. Chapter VIII) between the short-run fluctuations of the production index and those of the standard pattern.

The "best lag" can almost always be readily determined by simple graphic inspection of the link-relative charts. Formal computation is resorted to in doubtful cases.

[14] The standard pattern appearing on Chart 23 is that developed on the "ap-

composite chart is extremely illuminating. We observe first of all the close correspondence among the series in general form of short-time fluctuation. To be sure, the various series have their individual peculiarities and irregularities, with some of which definite disturbing influences can readily be identified — e.g., the behavior of commercial-paper rates at times of economic crisis, as in 1873, 1884, 1890, 1893, 1907; or at times of diplomatic, political, or military disturbance, as in 1895, 1896, and 1898, respectively: or in merchandise imports just before and following important tariff changes, as in 1897.[15] But, setting aside these relatively minor and incidental features of the picture, the general impression is one of striking congruence in the contours of short-run movement.

This concurrence of fluctuation, remarkable though it be, is not the most striking feature of Chart 23. The outstanding characteristic of the chart, and the one having the most important implications, is the strong and ubiquitous tendency for the various curves, within each sub-period, *to drift apart from one another in a comparatively smooth and gradual way, the vertical differences among the curves exhibiting change in a fashion suggesting a high degree of systematic continuity.* This characteristic is clearly discernible upon scrutiny of the graphic picture afforded by Chart 23; within each sub-period a notable fan-like tendency is displayed in the structure of the series — the several curves by slow degrees diverge until the fan-like form of distribution has definitely appeared.

This striking characteristic of our group of series suggests the statement of a theorem which may very well become the Fundamental Proposition of our investigation into the essential nature of time-series variations. We may now state this proposition explicitly.

*For the array of leading economic series which enter our present analysis and over our selected time period, it is a good first approximation to the truth to say that the time-series variations (setting aside seasonal and irregular fluctuations) are resolvable into*

---

propriate-lag" basis, as described in Chapter IV. The dotted lines on Chart 23 labelled "Prod. devs." should be ignored for the present, since they do not enter the argument until a later stage.

[15] The arrow on the curve for imports in 1897 indicates the truncation of the sharp peak due to the tariff changes of that year.

CHART 23

ORIGINAL ITEMS (ADJUSTED FOR SEASONAL VARIATION WHERE NECESSARY)
FOR TWELVE INDIVIDUAL SERIES, AND FOR THE STANDARD PATTERN —
ADJUSTED FOR LAG AND DIFFERENCES IN AMPLITUDE, AND ARRANGED
BY SUB–PERIODS: QUARTERLY ITEMS, 1866–1914 *

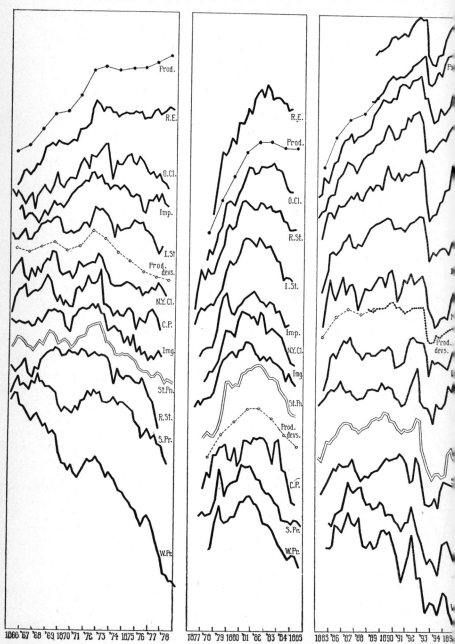

\* Logarithmic vertical scales. For explanation of arrangement, etc., see accompanying t
For key to captions, see opposite page.

CHART 23

ORIGINAL ITEMS (ADJUSTED FOR SEASONAL VARIATION WHERE NECESSARY)
FOR TWELVE INDIVIDUAL SERIES, AND FOR THE STANDARD PATTERN —
ADJUSTED FOR LAG AND DIFFERENCES IN AMPLITUDE, AND ARRANGED
BY SUB-PERIODS: QUARTERLY ITEMS, 1866–1914 (*Continued*)

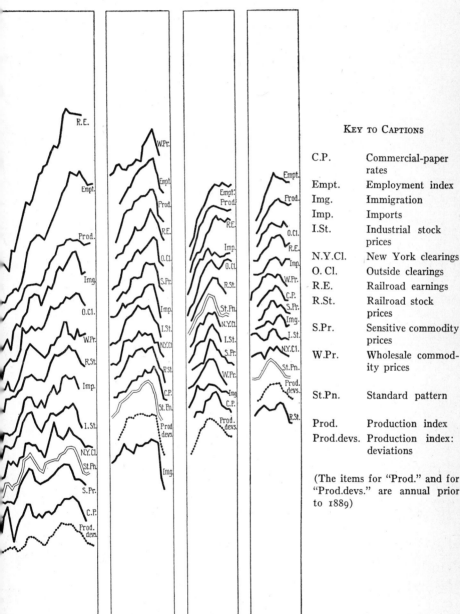

KEY TO CAPTIONS

| | |
|---|---|
| C.P. | Commercial-paper rates |
| Empt. | Employment index |
| Img. | Immigration |
| Imp. | Imports |
| I.St. | Industrial stock prices |
| N.Y.Cl. | New York clearings |
| O. Cl. | Outside clearings |
| R.E. | Railroad earnings |
| R.St. | Railroad stock prices |
| S.Pr. | Sensitive commodity prices |
| W.Pr. | Wholesale commodity prices |
| St.Pn. | Standard pattern |
| Prod. | Production index |
| Prod.devs. | Production index: deviations |

(The items for "Prod." and for
"Prod.devs." are annual prior
to 1889)

'97 '98 '99 1900 '01 '02 '03 '04    1904 '05 '06 '07 '08    1908 '09 1910 '11    1911 '12 '13 '14

*smooth, continuous, gradually-changing long-time movements* *which may appropriately be designated "secular trends," and* *wave-like short-time oscillations which may appropriately be desig-* *nated "cyclical variations"; and it is further a good first approxi-* *mation to assert that the relationship between these two types of* *variations is that of being logarithmically [16] additive.*

We speak of this as a *suggested* proposition, but why? In view of the striking and cogent evidence revealed by the system of logarithmic curves upon Chart 23, why be thus hesitant? Why not assert the proposition boldly, with entire confidence in its validity? The answer is that in two respects the demonstration lacks completeness, and until these two deficiencies in demonstration have been remedied we are not at liberty to regard the proposition as fully established. We consider these two deficiencies in turn.

In the first place, we have, to be sure, demonstrated smoothness and continuity of secular movements, but only *within* the sub-periods. For all that we have shown so far, there may be abrupt shifts in level of secular position at the termini of the sub-periods. There may be finite discontinuities, so to speak, in the course of these secular tendencies, as illustrated in the accompanying diagram (Sketch B).

This first deficiency in demonstration may readily be remedied. We do our experimental work over again, this time taking as boundary lines for the sub-periods, not the low points of the several swings of the production-index chain series of Chart 17, but instead the *high* points. If abrupt discontinuities of the sort we have just been considering are indeed present, we shall by this procedure quickly discover them. Carrying out this idea, we arrive finally at a chart corresponding to Chart 23, but with high points, rather than low points, taken as boundary dates for sub-periods.[17] This new chart completely confirms the conclusions of

[16] The reasons for expressing the proposition in terms of "logarithmically-additive," rather than merely "additive," relationships go back to the analytical investigations of the issue, "absolute versus relative fluctuations," described in Chapter III (see especially Chart 2).

[17] It is regretted that, because of considerations of expense, it has been impossible to reproduce this chart, or that on the more liberal "twelve sub-period" basis referred to just below. However, the reader may perhaps be able to infer the main features of these two charts from careful examination of Chart 1, or (later) Chart 34.

Chart 23; no evidence of abrupt discontinuity appears. The first methodological doubt connected with our fundamental proposition has thus been removed.[18]

The second deficiency in demonstration relates to a different matter. In making up our schedule of sub-periods we employed a

SKETCH B

ILLUSTRATION OF CONCEIVABLE TREND DISCONTINUITY

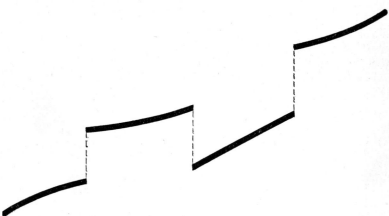

particular criterion. To be sure, effort was exerted to avoid arbitrariness and to make the selection on as logical a basis as the present stage of development in the investigation permitted. But the critical reader cannot fail to observe that, in spite of this laudable striving for objectivity in the choice of procedure, the *net effect* of the decision is to set up a list of sub-periods which is very much restricted — no interval of wave-movement can gain admission unless this movement takes place *around* the horizontal base line of Chart 17, and certain intervals which are commonly given independent treatment in statistical and economic literature (such as 1897–1900, for example) are here not accorded the dignity of individual representation. It seems desirable to check our conclusions by undertaking an experiment based upon a list of sub-periods not so severely restricted. Our need for a list of sub-periods established upon a more generous basis is most felicitously met by a schedule already available, drawn up after careful con-

---

[18] In the two following chapters, confirmatory evidence upon this matter will be presented.

sideration by an eminent investigator in the field of business
fluctuations — the "standard reference dates" prepared some years
ago by Professor Wesley C. Mitchell.[19] The part of the schedule
which is pertinent to our present purposes is shown in Table 11.

TABLE 11

STANDARD REFERENCE DATES, 1866–1914*

*(Taken from list arranged by Professor Wesley C. Mitchell)*

| Low | High |
|---|---|
| December 1867 | |
| | June 1869 |
| December 1870 | |
| | October 1873 |
| March 1879 | |
| | March 1882 |
| May 1885 | |
| | March 1887 |
| April 1888 | |
| | July 1890 |
| May 1891 | |
| | January 1893 |
| June 1894 | |
| | December 1895 |
| June 1897 | |
| | June 1899 |
| December 1900 | |
| | September 1902 |
| August 1904 | |
| | May 1907 |
| June 1908 | |
| | January 1910 |
| January 1912 | |
| | January 1913 |
| December 1914 | |

* For source, see accompanying text and footnote.

From this schedule, we obtain a new list containing twelve sub-
periods. This new list, constructed as it is on a decidedly more
liberal basis for admission of intervals of wave-like swing, is
admirably suited for contrast with our earlier, severely restricted
list.

We now apply our procedure to the new list of sub-periods, and

[19] Cf. the National Bureau of Economic Research's *Recent Economic Changes in
the United States* (New York and London: McGraw-Hill Book Company, Inc.,
1929), vol. II, p. 892.

we come out at the end of the analysis with a chart, similar to Chart 23, but broken into shorter time intervals. Examination of this chart completely substantiates the conclusions based upon Chart 23. And, if yet further confirmation is felt to be required, it may readily be obtained by trying out still different types of arrangements regarding the delimitation of sub-periods — e.g., taking intervals of fixed length, as five-year or ten-year periods. It is capable of demonstration, by tests as exhaustive as may be needed to produce complete and unqualified conviction, that our conclusions are not dependent upon, or resultant from, the choice of criterion for laying out sub-periods. The second of the two methodological doubts, consequently, is also removed.

The deficiencies in demonstration having thus been remedied, we may restate our Fundamental Proposition, now setting it forth without qualification.

*For the array of leading economic series which enter our present analysis and over our selected time period, it is a good first approximation to the truth to say that the time-series variations (setting aside seasonal and irregular fluctuations) are resolvable into smooth, continuous, gradually-changing long-time movements which may appropriately be designated "secular trends," and wave-like short-time oscillations which may appropriately be designated "cyclical variations"; and it is further a good first approximation to assert that the relationship between the two types of variations is that of being logarithmically additive.*

### Comments upon Fundamental Proposition

This statement of fundamental proposition calls for extended comment.

(1) There is, of course, nothing essentially new about the proposition itself. In a large part of the work which has been done in time-series decomposition, some proposition of this general nature has been implicit, even if not fully stated formally. The claim to novelty in our treatment rests not upon *statement* of the proposition but upon *demonstration* of it for an important range of data. Our contribution consists in transforming a postulate which is merely asserted into a theorem which has been established by cogent evidence with respect to at least a certain significant portion of the field of economic statistics.

(2) A word may now be said regarding the terms "secular trend" and "cyclical variations" themselves. From the time when (in Chapter III) we began the analytical work of the present volume up to now, we have avoided the use of these expressions, even at the cost of employing what may have appeared at times awkward circumlocution. This policy has been deliberate: as has earlier been set forth, in a statistical study of time-series variations which undertakes to proceed by the genetic method — *ab initio* — it is palpably improper to talk about "secular trends" and "cyclical variations" until it has been shown that such variations are inherent in the material and that the expressions are appropriate for the description of these variations. But now that this demonstration has been furnished (at any rate for a particular body of statistical material of substantial magnitude and considerable economic significance) we shall feel at liberty to employ the expressions more freely. In the interests of simplicity, we shall refrain from coining new expressions to denote the two types of variation just analytically shown to exist in our data, and shall rather utilize expressions already familiar. It is believed, however, that some contribution has now been made, and that before the conclusion of this volume is reached an appreciable further contribution will be made, to the definiteness of connotation of these terms.

(3) To avoid any possible misunderstanding, it must be said explicitly that the use of the expression "secular trend" is not to be construed as a denial of the possibility that these "trends" may be, in actuality, merely segments of very long wave movements, indicative of corresponding fluctuations in economic phenomena. Our position at present is simply this: within the limits set by the scope of our investigation, we are able to discern certain long-time tendencies which are capable of approximate description by smooth, gradually-changing lines, and we are therefore justified in going so far as definitely to attach to them the designation "secular trend." Quite possibly, further investigation with a broader temporal and geographical scope may show these trends to be parts of a system of long wave fluctuations extending over the centuries. Upon this question we are at this point obliged to take an agnostic position, for we have not as yet developed evidence sufficiently cogent to justify taking a stand.[20]

[20] Though we must call attention (as we have several times previously) to the

(4) As regards the term "cyclical variations," also, it is desirable to make certain explanatory statements with a view to avoiding possible misunderstanding. We have demonstrated the presence of a short-time wave-like form of fluctuation, systematically running through our body of statistical material, and we are therefore justified in going so far as to attach to these fluctuations the expression "cyclical variations." Now it is by no means inconceivable that a curve of "cyclical variation" is in fact intrinsically a *composite* — a composite embodying, let us say, for example, the combined effect of a "major-cycle" impulse and a "minor-cycle" impulse.[21] Here again, we are obliged for the time to take an agnostic position. We have so far found no analytical evidence in favor of the two-cycle (or multi-cycle) hypothesis; but, on the other hand, nothing in our results so far is definitively contradictory to such hypothesis. For the present, then, we shall speak of "*the* cyclical variation" of any particular series, without entering into the question whether such cyclical variation is essentially simple or compound.

(5) We may now pause to consider the *causal implications* of our fundamental proposition. Does the demonstration of this proposition indicate that we are dealing with two essentially distinct sets of causal influences — one set operating gradually over comparatively long periods of time and producing smooth long-time trends; the other set operating in a more rapid, oscillatory fashion and producing short-time wave-like fluctuations? Could we perhaps take a sheet of paper and list these sets of causal forces in two contrasting parallel columns? It is not likely that anyone would give unqualifiedly affirmative answers to these questions. But there may be those who, while not taking such position unconditionally, may nevertheless incline in that direction. Even those who have this leaning, however, would doubtless be willing to agree that the rate of change exhibited by the secular trend is, *to some extent at least*, a result of the presence of cyclical variations. And if, in sharp contrast to the preceding, one takes the view that the forces of progress which are inherent in the fluctuations of economic cycles are also primarily responsible for the emergence of secular trends, then clearly the neat simple notion

---

fact that the results so far obtained are at least consistent with the Kondratieff hypothesis.

[21] Cf. the corresponding discussion in Chapters VI and X.

of two essentially independent sets of causal influences, connected with secular and cyclical variations, respectively, must be abandoned.

In any event, then, it is clear that we should think here, not in terms of distinct sets of causal forces, but in terms of *lines of causal influence*. One might, for example, speaking very broadly and omitting qualifications, suggest that in the United States over the closing decades of the nineteenth century economic forces (working, to be sure, in the midst of a certain *environment* of other causal influences and of institutions) produced, in the physical volume of industrial and commercial production, short-time wave-like fluctuations of a particular contour, and at the same time a rapid sweeping upward movement; in wholesale commodity prices, much the same form of wave-like fluctuations as in production, and simultaneously a fairly strong downward drift; in commercial-paper rates, still once more essentially the same form of wave-like movement, and coincidentally a general trend which did not depart far from the horizontal.

(6) We come next to consider the implications of the statement that, for our given body of data, we can as a good first approximation assert that the relationship between the two types of variation — secular and cyclical — is essentially an additive one.[22]

In the first place, this clearly *is* a first approximation, and should not be taken as more than that. There is no desire to imply, for example, that a given set of causal impulses has affected during our period of investigation (or would affect at any particular stage of historical development) the *form*[23] of the curve of cyclical variation for, say, commercial-paper rates in exactly the same manner as the form of the curve of cyclical variation for, say, the physical volume of industrial and commercial production. We assert, merely as a *first approximation* to the truth, that within the geographical and temporal limits of our investigation a definite tendency toward such relationship has appeared, and we thus have some evidence which, combined with other suitable evidence and given proper theoretical consideration, may lead to the emergence of a generalization concerning the relationship and its significance. There is no thought of denying that, even within our

---

[22] Specifically, that of being logarithmically additive; cf. fn. 16 in this chapter.
[23] Setting aside, that is, the differences between the two series with respect to average amplitude of fluctuation and with respect to timing.

present body of material, divergencies from precise correspondence in general statistical relationship are continually appearing. On the contrary, opportunity is taken here expressly to urge that the investigation of such discrepancies and apparent anomalies (not only for the two series which happen to be named above for purposes of illustration, but for the wide array of available statistical material) is to the highest degree important; in fact, it may very well be that in an investigation of discrepancies and anomalies — which can be elaborated in various ways — we have a promising method of attack, enabling us to surprise economic forces in the course of their operation and to read much more clearly the implications of their statistical manifestations. And, finally, it may be suggested that a good first approximation not only has intrinsic usefulness, but also constitutes a prerequisite for the derivation of second and higher approximations; one must have a basis for comparison before one can successfully set out to discover and to interpret divergencies.

Let us make our example somewhat more complex. The statement, that as a first approximation the relationship between secular and cyclical variations in our series may be said to be logarithmically additive, is further not to be taken to imply a sympathetic view to such generalizations as, for example, that the relationships found between the cyclical variations of the volume of industrial production and commercial-paper rates in (let us say) an epoch during which industrial production has an accelerating rate of growth and interest rates have an upward-sloping secular trend must be supposed to persist in unmodified form into an epoch during which industrial production is experiencing severe retardation in its rate of growth and interest rates have a falling secular trend.[24] On the contrary, it is urged that here again we should anticipate finding discrepancies of behavior, and that the investigation of these discrepancies might be expected to constitute a fruitful line of research. And once more it is pointed out that good first approximations are valuable not only for their own sake, but

---

[24] Any more than (to turn to another phase of time-series decomposition) would the assertion, that for many statistical series it appears to be a good first approximation to consider the seasonal variation logarithmically additive with respect to the cyclical variations, imply that (for example) a given set of intra-yearly climatic conditions would exhibit exactly the same proportionate effects in a year of depression as in a year of prosperity. Deviations and discrepancies worthy of examination would appear here also.

also because they constitute a necessary foundation for more sophisticated analysis.

(7) We may, finally, give some attention to the *scope* of our fundamental proposition. To begin with, the conclusions summarized in this proposition rest upon a body of statistical data which is of substantial magnitude and of considerable economic significance. We have the standard pattern, based upon a group of important economic series and further confirmed as to its short-time fluctuations in a variety of ways, as set forth at length in Part Two. And, turning to those constituent series of the standard pattern which we have employed in the analyses of this chapter, we see that we have included statistical series relating to such important manifestations of general economic activity as the volume of clearance of business checks; the earnings of the leading section of the nation's transportation system, the steam railroads; the value of merchandise imports; the number of male immigrants; the prices of railroad and industrial stocks; the bank clearances in New York City, reflecting to a considerable extent (during this period at any rate) the volume of stock-exchange speculation; the movement of the general wholesale commodity-price level; the fluctuations in the average level of prices for commodities especially sensitive to changes in business conditions; and the interest rate in the New York commercial-paper market.

In addition to these series, taken over from the standard-pattern analysis, our present study also has as part of its basic material two widely comprehensive and fundamental series — our new index of industrial and commercial production (which is formed from two components, relating to the volume of manufacture, and of transportation and communication, respectively, and which is accompanied by way of confirmation by a "check production index," as previously set forth), and our new index of employment.

Though the statistical groundwork for the fundamental proposition is thus seen to be reasonably comprehensive within the limits of available data, with respect to leading, basic series, question still comes to mind regarding the possibility of extending the proposition to more detailed indicators of economic activity and relationships. In particular, there is the question whether it can be extended to the *individual series* which enter the production and price structures. Even though only preliminary, our previous investigations into these structures — with the discovery of the wide pervasiveness of the standard pattern of short-time fluctuation, apparently accompanied in general by fairly smooth long-run tendencies — offer strong suggestion that our fundamental proposition regarding the nature of time-series variations will hold for particular statistical series of this sort, over at least a part of each of these economic fields. And for most of the group of miscellaneous series discussed in the closing section of Chapter X, graphic examination gives rather definite indication that our fundamental theorem would be upheld almost as well by them as by the group considered in the present chapter.

Further, there is the question as to what we can say regarding those series which, while exhibiting some similarity of short-run fluctuation to that of the standard pattern, nevertheless fail to show simple and clear correspondence — such series as loans of New York banks, bond prices, and merchandise exports, mentioned earlier in this chapter. Sometimes careful economic analysis, or improvement of the series by eliminating defects in its statistical construction, may enable us to bring the series into the general standard-pattern scheme. But cases will remain where the failure to conform to the standard pattern is definitely intrinsic. With respect to these, the situation is more doubtful. We do observe, however, that such individualistic series seem to *mimic* the general style of behavior of those which are more nearly in accordance with the pattern; this observation gives some ground for supposing that the fluctuations of these individualistic series may conform to our fundamental proposition, though with cyclical movements of a different pattern, and possibly secular movements of a somewhat different sort, than appear in the body of more conventionally behaving series. But, for the present at least, our judgments about these individualistic series are more or less conjectural.

All things taken into account, consideration of the results of the preliminary studies described in Part Two of this volume, together with cursory examination of additional bodies of data not there treated, affords reason for suspecting that our fundamental proposition regarding the nature of time-series variations is capable of some extension beyond the territory claimed for it here in the explicit statement of the theorem — perhaps to other bodies of data, other countries, and other epochs. However, definite conclusions upon this point must await the carrying out of careful detailed studies.

In this chapter we have made an investigation into the essential nature of time-series variations. We have presented evidence that for the array of leading economic series shown on Chart 23 these variations, setting aside seasonal and irregular fluctuations, may be resolved into secular trends and cyclical fluctuations, related to each other in a particular fashion. In the next three chapters we shall move toward still more ambitious goals. We shall endeavor, for this group of series, to arrive at good first approximations to their statistical decomposition — the statistical separation, that is, of the secular and cyclical movements. We shall attack the problem by *two independent methods*, explicated in Chapters XIII and XIV, respectively.

# CHAPTER XIII

## THE FIRST METHOD: USE OF A PARTICULAR SERIES TO PRECIPITATE THE TREND–INDICATIONS

IN THE PRESENT CHAPTER we develop the first of the two independent methods for effecting the statistical decomposition of the group of leading economic time series treated in the preceding chapter (cf. Chart 23). This first method involves, as we shortly see more fully: (1) the selection, out of the group, of the one particular series for which the relationship between secular and cyclical variations is likely to be the simplest, and (2) the use of this series as a basis for precipitating the trend-indications of the other series.

### THE SELECTION OF THE BASIC SERIES FOR TREND-INDICATION ANALYSIS

We give attention now to the first of the two tasks just outlined. With the findings of Part Two and of the preceding chapter to assist us, we must select, from among the series of Chart 23, that one series for which the trend-cycle relationship is simplest, and easiest to represent in explicit statistical terms. Which of the series shall we choose?

The first possibility coming to mind is the original standard pattern for thirteen series, developed in Chapters III and IV. If, however, we go back and review the methodological decisions involved in its construction, as set forth on earlier pages, we are constrained to the view that this pattern, though affording an excellent picture so far as the contour of short-run fluctuation is concerned, in all probability lacks homogeneity as regards its long-time variations. That is to say, presumably this pattern is residually affected by heterogeneous elements in those long-time tendencies which we have already (cf. Chapter XII) demonstrated to exist for the individual constituent series — elements whose influence has been only incompletely removed by the simple adjustment for differences in average level of the link-relative series, made in the course of the original pattern analysis.[1] For our present purposes, then, we must reject the standard pattern.[2]

Setting aside the standard pattern, we have remaining the twelve individual series of Chart 23. How shall we choose among these? In the first place, we certainly want a series which is not from its very nature open to capriciousness in long-time variation; the adoption of this criterion immediately leads to the rejection of series largely dependent on speculative conditions, such as railroad and industrial stock prices, and (over our period at least) New York City bank clearings. Again, we want a series which has a broad scope with respect to *fields* of economic activity, for disturbance in some one economic field, or shift in economic activity from one field to another, may very well produce comparatively rapid and violent alteration in the form of long-time variation for the corresponding statistical series (perhaps even producing in a relatively short period a transition of secular movement to a new level); this criterion leads to the rejection of such series as merchandise imports and immigration. Further, though we do indeed want broad coverage from the point of view just indicated, we do not want a statistical series in which too many varying *aspects* of economic life are determinative, for this introduces the danger of heterogeneity in long-time tendencies; on such ground we reject the series outside clearings, merchandise imports, and railroad earnings — each of which is "compound," in the sense that it may be thought of as representing the product of a "physical-quantity factor" and a "price factor." Still further, we want a series which is free from frequent marked irregular fluctuations, for such fluctuations would destroy any possibility of precise measurement in our later steps; this criterion points to the elimination of the series for commercial-paper rates, which repeatedly exhibits sudden movements to extreme heights, sometimes connected with economic crises, sometimes related to diplomatic, political, or military disturbance.

These various deletions from the list of series leave us with

---

[1] See Chapter III, in the section entitled "Adjustment for Differences in Average Level." Conceivably, these long-time tendencies in the constituents may be bound together in some scheme of relationship which is at once so comprehensive and so simple that the elements should not deserve the adjective "heterogeneous." But this seems highly improbable, and at any rate we certainly have no right to assume it.

[2] [In the next chapter, however, we shall — employing a different mode of ap-

essentially two possibilities: (1) an index of commodity prices, either for the general wholesale price level or for sensitive wholesale prices; (2) the production index — i.e., our new index of the physical volume of industrial and commercial production.[3] We are, then, finally faced with the question whether it is in a wholesale price index or in the production index that we should expect to find the simpler relationship between secular and cyclical tendencies.

We may here very well turn to our accumulation of statistical evidence, as presented in Part Two. In the first place, our investigation of the structure of commodity prices over the pre-war years 1866–1914 suggests the presence (even after excluding agricultural prices) of a considerable degree of statistical heterogeneity in that structure, whereas in our extended study of the structure of production (again setting aside the field of agriculture) something much more nearly resembling unity makes its appearance.[4] In the second place, our link-relative analysis for commodity prices gave definite suggestion of lack of consistency in long-run movement; clear evidence appeared, it will be remembered, of a rather abrupt deflection just before the turn of the century (cf. the early pages of Chapter X, especially Chart 22). Our analysis for the production index, on the other hand, indicated a high degree of continuity in long-run tendencies; in fact, these tendencies expressed themselves mainly in a large average rate of growth, accompanied by very slight retardation.

This survey of the statistical evidence pertinent to the choice between a commodity-price index and the index of industrial and commercial production leads us, then, to prefer the latter. And so we have finally come to the selection of the production index as that series out of the array of Chart 23 which promises the simplest relationship between secular and cyclical variations. Our task is, however, far from complete. An entity may be entitled to the superlative degree of adjectival comparison without deserving

---

proach — find a way of using the standard pattern for purposes of trend-indication analysis.]

[3] We do not consider the employment index as a possibility, for the reason that this index (beginning in 1889) extends over only one-half of our period.

[4] Compare Chapters X and VII. We are here making a broad contrast between the two structures. To be sure, the price structure is by no means lacking in unifying elements, and the production structure contains numerous instances of individualistic or eccentric behavior. But in broad terms the contrast stands as valid.

the positive degree: the production index may very well be *the simplest* of the array of series from which it was selected — simplest, that is, as regards the relationship between secular and cyclical tendencies — without being in this respect *simple*. Obviously, we are under obligation to examine further into these tendencies.

## THE NATURE OF THE SECULAR MOVEMENT OF THE PRODUCTION INDEX

In investigating the secular movement of the production index we take as the starting point the fundamental proposition of the preceding chapter (arrived at after study of the data in such diagrams as Chart 23), which asserted that over our pre-war time interval and for a group of leading economic series — of which the production index was one — the time-series variations (seasonal and irregular fluctuations aside) were resolvable into smooth, continuous, gradually-changing long-time movements which might appropriately be designated "secular trends," and wave-like short-time oscillations which might appropriately be designated "cyclical variations." What now can we say as to the exact nature of the secular trend for the production index? What is the precise form of this "smooth, continuous, gradually-changing" secular movement which, on the basis of the analyses of the preceding chapter and of Part Two, we know to be present?

In the later sections of Chapter VIII, we reached the conclusions (1) that the short-time movements of the production index afford a very clear delineation of the contour of that general pattern of short-time fluctuation which we have found so widely pervasive throughout the economic structure, and (2) that the long-time tendencies of the production index seem very largely to exhaust themselves in a high annual average rate of growth, accompanied by very slight retardation in rate of growth. Reading these results in the light of the findings of the preceding chapter, the suggestion is palpable that we may, at least as a good tentative approximation, represent the secular trend of the production index over our pre-war time period by the logarithmic parabola

$$(\log y = a + bt + ct^2),$$

in which the notion of a fixed rate of retardation (or acceleration) in growth is implicit.[5] We did, in fact, carry out (see Chapter VIII, pages 205–206) a calculation which in effect implied a logarithmic-parabola secular trend, and we presented certain results (cf. the first line on Chart 17, page 207) whose derivation in effect amounted to elimination of such a secular trend.

While these results of Chapter VIII, interpreted in the light of the findings of Chapter XII, strongly suggest that the logarithmic parabola is appropriate as the trend-representation for our pre-war production index, there is nevertheless ground for at least one possible doubt: this doubt impinges upon the assumption, implicitly involved in the mathematical function, of a *constant* rate of retardation. This particular assumption, and its implications in the case of the production index, we must now examine with care.

## COMPARISON WITH FINDINGS OF EARLIER INVESTIGATION, RELATING TO INDIVIDUAL PRODUCTION SERIES

The necessity for examining this assumption impresses itself the more strongly upon us when we recall certain of our previous generalizations concerning the form of long-time movement for *individual production series*. It will be remembered that in the course of the investigation into the structure of production (as described in Chapter VII) we found through graphic examination of the various individual series that nearly all exhibited definite departure from a constant rate of growth. Most of the series, in fact, showed a high rate of retardation in growth. Specific evidence is afforded by Professor Burns' frequency chart of retardation rates for individual production series, which we here reproduce as our Chart 24.[6]

Further, we found unmistakable indication — through graphic and analytical study of the individual production series (Chapter VII, pages 146–151), supplemented by comparison of retardation

[5] For brief discussion of the properties of the logarithmic parabola, and a simple illustrative case, see pp. 144–146, in Chapter VII.

[6] For the original chart, see Arthur F. Burns, *Production Trends in the United States since 1870* (New York: National Bureau of Economic Research, Inc., 1934), p. 107. This chart is reproduced by permission of the National Bureau of Economic Research. Professor Burns' figures apply to a somewhat different time interval than ours, but this does not affect the broad conclusions we now draw. Professor Burns uses the *negative* sign to denote retardation. The notations at the foot of Chart 24, added by the present writer — "retardation rate of our production index" and "zero retardation rate" — will be discussed shortly.

# CHART 24

## Contrast between Retardation Rates for Individual Production Series, and Retardation Rate for the Production Index *

FREQUENCY DISTRIBUTION OF AVERAGE RATES
OF RETARDATION OF 142 PRODUCTION SERIES

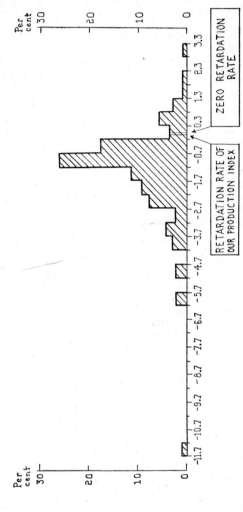

Average rate of retardation (per cent per decade)

* For explanation, see accompanying text.

rates for the two intervals 1866–1914 and 1870–1929 (Chapter VII, pages 165–166) — that in general the long-time tendencies of individual production series do not conform to the logarithmic parabola, i.e., that the assumption of a constant rate of retardation is in general untenable. Our analytical work with logarithmic differences of representative individual production series resulted, it will be recalled, in the definite emergence of curvilinear, rather than straight-line, tendencies in the long-run movements of the logarithmic first differences (cf. Chart 11, and the accompanying discussion).

A survey of individual production series, then, led to the conclusion that for a typical series the description of the long-time characteristics would run as follows: decided departure from a constant rate of growth, exhibiting itself in a high average retardation rate; and systematic variability over time with respect to the long-run tendencies of the retardation rate itself, evidenced by the results of such studies as have been described in Chapter VII. The widespread presence of such characteristics among individual production series points unquestionably to the general unsuitability of the logarithmic parabola for representation of the long-time movements of these series over extended intervals.

It is now altogether clear that if these typical characteristics of *individual production series* should appear in the *production index*, the use of the logarithmic parabola to represent its secular trend cannot possibly be defended. What is the reasonable expectation here? We may quite properly, of course, invoke the consideration that a broadly comprehensive index is likely to exhibit, in various senses, more stability than the individual series from which it is formed. This observation is not without weight, but obviously its mere citation cannot be taken as meeting the issue which has just been raised. After all, the real issue is whether those characteristics of typical individual production series, just set forth, which are destructive to the notion of a logarithmic parabola for secular-trend representation, are essentially present in the production index, even though perhaps with somewhat lessened intensity, or whether the differences in degree between individual production series and the production index are here sufficiently great to constitute in effect a difference in kind.

We turn at once, then, to investigation of this crucial question. And we begin by directing attention to the comparison of the average rate of retardation for the production index with corresponding rates for individual production series. Here the contrast is indeed striking. This is most forcefully brought out if we turn to the frequency distribution of average retardation rates for individual industries, just presented, and observe the narrowness of the space between the two thin vertical lines which have been superimposed upon the diagram (cf. our Chart 24) — one such line standing at "zero retardation" and the other standing at the retardation rate of the production index (0.07 per cent per decade) — as contrasted with the "spread" of the retardation rates for individual series.[7]   In fact, the retardation rate for the production index is by comparison so small that we are just barely able to make it visible upon the chart.  Here at least, there cannot be the slightest doubt that the difference in degree, between the production index and individual production series, *is* so great as to constitute a difference in kind.

The results of the comparison just presented unquestionably strengthen very materially the case for the use of the logarithmic parabola to represent the secular trend of the production index. The departure from constancy in long-run rate of growth is very slight for this index number.[8]   Further, it seems highly probable — taking into account that the total accumulated effect of retardation in growth for the production index over the whole pre-war period is so small (cf. Chart 14 in Chapter VIII) — that such *variations* as may have occurred over time in the rate of secular

[7] To be sure, the comparison is not precisely accurate, inasmuch as the retardation rate for the production index pertains to the pre-war period only (ending at 1914), while Professor Burns' rates for individual production series pertain to intervals running through the war and post-war years (up to 1929), and we have some evidence (see, in Chapter VII, the discussion of this point in sub-section entitled "Average rate of retardation") that retardation rates for individual series over the shorter period are in general somewhat lower than those for the longer interval. Quite possibly, this difference may affect somewhat the dispersion of the retardation rates for individual production series, but it cannot in any essential way affect the comparison drawn in the text above; even if we assume appreciable reduction in the dispersion of the frequency diagram for individual series, the sharp contrast with the production index remains.

[8] As has previously been suggested, it is very doubtful whether for the phenomenon itself there is any long-run retardation at all in the rate of growth (we may refer again to the contrast between retardation in the *index number* and retardation in the *phenomenon* which the index number attempts to represent). In fact, it will be remembered, for one of the two components of the production index — that is, the index of manufacturing production — no evidence of retardation in rate of growth could be discerned.

retardation have no significant effect upon the form of the trend line. However, in order to remove any remaining doubt, we proceed still further with our statistical tests: specifically, we shall test analytically the propriety of assuming *constancy* in the rate of retardation for the secular trend of the production index over our pre-war period.

We begin this new test by drawing up for the production index a pair of curves (Chart 25, Part A) which are cognate with those presented on a corresponding chart for typical individual production series in Chapter VII (Chart 11, Part A). Comparing the two charts, we see at once that they give essentially different indications regarding the behavior of the retardation rate. In decided contrast with the showing of the chart for the typical individual production series, there is in the chart for the production index no discernible tendency toward curvature in the long-run movements of the logarithmic first differences $(d')$.[9] This evidence of constancy in the secular rate of retardation serves further to reënforce the contrast between the production index and typical individual production series, and gives still additional confirmation as to the propriety of using the logarithmic parabola to represent the secular trend of the production index.

However, it may be felt that the work immediately under discussion rests upon a statistical basis which is not completely satisfactory. In particular, our attempts to reach a clear-cut judgment are interfered with by the wave-like fluctuations in the curve of logarithmic first differences for the production index (cf. Chart 25, Part A). May not these oscillatory movements conceivably operate to hide from casual inspection variable tendencies in the secular behavior of the retardation rate?

We proceed to further analysis in which, as will shortly be seen, we shall employ more delicate measuring instruments. And we take our point of departure here from these same wave-like fluctuations in the curve of logarithmic first differences. This curve is in effect nothing more than a graph of the link relatives plotted with logarithmic vertical scale;[10] and — since the movements of

---

[9] In fact, even the *straight-line* downward slope, indicative of the average rate of retardation, is barely perceptible. The equation of this straight line comes out $d' = 0.0225 - 0.000032\ t$ ($d'$ refers to logarithmic first differences, and $t$ represents time in years from the center of the period), reflecting an average annual rate of growth of 5.3 per cent, and an average annual rate of retardation of 0.007 per cent.

[10] The simple general mathematical point here involved may be illustrated by

# CHART 25

### LONG-RUN TENDENCIES OF THE PRODUCTION INDEX —
### COMPARISONS OF LOGARITHMIC DIFFERENCES:
### BASED UPON ANNUAL DATA, 1860–1914 *

*(In Part A, a straight line is fitted to the first differences, and for the second differences the horizontal line stands at zero: in Part B, the first differences are expressed as deviations from straight line, and the second differences are adjusted for amplitude and timing; the first differences are plotted below the second differences in such manner as to exhibit the close approach to parallelism between the two curves: in Parts C and D, the curves are adjusted for amplitude and timing)*

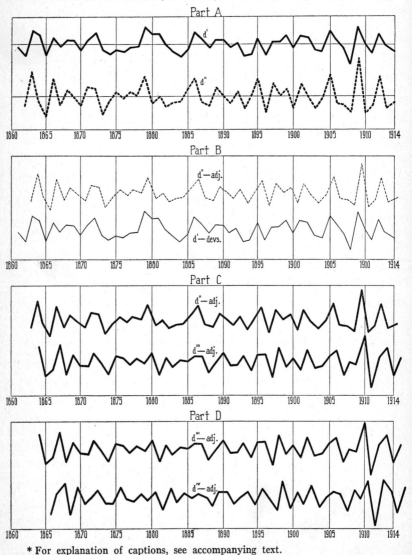

\* For explanation of captions, see accompanying text.

these link relatives are confined within a *very narrow* range upon
the logarithmic scale — this graph is for practical purposes virtually identical, as regards form of fluctuation over the period 1867–
1914, with the second curve of Chart 16 (page 197), which shows
for the production index the link relatives in average-deviation
units. The fluctuations of the link relatives of the production index
about their "line of average growth and retardation" are, then,
virtually the same in form whether we read from the arithmetic-
scale curve of Chart 16 or from the logarthmic curve of Chart 25,
Part A. Now, from our earlier investigations and comparisons we
know that these fluctuations are capable of description as constituting primarily and mainly a clear delineation of that general
pattern of *short-run* fluctuation which we have found to be so
widely pervasive in the economic structure of the United States
over our long pre-war period (cf. Chart 22). Still further, there
can be no doubt that it is this same general pattern of fluctuation,
observed in the *link relatives* on Chart 22 and upon various earlier
charts of Part Two, which manifests itself in the smooth, undulatory form of movement of the *original items* for leading economic
series, exhibited by Chart 23 — a form of movement which we, in
the course of the development of our fundamental proposition in
the preceding chapter, found it appropriate to designate by the
term "cyclical variations," in contrast with the other type of variation found in these series, to wit, secular trend. The outstanding
fact, then, about the wave-like fluctuations which we see in the
curve of logarithmic first differences of the production index
(Chart 25, Part A) is that these fluctuations are primarily and
mainly a manifestation of *cyclical* variation.

Granted that all of this is undeniably true, the possibility nevertheless still remains (as was suggested above) that the wave-like
fluctuations of the logarithmic first differences observed in Chart
25 may conceal from ordinary examination some systematic long-
time variation in the retardation rate. This possibility we must
now investigate. Our analytical procedure here will parallel that
earlier employed in connection with typical individual production
series, as described in Chapter VII (cf. pages 147–151, with which

---

reference to Table 4, of Chapter VII: in Table 4, if we transform the figures for
"annual ratio of growth" to percentages, through multiplication by 100, we have
the link relatives; and the figures for "first difference of logarithm" consequently
are logarithms of link relatives.

the ensuing discussion should be carefully compared, step by step).

Comparing the two curves of Chart 25, Part A, we note that here — as in the case of typical individual production series (cf. Chart 11, Part A) — there are oscillatory swings in the logarithmic second differences ($d''$) which have a contour rather similar to those in the logarithmic first differences, but exhibit systematic divergence as to timing. As in the earlier case, the short-run movements of the second differences precede those of the first differences by a time interval which may very roughly be described as one-quarter of the (variable) period of wave-like fluctuation in the first differences. And, once more, we find an analogy with the well-known relationship between the sine curve and its derivative.

Next, following the procedure previously employed for individual production series, we eliminate the average rate of growth and the average rate of retardation of the production index from the logarithmic first differences; we accomplish this by taking deviations from the straight line previously fitted to them (Chart 25, Part A), thus obtaining the lower curve of Chart 25, Part B, labelled "$d'$-devs." We now redraw the curve of second differences (see the upper curve of Chart 25, Part B, labelled "$d''$-adj.") making such change in vertical scale as to produce appropriate correspondence in average intensity of fluctuation with the new curve of first-difference deviations, and at the same time shifting the horizontal scale to accomplish proper compensation for the average difference in timing between the two curves.[11]

The results (Chart 25, Part B) are in very decided and striking contrast with those earlier obtained for typical individual production series (cf. Chart 11, Part B). In the earlier case, even after allowing for the fact that the timing lag was variable rather than constant, the two curves typically showed unmistakable departure from parallelism; the "band" between the two curves, as we passed in order of time across the chart, suffered gradual and systematic alteration — e.g., for the particular series of Chart 11, Part B, this band steadily widened over the first part of the period and then slowly narrowed — thus clearly demonstrating long-time variation in retardation rate. In sharp contrast, for the production index (once more bearing in mind that theoretically we should expect the lag to be somewhat variable) a very close

---

[11] As to the technical procedure, see the corresponding discussion in Chapter VII.

approach to parallelism between the two curves is maintained
throughout (cf. Chart 25, Part B), indicating virtual constancy
over the entire period in the rate of secular retardation. The
indications of this graphic comparison are unequivocal and unmistakable.[12] Once more, as between typical individual production series, upon the one hand, and the production index, upon the
other, the difference in degree is most emphatically a difference
in kind.

OTHER COMPARISONS

The findings of our analytical investigation of first and second
differences are so clear in their implications that it is perhaps
otiose to go on to comparisons involving higher orders of differences. With a view, however, to removing any possible doubt
which might impinge at this point, we carry out calculations —
with adjustments for timing and amplitude corresponding to those
described above — comparing the second and third logarithmic
differences of the production index (the two curves of Chart 25,
Part C), and the third and fourth logarithmic differences (the two
curves of Chart 25, Part D). The results, as will be seen, give
added confirmation to the previous conclusions.

Entirely as a digression, we may note that for the curves of
first and higher logarithmic differences, the "average period" of
wave-like swing comes out rather close to forty months. The
bearing of this upon the results of Professor W. L. Crum's peri-
odogram analysis for commercial-paper rates, and upon Mr.
Joseph Kitchin's conclusions regarding "minor cycles" averaging
forty months in length [13] — and, further, the bearing of the striking correlation between logarithmic differences of successive orders
— must, however, be postponed for consideration at some later
time.

Returning to the present main theme — the form of the pre-war
secular movement for the production index — we may seek cor-
roboration of our conclusions from a somewhat different point of

---

[12] For the mathematical basis of this analysis, and its application to production
data, see the corresponding discussion in Chapter VII.
[13] Both in the *Review of Economic Statistics*, v (January 1923), pp. 17–27, and
pp. 10–16, respectively.

view. We may apply the same process of analysis (involving the consideration of the average retardation rate and of first, second, and higher logarithmic differences) separately to each of the two constituents of the production index — i.e., to the manufacture index, and to the index for transportation and communication — and observe the results. We discover in each of the two cases a high degree of similarity, comparing with the findings of the analysis for the production index itself, as respects the general form of the graphical results obtained (setting aside systematic difference in amplitude of short-run fluctuation, which is to be expected, of course, in view of our earlier findings),[14] and also complete confirmation of the conclusions as to the secular constancy of the retardation rate. For the manufacture index, indeed, the situation is even simpler than for the production index itself, in that secular constancy is indicated not merely in the pre-war rate of retardation, but also in rate of *growth*.

### THE "CHECK PRODUCTION INDEX" AGAIN

There remains still a further point of view from which doubt concerning the essential validity of our conclusions may arise. In the course of certain discussions in the latter part of Chapter VIII,[15] attention was called to the facts that the present writer had been obliged to construct his own production index, and that this necessity had one unfortunate consequence: since in the construction of this index it was unavoidable that a great range of significant discretionary judgments should be made, the trustworthiness of the final results was to a certain degree prejudiced, in that even with the very best of intentions an analyst might, in the making of this range of judgments, unconsciously impress into the somewhat plastic mass of material confronting him certain preconceptions as to what his index *ought* to show. Briefly, there was danger of a *methodology bias*. As a safeguard against such bias, a "check production index" was set up, based upon production indicators which had been developed independently by *other investigators*. This "check production index" was indeed inferior to our own with respect to quality of basic material and technique of construction, but it had the one great virtue of being essentially *independent* in derivation, and hence was held to be suitable for

---

[14] Cf. Table 8, in Chapter VIII (p. 196).
[15] The section headed, "The 'Check Production Index.'"

use during the remainder of our general investigation as a safe-guard against "methodology bias" — as a "control," as a check from a certain point of view upon the validity of any conclusions we might later reach.

It is manifestly desirable to test for possible "methodology bias" the present conclusions regarding the nature of the pre-war secular movement of the production index. Accordingly, we put the "check production index" through the same analytical procedure as has been applied to our own production index, with quite simi-lar results. To be sure, the average rate of retardation for the "check production index" is appreciably larger than that for the production index itself, but even this larger rate is moderate as compared with those for most individual production series; and, in any case, it is primarily not the *average* magnitude of the re-tardation rate, but rather its *constancy over time*, which is signifi-cant for our present problem.

### CONCLUSION AS TO SECULAR TREND OF PRODUCTION INDEX

We began this line of inquiry by asking with reference to the production index the question, "What is the precise form of this 'smooth, continuous, gradually-changing' secular movement which, on the basis of the analyses of the preceding chapter and of Part Two, we know to be present?" Through the analytical work described in this section, we have arrived at an answer which may be set forth with some assurance: the secular trend of the produc-tion index over our pre-war period (i.e., up to 1914) can be represented with reasonably close approach to precision by a logarithmic parabola of such form as to indicate a rather high average rate of secular growth (5.3 per cent per year) accom-panied by very slight retardation (0.007 per cent per year) in such growth.

It is desired to emphasize that the choice of the logarithmic parabola for trend-representation here is *not* based merely upon comparisons of certain sets of curves for various orders of logarith-mic differences. Such comparisons indeed have an important rôle to play in the discussion, but if the basis comprised no more than this, the reasoning of this section would be intrinsically unsound; the argument, however, rests upon a much broader foundation. The findings of the earlier part of this volume, as summarized in Chapter XI, and the conclusions of the immediately preceding chapter as concisely suggested by Chart 23 and epitomized in the fundamental proposition, are essentially involved.[16]

We now proceed to fit the logarithmic parabola to the production index, to each of its two constituents — the manufacture index,[17] and the index of transportation and communication — and to the "check production index." These trend lines, just derived, have been plotted, in conjunction with the various series, upon Chart 14 (opposite page 180); also shown on Chart 14 are logarithmic parabolas fitted to the Day-Persons indexes for manufacture and for manufacture and mining combined.

We have now reached the point where we may think of the various production curves of Chart 17 (page 207), earlier obtained by a process which in effect amounted to elimination of logarithmic-parabola secular trends, as representing with a reasonably high degree of accuracy the *cyclical variations* of the several series. For the production index, these cyclical variations have been plotted by sub-periods upon Chart 23,[18] in order to facilitate comparison with the other series.

## "Laws of Growth" and "Growth Curves"

### is there a logarithmic-parabola "law of growth"?

But can we perhaps make a very broad generalization based upon the finding that the secular trend of our production index over the pre-war period ending with 1914 is well represented by a logarithmic parabola of such form as to indicate a rather high average rate of growth accompanied by slight retardation? Are we not of necessity led to the conclusion that there are in modern industry inherent forces which make for a nearly uniform rate of growth over long epochs? Must we not infer that there is a logarithmic-parabola "law of growth" which the course of industrial production is constrained to obey?

---

[16] [The conclusion of this section — that the secular trend of the production index can be suitably represented with rather close approach to precision by the logarithmic parabola — will be reached in the next chapter, independently, through analytical procedure following a quite different route.]

[17] For the manufacture index, the retardation constant comes out almost precisely zero, and is accordingly neglected; the logarithmic parabola in this case, then, degenerates into a compound-interest curve.

[18] See the lines upon the chart captioned "Prod. devs." — signifying deviations from secular trend of the production index.

The answer is definitely in the negative: we are led to no such conclusions. Even if one holds the view that increase in industrial production conforms essentially to the notion of a continuous, gradually-altering equilibrium situation (though, of course, with the superimposition upon this intrinsically continuous process, as phenomena of a secondary sort, of certain quasi-systematic and recurring maladjustment fluctuations), that such industrial increase is essentially a resultant and conforming phenomenon, flowing from the orderly development (to be sure, sometimes interfered with or deflected by "outside influences") of such supposedly basic forces as the gradual growth of population, the steady continuance of accumulation, the constant development of technical knowledge, and the incessant emergence of new tastes and desires — even if one accepts all this, it is a *non sequitur* to assert that the fundamentally smooth continuous process of growth thus envisaged is constrained to proceed in accordance with the particular mathematical curve, the logarithmic parabola, to show itself in terms of a constant rate of retardation in growth. And if, in contrast with the preceding, one takes the view that the wave-like fluctuations in the curve of industrial production are fundamentally the manifestation of those forces of progress which are mainly responsible for the upward course of industrial production over the generations, then still less reason exists for expecting the general movement of production over long periods to conform to a particular mathematical curve.

It follows, then, that — although our statistical results for the secular trend of the production index fit most neatly into the notion of inherent forces which make for a nearly uniform rate of growth over long periods of time — we must repudiate the suggestion that these results establish any such conclusion. What we *have* shown is that for the United States over the pre-war period 1866–1914 the forces of progress, joined with those of mere growth, did operate in such a way as to produce in the index number [19] a long-time secular movement characterized by a high annual average rate of growth, accompanied by very slight retardation; we do not infer from these results any generalized "law of growth."

[19] Bear in mind still once more the distinction between the *index number* and the *economic phenomenon* which the index number attempts to represent, previously set forth in this volume.

### OTHER TYPES OF "GROWTH CURVES" — THE LOGISTIC, THE GOMPERTZ, THE NORMAL-CURVE INTEGRAL

Objection may be raised, however, that we have failed to give proper consideration to the possibility of using some other "growth curve" than the logarithmic parabola — say, the logistic curve, the Gompertz curve, or the integral of the normal curve. Certainly it must be admitted at once that the statistical evidence presented has been just as consistent with the assumption of one of these curves for the pre-war secular trend of our production index as with the assumption of the logarithmic parabola. Sufficient irregularity appears in the indications of the curves of logarithmic differences (Chart 25, Parts A and B) that the assumptions as to the nature of retardation in rate of growth which would correspond to the fitting of the logistic curve (or, alternatively, the Gompertz curve, or the integral of the normal curve) to the original items of our production index over the pre-war period are equally plausible with the assumption implicit in the logarithmic parabola. For the specific series and time interval at hand, the retardation indications of these various other "growth curves" upon a chart of logarithmic first differences (such as Chart 25, Part A), exhibit only slight deviation from the straight-line retardation indication of the logarithmic parabola. Is there, then, any just ground for discriminating here in favor of the logarithmic parabola, as opposed to one of the other curves?

It may, of course, be pointed out that practically, so far as the form of the line of secular trend *for this particular index number over this particular time period* is concerned, it is not likely to be of great consequence which of the various curves — logarithmic parabola, logistic curve, Gompertz curve, integral of normal curve — we choose to fit. But the question of principle nevertheless still remains. Why choose the logarithmic parabola here in preference to the other possibilities?

We make this choice because the logarithmic parabola, taken in conjunction with reasonable interpretation, says with precision all that we have a right to say, on the basis of available evidence, about the nature of the secular trend of our production index over the pre-war interval ending with 1914, *and then stops*; no unwarranted *obiter dictum* is added. Reasonably interpreted in the light of our earlier discussion, the logarithmic-parabola trend equation tells us that the rate of retardation in secular growth for the production index over our period may as a good approximation to the truth be taken as constant, and that we are not justified in attempting to make any statement about this retardation rate implying a closer approach to precision.

In contrast with this, any one of the other three curves will *say too much* about the rate of retardation; their implications as respects the retardation rate are quite unwarranted on the basis of the statistical evidence. That is to say, each of the other curves carries with it the implication of a retardation rate varying from constancy *in a very special and peculiar manner*, conforming to the properties of a particular mathematical function, while the statistical evidence (cf. Chart 25, and the accompanying discussion) affords no ground whatever for such particularization; we have no statistical methodology, no measuring instruments, which will enable us to draw such refined conclusions for our present series.

The selection of a particular mathematical function for secular-trend representation in a given instance does not, of course, in itself carry any necessary implication that this trend is deemed capable of extension into the future. And for the case at hand, the implications of the selection of the logarithmic parabola to represent the secular trend of the production index over the half century from the Civil War to the World War of 1914 do not carry even so far as to signify that, over this pre-war period, forces were at work which (unless interrupted or deflected by the introduction of other, new forces) would, in conformity to a law embodied in a particular mathematical function, bring the trend of production up to some limiting maximum value, from which such trend would later progressively recede, still in accordance with this same law. We are under no compulsion to set up such an *obiter dictum*. Furthermore, we need not resort to it in order to translate our mathematical equation into words; we can accomplish this translation merely by saying, quite simply, that over our pre-war interval the forces of progress (along with those of mere growth) operated in such way as to bring about in the production index a rapid average rate of secular advance, accompanied by a rate of secular retardation which was very slight and which with reasonable approach to precision may be described as constant.

Now, of course, it must immediately be set down that equally the mere selection for trend representation in a particular case of the logistic curve, the Gompertz curve, or the normal-curve integral does not carry with it any necessary implication that this trend is thought to be projectable into the future. And, to continue the parallel with the preceding paragraph, the implications of the choice of one of these mathematical curves to represent the secular trend of the production index over the pre-war interval ending with 1914 would not extend even so far as to signify that, during this pre-war period, forces were at work which (unless interrupted or deflected by the introduction of other, new forces) would cause this trend, in conformity to a law embodied in a particular mathematical function, progressively to approach a limiting maximum value, which would constitute an upper asymptote for such secular movement. Once again, we are under no constraint to set up the *obiter dictum. But, and here lies the essential point, for any one of these curves (as opposed to the logarithmic parabola) it is extremely difficult, if not impossible, to translate sensibly into words the explicit trend equation without resort to the obiter dictum.*

The adoption of one of these three curves may, however, be urged on a quite different ground: to wit, that there is inherent in economic progress a "rational" logistic (or Gompertz, or normal-curve-integral) "law of growth." In this connection, the following statement by Professor Sewall Wright is pertinent.

"It is perhaps conceivable that an organism or population may continue growth according to the compound interest law until it bumps abruptly into a limiting condition. It is much more likely, however, that there will be increasing adverse pressure as growth goes on, leading to damping off and reversal of curvature, and ultimately, if conditions are uniform, to an asymptotic approach for an upper limit. In this we have simply described a general *S*-shaped curve, which may take various forms depending on the exact nature of the adverse pressure. Anything growing under constant or even changing conditions, provided the changes are sufficiently gradual, can hardly be expected to grow in any other way. Any flexible mathematical formula which gives this general shape can hardly fail to give an empirical means of fitting such a curve. The logistic curve is, perhaps, the most convenient but it is by no means the only mathematical form with this property." [20]

[20] Sewall Wright, *Journal of the American Statistical Association*, XXI (December 1926), pp. 493–494.

The present writer is inclined to adopt the point of view developed in this quotation; and further, to extend it to cover economic advance in such entities as total industrial and commercial production [21] and to apply it to such functions as the Gompertz and the normal-curve integral, as well as the logistic.

There is the further highly significant point that — even though we waive the above objection and agree to accept the logistic (or alternatively, one of the others) to represent secular growth under a given set of fixed or gradually-changing conditions — in actual economic life *important new factors and forces* may come into play, often rather abruptly, and render invalid the mathematical function adopted for the past. All things considered, the present writer is disposed to accept the conclusion of Professor A. B. Wolfe that "not a jot of real evidence has been given that the causes bearing on population growth are of such nature and composition that growth must, or will, follow the logistic curve" [or, he might well have added, the Gompertz curve or the normal-curve integral], and to extend this conclusion to such an economic entity as the rate of advance in total industrial and commercial production.[22]

## THE PRECIPITATION OF THE TREND-INDICATIONS

We have thus far set up the trend-cycle separation for the production index (as well as for its two components, and for the "check production index"). We come now to the second task of this chapter — the precipitation of trend-indications for the remaining eleven series of Chart 23.

### THE BASIC LINE OF REASONING

Our line of reasoning here goes back to the developments of earlier pages. In Part Two, we demonstrated the pervasiveness throughout the fabric of the nation's economic life of a certain general pattern of short-time fluctuation. This pattern repeatedly emerged, in highly consistent form, as we successively carried out pattern studies (cf. Chart 22) for the thirteen important economic series, for the structure of industrial and commercial production, for the composite index number of industrial and commercial pro-

---

[21] The problem with regard to *individual industries* is, of course, a different one.

[22] It is not possible to discuss this matter further here. Cf. the article by Professor Wolfe (from p. 593 of which the above quotation is taken), "Is There a Biological Law of Human Population Growth," *Quarterly Journal of Economics*, XLI (August 1927), pp. 557–594 — together with the publications referred to therein.

duction, for the employment index, for the commodity-price structure, for index numbers of wholesale commodity prices, and for a group of miscellaneous series. Further, we were able, in all these pattern studies, to find analytical evidence of the presence of one, and only one, such general pattern.[23] Still further, we encountered throughout definite manifestation of the existence of some disjoining force (or complex of forces), of a fairly long-run sort, which was operating upon our array of series, gradually over the course of time overcoming the cohesiveness which the pervasiveness of the general pattern of short-time fluctuation gave to them, and driving them away from one another. Then, as related in the chapter just preceding, for a group of a dozen leading economic series we demonstrated, as a good first approximation to the truth, a fundamental proposition: the variations of these series (setting aside seasonal and irregular fluctuations) were found to be resolvable into smooth, continuous, gradually-changing long-time movements which might appropriately be designated "secular trends," and wave-like short-time oscillations which might appropriately be designated "cyclical variations"; and the relationship between these two types of variations was shown, again as a good first approximation, to be logarithmically additive. In the earlier part of the present chapter we selected, from among the dozen leading economic series of Chart 23, the index number of industrial and commercial production as that series which gave promise of exhibiting the simplest relationship between the secular and cyclical variations; we derived a representation of its secular trend over our chosen time period and (through elimination of this secular trend) the curve of its cyclical variations. We now propose, in the next step of our investigation, *to employ this curve of cyclical variation for the production index as a basis for eliminating from the other series of Chart 23 the form of cyclical movement which is inherent in our general pattern of short-time fluctuation, thus effecting the precipitation of their trend-indications, which in turn will be revelatory as to the form and position of their lines of secular trend.*

Before we proceed to consideration of this next stage of our investigation, we may pause to suggest that the force of certain earlier observations will shortly be even more fully apparent: the

[23] Setting aside the field of agriculture as a special case.

force, that is, of statements upon previous pages to the effect that particular conclusions there set forth, based upon our prior investigations, constituted indispensable prerequisites for later methodological developments. As will soon become unmistakably clear, the plan of procedure which we now set up, and the subsequent analysis employing this procedure, would be altogether indefensible and deserving of no kinder description than "arbitrary and unwarranted manipulation of data," did we not possess the broad and solid foundation built up through our earlier work. Only because the new methodological architecture rests upon this foundation may we justly claim scientific validity for our procedure and results.

### THE SUB-PERIODS

We come now to the immediate task — the precipitation of the trend-indications for the eleven series. Here, as in certain preliminary investigations of the preceding chapter, it is desirable to split the interval 1866–1914 into sub-periods, for convenience of study. And here once more we turn for guidance to the fluctuations of the production index. But, though we employ the same curve as before (the top line of Chart 17, page 207), our use of this curve stands on an entirely different logical basis. Previously we designated the curve as "the production index with average rate of growth and average rate of retardation eliminated"; we felt its use to be justified only for purposes of rough, general analysis; and we described its wave-like fluctuations merely as "swings about the horizontal base line." [24] Now, on the basis of findings set forth in the earlier part of this chapter, we speak of the curve as representing "the cyclical variations of the production index"; we believe that the curve, taken with this designation, possesses a rather high degree of accuracy; and we describe its wave-like fluctuations as "cyclical variations." These alterations in terminology thus reflect a most decided change in our attitude toward the curve, in our estimate of its significance; this change in attitude and estimate flows from the results of the analysis of the secular-cyclical relationship for the production index, as worked out in preceding sections of this chapter. The selection of the seven time intervals — 1866–78, 1878–85, 1885–96, 1896–1904, 1904–08, 1908–11, and 1911–14 — to serve as sub-periods

---

[24] Cf. the discussion in the earlier pages of Chapter XII.

in the present investigation thus rests upon an altogether different and decidedly more secure basis than in Chapter XII.

### THE CYCLICAL VARIATIONS OF THE PRODUCTION INDEX AS A "DENOTATIVE" SERIES

We proceed now with the investigation. The general plan, as already indicated, is to employ the curve of cyclical variation for the production index as a means of eliminating from the other eleven series of Chart 23 that general form of cyclical variation which is inherent in the various patterns of short-run fluctuation derived in Part Two of this volume, and thus to effect the precipitation of the trend-indications for these eleven series. But before we undertake the process of formal calculation, it is essential that we should set forth carefully the chain of reasoning which forms the basis for the methodology.

In the first place, we take the form of short-time fluctuation shown by the production index to represent a much broader entity — to represent, that is, the *general* pattern of short-run fluctuation which we have found to be interwoven through the fabric of the nation's economic life over our period of analysis. It would appear that this decision is wholly proper and justified, in view of the very close similarity which we have previously discovered between the link-relative pattern for the production index and the various other manifestations of the broad general pattern to which reference has just been made — i.e., the link-relative patterns for the thirteen important series, for the structure of production, for the employment index, for the structure of wholesale commodity prices, for commodity-price indexes, and for the group of miscellaneous series.

Next we reiterate that we have been able to effect a satisfactory elimination of the secular trend of the production index, and consequently to isolate, with a reasonably high degree of accuracy, the *cyclical variations* of this index. We then take the final step in the present chain of reasoning and indicate that in the subsequent analysis of this chapter we shall use the curve of cyclical variation for the production index as *denotative* of the cyclical elements which (even though we have not been able to isolate *these latter* cyclical elements by any direct process) we know to be inherent in that general pattern of short-time fluctuation previously demonstrated to be present in the fabric of the nation's pre-war economic life.

We may pause to direct attention still once more to the dependence for validity of our methodological developments upon the basic foundations laid in earlier studies. The argument just set forth — which is crucial for the justification of the statistical operations now to be inaugurated — rests upon these foundations. Our procedure and our results could have no validity without them.

### THE MODIFIED SERIES

We now proceed to eliminate from each of our eleven individual series (for list of series, cf. Chart 23) the form of cyclical movement inherent in the general pattern of economic variation, employing the *denotative* cyclical series for the production index (cf. Chart 17) as a basis for such elimination. Our first operation is to calculate amplitude ratios for the several series. These ratios are readily developed by utilizing the dispersion measures (based upon average deviations of link relatives) derived as described in the preceding chapter; that is, for each sub-period we divide the dispersion measure for the given series by the corresponding measure for the production index. Thus, for example, in railroad earnings over the sub-period 1885–96, we divide the average deviation of the link relatives (5.25 per cent) by the corresponding average deviation of the production index (5.70 per cent), thereby obtaining the required amplitude ratio (0.92). We also make within each sub-period certain minor adjustments, connected with the presence of lags and leads among the various series.[25]

Dealing with each of the eleven series in turn and working by sub-periods, we now undertake to eliminate, from the fluctuations of the particular series, the general form of cyclical variation in economic activity as represented by the denotative production-index curve of Chart 17. And, since we have previously found the relationship between cyclical and secular variation to be (approximately) logarithmically additive, we shall work with logarithms as we proceed. Specifically, we multiply, year by year, the logarithms of the cyclical-variation curve for the production index (Chart 17)[26] by the proper amplitude ratio (in the case of railroad

---

[25] In each case, the given series is shifted backward or forward a sufficient number of quarters to compensate for the average lag or lead during the sub-period of its short-time fluctuations as compared with those of the production index. The procedure is analogous to that employed in Chapter XII (cf. especially fn. 13 in that chapter). For the most part, the lags or leads are small — one or two quarters.

[26] Our logarithms are expressed as simple positive or negative numbers. Thus,

earnings over the sub-period 1885–96, for example, the multiplier is 0.92, obtained as described just above). This multiplication brings the average amplitude of short-time fluctuation for the production index over the sub-period into correspondence with that of the particular series, and thus (on the basis of arguments previously presented) may be held essentially to do away with difference over the sub-period in average intensity of cyclical fluctuation as between the two series.

We then perform, year by year [27] within each sub-period, a subtraction of logarithms. That is, for each year we take algebraically the difference between (1) the logarithm of the actual item for the particular individual series [28] — e.g., railroad earnings — and (2) the figure just obtained through multiplication of the logarithm for the cyclical-variation curve of the production index by the appropriate amplitude ratio.

To see what sort of picture this operation has yielded, we may for each of the eleven series draw a graph of the successive differences, arranged in order of time; or, alternatively, we may plot the natural numbers corresponding to these differences, employing logarithmic vertical scale, as is illustrated in Chart 26. The line thus derived may be described, proximately, as the particular series (e.g., railroad earnings) with the general form of cyclical variation of the production index eliminated therefrom. But if our argument as set forth in the preceding sub-section is acceptable, we may place a wider interpretation upon the results: since we take the cyclical fluctuations of the production index as *denotative* of a more comprehensive entity, we may properly describe our present results as showing us the particular statistical series, with elimination therefrom of the form of cyclical variation inherent in that *general pattern* of fluctuation which we have previously found to be pervasive in the nation's economic life.

We now carry this reasoning still one stage further. We argue that for any particular series from the list of Chart 23 (say, railroad earnings), we, in eliminating from the series the form of

---

when the cyclical-variation curve for the production index stands at 1.05 (or 105 per cent), the logarithm is written as +0.0212; and when this curve stands at 0.95 (or 95 per cent), the logarithm is written as −0.0223, rather than as 9.9777–10.

[27] Over the interval 1904–14, when the cyclical fluctuations are rather rapid, these operations based upon annual items are supplemented by corresponding calculations based upon quarterly data.

[28] With proper timing adjustment for lag or lead, as explained just above.

# CHART 26

ORIGINAL ITEMS FOR (1) RAILROAD EARNINGS, AND (2) EMPLOYMENT INDEX,
WITH FORM OF CYCLICAL VARIATION OF PRODUCTION INDEX ELIMINATED:
BY YEARS, 1866–1914 *

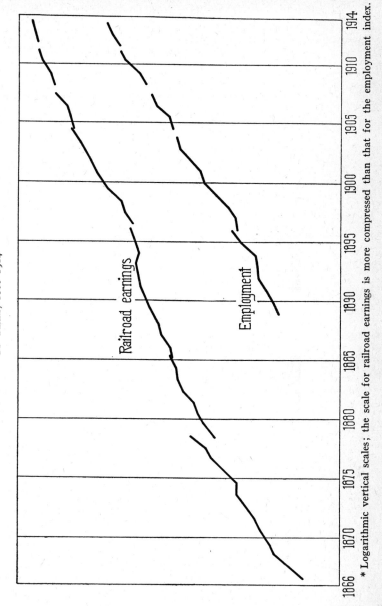

* Logarithmic vertical scales; the scale for railroad earnings is more compressed than that for the employment index.

cyclical variation of this general pervasive pattern, accomplish *approximately* the elimination of the cyclical movement *of the series itself.*

This statement calls immediately for two comments. In the first place, it cannot be said too emphatically that the conclusion is justified only because of the close correspondence which we have earlier demonstrated to exist between (1) the form of short-time variation in the general pattern of short-run movement for economic series, in its several manifestations — the standard pattern for the thirteen series, and the various others connected with production, employment, and commodity prices — and (2) the form of short-time variation in each of the individual series whose secular tendencies are now under examination, such close correspondence being evidenced by the various link-relative charts of Part Two (we may refer in particular to Charts 4, 5, and 22), as well as by such original-item charts as Chart 23. The application of our present procedure to a series not possessing this property of correspondence in short-run variation with the general pattern would be unjustified, and the results would in all probability be absurd and meaningless. We must take this earliest opportunity to enter an emphatic caveat against any such perversion of the methodology.

In the second place, the force and the implications of the word *approximately* in the above statement must not be overlooked. The insertion of this adverb is called for by a number of considerations. In each of the individual series, the picture of cyclical variation has doubtless some elements of error, traceable to statistical defects of the series connected with the basic material from which it is formed and perhaps with the technique of its construction; and the same is in some degree true, in spite of the care lavished upon its derivation, for the production index itself. Further, though we have devoted considerable attention to the methodology for determining the amplitude ratios by sub-periods and probably have achieved reasonably reliable measurements of these ratios, we cannot claim perfection for them; to the extent that imperfection is present, some degree of error (on the whole, probably minor) creeps into the results of the calculations. Still further, it must not be forgotten that these amplitude ratios are but *averages* over a sub-period; in so far as there is, *within the sub-period*, intrinsic variation in the amplitude ratio (and there

can be no doubt that such variations often do occur), the final
results of our calculations suffer some distortion. Also to be taken
into account is the timing of movement: the average lag or lead
(as compared with the production index) for a particular series
within a given sub-period is measured only to the nearest quarter
of a year, and (which is more significant) the intrinsic lag or lead
in general tends to alter within the sub-period; to a very considerable extent, the small oscillatory fluctuations in our results (cf.
Chart 26) are accounted for by this influence. Finally, and most
important of all, even though in each case the general correlation
between the form of short-time movement for the particular series
and that for the pervasive economic pattern has been shown to be
very high, departures from precise congruence of cyclical fluctuations nevertheless appear throughout; here again there is opportunity for some distortion of results.

In sum, then, we may say that we are justified in applying the
present procedure to this group of eleven leading series only
because of the close general correspondence which we have previously demonstrated to exist between the short-run movements for
these several series and those of the pervasive pattern of economic
fluctuation; that, for a variety of reasons, we may properly speak
of the results of the procedure only as approximations; and that
we are at liberty to regard these approximations as, on the whole,
satisfactory only because of this same close general correspondence to which reference has just been made. Furthermore, the
dependence of the procedure upon the basic foundation built up
through the analytical studies described in Part Two and in the
preceding chapter cannot be too much stressed; without this
foundation, no scientific validity could be claimed for the findings.

The results of the calculations just completed — in which we
have eliminated from each of the eleven leading economic series
the form of cyclical movement of the production index — we shall
regard, then, as yielding in each case a depiction of the individual
series (e.g., railroad earnings) modified by being freed, approximately, from *its own* cyclical variations. For the sake of brevity
we shall frequently hereafter refer to such depictions simply as
the *modified series*.

When we turn to an examination of these modified series, we
note at once a strong tendency toward continuity of movement
(cf., for example, the curves for railroad earnings and employ-

ment, presented on Chart 26) — as we should indeed have anticipated, taking into account our findings in Chapter XII regarding
the nature of secular variations. But the several curves of modified series are by no means perfectly smooth; some measure of
irregularity appears (cf., again, Chart 26), though the irregularities involved are of a distinctly lower order of magnitude than
the previously-eliminated cyclical variations. The emergence of
such irregularity we should also have anticipated, in view of the
considerations set forth in a preceding paragraph with respect to
those failures of precision in the methodology which require us to
attach the adverb "approximately" to our results, and further in
view of the fact that the individual series contain numerous
extraneous variations which, even though the cyclical elimination
were perfectly accomplished, would nevertheless cause irregularity
to appear in the final modified series.

### THE TREND-INDICATIONS

Now we know, from the findings of Chapter XII and of the
present chapter, and the reasoning based upon them, that our
present modified series are primarily and essentially representative of secular variations. But unfortunately the picture in each
case lacks clarity; it is blurred by the presence of those various
elements of error and irregularity to which allusion has been made
in preceding paragraphs. Is there any device by means of which
we can relieve the modified series from these irrelevant details,
and thus be able to see in clear relief the secular variations? A
plan of action for attack upon this problem readily suggests itself:
since for each of the several modified series the curve traces out,
within each sub-period, some fairly clear general tendency, (1)
give concrete expression to these tendencies by fitting, series by
series, a line to the points within each sub-period, and then (2)
assemble such lines for all eleven series upon a single chart, thus
facilitating their examination and intercomparison. In this way
the indications as to the nature of secular variations furnished by
the array of modified series may be condensed and epitomized.

We accordingly proceed to the systematic fitting of these lines.
It appears most expedient to confine ourselves for the time being
to the fitting of *straight lines* to the data on logarithmic scale,
which carry only the simple implication of a constant rate of
increase (or decrease) over the sub-period. In most of the cases
with which we are confronted the logarithmically-plotted points

within the sub-period show fairly close approach to straight-line movement, and it seems clear — especially in view of the considerations previously set forth with respect to the failure of complete precision in the modified series as representative of secular variations — that we are not at this stage of our analysis justified in going beyond the simple straight line in reading, from these logarithmic-scale charts, the secular-trend implications of any of the modified series over a given sub-period. To be sure, in a few instances — e.g., railroad earnings in 1885–96 (Chart 26) — the tendency toward curvature in the modified series over a particular sub-period seems fairly well marked, but cases of this sort are rare. All in all, it appears decidedly wisest, in view of the limitations (earlier set forth at length) which here attach to our measurements, to go very slowly in reading curved-line implications into the movements of the modified series within any sub-period. For the moment our examination is preliminary, and we are looking at each series, and indeed at each sub-period, in isolation, so to speak; judgments regarding the presence of curvilinear tendencies in secular variation can best be made at a later stage, after we have had a chance to study the assembled evidence as a connected whole.

Taking the modified series one by one, we fit a straight line (upon logarithmic scale) to the items falling within each sub-period.[29] In numerous instances the points lie so nearly upon a straight line that the fitting can readily be performed by eye; where this is not feasible, least-squares fitting is adequate. The various fitted straight lines are assembled upon Chart 27. These lines will hereafter be referred to as the *trend-indications*.[30]

The first characteristic of this array of lines to engage our attention is the general tendency toward continuity in the trend-indications. The conclusions of Chapter XII upon this point (cf. pages 250–251) have thus been confirmed by evidence derived through a new approach. To be sure, the straight lines upon Chart

[29] In fitting the trend-indication lines, certain conspicuous irregularities (e.g., the "tariff-change" peak in imports, 1897) have been ignored. (See also the next footnote.)

[30] For commercial-paper rates, quite obviously the modified series (and the several lines fitted thereto) are materially distorted by the frequent irregular fluctuations, connected with economic crises and other disturbances, to which reference was made in Chapter XII (cf. Chart 23). For this series, accordingly, we have fitted a revised set of lines, omitting the irregular items in the process of computing. These revised lines (dotted on Chart 27) will be used as the trend-indications for this series.

27 very seldom effect a precise joining at their extremities; there are throughout gaps at the points of junction. These gaps, however, are on the whole comparatively moderate in magnitude. And, in view of the strong tendency toward continuity appearing in the modified series from which these lines were derived (cf. Chart 26), it would seem that we should attribute these gaps to (1) the irremediable limitations of the methodology by which the curves of modified items were obtained, as set forth at length in preceding paragraphs; and (2) the fact that for certain series (e.g., railroad earnings, wholesale commodity prices) the underlying secular tendencies are really curvilinear, and hence are only imperfectly represented by the straight-line fittings to which we have felt it wise to confine ourselves in this preliminary attack.

Another outstanding feature of the array of lines upon Chart 27 is the indication that among the ten series which extend over the entire interval 1866–1914,[31] there are very few, if any, for which the secular variations are capable of satisfactory representation by a single simple mathematical curve. *This finding, taken in conjunction with conclusions earlier reached regarding individual production series and individual price series (cf. Chapters VII and X), strongly suggests that the secular movements of economic series over long periods do not in general tend to proceed in accordance with "laws" embodied in simple mathematical functions.*

Still another important feature of the array of lines upon Chart 27 is the appearance for many of the series of alteration, often rather abrupt, in the direction or slope of the secular movement around the turn of the century. The widespread tendency for such alteration to occur is definitely attested by the behavior of the trend-indication lines over the sub-period 1896–1904. Clearly, we must observe particular care when we come to set up secular-trend representations in this time interval and its immediate neighborhood.

We have selected the production index as that series of the group under treatment for which the relationship between secular

---

[31] The track of the trend-indications for the employment index suggests that the underlying secular movement is closely approximated by a straight line (upon logarithmic scale) — i.e., that the rate of secular growth of this *index number* (cf. fn. 12 in Chapter IX) is, for the time interval at hand, very nearly constant. (This, incidentally, confirms the tentative conclusion of Chapter IX.) The employment index, however, extends over only one-half of our pre-war period of analysis.

# CHART 27

TREND-INDICATIONS FOR INDIVIDUAL SERIES, BY FIRST METHOD
(USE OF CYCLICAL VARIATIONS OF PRODUCTION INDEX AS BASIS):
BY SUB-PERIODS, 1866–1914 *

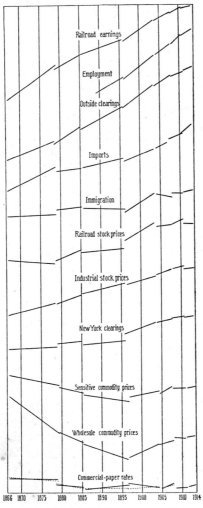

* Logarithmic vertical scales; to facilitate presentation within limited space, varying scales are employed for the several series. For explanation of chart, see accompanying text.

and cyclical variations is likely to be simplest. As regards the magnitude of the retardation rate and its constancy, we have found the production index to differ essentially from individual production series. On the basis of a new mathematical technique — which involves the study of first and second logarithmic differences, and the utilization of the relation between the sine curve and its derivative — we have established that the pre-war secular trend of the production index can be represented with a reasonably close approach to precision by a logarithmic parabola. Further, employing a new methodology involving the use of the cyclical variations of the production index, we have succeeded in precipitating the trend-indications for a group of leading economic series. We are now ready to proceed with the transliteration of these trend-indications into definitive lines of secular-trend representation. This task, however, we postpone to Chapter XV, turning our attention immediately, in Chapter XIV, to the derivation of the trend-indications *by an independent method.*

# CHAPTER XIV

## THE SECOND METHOD: GRADUAL ATTENUATION OF THE NON–CYCLICAL ELEMENTS IN THE STANDARD PATTERN

IN THIS CHAPTER we develop the second of the two independent methods for deriving the trend-indications of the group of leading economic time series entering Chart 23. In a desire emphatically to direct attention to the essential *independence* of the two lines of procedure, described in Chapters XIII and XIV, respectively, the writer has sought for some special device of presentation to accomplish this end. At one time the thought was seriously entertained of printing the two chapters in parallel columns to show that neither stood as a prerequisite for the other. This idea was finally rejected as bizarre. It was decided as a substitute device *to write the main body of Chapter XIV as if Chapter XIII had not been written*, even though the adoption of this device must (in spite of the essential independence of the two lines of procedure) inevitably involve at points a certain appearance of repetitiveness in the form of exposition.

However, since the reader must of necessity examine the chapters successively, it has seemed wise to insert, from time to time in the main body of the present chapter, *running comments* relating to similarities or contrasts between the methods or the results of the two lines of procedure; such comments will be placed in footnotes within square brackets.

Though we shall advance by a different route from that of Chapter XIII, our starting point is the same. We shall start, that is, from the position gained through our earlier studies — the search for patterns of fluctuation in economic data, as set forth in Part Two of this volume, and the investigation into the fundamental nature of time-series variations, as described in Chapter XII. And here, as in Chapter XIII, it is true that the validity of the procedure and conclusions is vitally dependent upon the findings of our earlier work.

### THE STANDARD PATTERN RECONSIDERED

We now revert to a situation which emerged at a quite early stage of our general investigation. It will be remembered (see

Chapter III, on pages 89–91) that we began the search for patterns of short-time fluctuation in the array of thirteen important
economic series by computing quarterly link relatives over the
pre-war period 1866–1914 for the several constituents (these
constituents being first, when necessary, adjusted for seasonal
variation), and then studying these link relatives in graphic form.
Such examination revealed a high degree of congruence among the
link-relative series as regards form of short-time fluctuation; but
this examination also brought to light the fact that there were
present in the data long-time tendencies which were to a certain
degree distorting, from the point of view of deriving the pattern
of short-time fluctuation. One evidence of such tendencies was the
appearance of differences among the several link-relative charts
with respect to average level of fluctuation. These differences in
level of link-relative curves obviously were traceable to the presence in the original items of long-time drifts, upward or downward (cf. Chart 1).

With reference to the problem then at hand, it was argued in
Chapter III that these long-time drifts in the original items were
mildly distorting in connection with the derivation of the general
pattern of short-time movement for the thirteen series — more
specifically (cf. footnote 44 in Chapter III) that had we failed to
make some adjustment for differences in average level of fluctuation among the link-relative series, the influence of the disturbing
element would have shown itself in a certain degree of blurring in
the measurement of central tendency for the various columns of
the multiple frequency table of link-relative items. It was further
argued that by applying to each individual series of link relatives
an adjustment for differences in average level of fluctuation (the
adjustment consisting simply in dividing the series through by its
average over the period of study) the effects of this distorting
influence, though of course not entirely removed, could be very
materially lessened — more specifically, the measurements of
central tendency in the multiple frequency table could be made
more nearly precise. Such adjustments for differences in level
of the link-relative series were accordingly carried out, as one of
the steps in the derivation of the standard pattern.

The phrase chosen in Chapter III to characterize this distorting, blurring influence was purposely somewhat vague — "long-
time drift." It was altogether appropriate that an indefinite

expression should be employed, for on the basis of the meager amount of relevant analytical evidence which had been developed at this very early stage of our investigation we could have knowledge only of the most general sort concerning the entity or entities behind the phrase. And, correspondingly, in the process of adjustment for this long-time drift we went only as far as we were at that point justified in going. It will be remembered that we expressly repudiated the idea of then setting up any attempt at more refined adjustment. Indeed, our anxiety to protect the final results of this pattern analysis from any possible implication of question-begging was so great that we refused even to take judicial notice of such well-known facts as, for example, the observation that the long-time movement of wholesale commodity prices shows a break around 1896. And further, it will also be remembered, we repudiated the notion that the simple adjustment employed was intended to be, or could be thought of as constituting, "elimination of secular trend." In fact, at that time we were unwilling even so much as to admit the term "secular trend" to our working vocabulary.

We now, on the basis of analytical work subsequent to that of Chapter III — notably, the various pattern studies of Chapters VII to X, and also the investigations and findings of Chapter XII — have greatly increased knowledge concerning both the short-run and the long-run tendencies which we were just beginning to discern in those tentative steps of Chapter III. We now know that the pattern of short-time fluctuation for the thirteen important economic series which we then discovered was simply one manifestation of a more general pattern of economic fluctuation permeating the fabric of the nation's economic life. And we now know — as a corollary of the fundamental proposition of Chapter XII — that those long-time drifts which we vaguely glimpsed in Chapter III are, for ten of the thirteen series at least, nothing more nor less than the manifestations of certain smooth, continuous, gradually-changing, long-run tendencies with which it is appropriate to connect the designation "secular trend."

A question crucial with respect to the purposes of the present chapter comes to mind. We realize (as has just been set forth) that the procedure employed in the derivation of the standard pattern — specifically, the application of the very simple adjustment for differences in average level among the link-relative series

— can scarcely have effected the *complete elimination* of the secular element from this standard pattern (which, if accomplished, would signify the virtual isolation of its cyclical element).[1] This adjustment, however, must certainly to some degree have *attenuated* such secular element — must have reduced the influence of this factor which is (from the point of view of securing a picture of "pure" cyclical variation for the standard pattern) an extraneous one. Our crucial question now is: How far-reaching in its effects has been the process of attenuation, as accomplished by the procedure of Chapter III in deriving the standard pattern (also applied, for the annual case, in Chapter IV); to what extent has the elimination of the extraneous trend element from the standard pattern of short-time fluctuation been accomplished by this earlier operation? We turn now to a line of analytical procedure which we hope will assist us in arriving at an answer to this question.

In this new line of analytical procedure, we shall endeavor to determine whether or not anything at all definite can be made out concerning the nature of the secular trends of the dozen leading economic series embraced by our study of Chapter XII.[2] And we shall begin by fixing attention upon the matter of consistency, or lack of consistency, over time in secular-trend behavior. This statement of immediate objective suggests a division of the whole interval of study, 1866–1914, into shorter sub-periods, for comparison of the secular characteristics of the several series.

## THE STUDY OF RANKS

We wish to make the selection of sub-periods independent of that which is given major prominence in Chapter XII and embodied in the lay-out of Chart 23 — the selection, that is, based upon certain properties of the production index.[3] It appears most expedient, for the purposes of a preliminary attack, to adopt the device of splitting the pre-war interval of study into sub-periods of *equal* length, having in mind to let our later methodological

---

[1] Since the constituent series have been where necessary adjusted for seasonal variation, and the procedure for deriving the standard pattern is such as largely to eliminate the influence of irregular variations.

[2] That is, ten series from the original standard pattern study, together with the production index and the employment index.

[3] [We are also actuated, of course, by the desire to keep the present path of investigation independent of that of Chapter XIII.]

developments (in this matter as well as in others) flow from thoughtful consideration of the results of the preliminary attack.

So far as the length of sub-period is concerned, the decade seems perhaps as good a choice as we could make: the decade is at once long enough to include several of those brief, oscillatory swings which we can readily observe in the various link-relative patterns (cf. Chart 22), and short enough to yield a number of sub-periods sufficient to permit decisive comparison among the individual series as to the character of their secular behavior over time. We accordingly set up the five sub-periods 1866–75, 1875–85, 1885–95, 1895–1905, 1905–14.[4]

We now construct a new chart, employing precisely the procedure used in setting up Chart 23 in Chapter XII, except that the chart is laid out with reference to the schedule of decade sub-periods, just set forth.[5] The new chart presents very much the same appearance as did Chart 23, and gives very much the same impression. It immediately furnishes complete confirmation of Chart 23 as respects the reading of the *fundamental proposition:* once more we may read from the graphic array of curves the proposition that the variations of our group of leading time series (seasonal and irregular fluctuations aside) are resolvable into smooth, continuous, gradually-changing long-time movements which we may appropriately call "secular trends," and wave-like, short-time oscillations which we may appropriately call "cyclical variations," the relationship between these two types of variations being capable of description (approximately) as logarithmically additive.

What now can we say as to the first of these two types of variation — the secular trend? Specifically, can we devise a procedure by means of which we may discern something of the nature of the secular trends for our dozen leading economic series?

We begin our examination into the nature of the secular movements of these series by making a study of their comparative *ranking* in the several decade sub-periods with respect to certain manifestations of their secular characteristics. More specifically, in the new chart — just as in Chart 23 — the several curves for

---

[4] The three central "decades" are, strictly speaking, eleven years in length. We thus have — as would seem desirable — allowed in each case an overlap of one year at the point of intersection of the sub-periods upon the time scale.

[5] This new chart has not been reproduced, but its form and arrangement can be inferred from examination of Chart 23.

each sub-period are arranged in order of the slopes which they exhibit over the sub-period. (The reader is urged to turn to Chart 23 and observe the arrangement there.)[6] It is consequently possible to set up, for the new chart, a table indicating in each of the five decade sub-periods the comparative ranking (on the basis of this criterion) for the eleven individual series which extend over the entire period 1866–1914.[7] In each sub-period, the curve hav-

TABLE 12

"Rank Numbers" and "Dispersion Measures" for Eleven Series: by Sub-Periods of Uniform Length (Decades)*

| Series | "Rank numbers" | | | | | "Dispersion measures" |
|---|---|---|---|---|---|---|
| | 1866–75 | 1875–85 | 1885–95 | 1895–1905 | 1905–14 | |
| Production index ........ | 1 | 2 | 1 | 2 | 3 | 0.64 |
| Railroad earnings ....... | 2 | 1 | 2 | 1 | 2 | 0.48 |
| Outside clearings ........ | 3 | 3 | 3 | 5 | 1 | 0.80 |
| New York clearings ..... | 6 | 8 | 6 | 9 | 9 | 1.12 |
| Commercial-paper rates .. | 7 | 9 | 8 | 11 | 10 | 1.20 |
| Sensitive commodity prices | 10 | 11 | 10 | 10 | 6 | 1.36 |
| Imports ................ | 4 | 7 | 4 | 7 | 4 | 1.44 |
| Immigration ............ | 8 | 6 | 9 | 3 | 7 | 1.68 |
| Industrial stock prices ... | 5 | 5 | 5 | 8 | 8 | 1.68 |
| Railroad stock prices .... | 9 | 4 | 7 | 6 | 11 | 2.08 |
| Wholesale commodity prices | 11 | 10 | 11 | 4 | 5 | 2.96 |

* For explanation, see accompanying text.

ing the strongest upward slope is assigned "rank number" 1, the next "rank number" 2, and so on. This ranking is presented in Table 12.

The tabulation of ranks is exhibited graphically in Chart 28, Part A, where the successive "rank numbers" 1 to 11 appear as ordinates, and the five sub-periods as abscissas. The outstanding feature of this chart (and as we shall shortly see, the one which is of the most vital importance for the present investigation) is the high degree of variability over time which appears for nearly all of the constituent series, as regards their position on the scale of ranks. This variability presents itself to us through the move-

---

[6] For detailed description of the procedure for constructing the sub-period diagrams, see Chapter XII.

[7] The twelfth series — the employment index — we omit from the tabulation, since this series is available only over the latter half of the period.

ments of the oscillatory "rank curves" for the several series; the fluctuations are so intense that the chart gives to the eye an impression of a confused network. This variability in rank among the several series is afforded numerical expression by the figures in the last column of Table 12, headed "dispersion measures." These "dispersion measures" — in each case, simply the average deviation (measured from the arithmetic mean) of the five "rank numbers" for the particular series in question — show large values for most of the series. (The *period-to-period* variability, also, is on the whole high — cf. the chart.)

We note, however, that the production index exhibits a strong tendency toward constancy in rank. This suggests that the production index may possess a fairly simple form of secular movement, at least as compared with most of the other ten series. Setting aside the production index, the series seem to divide themselves rather definitely into two groups: (1) railroad earnings and outside clearings, with comparatively low dispersions in rank, and (2) the other eight series, with relatively high dispersions. This suggests that the secular trends of the two series of the first group may come appreciably nearer to possessing the quality of simplicity than those of the eight series of the second group. These inferences, as regards the comparative simplicity or complexity of the form of trend movement for the various series, must, of course, be regarded as only suggestive, for the analytical treatment described in this paragraph is very rough and general.

### The Probabilities as to Attenuation of Secular Tendencies in the Standard Pattern

With the result of our "study of ranks" at hand to assist us, we return to the question, posed on an earlier page of this chapter: How far-reaching in its effects has been the process of *attenuation* of the secular elements in the standard pattern, as accomplished by the procedure of Chapters III and IV; to what extent has the elimination from this pattern of the trend element (extraneous with respect to our present purposes) been accomplished by this earlier procedure?

To take a simple point first, in so far as the manifestations of the secular influences for a particular series are capable of description in terms of a constant rate of growth (or decline) over the period of analysis, such influences have been almost completely

CHART 28

VARIATIONS IN "RANK NUMBERS" FOR ELEVEN INDIVIDUAL SERIES:
BY SUB-PERIODS, 1866–1914 *

Part A: Sub-Periods of Uniform Length (Ten-Year)

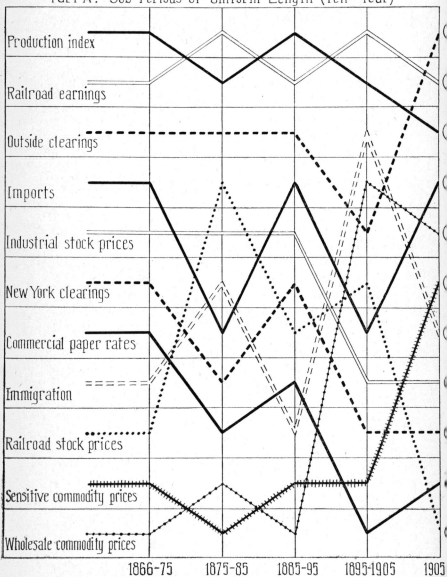

Production index

Railroad earnings

Outside clearings

Imports

Industrial stock prices

New York clearings

Commercial paper rates

Immigration

Railroad stock prices

Sensitive commodity prices

Wholesale commodity prices

1866–75    1875–85    1885–95    1895–1905    1905

* For explanation of chart, see text, pp. 299–301 and 318–321.

# CHART 28

VARIATIONS IN "RANK NUMBERS" FOR ELEVEN INDIVIDUAL SERIES:
BY SUB-PERIODS, 1866–1914 (*Continued*)

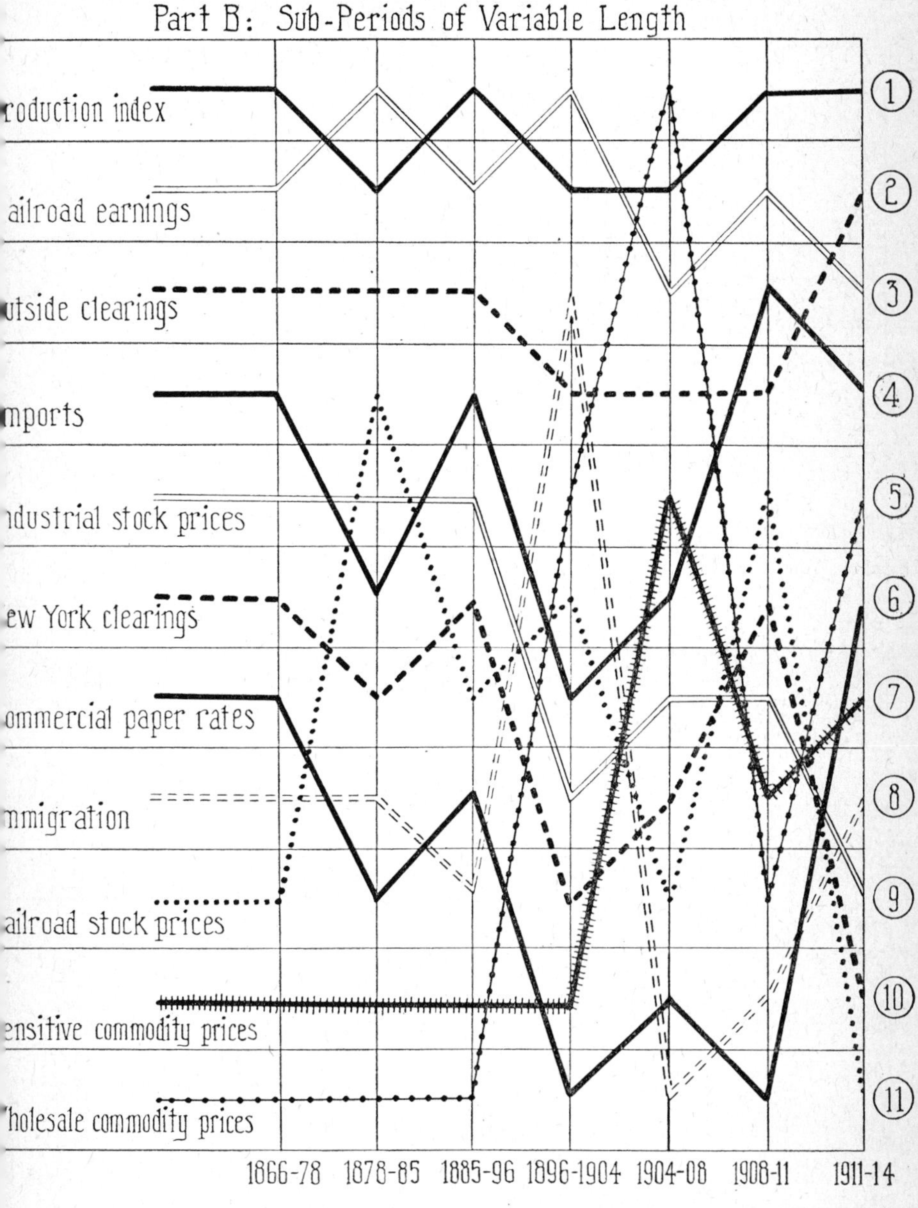

## Part B: Sub-Periods of Variable Length

roduction index ① 

ailroad earnings ② 

utside clearings ③ 

mports ④ 

ndustrial stock prices ⑤ 

ew York clearings ⑥ 

ommercial paper rates ⑦ 

mmigration ⑧ 

ailroad stock prices ⑨ 

ensitive commodity prices ⑩ 

holesale commodity prices ⑪ 

1866-78  1878-85  1885-96  1896-1904  1904-08  1908-11  1911-14

eliminated by the simple adjustment for differences in average level of fluctuation applied to the link relatives in the course of deriving the standard pattern.

But with regard to manifestations of secular tendency other than average rate of growth (or decline), what are the probabilities as to attenuation in the standard pattern? We have good reason to believe that a very substantial degree of attenuation has taken place. The strongest statistical testimony that we could perhaps hope to obtain is furnished by the picture of Chart 28, Part A, with the web-like, "criss-cross" movement which it shows. The indications of this chart are extremely important: this array of series exhibits nothing resembling a constant, or even a systematic relationship over time as to the direction and intensity of secular variation, but most decidedly the contrary. It is certain, then, that in the standard pattern — which is essentially an average — the diverse secular tendencies of the individual constituent series have very largely offset one another. And when we join with the striking indications of the "chart of ranks" the consideration that within each sub-period very great diversity of secular tendency appears among the several constituent series (as is brought out most vividly by the extent of the fan-like spread of the curves for each sub-period in the new logarithmic chart of original items by decades), it is obvious that this offsetting process must have gone very far indeed.[8] We can put the point negatively by saying that if the "rank curves" upon Chart 28, Part A, moved with an approach to parallelism, we should have much less reason for believing that the process of averaging had accomplished any very great attenuation of the secular element; and, in such a case, for us to contend — merely on the ground that the standard pattern is essentially an average — that such attenuation had occurred would put us in some uncomfortable analogy with the proverbial washermen who made a living by taking in one another's laundry.

The arguments of the immediately preceding paragraphs, though cogent, fail to put the case strongly enough. There is still more to be said. The standard pattern is not merely an average, but is an average of *a particular kind*. Specifically, the averaging process applied in obtaining the measure of central tendency within each

---

[8] While this chart has not been reproduced, the same phenomenon can readily be observed in Chart 23.

column of link-relative items in the multiple frequency table,[9] is to take the mean of the middle group of tally marks — those lying between the first and third quartiles. The significance of this with reference to our present question is easy to see. The nature of the averaging process involved in the calculation of the standard pattern is such as to reduce very materially (*over and above the reduction which would be accomplished by such an average as the arithmetic, geometric, or harmonic*) any distorting influences from non-typical, individualistic tendencies of particular constituent series. Consequently, if one (or even several) of the constituent series should experience within a given sub-period some violent deflection of secular movement, the abatement of the influence of this deflection would be notably greater for the standard pattern, with the special form of average there employed, than it would be were some such average as the arithmetic, geometric, or harmonic involved. We thus have still further ground for expecting attenuation of the secular element in the standard pattern.

Taking all things into account, the probabilities appear very high indeed that the secular influences of the individual series have been so weakened, so attenuated, that their rôle in the standard pattern is comparatively small. This conclusion must, of course, be stated in terms of probabilities. It is quite possible, looking at the matter abstractly as a problem in the handling of arithmetical processes, to build up sets of figures, pertaining to suppositional cases, for which the procedure would fail. If we posit the occurrence of some catastrophic event, of such nature as to bring about with comparative suddenness violent deflections of secular trends in the body of constituent series more or less simultaneously — and moreover the deflection of all (or nearly all) of them in the same direction, and quantitatively in a magnitude appreciable as relative to their respective measures of intensity in short-time movement [10] — we should arrive at a situation in which the "chart of ranks" would fail to give clear indication as to what was happening. The historical record of our pre-war period of analysis, 1866–1914, does not, however, suggest that any such catastrophic event took place. Moreover, even ignoring all historical knowledge regarding this specific time interval, it is not easy (especially if one puts aside the possibility of violent and rapid

---

[9] For detailed statement of the procedure, see Chapters III and IV.

[10] I.e., in relation to average deviation of link relatives.

monetary inflation) to conceive of, and to work out schematically the effects of, a cataclysm which would operate, upon the secular trends of the economic series within such diversified congeries as our present collection, with such a set of quasi-mathematical relationships as to make the "chart of ranks" furnish misleading indications.

For our particular body of statistical data and our pre-war time period, then, the probabilities appear very high indeed that in the standard pattern the secular element, though by no means reduced to insignificance, has nevertheless been very materially attenuated.

## The General Plan of Attack

Combining the conclusions just set forth and the various findings of Part Two and of Chapter XII, we are able to develop a procedure by means of which we shall derive *tentative* indications of the secular tendencies in the dozen leading economic series now under consideration. This statement requires elaboration.

In the first place, it may fairly be maintained that the cyclical element in the standard pattern (were we able completely to isolate it) could be taken as representative of a broader entity — the cyclical variation inherent in that *general* pattern of short-time economic fluctuation which in the course of the several pattern analyses of Part Two has been found so pervasive. We have in mind here, of course, the close similarity previously discovered between the link-relative standard pattern, as developed in Chapters III and IV, and the various other manifestations of the broad general pattern to which reference has just been made — i.e., the patterns for the structure of production, for production-group index numbers, for the employment index, for the structure of wholesale commodity prices, for commodity-price indexes, and for the group of miscellaneous series.

Further, we may argue that *if* in the standard pattern the form of cyclical movement *were* fully isolated, and if we should (by some appropriate methodological procedure) effect its elimination from the fluctuations of the original items [11] of the several individual series, we should by this means accomplish in each case approximately the elimination of the cyclical movement *of the series itself*, and thus derive an indication as to the form of secular

[11] Taken, say, in annual form; if quarterly items were employed, adjustment for seasonal variation (where needed) would, of course, be called for.

movement of the particular series. This conclusion is justified only because of the close correspondence which we have earlier demonstrated to exist between (1) the form of short-time variation in the general pattern for economic series, referred to just above, in its several manifestations — the standard pattern, and the various other patterns connected with production, employment, and commodity prices — and (2) the form of short-time variation in each of the dozen individual series whose secular tendencies are now under examination, such close correspondence being evidenced by the various link-relative charts of Part Two (we may refer in particular to Charts 4, 5, and 22), as well as by such original-item charts as Chart 23.

We have, then, concluded that *if* in the standard pattern the secular element *were* completely removed, and the form of cyclical variation for this pattern *were* therefore fully isolated, we should, through elimination of this form of cyclical variation from the fluctuations of the several individual series under consideration, accomplish in each case the approximate elimination of the cyclical movement of the series itself, and thus precipitate an indication of the form of the secular variation for such individual series. Now it is clear that in the standard pattern the influence of the secular element has in fact not been *completely* removed, and consequently the cyclical element has not been *fully* isolated. Nevertheless, if arguments presented earlier in this chapter are accepted, the secular element in the standard pattern must have been *very appreciably attenuated*, and consequently the pattern is *predominantly and mainly* indicative of cyclical variation. This last observation suggests that if (applying some appropriate methodology) we eliminate from the original items of our dozen leading economic series, each taken in turn, the form of the *total* fluctuation of the standard pattern (which, as we have seen, is made up of the predominant cyclical element, together with a residual secular element), we shall as a result of this statistical operation secure a *tentative* indication of the nature of the secular movement for the series in question. The picture which we thus obtain will not, to be sure, be a wholly true one; the indications of secular tendency for the individual series will have suffered some malformation resulting from the presence of a residuum of uneliminated secular element in the standard pattern. But taking into account two considerations — first, that, as our observations in connection with the "chart of ranks" (Chart 28, Part A) have made clear, each individual series in the list has its own, most definitely marked individualistic secular characteristics, and, second, that in the standard pattern the secular influence has been very materially attenuated — it may fairly be asserted that, in spite of the elements of malformation just referred to, the essential form of the secular variations for the several individual series will nevertheless be manifest, much as the essential form of a large and well-defined object is discernible from its image in a mirror, even though the glass be mildly warped by the presence here and there of moderate convexities and concavities.

## DERIVATION OF THE TREND-INDICATIONS BY DECADE SUB-PERIODS

### THE MODIFIED SERIES

We turn, then, to the problem of developing suitable methodology for derivation of trend-indications. We begin by setting up pairs of curves, illustrated by the three sets of lines upon Chart 29.[12] A discussion of the curves in the first section of the chart will make clear the nature of the general procedure here being applied. In this first section we make a comparison, upon a common grid background, of (a) the annual link relatives in average-deviation units for the production index, as derived in Chapter VIII, and (b) the annual link-relative standard pattern of Chapter IV (which, it will be remembered, is in average-deviation units). The link-relative standard pattern is that which was marked "$SP_1$" on Chart 12; this variation of the pattern is employed, in preference to that pertaining to calendar years ("$SP_0$"), because of the lag of approximately one-quarter of a year in the short-run movements of the standard pattern, as compared with those of the production index.

As we have earlier observed (cf. Chart 16, and the accompanying discussion in Chapter VIII), these two curves show a high degree of similarity in short-run movement. And if we scrutinize them carefully upon this common grid background against which they are now displayed, we see that their fluctuations exhibit a

---

[12] On Chart 29, the link-relative series for the production index, for the "check production index," and for railroad earnings have been reduced to average-deviation units, but have *not* in any case been adjusted for level by being divided through by the average link relative of the series — i.e., no correction for "long-time drift" of original items has been applied.

# CHART 29

### Link Relatives in Average-Deviation Units for (1) Production Index, (2) "Check Production Index," and (3) Railroad Earnings — Each Compared with Link-Relative Standard Pattern: by Years, 1867–1914

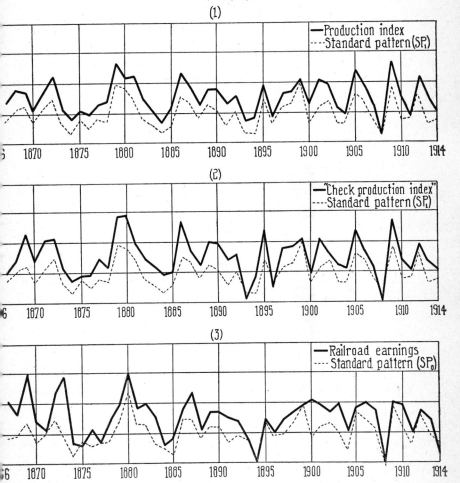

very close approach to parallelism, with, however, a barely perceptible tendency for the "band" — the vertical distance — between them to narrow in the course of the time period. This showing of the two curves, read in the light of our preceding argument, gives strong suggestion, as a tentative indication, of a logarithmic parabola for the secular trend of the production index — and specifically (in view of the magnitude of the gap between the curves,[13] and the extreme slowness with which this gap narrows over the period of analysis) a logarithmic parabola of such form as to involve a rather high average rate of growth accompanied by only slight retardation.[14]

The idea comes very readily to mind that we may give concrete expression to this tentative indication, afforded by the graph of *link relatives* comprising the first section of Chart 29, by the formation of a certain *chain series*, of such sort as to admit of ready comparison with the original items of the production index. Specifically, we (1) take the successive differences, year by year, 1867–1914, between the paired items of the two link-relative curves in the first section of Chart 29; (2) translate these differences into percentage ratios of change by multiplying them by the dispersion measure for the production index (the average deviation of the link relatives, 5.33 per cent) and then adding 100 per cent; and, finally, (3) form a chain series through successive multiplication of these ratios, taking the initial year (1866) as arbitrary base.[15]

We need some brief designation which may be applied to results obtained by methodology of this sort; and, since the broad purpose is to effect the modification of the series through elimination of their cyclical elements (to such an extent and as accurately as may be possible at any given stage of our progress), we have recourse to the term *modified series*.

The modified series, then, for the production index (obtained as above described, using the standard pattern as the basis of derivation) is shown as the top curve of Chart 30 (labelled "1a"). This curve completely confirms the suggestion yielded by the link-

---

[13] The gap averages roughly one "average-deviation unit," and the average deviation of link relatives for the production index is 5.33 per cent (cf. Table 8).

[14] For discussion of the properties of the logarithmic parabola and a simple illustrative case, see pp. 144–146; also see fn. 20 on p. 147 and fn. 37 on p. 163.

[15] For the purpose at hand, the choice of base period for the chain index is inconsequential.

# CHART 30

ORIGINAL ITEMS FOR (1) PRODUCTION INDEX,
(2) "CHECK PRODUCTION INDEX," AND (3) RAILROAD EARNINGS —
WITH FORM OF CYCLICAL VARIATION OF STANDARD PATTERN
(A, ORIGINAL; B, FIRST REVISION; C, SECOND REVISION) ELIMINATED:
BY YEARS, 1866–1914 *

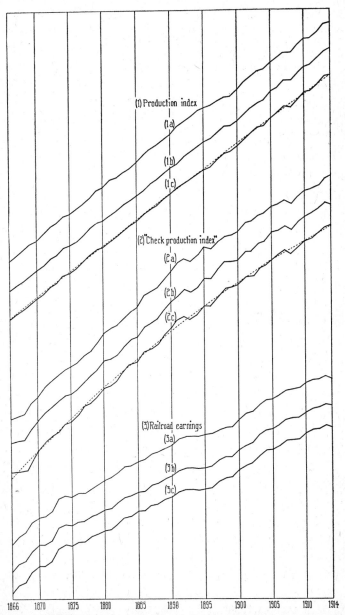

* Logarithmic vertical scales; the scale for railroad earnings is more compressed
than that for the two production indexes.

relative comparison in the first section of Chart 29 (as set forth just above) with respect to the tentative indication of secular trend for the production index. The modified series of Chart 30 (curve "1a") traces out a line which exhibits remarkable smooth-ness (in decided contrast with the wave-like fluctuations of wide amplitude in the original items of the series),[16] thus implying that we have had a considerable degree of success in freeing the series from its cyclical fluctuations. The first rough impression afforded by curve "1a" is that of a general straight-line movement (which, upon this logarithmic scale, would point to the compound-interest curve); but if we examine the line more carefully, we see that it has a slight but persistent curvature of such a simple sort as defi-nitely to suggest the logarithmic parabola.[17]

This tentative conclusion regarding the secular trend of the production index we now seek to verify from a particular point of view. In the latter part of Chapter VIII, it will be recalled, atten-tion was directed to the consideration that the present writer had been compelled to develop his own production index, and, since in the construction of this index a considerable body of discretionary judgments of necessity had to be made, the trustworthiness of the final results was to some extent prejudiced, in that even with the very best of intentions an investigator may unconsciously impress into the somewhat plastic mass of material confronting him certain of his preconceptions as to what the result *ought* to show. As a safeguard against such a *methodology bias* there was set up a "check production index" based upon production indicators which had been developed independently by other analysts.

We now, as a "control," put the "check production index" through the procedure which has just been applied to our own production index. The results emerging are essentially similar to those obtained for the production index itself. This is true as regards both the showing of the link-relative series (see the middle section of Chart 29) and that of the chain series (see the curve marked "2a" on Chart 30). The suggestion of a logarithmic-parabola secular trend is as clear for the "check production index" as for the production index; the only significant difference, in fact,

---

[16] Cf. Chart 14, in Chapter VIII.

[17] As to the appearance of the logarithmic parabola on charts drawn with logarithmic vertical scale, see fn. 19 in Chapter VII; also see the references indicated in fn. 14 of this chapter, just above.

is that the indications of retardation in rate of growth for the "check production index" are much stronger (cf. the comparatively rapid narrowing of the "band" between the curves, in Chart 29, and the more pronounced curvature in Chart 30). The difference between the two indexes with respect to indication of rate of retardation is largely explainable on technical grounds connected with their composition and construction. So far as tentative suggestion of the general form of secular trend is concerned, the "check production index" here affords full verification.

We now go on, and apply to each of the remaining eleven series under analysis the procedure which has just been carried out for the production index (as well as for the "check production index"). We may refer to the series railroad earnings for purposes of illustration. For railroad earnings, both the link-relative series (see the third section of Chart 29)[18] and the chain series (curve "3a" on Chart 30) give clear indication of general retardation in rate of secular growth; and there is here suggestion of a break in secular movement, somewhere in the late nineties.

We continue the computation of modified series until all of the dozen individual series under consideration have been treated. Before undertaking examination of the concrete results of these computations, it may be pointed out that — quite aside from the possible presence of "warping" tendencies having as their origin some residuum of secular influence in the standard pattern — several sources of approximation and irregularity are involved in our procedure. In each of the individual series, the picture of cyclical variation has doubtless some elements of error, traceable to statistical defects of the series connected with the basic material from which it is formed and perhaps with the technique of its construction; also, in some degree (though presumably much less significantly) certain of these elements of error may have affected the standard pattern. Further, the comparative amplitude measures (the average deviations) for the several series, as well as that for the standard pattern, are essentially *averages* of dispersion intensity over a long period; in so far as there is, within the time interval of analysis, intrinsic variation in the ratios of these amplitude

---

[18] For each individual series, we take proper account of the average lag or lead over the period of analysis, as compared with the standard pattern. Thus, for railroad earnings the "best lag" is zero, denoting concurrence. We therefore use the calendar-year link-relative standard pattern ("SP₀"); cf. Chart 12.

measures, one compared with another (and unquestionably such variations are present), our results suffer some distortion. Also to be taken into account is the timing of movement: the average lag or lead (as compared with the standard pattern) for each series is measured only to the nearest quarter of a year, and (which is more significant) the intrinsic lag or lead tends to vary over the period. Finally, and most important of all, even though in each case the general correlation between the form of short-time movement for the particular series and that for the pervasive economic pattern has been shown to be very high, departures from precise congruence of cyclical fluctuations nevertheless appear throughout; here again there is opportunity for some distortion of results.

When we turn to detailed examination of the modified series, we observe generally a strong tendency toward continuity of movement, thus confirming the findings of Chapter XII. The several curves for the modified series are indeed by no means perfectly smooth; we discover in them irregular movements. But such irregularities we may fairly attribute mainly to the elements of approximation involved in our procedure, set forth just above, as well as occasional extraneous variations present in the original items of the several individual series.

### THE TREND-INDICATIONS

In order to free the modified series from these irrelevant details we fit, for each series, a set of lines to the points on the modified-series curve — one line for each decade sub-period.[19] For the purposes of the present attack upon the problem of establishing trend-indications — which is only tentative — it appears most expedient to confine ourselves to the fitting of *straight lines* to the data on logarithmic scale, which carry only the simple implication of a constant rate of increase (or decrease) over the sub-period. Judgments regarding the presence of curvilinear tendencies in secular variation can best be made at a later stage of the investigation. In numerous instances the points within the sub-period lie so nearly upon a straight line that the fitting can readily be performed by eye; where this is not feasible, least-squares fitting is adequate. The various straight lines, which we shall designate as

---

[19] In fitting the trend-indication lines, certain conspicuous irregularities (e.g., the "tariff-change" peak in imports, 1897) have been ignored. (See also the next footnote.)

tentative *trend-indications*, are shown in collected form on Chart 31, Part A.[20]

It will be noted that we refer to the present array of trend-indications as *tentative*. We attach this adjective because the secular element is still present, to some degree at least, in the standard pattern. We shall feel at liberty to remove this modifier, which pointedly calls attention to the preliminary nature of the results, only if and when the freeing of the standard pattern from secular influences is substantially complete.

When we examine the array of tentative trend-indications in Chart 31, Part A, we first observe that we have obtained further general confirmation of our previous conclusions (set down in Chapter XII, and also in an earlier paragraph of the present chapter) with respect to general continuity in the secular tendencies of this group of series. To be sure, the lines upon the chart seldom "match up" precisely at the points of junction, but the various gaps are usually comparatively small. And, bearing in mind the essential continuity of the modified series from which the present trend-indications are derived, it appears that we should attribute these various failures of precise joining to the presence of irremediable defects having their origin in flaws of original data or limitations of methodology, and to the fact that (at certain points) the trend movement is intrinsically curvilinear and thus fails to receive adequate representation by the straight lines which have been fitted (cf. on Chart 31, Part A, the lines for railroad earnings, wholesale commodity prices).

The assemblage of trend-indications on Chart 31, Part A, affords conclusive verification of our preliminary judgment, based upon the study of ranks, that the series exhibit wide diversity and decided individuality as regards the form of secular variation. Our belief (set forth at length in the first part of this chapter) that in the standard pattern the secular element has been very materially attenuated is thus given further support.

Looking again at the chart, we see that the general indications, with respect to comparative simplicity of form of secular move-

[20] For commercial-paper rates, quite obviously the modified series (and the several lines fitted thereto) are materially distorted by the frequent irregular fluctuations, connected with economic crises and other disturbances, to which reference was made in Chapter XII (cf. Chart 23). For this series, accordingly, we have fitted revised lines, omitting the irregular items in the process of computing. These revised lines (dotted on Chart 31) will be used as the trend-indications for this series.

# CHART 31

### Tentative Trend-Indications for Individual Series, by Second Method (Gradual Attenuation of Secular Elements in Standard Pattern): by Sub-Periods, 1866–1914 *

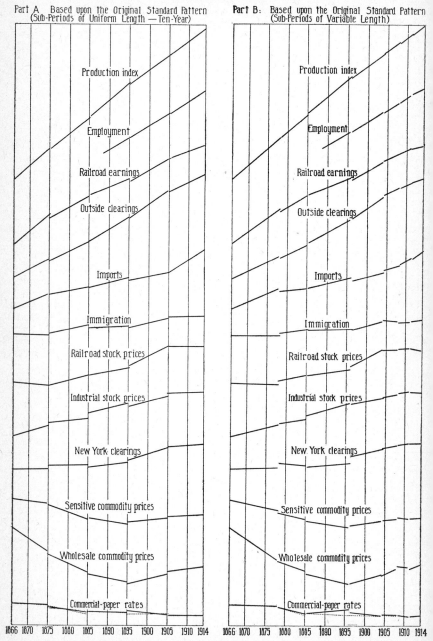

Part A  Based upon the Original Standard Pattern (Sub-Periods of Uniform Length — Ten-Year)

Part B:  Based upon the Original Standard Pattern (Sub-Periods of Variable Length)

Production index

Employment

Railroad earnings

Outside clearings

Imports

Immigration

Railroad stock prices

Industrial stock prices

New York clearings

Sensitive commodity prices

Wholesale commodity prices

Commercial-paper rates

1866 1870  1875  1880  1885  1890  1895  1900  1905  1910 1914

* Logarithmic vertical scales; to facilitate presentation within limited space, varying scales are employed for the several series.

# CHART 31

## TENTATIVE TREND-INDICATIONS FOR INDIVIDUAL SERIES, BY SECOND METHOD
### (GRADUAL ATTENUATION OF SECULAR ELEMENTS IN STANDARD PATTERN):
### BY SUB-PERIODS, 1866–1914 *(Continued)*

Part C. Based upon the Standard Pattern, First Revision

Part D Based upon the Standard Pattern Second Revision

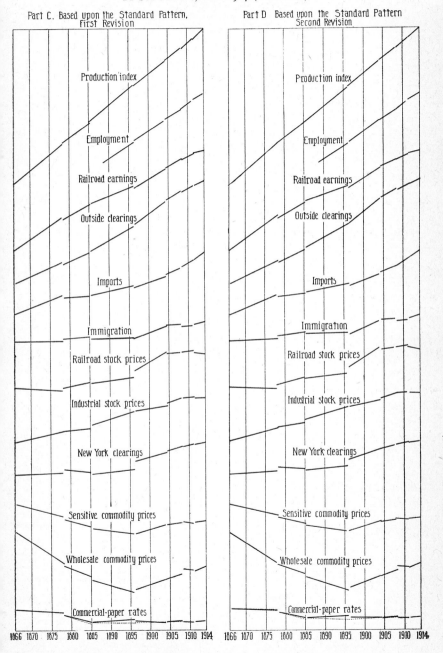

ment in the eleven series extending over the period 1866–1914,[21] are quite in accord with the inferences previously drawn from the dispersion measures derived for the table of decade rankings (Table 12), as well as from the "chart of ranks" (Chart 28, Part A). This study of ranks suggested, in the first place, that the production index had a relatively simple form of secular movement, as compared with most of the other ten series; the tentative trend-indications of Chart 31, Part A, are in accord with this earlier suggestion. In fact, the indication of this chart, like that of Chart 30 (curve "1a"), is that the pre-war trend of the production index over our period of analysis can be suitably represented by a single simple mathematical curve — the logarithmic parabola.

In this earlier study of ranks, the series (setting aside the production index) seemed to fall rather definitely into two groups — (1) railroad earnings and outside clearings, and (2) the remaining eight series. It appeared that the secular movements of the two series of the first group possessed the quality of simplicity in appreciably higher degree than those of the eight series of the second group (cf. Table 12, and also Chart 28, Part A). These previous observations, also, receive confirmation from the trend-indication lines of Chart 31, Part A.

Our methodology, as so far developed, is from some points of view unsatisfactory. The conclusions just set forth suggest a possibility of using the present results to effect an improvement, in one particular aspect at least, of this methodology: *viz.*, in the basis for choice of boundary dates of sub-periods. This statement may now be elaborated.

The present selection of sub-periods, though based upon cogent considerations, is nevertheless analytically unsatisfactory, inasmuch as it represents the arbitrary setting-up of a fixed time interval of analysis (the decade) — thus leading to the establishment of a schedule of sub-periods which may very well be, and in all probability is, Procrustean with respect to the intrinsic nature of those cyclical elements we know to be present in the several series. We wish to substitute for this arbitrary set-up some new arrangement having a more logical foundation. And, further, we wish to arrive at this new arrangement by a line of thought *inde-*

---

[21] We omit the employment index from the present discussion, since it covers only one-half the period of analysis.

*pendent* of that which was followed in obtaining the schedule of sub-periods employed for Chart 23, in Chapter XII.[22]

The idea comes to mind that we might utilize the two series of the "first group" just above — the group which we characterized as possessing, over the time period of analysis, the relatively simpler form of secular movement — to obtain a more logical basis for sub-period delimitation. If, on Chart 31, Part A, we examine the trend-indications for the two individual series of the "first group" — railroad earnings and outside clearings — we see that in each case the lines indicate definite departure from a straight-line movement (which, if present, would upon this logarithmic scale denote the compound-interest curve). For each of the two series, there is definite indication of curvature in form of secular movement, although the precise nature of this curvature is not quite clear.

Now we desire to use the tentative trend-indications for railroad earnings and outside clearings as an aid in arriving at preliminary judgments regarding the form of the respective secular trends of these two series; at the same time, having in mind the elements of unsatisfactoriness in our present procedure (and in particular the arbitrary, Procrustean criterion for delimitation of sub-periods), we feel constrained to be *very conservative* in reading the implications of the trend-indication lines of Chart 31, Part A, even for these two series. All things considered, the wisest decision seems to be in each of the two cases at hand to make no more complex assumption at this time than that of constancy in the *rate of change* of the ratio of secular growth; in other words, provisionally to employ the logarithmic parabola for trend representation. The secular trends thus obtained for the two series *are* indeed highly "provisional"; the chances are very good that we shall modify them appreciably before we reach the end of the present analysis. But these trends do represent a conservative reading of the trend-indications of Chart 31, Part A, and such a conservative reading is all that we are justified in making at this stage of our analytical progress.

We next fit a logarithmic-parabola trend to the annual original items of each of the two series railroad earnings and outside clear-

---

[22] [We are actuated also, of course, by the desire to keep the line of procedure for the present chapter independent of that of Chapter XIII.]

ings, and, through elimination of such trends,[23] obtain two curves representative of the cyclical variations of the respective series. These curves of cyclical variation, it need hardly be said, must also be regarded as highly provisional, and subject to possible later revision. The two cyclical curves show a rather high degree of correlation. Now if, taking a simple arithmetic mean,[24] we average the two curves, year by year, we obtain a new curve which exhibits seven distinct wave-like swings about the horizontal base line (100 per cent): 1866–78, 1878–85, 1885–96, 1896–1904, 1904–08, 1908–11, 1911–14.[25]

The list of sub-periods thus suggested turns out to be identical with that of Chart 23, arrived at in Chapter XII; *but the path of analysis in derivation is independent.* And it may further be remarked that, keeping strictly within the confines of the analytical work of the present chapter, we could obtain this same list of sub-periods in yet another way, *still independently of the developments of Chart 23 in Chapter XII.* We could, that is, adopt provisionally the suggestion — furnished by the curves of Chart 29 (first section) and Chart 30 (the line "1a"), as well as by the trend-indication lines of Chart 31, Part A — of a logarithmic-parabola secular trend for the production index; eliminate such trend from the original items; and then, from the resulting curve of cyclical variations, read off the seven cycle periods. To be sure, the curve of cyclical variation for the production index, just referred to, would be identical with the top line on Chart 17 (used in the analysis of Chapter XII), but the *logical derivation* would be independent.[26]

Though the new selection of sub-periods — set up on the basis

[23] In conformity with the finding of Chapter XII as regards logarithmically-additive relationships (cf. also Chapter III, especially Chart 2), we employ the conventional process for trend elimination, i.e., division of original items by their respective trend ordinates, expressing the results as percentages.

[24] In view of the concurrence between the two series, no more elaborate procedure seems called for.

[25] The first swing (possibly the last also) is incomplete (cf. fn. 4 in Chapter XII).

[26] [Comparing our current route of analysis with that of Chapter XIII, we see that, since the derivation of the variable-length sub-periods in the present chapter is made without reference to the production index, full independence of the path of procedure between the two chapters has been maintained. But, *even if* in the present chapter we had used the production index (employing the trend-indications of Chart 31, Part A, as pointing toward the logarithmic-parabola trend), the procedure would nevertheless have been wholly deserving of the characterization "independent," for the establishment of the logarithmic parabola as the secular trend

of certain characteristics of the two series, railroad earnings and outside clearings — can thus be given confirmation, we must nevertheless regard such selection (like the cyclical curves and the

TABLE 13

"Dispersion Measures" for Eleven Series:
by Sub-Periods of Variable Length*

| Series | "Dispersion measures" | |
|---|---|---|
| | Simple | Weighted |
| Production index ........................ | 0.49 | 0.49 |
| Railroad earnings ....................... | 0.57 | 0.66 |
| Outside clearings ........................ | 0.61 | 0.60 |
| Imports ............................... | 1.27 | 1.27 |
| New York clearings ..................... | 1.34 | 1.30 |
| Industrial stock prices .................. | 1.34 | 1.43 |
| Commercial-paper rates ................. | 1.59 | 1.63 |
| Immigration .......................... | 1.59 | 1.71 |
| Sensitive commodity prices .............. | 1.63 | 1.53 |
| Railroad stock prices ................... | 2.04 | 2.03 |
| Wholesale commodity prices ............. | 3.34 | 3.19 |

* These "dispersion measures" are analogous to those of Table 12. In the present case, however, two sets of results are presented: (1) simple average deviations, regarding the sub-periods as of equal importance, and (2) weighted average deviations, weighting by length of sub-period, in years.

trend-indications upon which it rests) as *provisional*, and we shall in fact hold the list subject to amendment should later analytical developments point that way.

## Derivation of the Trend-Indications by Sub-Periods of Variable Length

Our first use of the new list of sub-periods is to employ it in a study of ranks, along the same lines as that earlier carried out, but substituting the new list of "variable-length" sub-periods for the old list based upon decades. The results for the present case are presented in Table 13 and in Part B of Chart 28. These results substantiate the findings of the corresponding study by decade sub-periods, as set down previously.

We now, working with the same modified series as before,

of the production index is reached in the present chapter by an analytical route distinct from that of Chapter XIII.]

develop new trend-indications for the several series (Chart 31, Part B), this time fitting the lines with reference to the sub-periods of variable length. With respect to these results we may state certain conclusions. (1) We observe (ignoring for the moment the production index) that among the series which extend over the entire period 1866–1914 [27] there is none for which the trend-indications suggest that the secular movement can be satisfactorily represented by a single simple mathematical curve. (2) We note, further, the appearance for many of the series around the turn of the century (cf. the behavior of the lines of Chart 31, Part B, for the sub-period 1896–1904) of alteration, in some instances rather abrupt, in the direction or slope of trend. (3) The new trend-indications — though doubtless superior to the old, since the delimitation of sub-periods has been made on a more logical basis — must nevertheless be designated (as in the earlier case) "tentative," inasmuch as our attempts to discern the precise nature of the secular movements for the several individual series are still interfered with by the residuum of secular influence present in the standard pattern.

We now undertake to establish tentative secular trends for the ten series.[28] And in our successive decisions as to procedure we shall be particularly guided by the findings enumerated in the preceding paragraph: *first*, that for no one of these ten series is the secular trend capable of satisfactory representation by a single simple mathematical curve; *second*, that there is in the neighborhood of the turn of the century a widespread tendency among these series toward alteration in the direction or slope of trend; and, *third*, that the trend-indications of Chart 31, Part B, must be regarded as tentative, since they are subject to some degree of malformation on account of the residuum of secular influence still present in the standard pattern.

Having in mind the *first finding*, as just set forth, we decide not to attempt in any instance the representation of the secular movement over the period 1866–1914 by a single curve, but rather for each series to break that long interval into parts and deal with

[27] We again set aside the employment index, which is available for only one-half the period. For the employment index, the trend-indications of Chart 31, Part B, trace out very nearly a straight line (upon the logarithmic scale), thus suggesting a compound-interest curve.

[28] In addition, that is, to the production index and the employment index, already discussed.

these parts separately. And, having in mind the *second finding*, we deem it wisest to begin for each series by studying the secular tendencies of the two periods 1866–96 and 1904–14, respectively, and then (in the light of the information gained from this examination) to make an attack on the more troublesome case of 1896–1904. Finally, having in mind the *third finding*, we shall be careful to adopt at this stage of our procedure a rather conservative attitude in reading the implications of the trend-indication lines: we shall infer curvilinear trend movements and breaks in trend only when the evidence is very convincing, and if there be doubt as to a choice between a simple and a complex trend-representation, we shall give preference to the former. We shall, in fact, confine ourselves here to straight lines and second-degree parabolas (which, drawn upon these graphs with logarithmic vertical scale, denote of course compound-interest curves and logarithmic parabolas, respectively).

We may illustrate the procedure by reference to the series railroad earnings (cf. Chart 31, Part B): for the period 1866–96, rather than make a break at 1878 we fit a single parabola,[29] thus giving preference to the more conservative reading; for the period 1904–14, the indication of curvature is clear, and we fit another parabola; so far as the intermediate period 1896–1904 is concerned, the suggestion of the trend-indication lines is that the secular movement can be satisfactorily represented by the backward extension of the 1904–14 parabola. For the series imports (to illustrate further), in the first long period, 1866–96, the evidence is rather strong for the assumption of a trend break at about 1878,[30] but, conforming to our policy of conservatism, we content ourselves with the fitting of a single straight line, 1866–96; in the period 1904–14, the indications are fairly definite for a parabolic trend; for the period 1896–1904, we extend the 1904–14 trend backward, rather than accept the suggestion of a possible "gap" at 1904.

---

[29] For the sake of brevity, we shall throughout the remainder of this chapter describe the trends as they would appear upon a chart with logarithmic vertical scale. The reader can readily make mentally the transliteration to an arithmetic-scale basis.

[30] In fact, the sharp movement of 1866–78 appears to be the continuation of a rapid upward tendency which had its beginning in the fifties. See the article by C. J. Bullock and H. L. Micoleau, "Foreign Trade and the Business Cycle," *Review of Economic Statistics*, XIII (November 1931), pp. 138–159.

The tentative secular-trend lines for the several series, derived as just illustrated, are listed in Appendix XIV–A, Part I. These trends are based upon *conservative* readings of the tentative trend-indications of Chart 31, Part B; and it is perhaps unnecessary to add that — for reasons which have been fully set forth above — we regard these lines of secular trend as themselves decidedly provisional; we shall hold them open to revision as later methodological developments may require.

### REVISION OF THE STANDARD PATTERN

We are now in position to derive a revised standard pattern which will undoubtedly be superior to the original standard pattern, in that even the small residuum of secular influence there present will be very largely eliminated, and the cyclical element will thus be much nearer to complete isolation. Specifically, we plan to recompute the standard pattern, basing it upon the ten individual series now under analysis, and substituting (in place of the crude correction for "long-time drift" employed in the original computation) adjustments for secular trend of the several series, employing the tentative trends decided upon as described in the preceding section and listed in Appendix XIV–A, Part I.

The new standard pattern is shown upon Chart 32 (the second curve) in comparison with the original standard pattern (the first curve). The trend elimination in the new pattern is without question much further advanced than in the old: this can easily be appreciated by making a mental comparison, for each series of the array of Chart 31, Part B, of (a) the actual trend-indications there plotted, with (b) an imagined straight line drawn through for the entire period 1866–1914 to represent the constant rate of growth implied in the crude correction for "long-time drift" of Chapters III and IV. Certainly, the process of attenuation of the secular element, which even in the original computation of the standard pattern had been to a considerable degree accomplished (cf. the arguments of earlier pages in this chapter), has now been markedly advanced. We may feel confident that only in very minor degree is the essentially *cyclical* picture presented by the revised standard pattern subject to any malformation due to secular elements.

These conclusions suggest that if we were now to repeat our preceding analysis, taking the new revised standard pattern as

THE STANDARD PATTERN

COMPARISON OF (1) ORIGINAL, FIRST REVISION, AND SECOND REVISION: BY YEARS, 1866–1914
AND (2) ORIGINAL AND SECOND REVISION: BY QUARTERS, 1866–I TO 1914–II *

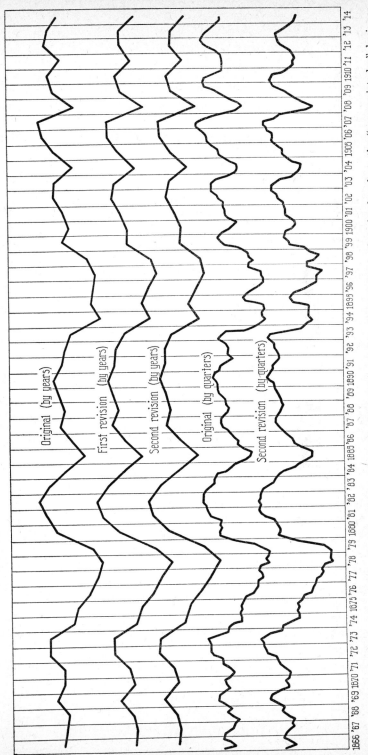

Original (by years)

First revision (by years)

Second revision (by years)

Original (by quarters)

Second revision (by quarters)

1866 '67 '68 '69 1870 '71 '72 '73 '74 1875 '76 '77 '78 '79 1880 '81 '82 '83 '84 1885 '86 '87 '88 '89 1890 '91 '92 '93 '94 1895 '96 '97 '98 '99 1900 '01 '02 '03 '04 1905 '06 '07 '08 '09 1910 '11 '12 '13 '14

* Uniform logarithmic vertical scales. The "original standard pattern," annual and quarterly, is that developed on the "appropriate-lag" basis, as described in Chapter IV.

basis in place of the original standard pattern, we should obtain results in which we could have decidedly greater confidence. We accordingly refashion the essential portions of our earlier work, with the alteration of methodology just indicated.[31]

The changes in the appearance of the results — whether one looks at the modified series (compare curves "1b," "2b," and "3b," of Chart 30 with curves "1a," "2a," and "3a," respectively), or at the trend-indications (compare Part C of Chart 31 with Part B) — are but slight. And this is despite the fact that (as we have just seen) in the revised standard pattern the underlying judgments as to the nature of the secular movements for the several constituent series are most decidedly at variance with the assumption, implicit in the crude correction for "long-time drift" of the original standard pattern, of a constant rate of growth for each series; and further despite the fact that the alteration produced in the standard-pattern curve by the revision, while by no means pronounced, is nevertheless sufficient to be observable in the chart (cf. Chart 32). The explanation of this seeming anomaly lies in the consideration that the inherent secular tendencies of the several constituent series are in each case so pronounced and so individualistic that by comparison the changes in their trend-indications occasioned by the revision of the standard pattern are minor, and are graphically barely discernible (once more, compare Parts B and C of Chart 31).

Though the revision of the standard pattern thus produces only slight alteration in the outward form of results — for modified series and for trend-indications, as exhibited in Charts 30 and 31, respectively — nevertheless in one sense the results have changed substantially. That is to say, inasmuch as the attenuation of the secular influences in the standard pattern, already far advanced, has now to a very large extent been completed (and, consequently, the isolation of the cyclical element almost accomplished), we may have a very much higher degree of confidence than before in the dependability of these results as indicators of form of secular movement. We therefore feel less constraint — less compulsion toward conservatism — in drawing from the trend-indications inferences as to the nature of secular tendencies.[32]

---

[31] In particular, we reconsider the schedule of sub-period delimitation dates, and come out with the same conclusions as before.

[32] Though of course we should not (even positing the absolutely complete

We may, then, in the light of our present increased confidence as to dependability of the trend-indication lines, reconsider the earlier decisions with respect to tentative secular trends for the several series, endeavoring to achieve clearer definition. When we systematically survey the series, however, we find that in only three of the ten cases does the evidence appear sufficiently strong to justify us in revising the previous judgments. As is set forth in Appendix XIV–A, Part II, the three series in question are imports, immigration, and railroad stock prices. The revisions have only moderate effects: in the case of imports, for example, the change consists in introducing a break in trend at 1878; two straight lines are fitted (upon logarithmic scale) — one for 1866–78 and one for 1878–96 — in place of the single line previously fitted for 1866–96.

## FURTHER REVISION OF THE STANDARD PATTERN

The refinements which we have been able to make in the tentative secular trends for the three series — imports, immigration, and railroad stock prices — suggest that we may still further improve the standard pattern by recomputing it once more, substituting the new trends for the old in these three series. The annual pattern resulting from this computation — which we may designate "standard pattern, second revision" — is shown as the third line on Chart 32. We also develop a *quarterly* series for the "standard pattern, second revision"; this is shown as the last curve on Chart 32, in comparison with the original quarterly standard pattern.[33] The numerical values of the "standard pattern, second revision," annual and quarterly, are given in Table 14.[34]

It will be noted that this new annual pattern exhibits only minor differences in movement from that obtained in the earlier revision (compare the second and third lines of Chart 32). It would ap-

---

elimination of secular influences from the standard pattern) be justified in a mere slavish adherence to the track of these trend-indication lines; we should still have to be guided by judgments as to reasonable probabilities.

[33] Developed in Chapter IV. See fn. 14 in Chapter IV.

[34] The original standard pattern, annual and quarterly — together with its subsequent revisions — has been calculated with arbitrary base period. This has so far been quite satisfactory, for in our analytical work up to this point the base period of the standard pattern has been entirely inconsequential. For the purposes of formal presentation in Table 14, however — as well as in Chart 34, in the next chapter — it has seemed best to show the standard pattern on a broader base and accordingly it has been shifted to the base, average for 1866–1913 = 100.

# TABLE 14

## STANDARD PATTERN, SECOND REVISION: BY QUARTERS AND BY YEARS, 1866–1914

### (Average for 1866–1913 = 100)

| Year | Quarterly | | | | | Year | Quarterly | | | | |
|------|-----------|---|---|---|---|------|-----------|---|---|---|---|
| | First quarter | Second quarter | Third quarter | Fourth quarter | Annual | | First quarter | Second quarter | Third quarter | Fourth quarter | Annual |
| 1866 | 104.0 | 97.1 | 99.9 | 104.9 | 101.4 | 1891 | 108.8 | 108.6 | 106.6 | 105.2 | 107.2 |
| 1867 | 103.2 | 101.2 | 98.4 | 98.8 | 100.3 | 1892 | 106.2 | 106.7 | 107.6 | 108.1 | 107.2 |
| 1868 | 97.5 | 102.2 | 106.1 | 104.1 | 102.6 | 1893 | 112.8 | 110.7 | 96.8 | 91.3 | 103.0 |
| 1869 | 109.6 | 114.1 | 113.0 | 107.7 | 111.1 | 1894 | 88.3 | 84.6 | 87.1 | 87.1 | 86.8 |
| 1870 | 100.9 | 101.3 | 103.1 | 101.1 | 101.7 | 1895 | 86.6 | 87.4 | 96.6 | 98.4 | 92.3 |
| 1871 | 99.9 | 102.3 | 107.2 | 108.3 | 104.4 | 1896 | 94.8 | 90.9 | 85.7 | 83.2 | 88.6 |
| 1872 | 108.6 | 115.5 | 117.1 | 117.5 | 114.7 | 1897 | 83.4 | 81.8 | 80.5 | 88.4 | 83.5 |
| 1873 | 118.0 | 120.9 | 112.6 | 105.3 | 114.2 | 1898 | 88.4 | 84.5 | 82.4 | 86.0 | 85.3 |
| 1874 | 104.1 | 99.4 | 94.0 | 93.7 | 97.8 | 1899 | 90.5 | 97.7 | 99.4 | 101.5 | 97.3 |
| 1875 | 94.8 | 94.0 | 94.9 | 92.9 | 94.2 | 1900 | 100.1 | 96.4 | 94.0 | 94.2 | 96.2 |
| 1876 | 91.5 | 86.9 | 86.1 | 85.1 | 87.5 | 1901 | 98.2 | 100.3 | 100.4 | 101.0 | 100.0 |
| 1877 | 84.5 | 81.6 | 80.7 | 81.7 | 82.2 | 1902 | 102.2 | 105.0 | 106.5 | 109.0 | 105.9 |
| 1878 | 80.1 | 75.7 | 77.2 | 77.2 | 77.6 | 1903 | 109.1 | 107.3 | 102.8 | 96.1 | 103.8 |
| 1879 | 77.1 | 80.2 | 86.1 | 96.1 | 84.9 | 1904 | 91.9 | 91.0 | 91.1 | 96.0 | 92.5 |
| 1880 | 107.1 | 106.3 | 105.7 | 107.0 | 106.7 | 1905 | 100.4 | 101.8 | 102.5 | 105.8 | 102.6 |
| 1881 | 108.8 | 117.2 | 120.2 | 121.0 | 116.8 | 1906 | 108.7 | 107.8 | 107.9 | 112.0 | 109.1 |
| 1882 | 120.1 | 120.6 | 120.3 | 120.1 | 120.3 | 1907 | 115.0 | 115.0 | 106.8 | 103.2 | 110.0 |
| 1883 | 118.0 | 114.0 | 110.0 | 108.7 | 112.4 | 1908 | 86.8 | 84.0 | 87.6 | 91.7 | 87.6 |
| 1884 | 106.4 | 103.1 | 96.5 | 93.4 | 99.9 | 1909 | 96.4 | 99.2 | 103.2 | 97.9 | 101.8 |
| 1885 | 87.8 | 86.2 | 86.4 | 91.2 | 88.0 | 1910 | 110.0 | 108.4 | 102.3 | 97.8 | 104.6 |
| 1886 | 95.6 | 97.2 | 99.5 | 101.2 | 98.5 | 1911 | 94.9 | 95.1 | 93.7 | 94.6 | 94.7 |
| 1887 | 105.3 | 107.2 | 108.4 | 107.5 | 107.1 | 1912 | 97.3 | 100.0 | 104.1 | 105.3 | 101.7 |
| 1888 | 105.2 | 103.9 | 102.7 | 104.2 | 104.0 | 1913 | 106.3 | 103.2 | 99.7 | 97.3 | 101.6 |
| 1889 | 104.6 | 105.9 | 107.2 | 108.4 | 106.5 | 1914 | 93.7 | 93.4 | ... | ... | 93.6* |
| 1890 | 109.1 | 111.0 | 113.7 | 112.4 | 111.4 | | | | | | |

pear that the process of gradual attenuation of the secular elements in the standard pattern has now eventuated in virtually complete elimination of such elements, and that we may regard the standard pattern curves — annual and quarterly — emerging from our second revision as constituting a rather faithful picture of *the cyclical element in isolation.*

We now recompute the modified series, this time, of course, employing the latest revised standard pattern as basis; again no essential change appears in the results (cf. the pertinent curves of Charts 30 and 31). In particular, we note that the suggestion of logarithmic-parabola secular trends for the production index and for the "check production index" is definitely maintained. This fact has been brought out explicitly by fitting such parabolas to the two curves (cf. the thin lines drawn through them on Chart 30). As will be seen, the fit (barring small irregularities) is close in both cases.[35]

In the second revision of the trend-indications certain slight modifications appear, but, as before, the underlying individualistic secular tendencies of the individual series are so pronounced that the eye is scarcely able to detect any change in the appearance of the trend-indication lines (compare Parts C and D of Chart 31). Our confidence in these lines has notwithstanding been still further increased, inasmuch as now we know that the standard pattern is virtually free from the extraneous secular element, which previously interfered with our judgments. We once more reconsider the schedule of tentative trends in Appendix XIV–A. We do not, however, find (either in the new statistical array of curves or in our attitude of increased confidence) sufficient ground for altering any of the previous decisions.

Manifestly, we have reached the logical stopping place in the present line of procedure. The process of gradual attenuation of the secular elements in the standard pattern has been carried to the point of practically complete elimination, resulting in the emergence of a pattern for which the isolation of the cyclical element has in effect been fully accomplished.

The main body of Chapter XIV is now concluded. In the introductory pages of this chapter it was indicated that we took

---

[35] [And, incidentally, the logarithmic-parabola equations just derived are very nearly the same (except for the constant term in each case, of course) as those we

our departure from the same starting point as in Chapter XIII —
we started, that is, from the position gained through the systematic search for patterns in economic data, as described in Part
Two of this volume, and the investigation into the fundamental
nature of time-series fluctuations, as described in Chapter XII.
From this common starting point the routes of Chapters XIII and
XIV diverged, and traced out their independent courses. Now
their paths join again. By independent analyses we have obtained
results closely agreeing in their indications as to the form of secular movements (compare the trend-indications of Chart 27 in
Chapter XIII with those of Chart 31, Part D, in the present chapter).[36] And it goes without saying that the warnings and reservations set down in Chapter XIII (see pages 283 and 288–289)
should be considered as brought forward and repeated here —
most especially the "caveat" against "perversion of the methodology" by applying our procedure to a series not possessing the
property of correspondence in short-run variation with that general pattern of short-run movement which we, in Part Two, found
so pervasive in the nation's economic life.

Before closing the present discussion, we should take one further
step. So far as the derivation of trend-indications by the procedure developed in the main body of this chapter is concerned,
we could not profitably have gone further in attempts to improve
our judgments, or to refine our results. And yet we know that this
procedure has, so to speak, specific organic weaknesses which
could not be removed, or even remedied, merely through improvement of the standard pattern. These weaknesses flow from certain
limitations of the methodology which, in turn, are connected with
the facts that in its application (1) we have implicitly assumed
for each series *constancy of amplitude ratio* over the entire period
1866–1914; (2) we further have assumed *constancy of lag* over
the entire period; (3) we have — in the course of obtaining our

---

obtained by a different path of analysis and computation in Chapter XIII, thus
affording confirmation by an independent procedure.]

[36] Attention may incidentally be called to the very close resemblance (differences
in lag and in amplitude of fluctuation aside) between the cyclical variations of the
standard pattern — "second revision" — and of the production index (as derived in
Chapter XIII). See the first two curves of Chart 34, in the next chapter. This
resemblance is all the more striking in view of the fact that these two cyclical curves
are based upon entirely distinct sets of statistical series and have been developed
independently of each other.

# CHART 33

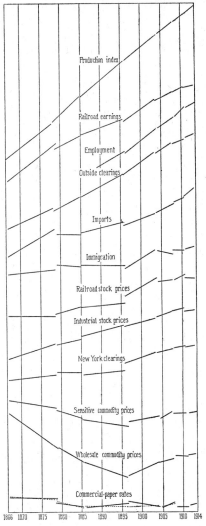

* Logarithmic vertical scales; to facilitate presentation within limited space, varying scales are employed for the several series.

various tentative secular trends, essentially involved in the process of successively revising the standard pattern — from necessity fitted such trends to the original items of the several series, rather than to the trend-indications or to the modified series.[37]

But now that we have succeeded in finally developing a standard pattern in which the cyclical element has been essentially isolated, it is possible to apply a different methodology, embodying the idea of *variable amplitude ratios* and *variable lags* as among the sub-periods, and permitting the fitting of lines of trend-representation to the *derived entity* — to the trend-indications or to the modified series [38] — rather than to the original items: in a word, to apply the procedure outlined in the latter half of Chapter XIII, but substituting the cyclical variations of the standard pattern ("second revision," of course) in place of those of the production index. The resulting trend-indications, presented in Chart 33, are almost precisely identical with those obtained in the preceding chapter (cf. Chart 27).

We have thus secured, by two independent methods, an array of *trend-indications* for our group of leading economic series. We shall have before us in the next chapter the task of transliterating these trend-indications into *trend-representations* explicitly tracing out the secular trends of the respective series.

[37] It would not have worked out to try to fit to the trend-indications or to the modified series, for these were "warped" by the residuum of secular influence present in the standard pattern until after the "second revision" was completed, and consequently any trends fitted to them would correspondingly have been systematically subject to mild deflection.

[38] See p. 334, in Chapter XV.

THE ARRAY OF SECULAR TRENDS AND CYCLICAL VARIATIONS
FOR LEADING ECONOMIC SERIES

THE TASK now before us is, with the aid of the information given by a composite chart of trend-indications (Chart 27 or, alternatively, Chart 33) and of inferences drawn from the various curves of modified series (e.g., those of Chart 26), to set up lines of secular trend for the several leading economic series which we have had under analysis in the last three chapters, and thus to obtain an explicit representation of their secular and cyclical variations.

### DERIVATION OF THE SECULAR TRENDS

In attacking this task, we take as our starting point the trend-indications of Chart 27 [1] — together with the modified series upon which they are based. Knowing as we do the methodological and other limitations upon the precision of the trend-indications — set forth in Chapter XIII (and also in Chapter XIV) — we shall avoid mere slavish adherence to the track of these indications. On the other hand, reviewing all the previously derived pertinent evidence and especially remembering the generally close correspondence among the series in respect to contour of short-time movement (as revealed in Chart 23), we do not feel justified in departing very far from the suggestions afforded by the trend-indications as to the form of continuous secular movement. We are confronted here with a problem in probabilities; we must in each case weigh the available pertinent evidence, and endeavor to make the soundest judgment we can.

When we come specifically to the choice of functions to represent the secular trends of the several series, we are guided in particular by certain general characteristics of our array of trend-indications, stated and discussed at length in Chapter XIII (and

[1] We might equally well use the trend-indications of Chart 33, which are virtually identical with those of Chart 27. It is practically a matter of indifference whether we take as our starting point, in the analyses of this chapter, the conclusions of Chapter XIII, as epitomized in Chart 27, or those of Chapter XIV, as epitomized in Chart 33.

also in Chapter XIV): the tendency toward continuity in these trend-indications, which we can definitely see to be generally operative, in spite of occasional minor, probably non-significant gaps, attributable to irremediable limitations of the methodology and for certain series to the presence of underlying curvilinear movements; the indication that among the series which extend over the entire interval 1866–1914 there are very few, if any, for which the secular variations are capable of satisfactory representation by a single simple mathematical curve; the appearance for many of the series of alteration, often rather abrupt, in the direction or slope of the secular movement around the turn of the century.

In the case of railroad earnings, for example, the most reasonable transliteration of the trend-indications (the first curve of Chart 27), and of the general picture presented by the modified series (the first line of Chart 26), would seem to consist in fitting two smooth curves, each of parabolic form, one embracing the first three sub-periods and the other the last three — extended to meet in 1897. We thus disregard as non-significant the "break" in the trend-indications at 1878. For the employment index, to illustrate still further, both the trend-indications (the second curve of Chart 27) and the modified series (the second line of Chart 26) strongly suggest the fitting of a straight line over the period for which the index is available, 1889–1914.[2]

As regards the technique for fitting the lines of secular trend, it is expedient to fit to the *derived entity* — to the trend-indications, or perhaps better still, to the modified series upon which the trend-indications are based — rather than to the *original items* of the series; we thus in very large measure avoid the effect of those extraneous influences which, in the conventional process of trend fitting, are so likely to distort the level and slope of the computed trend-representations.[3] While the principal methodological advantage of the present procedure does not, as may easily be appreciated, attach at this point, nevertheless even this gain in closeness of approach to precision is of appreciable importance.

---

[2] The reader will bear in mind that the various fittings just referred to are in terms of series plotted with *logarithmic vertical scale*. Described with reference to the arithmetic scale, the two suggested trend lines for railroad earnings are logarithmic parabolas, and that for the employment index is a compound-interest curve (as to the implications of this latter trend, cf. fn. 12 in Chapter IX).

[3] Cf. the discussion in W. L. Crum, A. C. Patton, and A. R. Tebbutt, *Introduc-*

Furthermore, in view of the lack of anything resembling a precise quantitative knowledge regarding the operation of the causal forces behind secular trends, we may well confine ourselves to simple mathematical curves. Indeed, we are now at last in position to state a conclusion as to the true place of mathematical curve fitting in secular-trend derivation for economic time series. Our reasoning and our results indicate that the rôle of mathematical curve fitting is minor. Far from being the principal element of the methodology (we can surely no longer speak of the secular trend as being "*determined* [e.g.] by the method of least squares"), its part is altogether subordinate and incidental. It enters not as the first step, but as the last in a long analytical process. It has its modest function, but it is in no way fundamental.

We limit ourselves, therefore, to the fitting of simple types of curves — straight lines and parabolas (upon logarithmic scale). For all of the series except the employment index (which covers 1889–1914 only) we find it necessary, as was previously anticipated, to break the time interval into two or more parts, fitting each separately. The equations for the *trend-representations* of the several series are given in Table 15, and the trends are plotted as thin dotted lines on Chart 34, in conjunction with original items (adjusted for seasonal variation where necessary) of the several series.[4] For purposes of comparison, we show the production index, together with its secular trend derived as described in Chapter XIII (or independently in Chapter XIV); and also the cyclical-variation curve for this index, obtained by elimination of the secular trend. We also present the standard pattern — "second revision" — as developed in Chapter XIV.

## Consideration of the Results

When we examine Chart 34 as a connected whole, we are immediately struck by the elements of *consistency* displayed by the array of secular trends and cyclical variations and easily readable

---

*tion to Economic Statistics* (New York and London: McGraw-Hill Book Co., Inc., 1938), p. 304.

[4] The logarithmic vertical scales for the various series of Chart 34 are so chosen as to be *inversely proportional* to the respective dispersion measures (average deviations of link relatives), and hence differences in average amplitude of fluctuation among the series have been eliminated. As to original sources, etc., of individual series see Appendix III–A, except for outside clearings and railroad earnings (see Appendix XII–A), and production and employment (see Chapters VIII and IX, respectively).

## TABLE 15

### SECULAR-TREND EQUATIONS FOR LEADING ECONOMIC SERIES, 1866–1914

| Series | Period | Center | Unit | Equation* |
|---|---|---|---|---|
| Employment index .......... | 1889–1914 | 1901–02 | Av. for 1899 = 100 | $\log y = 0.01626t + 2.0054$ |
| Railroad earnings ......... | 1866–96 | 1881 | \$1,000,000 | $\log y = -0.000489t^2 + 0.02608t + 1.3464$ |
| | †1904–14 | 1909 | | $\log y = -0.000569t^2 + 0.02131t + 1.9854$ |
| Outside clearings ......... | 1866–96 | 1881 | \$1,000,000 | $\log y = 0.000170t^2 + 0.01968t + 2.7118$ |
| | ‡1897–1902 | 1899–1900 | | $\log y = 0.02957t + 3.1464$ |
| | 1904–14 | 1909 | | $\log y = -0.000179t^2 + 0.02088t + 3.3784$ |
| Imports ......... | 1866–78 | 1872 | \$1,000,000 | $\log y = 0.02498t + 1.6003$ |
| | 1878–96 | 1887 | | $\log y = 0.00779t + 1.7572$ |
| | †1904–14 | 1909 | | $\log y = 0.000455t^2 + 0.02775t + 2.0718$ |
| Immigration ......... | 1866–85 | 1875–76 | 1,000 persons | $\log y = 0.001387t^2 + 0.01210t + 1.1461$ |
| | 1885–96 | 1890–91 | | $\log y = -0.00686t + 1.3222$ |
| | ‡1898–1903 | 1900–01 | | $\log y = 0.06915t + 1.4816$ |
| | 1904–14 | 1909 | | $\log y = 0.01075t + 1.7482$ |
| Railroad stock prices ......... | 1866–85 | 1875–76 | \$1 | $\log y = 0.001134t^2 + 0.00512t + 1.5798$ |
| | 1885–96 | 1890–91 | | $\log y = 0.00355t + 1.7259$ |
| | ‡1897–1900 | 1898–99 | | $\log y = 0.05950t + 1.8662$ |
| | 1904–14 | 1909 | | $\log y = -0.000609t^2 + 0.00402t + 2.0634$ |
| Industrial stock prices ......... | 1866–1904 | 1885 | \$1 | $\log y = 0.01218t + 2.0233$ |
| | 1904–14 | 1909 | | $\log y = -0.001746t^2 + 0.00780t + 2.3391$ |
| New York clearings ......... | 1866–96 | 1881 | \$1,000,000 | $\log y = 0.00367t + 3.3892$ |
| | ‡1897–1900 | 1898–99 | | $\log y = 0.07092t + 3.5876$ |
| | 1904–14 | 1909 | | $\log y = -0.001076t^2 + 0.00945t + 3.8871$ |

| | | | | |
|---|---|---|---|---|
| Sensitive commodity prices ......... | 1866–96 | 1881 | Av. for 1890–99 = 100 | log y = 0.000092t² − 0.01190t + 2.1378 |
| | †1904–14 | 1909 | | log y = −0.005552t² + 0.00509t + 2.1304 |
| Wholesale commodity prices......... | 1866–96 | 1881 | Av. for 1926 = 100 | log y = 0.000232t² − 0.01208t + 1.8835 |
| | †1904–14 | 1909 | | log y = −0.000347t² + 0.00619t + 1.8228 |
| Commercial-paper rates ............. | 1866–85 | 1875–76 | 1% | log y = −0.004450t² − 0.01074t + 0.7959 |
| | 1885–1914 | 1899–1900 | | log y = 0.00097t + 0.6609 |

* For each equation, time (t) on the abscissa is measured in years from the center of the period, as given in the third column of the table. For series relating to dollar volume of activity — railroad earnings, outside clearings, imports, and New York clearings — as well as immigration, the ordinate (y) is in terms of annual averages of monthly totals.

Except as otherwise indicated in succeeding footnotes, the transition from one trend line to another is taken at their intersection (one of them being extrapolated if necessary).

† For these series, the trend line over the period intermediate between 1896 and 1904 is obtained in each case by extending the 1904–14 trend line backward until it meets the trend line — extrapolated, if necessary — fitted for the period 1866–96 (1878–96, in the case of imports).

‡ For these series, the handling of the period between 1896 and 1904 is as follows (cf. Chart 34). In each case, there unquestionably is around the turn of the century a definite shift in level of secular movement, but the precise transition dates are not certain. After careful graphic examination of the series, and comparison of their movements over this time interval with those of the production index and its deviations from trend, as well as those of the revised standard pattern, we finally decide to make the transition from the immediately preceding trend line, extrapolated forward if necessary, to the succeeding trend line, extrapolated backward if necessary, by means of a straight line (upon logarithmic scale), extending:

for immigration, from January 1, 1898 to December 31, 1903;
for outside clearings, from January 1, 1897 to December 31, 1902;
for New York clearings, from January 1, 1897 to December 31, 1900;
for railroad stock prices, from January 1, 1897 to December 31, 1900.

It is scarcely necessary to say that these decisions regarding transition points in the interval 1896–1904 represent somewhat arbitrary readings of a difficult picture. But there can be no doubt at all that there is in each instance a clear transition in trend level, bounded roughly by the terminal dates selected and capable of at least approximate representation by the straight line upon logarithmic scale.

therefrom. We obtain from mere inspection of the chart a clear impression that the array represents at least so much as a *unified interpretation* of the general picture presented by this assemblage of economic series. Now, of course, these indications of consistency and uniformity are not in themselves adequate to constitute demonstration of the validity of the statistical procedure; such demonstration must rest upon the long chain of reasoning which has been developed in this volume, and the accompanying accumulation of evidence. Nevertheless, the indications of the chart are by no means lacking in cogency. Here, as in all scientific investigation — no matter how great the care with which the successive links in the chain of reasoning have been forged, or how great the confidence as to the essential soundness of the procedure — it is desirable to put the results to the final test of critical examination for internal consistency. And for the case at hand this test is met with entire satisfaction.

We present these results of Chart 34, relating to the form of secular trend and cyclical variation for the several individual series, as *approximations* to the truth. The trend-indication lines of Chart 27 (or Chart 33) are subject to certain reservations, as has previously been recited at length in Chapter XIII (and also in Chapter XIV). Further, we know that (only in limited degree, to be sure, but nevertheless not negligibly) certain elements of discretionary judgment have entered the transliteration of the trend-indications into definitive lines of trend-representation; such exercise of discretionary judgment has been, it would appear, of but minor significance for series like railroad earnings, employment, or wholesale commodity prices, but cannot be dismissed as wholly unimportant for such a series as immigration, where various alternative readings of the trend-indications would have been perhaps equally plausible, nor for the readings in the 1896–1904 interval for certain series, where the decisions as to transition dates were admittedly somewhat arbitrary (cf. Table 15, fn. ‡). Still further, even waiving all technical difficulties, the more fundamental consideration remains that the whole conception of time-series variations (seasonal and irregular fluctuations set aside) as resolvable into secular and cyclical movements, logarithmically additive, can itself be accepted only as an approximation.[5]

[5] Cf. the discussions of Chapter XII upon this point.

It will, of course, also be borne in mind that the lines of trend-representation of

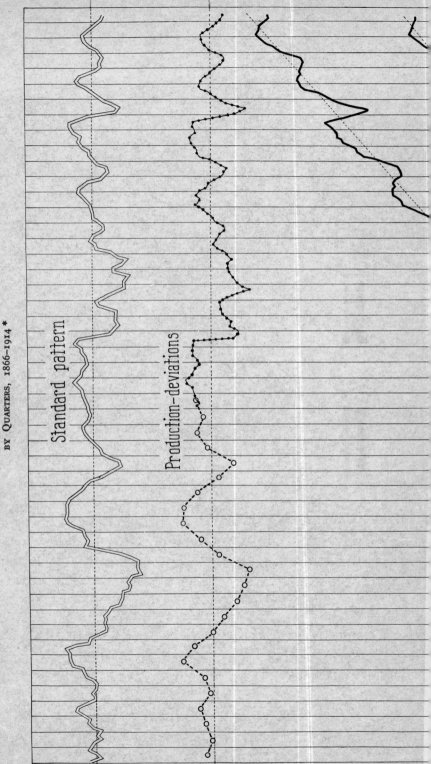

ORIGINAL ITEMS (ADJUSTED FOR SEASONAL VARIATION WHERE NECESSARY) AND LINES OF SECULAR TREND FOR TWELVE LEADING ECONOMIC SERIES, TOGETHER WITH THE STANDARD PATTERN AND DEVIATIONS FROM TREND OF THE PRODUCTION INDEX: BY QUARTERS, 1866–1914*

Standard pattern

Production-deviations

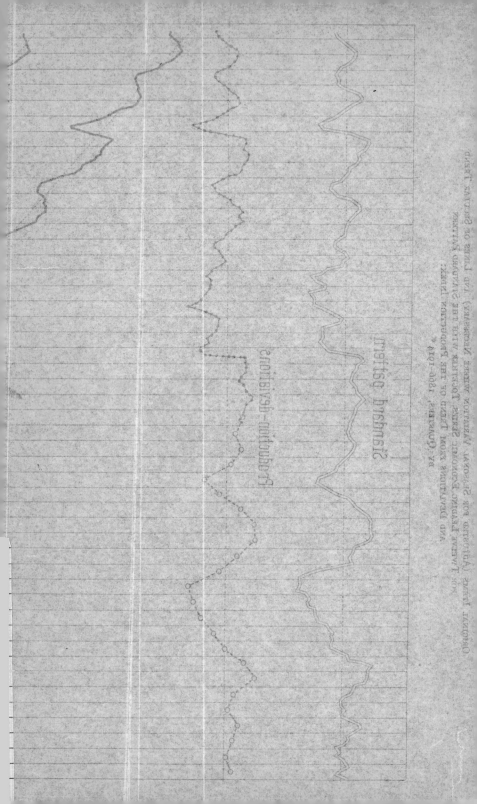

We set forth our results in Table 15 and Chart 34, then, as first approximations to the truth; and, on the basis of the reasoning and analytical evidence developed in this volume, we believe that they are good approximations. We present these results in the hope that they may be of assistance to other workers in the field of economic fluctuations, and with the intention of using them as guides in further, more detailed investigations into the structure of economic time series.

## A Note on the Scope of "Discretionary Judgment" in Trend Determination

Just here an objection may possibly be raised. It may be called to attention that our development of methodology for time-series decomposition took its very point of departure from a criticism, rather severe, of the conventional procedure of fitting trend lines on the basis of discretionary judgment and then taking the deviations therefrom as denoting "cycles." Yet now, in the application of the new methodology to the group of leading economic series, we have come in the end to the fitting of trend lines in which, as we have just seen, discretionary judgment is involved. It may be asked whether this is not inconsistent.

Such a charge of inconsistency would seem not to be well founded. The scope for the exercise of discretionary judgment in the two cases is essentially different. In the conventional procedure, discretionary judgment is almost completely determinative; in our present methodology, its rôle is in general comparatively minor. We here have once more an instance where the difference in degree is veritably a difference in kind.

Our point may be emphasized by inviting a contrast — "Look here, upon this picture, and on this." Go back to Chapter II, and "the pig-iron production case." Imagine the twenty-nine different trends there listed to be superimposed, in a single graph,

---

Table 15 and Chart 34 relate to the secular trends of *particular statistical series*, and consequently care must be exercised in reading their implications. Thus, the trend-indications presented for outside clearings pertain to the bank clearings for a group of seven selected cities, and cannot be taken as yielding the secular trend for aggregate clearings of all centers, nor for the total volume of all monetary transactions in the United States. Again, the trend-indications for the industrial stock price series which we have used (the Clement-Burgess and Axe-Houghton indexes, joined) show no alteration in level of secular movement around the turn of the century; but many of the other published indexes of industrial stock prices show a distinct shift in trend level between 1896 and 1904.

upon the chart of original items. A veritable network of lines would appear, yielding a decidedly confused impression, and indicating the greatest diversity of results from the exercise of the several discretionary judgments involved in the respective trend-representation selections. By way of contrast with this suppositional graph, consider Chart 35, which shows the application of the present methodology to the series pig-iron production, 1866–1914. The indications of this chart are quite definite: either the logarithmic parabola, or something giving nearly equivalent results, is *required* if we are to trace out the secular trend over this half-century.[6] The need for the exercise of discretionary judgment is here reduced until it becomes almost a negligible factor in the fitting.

Admittedly, in the array of leading economic series of Charts 27 and 34, the transliteration from trend-indications to trend-representations is not always so simple nor so clear-cut as it is for pig-iron production. Nevertheless, even for that array, the difference in degree, as to dependence upon discretionary judgment, between the conventional procedure and our present methodology, is unquestionably still great enough to constitute a difference in kind.

### A Note as to the Bearing of Our Results upon the Kondratieff Hypothesis

While our time period of analysis is (as we have previously indicated) too short to afford any decisive test of the Kondratieff long-wave hypothesis, we may nevertheless note in passing that the showing of the trend-indication lines of Chart 27, and especially the behavior of these lines around the turn of the century, is at least consistent with this hypothesis (the upward movement of Kondratieff's third wave is scheduled as beginning around 1890–96); and the array of evidence upon this chart can be made to fit into his statistical scheme. In fact, if, in accordance with Kondra-

---

[6] Pig-iron production easily passes the necessary qualifying test for application of our methodology, to wit, close correspondence of the form of short-time fluctuation with that of the pattern for the production index, as well as with those of the various other patterns of Part Two to which we have so often referred. (This can readily be demonstrated explicitly, both with reference to the link relatives and to the original items.) Incidentally, pig-iron production is one of the few individual production series whose pre-war secular trend (say, 1866–1914) *can* be suitably represented by the logarithmic parabola.

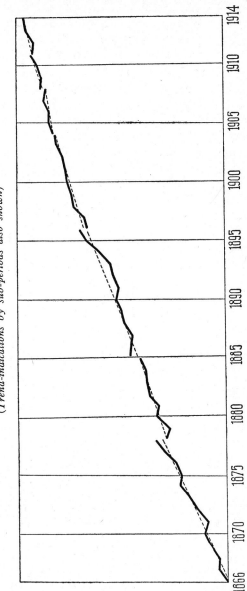

CHART 35

ORIGINAL ITEMS FOR PIG-IRON PRODUCTION

WITH FORM OF CYCLICAL VARIATION OF PRODUCTION INDEX ELIMINATED:
BY YEARS, 1866–1914 *

*(Trend-indications by sub-periods also shown)*

* Logarithmic vertical scale.

tieff's practice of employing *arithmetic-scale* charts, we redraw the trend-indications of Chart 27 upon a new diagram, with arithmetic vertical scales — as in Chart 36 — conformity to the general statistical scheme of Kondratieff appears (compare these graphic series with his curves in the *Review of Economic Statistics* for November 1935, pages 105–115). Since we have yet to develop evidence sufficiently cogent to justify our taking a stand, we are obliged (as we have earlier said) to assume an agnostic position with reference to the Kondratieff hypothesis. For the time being, we content ourselves with presenting such pertinent evidence as we may incidentally have obtained, and letting it speak for itself.

In this chapter, through transliteration of the trend-indications, we have obtained the trend-representations for our group of leading economic series. We have set up, in Chart 34, an array of secular trends fitted to original items (previously adjusted for seasonal variation where required), thus permitting the cyclical fluctuations to stand out in clear relief. We have thus in effect accomplished the statistical decomposition of these time series.

## CONCLUDING STATEMENT

In the Introduction we enunciated certain basic principles and laid down a broad, general program for attack upon the problem of time-series decomposition, and indicated that the present volume is intended as a contribution toward the fulfillment of that program.

This contribution clearly has *not* consisted in the development of a quasi-mechanical method for separating secular and cyclical movements which can be employed lightheartedly, without forethought or discrimination, to all data for all countries over all time intervals. In fact, the author's great misgiving in presenting this study is that there may somehow be supposed to be such a thing as the "Frickey method" for analyzing time series, capable of being applied automatically and universally. This writer is firmly of the opinion that in the methodology of economic statistics universalistic notions are unacceptable, that our tools must be fashioned with an eye to the needs of particular problems. And for the field of time-series decomposition in particular, the worker to be successful must be something of an opportunist — using his ingenuity, looking for openings, seizing upon the chance to strike

CHART 36

THE TREND-INDICATIONS OF CHART 27,
REDRAWN WITH *Arithmetic* VERTICAL SCALES:
BY SUB-PERIODS, 1866–1914 *

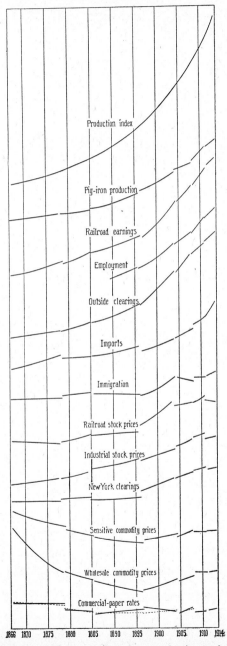

\* Together with trend-indications of pig-iron production and the secular trend
of the production index (also plotted on arithmetic vertical scales). To facilitate
presentation within limited space, varying scales are employed for the several series.

at the heart of the problem. Analysis of other time periods than ours here, or of other bodies of data, will in all probability necessitate at least variation in the procedure, and possibly will require essential change in the strategy.

The contribution which we have endeavored to make in this volume may perhaps be summed up under three heads. First, we have developed a way of looking at things, a manner of attacking problems, a system of procedure, which it is hoped may be suggestive and helpful in the planning of programs of research in time-series analysis generally. Secondly, we have devised specific tools of analysis, methodological procedures, which — while not to be thought of as universalistic nor to be employed carelessly — are nevertheless capable of wide applicability in the hands of discriminating workers. Thirdly, we may fairly claim to have made a substantial contribution toward the carrying out of those "early, comprehensive statistical analyses for the basic data," the indispensability of which was so strongly emphasized in the closing pages of our statement regarding "the nature of the problem" in the Introduction. We have made a highly elaborate analysis, covering a long time period, of an extensive and significant body of data.

But, of course, much more work remains to be done. Even within the temporal and geographical limits set for the present study, it is requisite to go on to consider material which is treated only broadly in this volume — e.g., the price and production data for individual commodities; also we have still before us the problem of how to deal with the trend-cycle separation for those series which do not conform to our general pattern. All of this is not to mention the extension of the analysis to other countries and other time periods. The issue involved in the dispute about "long," "intermediate," and "short" cycles deserves more attention than we could give it here. And it goes without saying that before the findings of these various statistical studies — accomplished and projected — can in any intrinsic sense be regarded as complete, they must (as a connected whole) be interpreted with the aid of economic theory and economic history, and reconsidered in the light of a synthesis of the elements provided by the several investigations — statistical, theoretical, and historical.

APPENDICES

| Description of series | Sources of data |
|---|---|
| **Bank clearings outside New York City:** | |
| (a) Philadelphia, monthly, 1866–1914 | 1866–78: The Philadelphia Clearing House Association |
| (b) Seven selected cities, monthly, 1875–1914 | 1875–1914: *The Public* and the *Commercial and Financial Chronicle* |
| Gross earnings of railroads, quarterly, 1866–1914† | 1866–69: The present author's computations‡ |
| | 1869–1914: J. E. Partington, *Railroad Purchasing and the Business Cycle* (Washington: The Brookings Institution, 1929), pp. 302–305 |
| Merchandise imports into the United States, monthly, July 1866–December 1914 | 1866–1911: United States Department of Commerce and Labor, Bureau of Statistics, *Monthly Summary of Commerce and Finance of the United States*, December 1911, pp. 1060–1066 |
| | 1912–14: United States Department of Commerce, Bureau of Foreign and Domestic Commerce, *Monthly Summary of Commerce and Finance of the United States*, December 1914, p. 513 |
| Male immigration into the United States, quarterly, 1866–92, and monthly, 1892–1914 | 1866–92: United States Treasury Department, Bureau of Statistics, *Monthly Summary of Commerce and Finance of the United States*, June 1903, p. 4362 |
| | 1892–1914: H. Jerome, *Migration and Business Cycles* (New York: National Bureau of Economic Research, Inc., 1926), p. 246 |
| Index of railroad stock prices (Harvard Economic Society's series, shifted to the level of the Dow-Jones averages††), monthly, 1866–1914 | 1866–96: Harvard Economic Society's files |
| | 1897–1914: W. M. Persons, "An Index of General Business Conditions," *Review of Economic Statistics*, 1 (April 1919), pp. 171, 169 |

For all footnotes, see end of table.

FOR QUARTERLY STANDARD-PATTERN STUDY

| References to discussions of source and nature of data | Geometric average of quarterly link relatives, 1867-II to 1914-I | Quartile deviation of quarterly link relatives, 1867-II to 1914-I |
|---|---|---|
| E. Frickey, "Bank Clearings Outside New York City, 1875–1914," *Review of Economic Statistics*, VII (October 1925), pp. 252–253 | Philadelphia (1867-II to 1914-I), 1.0089 | 3.00* |
| E. Frickey, "A Statistical Study of Bank Clearings, 1875–1914," *Review of Economic Statistics*, XII (May 1930), pp. 92–94; (August 1930), pp. 120–131 | Seven selected cities (1875-II to 1914-I), 1.0121 | |
| J. E. Partington, *Railroad Purchasing and the Business Cycle* (Washington: The Brookings Institution, 1929), pp. 293–299 | 1.0164 | 2.20 |
| W. M. Persons, "Indices of Business Conditions," *Review of Economic Statistics*, I (January 1919), p. 42 | 1.0088 | 4.48 |
| H. Jerome, *Migration and Business Cycles* (New York: National Bureau of Economic Research, Inc., 1926), pp. 29–30 and pp. 245–246 | 1.0060 | 10.90 |
| W. M. Persons, "An Index of General Business Conditions," *Review of Economic Statistics*, I (April 1919), p. 147 | | |
| Ada M. Matthews, "New York Bank Clearings and Stock Prices, 1866–1914," *Review of Economic Statistics*, VIII (October 1926), pp. 189, 192 | 1.0056 | 3.30 |
| A. H. Cole and E. Frickey, "The Course of Stock Prices, 1825–66," *Review of Economic Statistics*, X (August 1928), p. 139 | | |

| Description of series | Sources of data |
|---|---|
| Index of industrial stock prices:<br>(a) Clement-Burgess index, monthly, 1866–82¶<br>(b) Axe-Houghton i n d e x, monthly, 1883–1914 | 1866–82: C. P. Burgess, "Clement-Burgess Stock Market Average Carries the Record Back to 1854," *Annalist*, October 28, 1932, p. 580<br>1883–1914: E. W. Axe, "Generally Low Prices and Cheap Money Suggest a Bull Market This Year," *Annalist*, January 16, 1931, p. 177 |
| New York City bank clearings, monthly, 1866–1914 | 1866–1902: Ada M. Matthews, "New York Bank Clearings and Stock Prices, 1866–1914," *Review of Economic Statistics*, VIII (October 1926), p. 188<br>1903–14: W. M. Persons, "Indices of Business Conditions," *Review of Economic Statistics*, I (January 1919), p. 64 |
| Sensitive commodity prices:§<br>(a) Weighted average of Snider's "Cyclical A," "Cyclical B," "Cyclical C" groups, first month of each quarter, 1866–89**<br>(b) Persons-C o y l e commodity price index of business cycles, monthly, 1890–1914 | 1866–89: Computed by present writer from data in J. L. Snider, "Wholesale Prices in the United States, 1866–91," *Review of Economic Statistics*, VI (April 1924), pp. 105–107<br>1890–1914: W. M. Persons and E. S. Coyle, "A Commodity Price Index of Business Cycles," *Review of Economic Statistics*, III (November 1921), p. 369 |
| Index of wholesale commodity prices:<br>(a) Warren-Pearson index, shifted to U.S.B.L.S. base, monthly, 1866–89 | 1866–89: United States Department of Labor, Bureau of Labor Statistics, *Bulletin No. 572*, p. 114 |
| (b) United States Bureau of Labor Statistics index, monthly, 1890–1914 | 1890–1914: *Ibid.*, *Bulletin No. 543*, pp. 3–7 |
| Rates on prime commercial paper in New York, monthly, 1866–1914 | 1866–1914: W. L. Crum, "Cycles of Rates on Commercial Paper," *Review of Economic Statistics*, V (January 1923), p. 28 |

For all footnotes, see end of table.

| References to discussions of source and nature of data | Geometric average of quarterly link relatives, 1867-II to 1914-I | Quartile deviation of quarterly link relatives, 1867-II to 1914-I |
|---|---|---|
| C. P. Burgess, "Clement-Burgess Stock Market Average Carries the Record Back to 1854," *Annalist*, October 28, 1932, pp. 579–580 | 1.0066 | 4.02 |
| Ada M. Matthews, "New York Bank Clearings and Stock Prices, 1866–1914," *Review of Economic Statistics*, VIII (October 1926), pp. 187–189<br>W. M. Persons, "Indices of Business Conditions," *Review of Economic Statistics*, I (January 1919), p. 39 | 1.0071 | 7.15 |
| J. L. Snider, "Wholesale Prices in the United States, 1866–91," *Review of Economic Statistics*, VI (April 1924), pp. 94–99<br>W. M. Persons and E. S. Coyle, "A Commodity Price Index of Business Cycles," *Review of Economic Statistics*, III (November 1921), pp. 357–358 | 0.9974 | 3.20 |
| G. F. Warren and F. A. Pearson, "Wholesale Prices in the United States for 135 Years, 1797 to 1932," *Memoir No. 142*, Cornell University Agricultural Experiment Station (November 1932), pp. 120–162<br>United States Department of Labor, Bureau of Labor Statistics, *Bulletin No. 493*, pp. 2–6 | 0.9973 | 1.92 |
| W. L. Crum, "Cycles of Rates on Commercial Paper," *Review of Economic Statistics*, V (January 1923), p. 29 | 0.9972 | 8.02 |

| Description of series | Sources of data |
|---|---|
| Merchandise exports from the United States, monthly, July 1866–December 1914 | 1866–1911: United States Department of Commerce and Labor, Bureau of Statistics, *Monthly Summary of Commerce and Finance of the United States*, December 1911, pp. 1060–1066 |
| | 1912–14: United States Department of Commerce, Bureau of Foreign and Domestic Commerce, *Monthly Summary of Commerce and Finance of the United States*, December 1914, p. 513 |
| Loans of New York City clearing house banks, monthly, January 1866–June 1914 | 1866–78: W. M. Persons, P. M. Tuttle, and E. Frickey, "Business and Financial Conditions Following the Civil War in the United States," *Review of Economic Statistics*, II (July 1920 Supplement), p. 49 |
| | 1879–1914: W. M. Persons, "An Index of General Business Conditions," *Review of Economic Statistics*, I (April 1919), pp. 176–177 |
| Moody's "typical corporation bond prices," monthly, 1866–1914 | 1866–1914: *Moody's Investors Service*, November 20, 1924, pp. 426–427 |

* Employing deviations from average of link relatives for Philadelphia clearings, 1867-II to 1875-I, and for clearings of seven selected cities, 1875-II to 1914-I.

† The five sections of the series for 1866–69, 1869–73, 1872–83, 1882–1911, and 1910–14 are adjusted to form a continuous series on the basis of data for the overlapping periods 1869, 1872–73, 1882–83, and 1910–11.

‡ Computed from data for the following nine roads in various issues of the *Financial Review*: Central Pacific; Cleveland, Columbus, Cincinnati & Indianapolis; Pacific of Missouri; Chicago & Northwestern; Illinois Central; Marietta & Cincinnati; Michigan Central; Ohio & Mississippi; and Toledo, Wabash & Western.

| References to discussions of source and nature of data | Geometric average of quarterly link relatives, 1867-II to 1914-I | Quartile deviation of quarterly link relatives, 1867-II to 1914-I |
|---|---|---|
| C. J. Bullock, J. H. Williams, and R. S. Tucker, "The Balance of Trade of the United States," *Review of Economic Statistics*, I (July 1919), p. 266 | 1.0102 | 6.18 |
| W. M. Persons, P. M. Tuttle, and E. Frickey, "Business and Financial Conditions Following the Civil War in the United States," *Review of Economic Statistics*, II (July 1920 Supplement), p. 49 <br> W. M. Persons, "An Index of General Business Conditions," *Review of Economic Statistics*, I (April 1919) p. 149 | 1.0092 | 2.25 |
| *Moody's Investors Service*, November 20, 1924, pp. 425–426 | 1.0016 | 0.90 |

¶ Not strictly an industrial index in the earlier period (see Burgess, *loc. cit.*).

§ Adjusted to form a continuous series on the basis of overlapping data for the first quarter of 1890.

** Weights are 1, 1, and 2, respectively, approximately proportional to the number of series in the three groups.

†† Based upon the following three series: (1) Frickey's index, 1866–80; (2) Miss Matthews' index, 1880–97; (3) Dow-Jones index, 1897–1914 (adjusted to form a continuous series on the basis of data for overlapping years).

# APPENDIX III-B

*Original items.* For New York clearings, straight-line interpolation, applied to seasonally-adjusted data, is employed to fill a short gap in the year 1873 (cf. Chart 1).

*Link relatives.* Because of deficiency in the original data for the first half of 1866, it is not possible to obtain link relatives for merchandise imports and merchandise exports, 1866–II and 1866–III.

*Adjustment for differences in average level among the link-relative series.* In the actual process of computation it is sufficient to take the deviations from average by subtraction, rather than by division; this occasions only insignificant differences in results, and affords a considerable saving of time and expense.

The exact period for the geometric averages is 1867–II to 1914–I, thus omitting from the calculation data for 1866, whose figures were incomplete for certain series (see above), and most of the disturbed year 1914.

*Adjustment for variations in amplitude among the series.* The period for the quartile deviations, also, is 1867–II to 1914–I.

*Handling of outside clearings.* For outside clearings, a continuous series of "link relatives adjusted for differences in average level" is obtained as follows: over the interval 1866–II to 1875–I, the quarterly link relatives for Philadelphia clearings are divided through by the average of such link relatives for the period 1867–II to 1914–I (1.0089); over the interval 1875–II to 1914–II, the quarterly link relatives for clearings of seven selected cities are divided through by the average of such link relatives for the period 1875–II to 1914–I (1.0121).

*Multiple frequency tables.* For the first two quarters and the last two quarters of the period 1866–II to 1914–II, there are of necessity a few gaps in the items, making the number of entries less than thirteen. These gaps appear partly because of missing original data for certain series, partly because of our lead and lag shiftings. In these instances, the number of items falling within the first and third quartiles is, of course, less than seven. It does not appear that these few deficiencies in data exert any important effect upon the results.

# APPENDIX III–C

## Formal Statistical Measurement of Lags for Quarterly Link-Relative Series

Upon the completion of the graphic examination of the data (as described in the text, in the section entitled "Adjustment for Lags") it is desirable to confirm the conclusions by means of formal statistical tests. We turn first to the conventional analysis employing the Pearsonian correlation coefficient.[1] This method of analysis, however, soon proves to be highly unsuited for use in the problem at hand, for two reasons: (1) in many cases, the results are clearly controlled by the accidental position of a few extreme items;[2] (2) examination of the "cross-products" $(xy)$ reveals that in many instances the sub-total of such products over a comparatively small part of the time interval 1867–1913 dominates the grand total of the products, regardless of the situation as to lag during the remainder of that interval.

To avoid these difficulties, we devise a special method and apply it to the several series. The time period 1867–1913 is divided into intervals which, except for the two terminal intervals of 1867–70 and 1911–13, are five years in length. For each interval, five lags are measured, derived from a comparison of each series with the basic series ("the average of the four volume series"). These five are made up of the lag which the earlier graphic inspection has indicated to be the best, and the two lags immediately adjacent on either side. This special method is illustrated in the accompanying table, the particular series under test here being sensitive commodity prices. Graphic inspection has suggested the best lag to be 0 quarters, i.e., concurrence; accordingly, the other four lags to be measured are −2, −1, +1, and +2.[3]

For each of the time intervals, we make a count of cases of agreement and of disagreement in algebraic sign, pairing the items for the particular series under consideration with the appropriate corresponding items for the basic series, and trying out in turn the five lags under scrutiny. More specifically, this count is made in each instance by finding (a) the number of cases of *agreement* in algebraic sign; (b) the number of cases of *disagreement* in algebraic sign; and (c) the number of *zero* cases — i.e., cases where the item for one or both series is zero. The results of these counts for the illustrative series are presented in the various columns (a, b, c) of the table.

---

[1] An explanation of this procedure may be conveniently found in W. L. Crum, A. C. Patton, and A. R. Tebbutt, *Introduction to Economic Statistics* (New York and London: McGraw-Hill Book Company, Inc., 1938), pp. 365–367.

[2] Among these series of *link relatives* — quarter-to-quarter changes — extreme items are, as might be expected, of frequent occurrence (see Chart 3).

[3] In the notation here adopted, a "negative lag" denotes a precedence, in order of time movement, of the given series over the basic series. In the dating of the pairs of items, the dates for the basic series are determinative. Thus, the entries for the lag −1 over the interval 1871–75 in the table apply to 1871–I to 1875–IV for the basic series, and to 1870–IV to 1875–III for sensitive commodity prices.

Next, for each complete five-year period we select the "best lag." This selection is made for each time interval simply by determining the maximum excess, among the five possible lags, of "cases of agreement in algebraic sign" over "cases of disagreement in algebraic sign."[4] Thus, in the particular series

ILLUSTRATION OF THE SPECIAL METHOD FOR DETERMINING "BEST LAG": SENSITIVE COMMODITY PRICES COMPARED WITH THE BASIC SERIES

| Period | Lag | | | | | | | | | | | | | | | "Best lag" |
|---|---|---|---|---|---|---|---|---|---|---|---|---|---|---|---|---|
| | −2 | | | −1 | | | 0 | | | +1 | | | +2 | | | |
| | a | b | c | a | b | c | a | b | c | a | b | c | a | b | c | |
| 1867–70 .... | 5 | 7 | 2 | 6 | 7 | 2 | 9 | 5 | 2 | 8 | 5 | 2 | 5 | 8 | 1 | ..... |
| 1871–75 .... | 9 | 11 | 0 | 8 | 12 | 0 | 14 | 6 | 0 | 10 | 10 | 0 | 9 | 10 | 1 | 0 |
| 1876–80 .... | 11 | 9 | 0 | 11 | 9 | 0 | 14 | 6 | 0 | 11 | 9 | 0 | 7 | 13 | 0 | 0 |
| 1881–85 .... | 14 | 5 | 1 | 13 | 6 | 1 | 15 | 4 | 1 | 12 | 7 | 1 | 12 | 7 | 1 | 0 |
| 1886–90 .... | 5 | 12 | 3 | 5 | 12 | 3 | 9 | 8 | 3 | 10 | 7 | 3 | 10 | 7 | 3 | +1½* |
| 1891–95 .... | 9 | 8 | 3 | 12 | 5 | 3 | 12 | 6 | 2 | 6 | 12 | 2 | 7 | 11 | 2 | −1 |
| 1896–1900 .. | 9 | 9 | 2 | 13 | 5 | 2 | 11 | 7 | 2 | 12 | 5 | 3 | 13 | 4 | 3 | +2 |
| 1901–05 .... | 10 | 7 | 3 | 13 | 4 | 3 | 13 | 4 | 3 | 12 | 5 | 3 | 13 | 5 | 2 | − ½† |
| 1906–10 .... | 13 | 7 | 0 | 16 | 4 | 0 | 17 | 3 | 0 | 14 | 6 | 0 | 10 | 9 | 1 | 0 |
| 1911–13 .... | 7 | 3 | 2 | 6 | 4 | 2 | 8 | 2 | 2 | 9 | 1 | 2 | 6 | 4 | 2 | ..... |
| Median ..... | | | | | | | | | | | | | | | | 0 |

* "Tie" between +1 and +2.
† "Tie" between −1 and 0.

here selected for illustration, such excesses for 1906–10 are 6, 12, 14, 8, and 1 for lags of −2, −1, 0, +1, and +2 quarters, respectively, indicating for that period a "best lag" at 0 quarters, i.e., concurrence. Whenever there is a "tie" for any particular five-year period, a compromise figure is set down (also illustrated in the table).

Finally, the median of the eight "best lags" for the several periods (cf. the last column of the table) is taken as the statistical measure of "best lag" for the series as a whole. In the few instances where this median falls between two integral values, the indeterminateness of result is removed by selecting the lag for which summation over the period as a whole yielded the maximum difference between "cases of agreement" and "cases of disagreement."

The special statistical method, just described, appears to be a quite satisfactory one, and to avoid the difficulties which for the problem at hand are connected with employment of the conventional correlation-coefficient approach. The results of the special statistical test in every case agree with those previously obtained through graphic intercomparison of the series, as set forth in the text.

[4] In tests for inverse correlation, it is of course the excess of "cases of disagreement" which serves as a criterion for determining the "best lag."

# APPENDIX IV–A

## BASIC DATA FOR THE ANNUAL STUDY

Except for two series, outside clearings and railroad earnings, the basic data for the annual study are the same as those for the quarterly (cf. Appendix III–A).

*Outside clearings.* As our annual series for bank clearings outside New York City, we take the totals by years for *six* cities — Boston, Chicago, Cincinnati, Philadelphia, Pittsburgh, and Worcester. Over the interval 1875–1914, this series displays short-time movements which are closely similar to those of the series for *seven* selected cities — Baltimore, Chicago, Cincinnati, Cleveland, Philadelphia, Pittsburgh, and San Francisco — used in the quarterly study. Neither series is obtainable on a quarterly or monthly basis back of 1875, and the series for seven cities cannot be extended back even annually.

For the period 1883–1914, the series for six cities has been compiled by the present writer from data in the *Commercial and Financial Chronicle* and *The Public*; for the years 1866–82, the series has been supplied by the Federal Reserve Bank of New York.

*Railroad earnings.* In the annual analysis, we are able to employ, through the kindness of Professor Arthur H. Cole, the series developed by him and described in his article, "A Monthly Index of Railroad Earnings, 1866–1914," *Review of Economic Statistics*, XVIII (February 1936), pp. 31–41. [At the time of the quarterly analysis of Chapter III, this series had not been developed.]

## APPENDIX IV–B

### Technical Details Relating to Annual Standard-Pattern Study

*Annual averages.* For the two series imports and exports, no data are available for the first half of 1866; we take as the 1866 item, in each case, the average of the seasonally-adjusted figures for the third and fourth quarter of the year.

*Adjustment for differences in average level among the link-relative series.* Since the geometric averages for the annual link-relative series exhibit divergencies from 100 per cent which are approximately four times those of the corresponding averages for quarterly series, it seems wise, in calculating the deviations from average for the annual data, to employ the precise division method, rather than the short-cut subtraction method, which was found to be adequate in the quarterly case (cf. Appendix III–B).

*Statistical measurement of lags.* For the annual investigation, as opposed to the quarterly (cf. Appendix III–C), the problem of statistical lag measurement presents little difficulty. Inasmuch as we are here not troubled by the presence of highly extreme items (cf. Chart 5), we are able to adopt the conventional procedure involving the use of the Pearsonian correlation coefficient. As a check, however, we verify the results thus obtained by employing, with certain necessary modifications, the principle of the special method earlier developed and applied in the quarterly investigation: that is to say, we here, as before, classify the cases under the rubrics (a) "agreement," (b) "disagreement," and (c) "zero" — cf. the table of Appendix III–C — but in view of the smaller number of items now involved it is not feasible to divide our time period into sub-intervals; instead, we make our criterion for "best correlation" simply the maximum difference between cases of "agreement" and of "disagreement," over the entire interval of study.

# APPENDIX IV–C

STATISTICAL CONSTANTS FOR ANNUAL STANDARD-PATTERN STUDY

*(Unit: one per cent)*

| Series | Geometric average of annual link relatives, 1867–1913 | Average deviation of annual link relatives, 1867–1913 |
|---|---|---|
| Outside clearings ................. | 105.2 | 7.71 |
| Railroad earnings ................ | 106.2 | 5.94 |
| Imports ......................... | 103.6 | 10.13 |
| Immigration ..................... | 102.4 | 29.27 |
| Railroad stock prices ............ | 102.3 | 10.29 |
| Industrial stock prices ........... | 102.7 | 11.27 |
| New York clearings .............. | 102.9 | 16.51 |
| Sensitive commodity prices ........ | 99.0 | 8.19 |
| Wholesale commodity prices ....... | 98.9 | 4.79 |
| Commercial-paper rates .......... | 98.9 | 17.48 |
| Exports ......................... | 104.1 | 8.05 |
| Loans, New York banks .......... | 103.7 | 6.08 |
| Bond prices ..................... | 100.6 | 2.86 |

## APPENDIX V–A

*Basic data.* The basic materials for the analyses of Chapter V are the annual series, obtained as described in Appendix IV–A and the first paragraph of Appendix IV–B; also note, with particular reference to the handling of the 1914 item, the statement in the third paragraph of Chapter IV.

*Delimitation of time intervals.* The delimitation of time intervals for the several sets of averages of Chapter V is as follows:

2Y   . . .  1866–67, 1868–69, . . . . . . . . . . . . . . . , 1910–11, 1912–13.
3Y–A . . .  1866–68, 1869–71, . . . . . . . . . . . . . . . , 1908–10, 1911–13.
3Y–B . . .  1867–69, 1870–72, . . . . . . . . . . . . . . . , 1909–11, 1912–14.
3Y–C . . .  1868–70, 1871–73, . . . . . . . . . . . . . . . , 1907–09, 1910–12.
6Y–A . . .  1866–71, 1872–77, . . . . . . . . . . . . . . . , 1902–07, 1908–13.
6Y–B . . .  1868–73, 1874–79, . . . . . . . . . . . . . . . , 1904–09, *1910–14.*
6Y–C . . .  *1866–69,* 1870–75, . . . . . . . . . . . . . . . , 1900–05, 1906–11.
9Y–A . . .  1866–74, 1875–83, 1884–92, 1893–1901, 1902–10.
9Y–B . . .  1869–77, 1878–86, 1887–95, 1896–1904, 1905–13.
9Y–C . . .  *1866–71,* 1872–80, 1881–89, 1890–98, 1899–1907, *1908–14.*

It will be observed that in certain instances, indicated by italics above, averages are taken for periods of less than full length, with a view to enlarging our brief link-relative series by utilizing available data within their usable limits.

*Convention for dating of link relatives and for horizontal plotting on charts.* The convention for dating of link relatives and for horizontal plotting of link-relative series [1] on Charts 7 to 10, inclusive, may be illustrated by the handling of the first link-relative item of the "3Y–A" case. The first link relative for each series in the "3Y–A" analysis $\left( \dfrac{1869\text{–}71}{1866\text{–}68} \right)$ is, following our established procedure, given the date of the *later* of the two time intervals involved; that is, 1869–71. And in plotting, the point for this link relative is centered within the interval 1869–71; that is, at 1870 (see Chart 8, Part A).

*Measurement of lags* (cf. Appendix III–C and Appendix IV–B). For series containing so few items as those of Chapter V, the employment of the special method of lag measurement which was developed in the quarterly analysis and which also was used as a check in the annual analysis, is, of course, quite out of the question. It appears that here the conventional procedure, involving the $(xy)$ test and the Pearsonian correlation coefficient, is as satisfactory as any that could be set up. Obviously, regardless of the methodological device employed the statistical measurements of correlation must become more and

---

[1] The horizontal plotting, on Chart 6, of the corresponding *chain series* presents no special complexity. The procedure is simply to center each point within the time interval to which it applies.

more uncertain as the length of the period of link relatives becomes longer and the number of items in the series correspondingly fewer. Comment as to this increasing undependability of results has been made in the text of Chapter V.

For the most part, the indications of the statistical tests are "positive correlation, and zero lag (concurrent)." The exceptions are noted below (the basic series for comparison is, in all cases, "the average of the four volume series").

2Y  . . . . Bond prices, negative correlation, two years lag.
         Exports, negative correlation, two years lag.
3Y–A . . . . Bond prices, positive correlation, three years lead.
         Exports, negative correlation, three years lag.
3Y–B . . . . Bond prices, positive correlation, three years lead.
         Exports, negative correlation, three years lag.
3Y–C . . . . Bond prices, negative correlation, three years lag.
         Exports, negative correlation, three years lag.
6Y–A . . . . Bond prices, negative correlation, six years lag.
         Exports, positive correlation, six years lead.
6Y–B . . . . Bond prices, negative correlation, six years lag.
         Exports, positive correlation, six years lead.
6Y–C . . . . Bond prices, negative correlation, six years lag.
         Exports, positive correlation, six years lead.

In the nine-year analysis, no tests are made for lags; the following cases, on the basis of the scanty and somewhat ambiguous evidence afforded by the brief link-relative series, are formally classified as "negative correlation."

9Y–A . . . . Bond prices and exports.
9Y–B . . . . Bond prices, exports, and railroad stock prices.
9Y–C . . . . Exports.

These results for the nine-year case reveal certain anomalies in the correlation measurements. These anomalies doubtless have their source partly in certain factors previously discussed, partly in the brevity of the time series analyzed in this chapter.

# APPENDIX XII–A

## SOURCES OF DATA, AND METHOD OF DERIVATION OF SERIES: OUTSIDE CLEARINGS AND RAILROAD EARNINGS

### OUTSIDE CLEARINGS

*1875–1914.* Over this period, we use the series developed by the present writer some years ago: the aggregate bank clearings for seven selected cities — Baltimore, Chicago, Cincinnati, Cleveland, Philadelphia, Pittsburgh, and San Francisco — adjusted for seasonal variation (including calendar irregularities). See Edwin Frickey, "Bank Clearings Outside New York City, 1875–1914," *Review of Economic Statistics*, VII (October 1925), pp. 252–262; and "A Statistical Study of Bank Clearings, 1875–1914," *Review of Economic Statistics*, XII (May 1930), pp. 92–94.[1] For the interval 1875–78, however, the series has recently been revised. The occasion for this revision was the discovery of a systematic error over these four years in the figures for Philadelphia clearings employed in the original 1925 and 1930 computations.[2] The effect of the correction of this error was more or less systematically to reduce the indicated level of fluctuation of Philadelphia clearings over these years by about 17 per cent, and to lower the calculated totals for seven selected cities by about 7 per cent. These revised items for the series pertaining to seven selected cities, 1875–78, properly adjusted for seasonal variation, are used in Chart 23 (also, later, in Chart 34).

*1866–74.* It is not possible to make a direct extension back from 1875 of our series of bank clearings for seven selected cities. We are obliged to resort to a process of estimation. We begin by developing estimates of *annual* data. It is possible to obtain, over the entire interval 1866–1914, an annual series pertaining to a group of *six* cities — Boston, Chicago, Cincinnati, Philadelphia, Pittsburgh, and Worcester.[3] It will be seen that the two groups have in common the four important cities Chicago, Cincinnati, Philadelphia, and Pittsburgh. In view of this overlapping of basic data — together with the generally high intercorrelations among the short-run variations of clearings for individual

---

[1] In the present study the corrections for calendar irregularities are applied directly to the original items adjusted for ordinary seasonal variation. The correction for variable number of Sundays is as follows: for five-Sunday months (except February 1880), divide by 0.98; for four-Sunday months (except February), divide by 1.01. The correction for February items is as follows: in leap years (except February 1880), divide by 1.03; in non-leap years, divide by 0.99. February 1880 (which had five Sundays) is treated as a non-leap-year February; i.e., the item is divided by 0.99. For further explanation, see the second reference in the text above.

[2] The correction of the error was made possible through the kindness of Mr. C. H. Batten of the Philadelphia Clearing House Association, who furnished the revised figures.

[3] Cf. Appendix IV–A.

cities (cf. the articles by the present writer, referred to above) — it is not surprising that over the period for which both are available, 1875–1914, the *short-time* fluctuations for the two sets of aggregate-clearings series are closely similar. So far as the *long-time* movements of the two series are concerned, the only essential difference is in average rate of growth. The seven-city aggregate rises appreciably faster than the six-city aggregate. Contrasting 1875 and 1913 (the precise choice of comparison dates is not material, since the divergence between the two series develops quite systematically), we find that the series for seven cities rises per year, on the average, in the ratio 1.053, and that for the six cities in the ratio 1.048.[4] Dividing the first of these figures by the second, we obtain the constant 1.005. Accordingly, in making the estimated extension of our seven-city aggregate back from 1875 to 1866, we assume that in each year-to-year movement the ratio of change in the seven-city aggregate (going *backward*) is equal to the corresponding ratio for the six-city aggregate divided by the constant 1.005.

We next estimate the *quarterly* items, adjusted for seasonal variation, of clearings of seven selected cities, 1866–74, by taking each annual total, derived as just described, and distributing it among the four quarters of the year in proportion to the values of the respective quarterly items, adjusted for seasonal variation, of Philadelphia bank clearings (we know from examination of annual data that Philadelphia clearings constituted in this epoch a very high proportion of the seven-city aggregate).

### RAILROAD EARNINGS

For the series railroad earnings, we show on Chart 23 (and, later, on Chart 34) quarterly averages of the monthly items adjusted for seasonal variation derived by Professor Arthur H. Cole, and described by him in his article, "A Monthly Index of Railroad Earnings, 1866–1914," *Review of Economic Statistics*, XVIII (February 1936), pp. 31–41. [At the time of the analysis of Chapter III, including the construction of Chart 1, this series had not been developed.]

[4] Or, in terms of annual *percentage rates* of increase between 1875 and 1913, we have 5.3 per cent and 4.8 per cent, respectively.

# APPENDIX XIV–A

List of Tentative Trend-Indications for Ten Individual Series, 1866–1914
(*Described as they would appear upon logarithmic vertical scale*)

**(I) Based upon Trend-Indications Derived by Use of the Original Standard Pattern**

| Series | Period, and trend |
|---|---|
| Railroad earnings | 1866–96......parabola |
| | 1904–14......parabola |
| | 1896–1904....backward extension of 1904–14 trend |
| Outside clearings | 1866–96......straight line |
| | 1904–14......parabola |
| | 1896–1904....straight line connecting extremities of 1866–96 and 1904–14 trends |
| Imports | 1866–96......straight line |
| | 1904–14......parabola |
| | 1896–1904....backward extension of 1904–14 trend |
| Immigration | 1866–96......straight line |
| | 1904–14......straight line |
| | 1896–1904....straight line connecting extremities of 1866–96 and 1904–14 trends |
| Railroad stock prices | 1866–96......straight line |
| | 1904–14......parabola |
| | 1896–1904....straight line connecting extremities of 1866–96 and 1904–14 trends |
| Industrial stock prices | 1866–96......straight line |
| | 1904–14......parabola |
| | 1896–1904....backward extension of 1904–14 trend |
| New York clearings | 1866–96......straight line |
| | 1904–14......parabola |
| | 1896–1904....straight line connecting extremities of 1866–96 and 1904–14 trends |
| Sensitive commodity prices | 1866–96......parabola |
| | 1904–14......parabola |
| | 1896–1904....backward extension of 1904–14 trend |
| Wholesale commodity prices | 1866–96......parabola |
| | 1904–14......parabola |
| | 1896–1904....backward extension of 1904–14 trend |
| Commercial-paper rates* | 1866–85......straight line |
| | 1885–1914....straight line |

For footnote, see end of table.

(II) Based upon Trend-Indications Derived by Use of the Standard Pattern,
First Revision

| Series | Period, and trend |
| --- | --- |

*With the exception of the three series indicated below, the trends are the same
as those listed under Part (I).*

Imports .................. 1866–78......straight line
1878–96......straight line
1904–14......parabola
1896–1904....backward extension of 1904–14 trend

Immigration .............. 1866–96......parabola
1904–14......straight line
1896–1904....straight line connecting extremities of
1866–96 and 1904–14 trends

Railroad stock prices ....... 1866–85......parabola
1885–96......straight line
1904–14......parabola
1896–1904....straight line connecting extremities of
1885–96 and 1904–14 trends

---

\* For this series the break in trend appears to come at 1885, rather than around
the turn of the century.

# INDEX

# INDEX

*(Arabic numerals refer to pages of this volume. Insert charts are listed according to the text page preceding; thus for "ch. 66," read "chart opposite page 66.")*